"Unique, highly selective Southwest travel guide."
—Home & Away

"Morris . . . points out the particular pleasures, characteristics, and cuisines of each of the . . . inns in the book . . . so travelers can make an informed decision about where they want to stay."
—Longview *(Texas)* News Journal

"For those regular or intermittent travelers with a taste for homey layovers, this guide is a must."
—Books of the Southwest

"This carefully researched and written guide describes . . . unique inns . . . in the three states . . . Morris vividly notes the inn's specialty, whether architecture, menu, view, history, or atmosphere."
—Review of Texas Books

"Home baked muffins, gourmet meals, flowers in the room, a rocking chair on the front porch so visitors can watch the wildlife or chat with the amiable innkeeper—all these amenities are available when travelers are in-the-know. To locate non-clone travel lodging, this carefully written guide introduces and describes . . . unique inns . . . in vivid and colorful language."
—Beaumont *(Texas)* Enterprise

"An absolute necessity for even the most infrequent Southwest traveler."
—Northside People *(San Antonio, Texas)*

RECOMMENDED COUNTRY INNS® SERIES

"These guides are a marvelous start to planning the leisurely trek,
romantic getaway, or time-off for reflection."
—Internet Book Review

The Recommended Country Inns® series is designed for the discriminating traveler who seeks the best in unique accommodations away from home.

From hundreds of inns personally visited and evaluated by the author, only the finest are described in depth here. The inclusion of an inn is purely a personal decision on the part of the author; no one can pay or be paid to be recommended in a Globe Pequot inn guide.

Organized for easy reference, these guides point you to just the kind of accommodations you are looking for: Comprehensive indexes by category provide listings of inns for the sports-minded, inns that serve gourmet meals, inns for the business traveler . . . and more. State maps help you pinpoint the location of each inn, and detailed driving directions tell you how to get there.

Use these guidebooks with confidence. Allow each author to share his or her selections with you and then discover for yourself the country inn experience.

EDITIONS AVAILABLE:

Recommended Country Inns®

New England · Mid-Atlantic and Chesapeake Region

The South · The Midwest · West Coast

The Southwest · Rocky Mountain Region

also

Recommended Romantic Inns

Recommended
COUNTRY
INNS®

THE SOUTHWEST

Arizona / New Mexico / Texas

Seventh Edition

by Eleanor S. Morris

illustrated by Bill Taylor, Jr.

The Globe Pequot Press

OLD SAYBROOK, CONNECTICUT

About the Author

ELEANOR S. MORRIS is a freelance travel writer living in Austin, Texas—a "refugee," she says, from the big cities of Houston and Dallas. A member of the Society of American Travel Writers and the American Society of Journalists and Authors, she has published widely in national newspapers and magazines. Eleanor has stayed at country inns in such diverse places as Australia, Portugal, England, Canada, Mexico, and Japan. She says a country inn is a place where you are never a stranger, no matter how far you are from home.

ISBN 0-7627-0300-8
ISSN 1078-5515

Cover photo: Michael Gesinger/Photonica
Cover, text, and map design: Nancy Freeborn/Freeborn Design

Manufactured in the United States of America
Seventh Edition/First Printing

Contents

A Few Words about Visiting Southwestern Inns

Webster's Dictionary says that an inn is a hotel, usually a small one. *Thorndike Barnhart* says that an inn is a public house for lodging and caring for travelers. In my travels in the Southwest, I have found that an inn, or at least what we understand down here as a country inn, is much more. It is a place where, away from home, you feel at home—not necessarily because of the physical attributes of a place (although that's important, too), but more likely because of the people you find there, both the innkeepers and the guests.

Many of my innkeepers say, "Our guests are a special breed." I maintain that the reason is that country innkeepers themselves are a special breed. As in a family, sharing your home with others makes for companionship along with sensitivity to another's moods, a concern with well-being, comfort, and need. Almost without exception my innkeepers really like other people; they are interested in them and want to interact with them. (Those who find they do not soon drop out of this fast-growing industry.) And since like attracts like, innkeepers attract as guests people who are also open, adventurous, and interested in other people.

I think this people-interest, this interaction, is why the inn movement is growing so rapidly, at least in my section of the country, where just a short time ago such a thing as a country inn was almost impossible to find. Even when people travel on business, they're learning what it means to come "home" at the end of the day to someone's home, to someone who greets them with genuine interest on a personal basis. The world is becoming so hectic, so rushed, that we often feel it's passing us by; we'd better hurry just to catch up. Along the way, how nice to stop for a breather to stay with people who are interested in us and whom we can be interested in, too. It's as simple as that.

Inns of the Southwest range from romantic Victorian cottages to sprawling haciendas secluded behind high adobe walls, from grand old-time mansions to rustic country cottages, and their number is growing. Although some lodgings may disappoint you, innkeepers seldom will. Their guests become their extended family, many returning again and again. The inn movement in the Southwest is definitely "in."

—Eleanor S. Morris

How to Use This Inn Guide

Without exception, every innkeeper in this book to whom I posed the question "Why are you doing this?" answered, "The people. We love the people."

"The people" is you, the traveler, and here are some pointers that will smooth your path to better and more beautiful inn experiences:

Inns are arranged by states in the following sections: Arizona, New Mexico, and Texas. Because it is so large, Texas is divided into five geographical areas: North Texas, East Texas, Central Texas, Gulf Coast/Border Texas, and West Texas.

At the beginning of each section is a map and an index to the inns in that section, listed alphabetically by town. At the back of the guide is a complete index to all the inns in the book, listed alphabetically by name. Additional indexes list inns by special categories.

There is no charge of any kind to an inn to be described in this guide. The inclusion is a personal decision on the part of the author, who visited each inn described at length as well as many others that were not included. Address any questions or comments to Eleanor S. Morris, The Globe Pequot Press, P.O. Box 833, Old Saybrook, CT 06475.

CAVEATS

Menu Abbreviations:

EP: European Plan. Room without meals.

EPB: European Plan with Breakfast. Room with full breakfast. Where room rate includes continental breakfast only, this is mentioned in text.

MAP: Modified American Plan. Room with breakfast and dinner.

AP: American Plan. Room with meals.

Rates: I have listed the range from low to high, double occupancy (single where applicable), at the time I visited, realizing that it's up to you to decide how many in your party and what level of accommodation you wish. Rates change without notice, however, sometimes overnight, so I cannot promise that there will be no surprises. Always check beforehand. The rates given do not include taxes.

Reservations/Deposits: These are uniformly required, and if you do not show up and the room is not rented otherwise, you will most likely be charged. Expect to pay a deposit or use a credit card.

Minimum Stay: I have noted this wherever necessary, but most inns in this guide have no such restrictions. Check when you make your reservation, though, because policies change. Often during slow times minimum stay can be negotiable. And special rates are often available for an extended stay.

Personal Checks: All the inns in this book accept personal checks.

Credit Cards: Most inns accept the major credit cards. The few that do not are so noted in the text.

Children: Inns that especially welcome children are listed in an index at the end of the guide. With others, it's always a good idea to ask, since many simply do not have the facilities to offer children a comfortable and happy visit.

Pets: A number of inns are prepared to deal with pets, with some restrictions. I have listed them in an index at the back of the guide as well as in the text.

Food: I have noted which inns serve food, whether food is included in the rates as in a bed-and-breakfast inn, or whether there is restaurant service on the premises. Where there is food service for meals other than breakfast, the "Facilities and Activities" item for the inn explains this. Where there is not, most of your innkeepers will have an assortment of menus on hand for your perusal and are happy to make recommendations.

BYOB: It is usually all right to bring your own bottle, especially to an inn that has no bar or lounge facilities. Often the innkeeper will provide setups (ice and mixes), and many serve wine where licensing laws permit.

Smoking: Many inns, particularly in Texas, have restrictions as to where, when, and if their guests may smoke. This information appears in the text.

King, Queen, Double, or Twin Bed: If you have a preference, always ask when you make your reservation.

Television and Telephones: I have listed where these are available, although I imagine that, like me, you may want to get away from it all when you go inning. Many inns have both television and phone located in the common rooms.

Air-Conditioning/Heating: I have not listed these amenities, because almost without exception they are taken for granted in the Southwest if the climate warrants. I have noted if the climate does not.

Wheelchair Access: Most of the inns in this book unfortunately do not have total handicapped facilities, since so many of them are located in older (and often two-story) buildings. But many of them do have at least one guest room, usually a downstairs one, that can accommodate a wheelchair; in this case there will also be a ramp. It's best to ask ahead of time exactly what facilities are available.

Key to Icons Used in This Book

 a top pick

 caters to business travelers

 a best buy

 especially family friendly

 romantic inn

Recommended

COUNTRY
INNS®

THE SOUTHWEST

Arizona

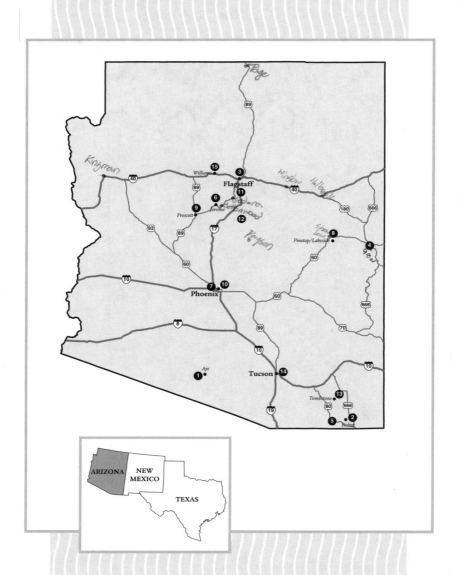

Arizona

Numbers on map refer to towns numbered below.

*Top Pick Inn

*Top Pick Inn

The Guest House Inn
Ajo, Arizona 85321

INNKEEPERS: Norma and Michael Walker

ADDRESS/TELEPHONE: 700 Guest House Road; (520) 387–6133

ROOMS: 4; all with private bath. No smoking inn.

RATES: $79, double; $10 extra person; EPB.

OPEN: All year.

FACILITIES AND ACTIVITIES: Patio with picnic table. Nearby: restaurants and shops in Ajo, museum, open-pit copper mine, golf, scenic drives, Organ Pipe Cactus National Monument, Cabeza Prieta Game Refuge, bird-watching.

This house is unusual: The four guest rooms are square in the middle. Each room has French doors opening onto the light, bright glassed-in porch that makes a U-shape around the center rooms. The inn was designed in 1925 as a guest house for visiting officials of the Phelps Dodge Corporation, whose copper mines were the town's main industry. Now the mining is over, and Norma Walker has sort of "inherited" the lovely house. "I was the housekeeper; I was in charge of this place until the mine closed down in 1985," she says.

Norma is a born hostess, coming from a home where, she says, hospitality was the rule. Breakfast on the long table in the bright dining room at the back of the house varies from pecan waffles to *huevos rancheros* with chorizo sausage. There are always fresh muffins with homemade jams and, for late risers, perhaps quiche. "Too heavy for early risers," says Norma.

Guest rooms are large and uncluttered, with lamps on nightstands for bedtime reading and dressers and chairs to put things on. Each room is furnished individually, from Victorian marble–topped antiques to handcrafted Southwestern pieces.

HOW TO GET THERE: From Phoenix take I–10 west to Highway 85 and 85 south to Ajo. From Tucson take Highway 86 west to Highway 85 and 85 north to Ajo. In Ajo turn south at La Mina Avenue (the only traffic light in town) to Guest House Road. Turn right, and the inn is at the end of the road. There is a sign.

Copper Mines and Birds

Ajo is a small town in the middle of a desert, 10 miles north of a town called Why. Why Ajo was chosen for the name is not certain, but it may come from the Tohono O'odham Indian word for paint—the Indians painted their bodies with the copper found here. In 1874 prospectors arrived, and in 1917 the New Cornelia Copper Company made this the birthplace of Arizona's mining industry.

The small town was a railroad and airline stop back then, but now you pretty much have to drive, either from Tucson or Phoenix. The Mine Manager's House Inn was exactly that, the home of the manager of the New Cornelia Company copper mine in 1919. Eventually part of the Phelps Dodge Corporation, the mine closed in 1985.

Bird-watchers are in for a real treat here in the Sonoran Desert, where Gambel's quail and the cactus wren are plentiful. And there's always a chance you might spot a wild javelina trotting along—just don't get in the way!

The Mine Manager's House Inn
Ajo, Arizona 85321

INNKEEPERS: Jean and Micheline Fournier

ADDRESS/TELEPHONE: One Greenway Drive; (520) 387–6505; fax (520) 387– 6508

ROOMS: 5, including 2 suites; all with private bath; wheelchair accessible. Smoking in Catalina Suite only.

RATES: $75 to $105, double; $15 extra person; EPB.

OPEN: All year.

FACILITIES AND ACTIVITIES: Jacuzzi and covered patio with refrigerator, coin laundry facilities, VCR, gift shop. Nearby: restaurants and shops in Ajo, pet care, museum, open-pit copper mine, golf, scenic drives, Organ Pipe Cactus National Monument, Cabeza Prieta Game Refuge.

The inn is situated on the top of a hill with a view of the southwestern Arizona desert and the huge open-pit mine, giving a lesson in how miners dug copper ore from the earth. The inn's enclosed front porch is a small shop full of local crafts. "Indian crafts, and those made by local ladies," Jean explains. The back porch, also enclosed, is the reading room. In between, the New Cornelia Suite, the Greenway Suite, the Early American Suite, and the Nautical Room offer different motifs, with a harmonious mix of antiques and contemporary furniture, old photographs, and comfortable space. The Early American Suite overlooks the

town and a lovely jacaranda tree; from the Honeymoon Suite there's a view of the mountains toward Organ Pipe Cactus National Monument. The Nautical Room is accessible for wheelchairs, and the Catalina Suite is detached, off the patio, and available to smokers.

For breakfast it's Jean who does the cooking, says Micheline: eggs Benedict, low-cholesterol Belgian waffles served with strawberries and yogurt, or tortillas stuffed with scrambled eggs and vegetables (in deference to the Southwest), orange juice, fruit cup, and blueberry muffins. On major holidays, when Ajo restaurants are closed, guests can reserve a place at the family table. "They become part of the family; they're included," the Forniers say.

HOW TO GET THERE: From Phoenix take I–10 west to Highway 85 and 85 south to Ajo. From Tucson take Highway 86 west to Highway 85 and 85 north to Ajo. In Ajo turn south at La Mina Avenue (the only traffic light in town) to Greenway Drive and follow the road up to the top of the hill. There is parking in front of the inn.

Bisbee Grand Hotel
Bisbee, Arizona 85603

INNKEEPER: Bill Thomas

ADDRESS/TELEPHONE: 61 Main Street (mailing address: P.O. Box 825); (520) 432–5900 or (800) 421–1909

ROOMS: 12, all with private bath. No smoking inn.

RATES: $55 to $110, double; $15 extra person; EPB.

OPEN: All year.

FACILITIES AND ACTIVITIES: Grand Western Saloon with complimentary snacks, pool table, large TV screen, and Ladies' Parlor; Murder Mystery weekends. Nearby: Old Bisbee Tour, City Mine Tour, Bisbee Mining and Historical Museum, antiques shops, art galleries.

*O*pulence—extraordinary, almost out-of-this-world opulence—is what you'll find at the well-named Bisbee Grand. *Grand* is a perfect adjective for this inn; so is *elegant*. From the red-velvet Victorian Suite to the otherworldly Oriental Suite, exotic luxury abounds in this posh, treasure-filled inn.

The modest, small black marquee over the double doors, squeezed in between two storefronts, hardly prepared me for what awaited as I climbed the red-carpeted stairs leading from the narrow entrance to the second floor and the inn rooms. Once there, faced with an iridescent stuffed peacock at the head of the stairs, I found myself in a world I certainly had never expected in the quaint and charming Old West mining town of Bisbee.

Each of the eight guest rooms is a world in itself, full of beautiful furniture and decorative details. "These antiques were collected for thirty years," innkeeper Bill says with justifiable pride. As for the four suites, they are extravaganzas, excitingly imaginative and full of unexpected appointments, such as a working fountain next to a lovely large flower arrangement in the Garden Suite.

The Oriental Suite is unashamedly opulent, with walls covered in black, pink, and gold fabric depicting Chinese scenes. The brass bed is adorned with onyx and alabaster. "It's a unique, one-of-a-kind honeymoon bed," Bill explains. The room is wide and high, with an oval mirror and paintings. Bronze dragon vases and black lacquer vie with other choice collectibles.

The Victorian Suite is dripping with deep-red velvet hangings, not only on the windows but also making a cozy nest of the canopied bed. The Garden Suite is a bower of flowers; as for the rest of the rooms, like the Coral and the Gray rooms, Deer Springs and Crow Canyon, well, I'm going to let you see for yourself. Just take my word for it: It's all outstanding.

On the main floor, adjacent to the Grand Western Saloon, the inn's old-fashioned Victorian parlor has an antique piano that you may play if you're careful. The saloon's 35-foot bar came from Wyatt Earp's Oriental Bar by way of the Wells Fargo Museum.

Breakfast will satisfy both the most eager gourmet and the health food aficionado. "All our food is from Tucson Cooperative Warehouses," Bill notes, "and we recycle and compost everything." The fruit course consisted of watermelon, cantaloupe, pineapple, and white grapes; the delicious quiche was full of cheese and mushrooms, with ham on the side; the homemade bread was delicious; and for sweets, there were cheese Danish and cinnamon rolls.

"We treat our guests very special, with all the grace and elegance of the best of a Victorian mining town," Bill says. Morning coffee, hot tea, iced tea, and a plateful of gingersnaps, lemon bars, and peanut butter and chocolate chip cookies are available in the saloon practically around the clock. And not the least of the pleasures of this small, elegant inn is watching the sunset, or the rainbow after it rains, over the mountains facing the front balcony.

HOW TO GET THERE: From Highway 80 east take Tombstone Canyon Road for approximately 2½ miles until it becomes Main Street. You can't miss the Bisbee Grand on the left.

Hotel La More/The Bisbee Inn
Bisbee, Arizona 85603

INNKEEPER: Katherine Anderson

ADDRESS/TELEPHONE: 45 OK Street (mailing address: P.O. Box 1855); (520) 432–5131 or (888) 432–5131; fax (520) 432–5132

E-MAIL: bisbeeinn@aol.com

ROOMS: 19; 14 with private bath, 5 share; all with washbasin. Pets permitted. No smoking inn.

RATES: $45 to $75, double; $5 extra person; EPB.

OPEN: All year.

FACILITIES AND ACTIVITIES: TV room, laundry facilities. Nearby: Brewery Gulch, Copper Queen Mine Tour, Lavender Pit Mine Tour, Bisbee Mining Museum.

his historic inn first opened its doors in 1917 as the La More Hotel, and it's come into its own name again, after being The Bisbee Inn for many years. The inn overlooks Brewery Gulch, back then a wild boomtown street. "We're adding Hotel La More to our name as a reminder of our beginnings," new inn owner Elissa Strati says. "It was named after its proprietoress, Mrs. Kate La More." Original owners Joy and John Timbers kept the mining hotel's spartan but comfortable Victorian atmosphere when they undertook the certified historic restoration, and new owners Elissa and Alfred Strati have carried on. I like the spare but clean look that solid light oak, lace curtains, and brass bedsteads can give. It's real Victorian, all right—the brass-painted beds (innkeepers point out that they're not really brass) and oak furniture are the original hotel pieces, in excellent condition. In the closets I found flowered and plain flannel robes hanging for guests' use, a thoughtful touch.

Both lounge and dining rooms are homey. Three rooms form the dining area, the center one a small atrium. Look up and you'll see a set of stairs and a wrought-iron balcony under the skylight. Lace cloths are on the tables, with places marked by pretty ruffled mats. Furnishings are carefully restored, original oak pieces.

Breakfast, made in quantity and of quality, consists of "all you can eat": two kinds of juice, fruit salad, whole-wheat bread, scrambled or fried eggs, bacon, pancakes, potatoes, waffles, and French toast made with homemade bread.

The inn is cooled in summer by evaporative coolers and is centrally heated during the winter. To add to guests' comfort, there are custom-made quilts on the beds. "A local lady hand-quilts them for us," says live-in innkeeper Katherine Anderson, and all the crew will recommend good Bisbee eateries. (The town is really three small towns strung out along the copper mountains. Get a map, brochures, and a walking-tour map from the Chamber of Commerce on Commerce Street.)

HOW TO GET THERE: From Highway 80 take the business exit into the heart of Old Bisbee and go straight up the hill, which is OK Street. The inn is 200 yards up the steep and narrow street, and there's parking to the right, just beyond the inn building.

From Mining Camp to Wealthy Town

Between 1877 and 1910 Bisbee grew from a tiny mining camp to a wealthy town with fine Victorian houses and a reputation for the best eating and drinking establishments in the territory. More than fifty saloons ensured that it stayed that way as the land continued to yield its rich copper ore.

The first prospector to discover the mineral left in disgust—he was hunting gold. But Judge DeWitt Bisbee and a group of other San Francisco business men realized that the new electrical industries being developed needed copper, and they bought the Copper Queen Mine in 1880.

Along came Dr. James Douglas of the Phelps Dodge Company, who bought land adjacent to the Copper Queen, and the two factions sensibly merged instead of fighting it out. As for the judge, he never headed east to see the town named for him.

Park Place
Bisbee, Arizona 85603

INNKEEPERS: Janet and Bob Watkins

ADDRESS/TELEPHONE: 200 East Vista; (520) 432–3054 or
(800) 388–4388; fax (520) 459–7603

ROOMS: 4; 2 with private bath. Pets at discretion of innkeepers.
No smoking inn.

RATES: $50 to $70, double; EPB.

OPEN: All year.

FACILITIES AND ACTIVITIES: Lunch and dinner by reservation;
workshops in weaving, spinning, fibers. Nearby: Historic Old
Bisbee, shops and restaurants, Lavender Mine tours, Bisbee
Mining and Historical Museum, bird-watching, golf, bike rental,
horseback riding, rockhounding.

I didn't have to ask the reason for Park Place's name once I turned the
corner and saw the large, 1910 Mediterranean-style home facing the
park. Bisbee natives into the fourth generation, Janet and Bob were
in the real estate business when they got the inn by trade. The house has windows everywhere, and every room is exceptionally large in the 5,000-square-
foot house. The glassed-in
solarium, known in these parts
as an Arizona room, is a
favorite gathering place. The
dining room is spacious, too,
with antique walnut furniture.
The library has a fireplace to
make you cozy while you read,
and more bright windows.

Each guest room is a corner
room, with large windows let-
ting in the view of the broad park across the street or the rose garden on the
grounds. The Green Room, in pastels and with twin beds that can be made
into a king, opens onto a large side porch. Both the Yellow Room and the
Blue Room also open onto the porch. The Pink Room is a spacious suite with
a queen bed. Janet and Bob are becoming absolutely famous for their breakfasts. One guest was so carried away that she exclaimed, "I have never eaten
that well for breakfast!" The meal is an hour- to an hour-and-a-half-long,

four-course feast of fresh fruit compote, German pancakes, ham, bacon, breakfast steaks or pork chops, and homemade muffins. From food to table, the presentation is worthy of a gourmet magazine.

HOW TO GET THERE: From the circle where Highways 80 and 92 meet, take the fourth road (Bisbee Road) to Congdon. Turn left to East Vista. Turn right; the inn is on the left, on the corner of East Vista and Tener.

Schoolhouse Inn
Bisbee, Arizonza 85603

INNKEEPERS: Jeff and Bobby Blankenbecker

ADDRESS/TELEPHONE: 818 Tombstone Canyon (mailing address: P.O. Box 32); (520) 432–2996 or (800) 537–4333; fax (520) 432–2996

ROOMS: 6, plus 3 suites; all with private bath; wheelchair accessible. No smoking inn.

RATES: $55 to $75, double; $10 extra person; EPB.

OPEN: All year.

FACILITIES AND ACTIVITIES: Lunch by reservation, groups only; cable TV; board games and chess; basketball, volleyball, horseshoes. Nearby: historic Old Bisbee, shops and restaurants, Lavender Mine tours, Bisbee Mining and Historical Museum, bird-watching, golf, bike rental, horseback riding, rockhounding.

*T*his is a fascinating place, a big, old-fashioned schoolhouse—really! Built in 1918 at the height of Bisbee's prosperous mining days, Garfield School accommodated grades one through four in four huge classrooms. When things died down in Bisbee in the 1930s, the school was converted into apartments. Now you can pick your favorite subject: Music? History? Geography, Art, Reading, Writing, maybe Arithmetic? You can "cut class" in the Library or play chief in the Principal's Office. Check out the original school blueprints hanging along the walls of the main stairway.

Rooms are decorated in pastel colors; there are pretty quilts on the beds; the 12-foot ceilings make everything seem extremely spacious. In the suites, cozy sitting areas are separated from the bedrooms by arched openings, and the writing desks are perfect for your "homework": writing postcards home, describing quaint Bisbee.

Breakfast is fulsome, with three fruits, cereals, and cook's choice of pancakes or quiche and muffins, or baked eggs, Mexican cornbread, or French toast.

HOW TO GET THERE: On Highway 80 pass through the Mule Pass Tunnel and take the Tombstone Canyon exit. Go 1 block on Tombstone Canyon and turn right onto Pace Avenue. The inn is up the hill, past the fenced-in school playing courts on the left.

Birch Tree Inn
Flagstaff, Arizona 86001

INNKEEPERS: Donna and Rodger Pettinger, Sandy and Ed Znetko

ADDRESS/TELEPHONE: 824 Birch Avenue; (520) 774–1042 or (888) 774–1042; fax (520) 774–8462

E-MAIL: birch@flagstaff.az.us

ROOMS: 5; 3 with private bath; no air-conditioning (elevation 7,000 feet). No smoking inn.

RATES: $69 to $109, double; $10 extra person; EPB.

OPEN: All year.

FACILITIES AND ACTIVITIES: Bicycles, tennis rackets (tennis courts nearby), pool table, game room, piano. Nearby: restaurants and Downtown Historical District, cross-country skiing, Grand Canyon, Museum of Northern Arizona, Coconino Center for the Arts, Lowell Observatory, Pioneer's Historical Museum, Northern Arizona University.

How do two women decorate one house? Good friends for years, Sandy and Donna hit on a perfect plan when they decided to go into the inn business together. "I have an idea," one of them said. "You take two rooms and I do the same, and no questions asked!"

The result is a lovely inn that everyone is happy with. The house was built in 1917 by a Chicago contractor who moved to Flagstaff with a large family.

"It was never considered a mansion, so we decided to decorate in comfortable country," Sandy says. All four innkeepers are from Southern California, and the ties go back, since Donna and Ed knew each other in the fifth grade!

They work together well, with Sandy doing the cooking and Donna taking care of the artistic touches. "She does the flowers, folds the napkins, decorates real pretty," Sandy says. Sandy's specialty is a Farmer's Breakfast, with skillet potatoes and a healthful frittata of eggs, cheese, broccoli, carrots, and green beans, served with fresh fruit and muffins. "Depends upon the mood I'm in, maybe they'll be banana-apple with nuts and orange." Sometimes there will be German pancakes with apples and syrup or strawberries and whipped cream. The newest delicacy is Texas-size toast in batter, baked in orange juice and served with a fresh orange sauce.

"We like to serve afternoon refreshments in the parlor," both Donna and Sandy say. "It gives us a chance to know our guests." Pella's Room has Dutch lace curtains and a handmade quilt. In Carol's Room they let a daughter pick out the wallpaper. The antique armoire was hauled all the way from California. The pale lemon–painted Wagner/Znetko Room, named after Ed's grandparents, has a basin in the room and a private bath attached.

The Wicker Room speaks for itself, in blue and white and with a queen-size bed. The aqua Southwest Suite has a king-sized bed, corner windows, and a huge bath with the house's original fixtures on a black-and-white tile floor. Downstairs, the soft rose-and-blue color scheme is restful—and so is the swing, out on the veranda. A wheelbarrow in the front yard is filled with bright flowers.

The innkeepers keep a book of restaurant menus handy for guest information; but in desperate situations, "like being snowbound," Sandy says with a laugh, they've served guests soup and fresh bread. "Donna is a good tour guide," she adds, which is a handy thing to know if you want to see some of the many attractions of the area. And during the summer months, you can see them via trolley, driven by your very own innkeeper, Ed Znetko.

HOW TO GET THERE: At the intersection of I–17 and I–40, take exit 195B (which becomes Milton Road). Follow it around to Highway 180 (which becomes Humphry's Street) and go left 2 blocks to Birch Avenue.

Dierker House
Flagstaff, Arizona 86001

INNKEEPER: Dorothea (Dottie) Dierker

ADDRESS/TELEPHONE: 423 West Cherry Avenue; (520) 774–3249

ROOMS: 3 share 1 bath; no air-conditioning (elevation 7,000 feet). No smoking inn.

RATES: $50 single or double, $21 extra person; no credit cards.

OPEN: All year.

FACILITIES AND ACTIVITIES: Lightly equipped kitchen, microwave. Nearby: tennis courts, Downtown Historic District, museums, Indian ruins, skiing, white-water rafting on Colorado River, Grand Canyon.

ottie was a nurse before she retired. She also raised six children. "I kind of like taking care of people," she says. "And my house really helps. It gives everybody privacy. I can go to market and leave it open, leave a note." The inn has the flavor of a European inn, and with good reason. "I've been in bed-and-breakfasts in other parts of the world—in Budapest, all over Greece, Europe, and the Mediterranean."

Wherever her guests may have been, they certainly enjoy Dierker House and keep coming back. Dottie lives downstairs in her house, and guests have the run of the upstairs. It's so cozy that guests sit around in the kitchen and raid the cookie jar or the refrigerator for refreshments. "They get together and exchange addresses," Dottie says with satisfaction. The single bath is large, with a skylight, plants, a scale, and a stocked medicine chest. "It's the nurse in me, I guess," Dottie confesses. The three

guest rooms, cozy under the eaves with down comforters and antiques and filled with green plants, are a travelogue in themselves. Would you rather sleep in France, Germany, or Greece? Posters and other mementos will take you there in your dreams.

For breakfast in the dining room, Dottie will serve one of four menus ("If you stay longer, you get a repeat," she warns): bran muffins, blueberry muffins, a meat dish, or an egg dish, all served at 8:00 A.M. "That's the only time I cook." But not to worry if you're early or late: "There's the option of a big continental breakfast in the guest kitchen."

HOW TO GET THERE: At the intersection of I–17 and I–40, take exit 195B (which becomes Milton Road). Follow it around to Highway 180 (which becomes Humphry's Street), turn left, and go 3 blocks to Cherry Avenue.

The Inn at Four Ten
Flagstaff, Arizona 86001

INNKEEPERS: Sally and Howard Krueger

ADDRESS/TELEPHONE: 410 North Leroux; (520) 774–6354 or (800) 774–2008; fax (520) 774–6354

ROOMS: 8; all with private bath; wheelchair accessible. No smoking inn.

RATES: $110 to $155, double; $10 extra person; EPB and afternoon refreshments.

OPEN: All year.

FACILITIES AND ACTIVITIES: Box lunches available. Nearby: Northern Arizona University, Museum of Northern Arizona, Lowell Observatory, Pioneer's Historical Museum, Arizona Snow Bowl with skiing and other winter sports, golf.

The Inn at Four Ten is a pretty gray-and-white house enclosed by a rock fence. The porch railings are painted white; so is the pretty gazebo in the yard to the right. Welcoming—and tempting—are the cookies waiting in the jar by the front door.

"This is certainly a lot friendlier than manufacturing!" Howard says happily, delighted to be finished with his past as a maker of purchase displays to advertise products in stores. "Indeed it is a friendlier industry. We've already made friends," Sally adds. "It took me ten years to do that in a Chicago suburb!" The Krueger motto is "There's no such thing as too much service," which may be part of the reason Sally and Howard find everyone so friendly. "We've liked to go on vacation ourselves, so we thought we'd like to help others enjoy their vacations." Howard says that he had a fortunate childhood, with help in the house, so he knows what service is. "We don't call for Jeeves; Jeeves is already here," he says with a laughing reference to the famous P. G.

Wodehouse butler. "We can see the comings and goings in the parking lot, and I stop what I'm doing so that I can welcome guests at the door. We want our guests to know they're appreciated."

Well, that explains how Howard is able to fling open the door almost before I have my hand on the doorknob! The entrance opens onto a large living/dining area with cozy ticking-covered sofas and white wicker. Little touches make the inn cozy and friendly: Birdcages are suspended from the ceiling and doilies decorate tables, even the newel post of the staircase. An old sewing-machine cabinet is used as a sofa table, and pretty flowers in a white china pitcher bloom over an assortment of antique children's boots on the linen doily.

Sally and Howard are concerned with the health of their guests. "I won't serve quiche!" he says rather vehemently. But you won't miss it when you see the bountiful basket of fresh-baked goods such as popovers and lemon-pecan muffins, pumpkin–chocolate chip muffins, and toasted homemade bread. There's French toast, too, and toasted bagels. All this is accompanied by a fresh fruit compote, and there's pineapple shrub to drink. This latter item sounds to me like something in an old-fashioned novel, and it turns out to be fruit juices blended with pineapple sherbet—delicious!

Sally and Howard coddle their guests with cookies in the afternoon, and wait until you taste the recipes that Sally brought with her from Chicago. Two favorites are cinnamon kiss cookies and Mrs. King's Cookies, concoctions of white and dark chocolate chips, oatmeal, and granola—you'd never know they were healthful. Hot chocolate, coffee and tea, and apple cider are available for "whoever's around in the afternoon," Sally says. "We love to eat, so we love to recommend restaurants."

Box lunches are a great option when you want to go sightseeing—the crowds at the Grand Canyon restaurants are daunting. Howard says, "This way you can unpack your lunch and enjoy it at the edge of the canyon away from the crowds."

HOW TO GET THERE: From the east on I–40 (or the south on I–17 to I–40), take exit 195B, and go about 11⁷⁄₁₀ miles through town. After you go under an overpass, take the third street on the left, which is Leroux. Go up the hill, and the inn is on the right. There's a sign.

Jeanette's
Flagstaff, Arizona 86004

INNKEEPERS: Jeanette and Ray West

ADDRESS/TELEPHONE: 3380 East Lockett Road; (520) 527–1912, (800) 752–1912; fax (520) 527–1713

ROOMS: 4; all with private bath. No smoking inn.

RATES: $95 to $125, double; $20 extra person; EPB.

OPEN: All year.

FACILITIES AND ACTIVITIES: Nearby: Northern Arizona University, Museum of Northern Arizona, Lowell Observatory, Pioneer's Historical Museum, Arizona Snow Bowl with skiing and other winter sports, golf, the Grand Canyon.

Although the inn is new, "even local people think we've renovated an older house," Jeanette says. That's because she and Ray did enough research on the early twentieth century to totally re-create another, more serene time. She and Ray have brought flapper and speakeasy days alive without the inconveniences of old plumbing, tiny bathrooms, and rickety stairs that they might have found if they'd attempted to restore an older home. Their aim was a quiet, romantic house, and "the only modern things are in the kitchen. We have a commercial stove and a three-compartment sink, because we are a commercial kitchen."

The four guest rooms, named after Jeanette and Ray's grandparents, have broad oak-plank floors, with furnishings representing other times, as well. Grandma Amelia's Room is furnished in oak. The marble-lined fireplace, trimmed with polished brass, is a real wood-burner. Stella's Room is influenced, as was Stella, by San Francisco, and her room is rich in maple. You can relax (but don't faint) on the 1894 San Rafael fainting couch or on the balcony overlooking Eldon Mountain.

Jeanette calls Icie Vean's Room "heavy metal" because of two metal beds, a metal dental cabinet "pretending" to be an armoire, and a six-foot solid vitreous-china bathtub "rescued" from Denver's Broadmoor Hotel.

These three rooms are upstairs; Mamie's is downstairs, and so has easy access to the inn's wraparound porch. Furnished with treasures of walnut, the large (6½-foot) claw-foot tub was manufactured in 1914.

Jeanette's breakfast sauces and smoothies are a tasty way to start the day. You might have fresh cantaloupe with ginger sauce, whole-wheat sour-cream pancakes with a banana cream sauce, and an apricot smoothie; or eggs Benedict with a balsamic cherry-tomato sauce and a three-orange smoothie of orange juice, Texas Ruby Red grapefruit, and grape juice.

HOW TO GET THERE: Take I–40 to exit 201. Turn left at the light and cross the overpass. Turn right on Lockett from the overpass lane. Go half a mile on Lockett and the inn will be on the north (right) side of the road.

Greer Lodge
Greer, Arizona 85927

INNKEEPER: Gerald Scott

ADDRESS/TELEPHONE: P.O. Box 244; (520) 735–7216; fax (520) 735–7720

ROOMS: 26; 9 with 9 baths in Main Lodge; 17 in 8 cabins; no air-conditioning (elevation 8,500 feet); cabins wheelchair accessible. Smoking permitted except in dining room.

RATES: Main Lodge: $75 to $280, double; $15 extra person; EPB in Main Lodge only; two-night minimum stay on weekends, three nights on holidays.

OPEN: All year.

FACILITIES AND ACTIVITIES: Restaurant serving breakfast, lunch (May to October), and dinner; weekends only in winter. Cocktail bar, stocked trout pond, hiking, horseback riding, skiing, bobsledding, bird-watching, canoeing; corporate meeting space.

*H*ere's another great place for communing with nature. On the inn grounds you might spot a blue heron or two, or perhaps an owl zooming down and buzzing the pond, catching its dinner. If it doesn't get a fish it'll get a duck; owls have been seen pulling full-size ducks out of the water. Such is the view from Greer Lodge's magnificent two-story greenhouse lounge at the back of the inn, all glass with plants everywhere. The room overlooks the pond and away to the pine-covered mountains in the distance, where you can strike out for a hike or horseback ride into the National Forest.

The inn's spacious, comfortable rooms also have windows with views. The color scheme is rust and white: rust carpets, rust curtains and coverlets with little white flowers sprinkled all over, fresh comforters, linens, and towels. "The whole atmosphere is bright," says Gerald Scott, who prides himself on the way the inn sparkles, bright and shiny.

Breakfast is ordered off the menu, and you can have homemade croissants with your "eggs any way," or waffles, or pancakes. (Breakfast is not included in the rate for Little Lodge.) Lunches are available, packed for picnic, hiking, or fishing trips.

Homemade soups are wonderful here, soups such as clam chowder or, my favorite, cream of cauliflower or broccoli soup. Fresh homemade Kaiser rolls or whole-wheat bread makes the thick roast beef, turkey, or ham sandwiches special.

Come winter, the inn's one-hundred-dred-year-old Mennonite sled is available for romantic rides. "We had two marriage proposals right away!" chef Brandon Bell says.

After lunch (or maybe early in the morning?) in the summer, sit on the back porch and just throw your line in the stream feeding the pond, which is stocked with two-pound rainbow and German brown trout, as well as Canloupes fresh from the Canadian lake of the same name. Fly-fishing schools have become popular at the lodge, taught both on the pond and on the Little Colorado River nearby. Sitting out on the sundeck facing the pond, I see fish jumping out of the water, just waiting for Greer Lodge guests to catch them. Horses graze in the meadows in the distance. Elk and deer graze in the sunny alpine meadows. The hurly-burly of the city is far, far away. "This is Arizona's most beautiful setting," Gerald says, bragging that "even the governor thinks so!"

HOW TO GET THERE: Greer is at the end of Highway 373, a short road that runs south from Highway 260 between Eager and Indian Pine. The inn is at the end of the road on the left.

Red Setter Inn
Greer, Arizona 85927

INNKEEPERS: Jim Sankey and Ken Conant

ADDRESS/TELEPHONE: 8 Main Street (mailing address: P.O. Box 133); (888) 99–GREER; fax (520) 735–7425

ROOMS: 9; all with private bath and phone; no air-conditioning (altitude 8,500 feet); wheelchair accessible. No smoking inn.

RATES: $110 to $155, double; $25 extra person; EPB and sack lunch.

OPEN: All year.

FACILITIES AND ACTIVITIES: Game room, decks overlooking river. Nearby: White Mountain Apache Indian Reservation, Little House Museum, cross-country and downhill skiing at White Mountains Ski Area, fishing, hiking on nature trails, boating, bird-watching, sleigh rides, horseback riding, llama trekking.

*G*reer is in the White Mountains of Arizona below the Mogollon Rim (where Zane Grey lived and wrote his westerns). The Red Setter Inn, on the west fork of the Colorado River, is a real getaway. The name is in memory of a beloved Irish setter of Jim's—and big, black "Dude," the friendly dog in residence now, doesn't mind a bit! The inn, logs inside and out, is built in three levels, with balconies and decks from which to savor the serenity of the surrounding woods. Inside, there is lots of public space, with soaring, angled ceilings in the great room. The stone fireplace, the French doors flanking it, the solidly comfortable striped sofas, and two easy chairs make it very inviting. There's a piano, too, in case guests feel musical.

Guest rooms are furnished in an interesting mix of styles. A rustic bed, covered with a geometric quilt, faces a sophisticated wood secretary/bookcase piece. Walls are soft white, a contrast to the yellow pine doors and woodwork. Bathrooms have handpainted tiles of regional flowers—and red setters. The lower-level game room has one of the two televisions in the entire inn. It also contains a bowling alley, the only one in Greer. But don't get too excited—it's one of Jim's antique toys, manufactured circa 1920 and only a couple of feet high and wide! But there are videos galore there, including quite a collection of *I Love Lucy* programs.

The dining room is bright, with large windows opening onto a porch. Breakfast on the 8-foot-long table is a feast: salmon and eggs Benedict, stuffed French toast (with strawberries and cream), peach cobbler, and blueberry pancakes. And to make sure you won't starve later in the day, "there's always something in the kitchen for a do-it-yourself lunch," Jim says. He also provides sack lunches—light fare in warm weather and steaming stew, chili, or soup come fall and winter—for adventuring around Greer.

HOW TO GET THERE: Greer is at the end of Highway 373, south of Highway 260 between Eagar and Pinetop/Lakeside. The inn is at the very end of Highway 373. It's on your left—look for the red "tin roof."

White Mountain Lodge
Greer, Arizona 85927

INNKEEPERS: Mary and Charlie Bast

ADDRESS/TELEPHONE: 140 Main Street (mailing address: P.O. Box 139); (520) 735-7568; fax (520) 735-7498

ROOMS: 7; all with private bath; wheelchair accessible; no air-conditioning (elevation 8,500 feet). Pets permitted.

RATES: $75 to $95, double; cabin $85 to $150; $10 extra person; EPB. No credit cards.

OPEN: All year.

FACILITIES AND ACTIVITIES: Nearby: fishing, hunting, and downhill and cross-country skiing at Sunrise Ski Area 13 miles away.

Mary is the daughter of original owners Sophie and Russ Majesky, and she and Charlie have taken over from the "old folks." I had loved Russ's answer when I asked why he liked being an innkeeper after supervising in Tucson's main post office. Not only did he say that both he and Sophie liked caring for people and that, although a lot of work, it was enjoyable, he also added energetically, "and—I gotta have something to do!" Now he's finding that he's just as happy with "a little less work to do."

Mary and Charlie say they are "refugees" from busy Tucson, where Mary was a health care administrator and Charlie also was in public administration. "Mom kept asking us when we were going to come up and take over, and I kept telling her to wait until our kids were grown." She laughs. "When I told her and Dad that finally we were ready, Dad said, 'I'm going to bed early!'"

White Mountain Lodge, the oldest building in Greer, began as a farmhouse, built in 1892 by one of the first Mormon families to settle in Greer. The Majeskys have preserved a wonderful landmark in a cozy and comfortable way, and Mary and Charlie have done nothing to change it, except for enhancing the breakfast menu a little.

The enclosed front porch and the main lodge room are comfortably furnished, and the word *cozy* keeps returning to my mind. The feeling is of warmth and interest in guests—genuine hospitality. "We've never charged a single cent for a cup of coffee in the years we've been in business," Charlie says. And the pot is on as early as 5:30 in the morning. This is the place for people who wake up early just dying for a cup of coffee. The full breakfast is served in the family dining room. In addition to orange juice, coffee, and toast and jam,  you'll have fresh fruit, a hot main entree, and homemade breads and rolls. "I'm the baker, Charlie's the cook," Mary explains as she serves honey-wheat bread, an apple or cherry coffeecake, melt-in-your-mouth butterhorns, and, maybe, a German sour-cream coffeecake.

"It really is a partnership. Wait until you taste Charlie's Grand Slam Breakfast!" It's a humdinger of a Mexican chorizo sausage casserole, served with hot tortillas and refried beans, and a fruit salad to cool things down a little. Breakfasting together with other guests, the Basts believe, "provides spontaneity in talk and in striking up friendships while at the lodge." And they find that such friendships often are ongoing. They say that they're seeing people from an entirely different perspective than from their former work: "As guests in your home," Charlie says. Mary finds that innkeeping in no way compares with what she used to do. "Putting on heels and a dress and going to an office? We love the independence of the lifestyle here! We have been blessed with seeing more elk, deer, and antelope grazing in the surrounding meadows," Mary says, "and of course the beaver continue to play in the ponds created by the Little Colorado River." "The elk kept me up, bugling last night," Charlie adds. "They say two things—baby, come my way, and hey, stay outa my way!"

HOW TO GET THERE: Greer is at the end of Highway 373, south of Highway 260 between Eager and Indian Pine. The inn is on the left as you enter the village.

Ramsey Canyon Inn
Hereford, Arizona 85615

INNKEEPERS: Shirlene and Ron DeSantis

ADDRESS/TELEPHONE: 31 Ramsey Canyon Road; (520) 378–3010

ROOMS: 6, all with private bath; 2 one-bedroom housekeeping cottages; no air-conditioning (elevation 5,400 feet); handicapped accessible. No smoking inn.

RATES: $90 to $125, double; EPB. Cottages: $85 to $105, double; $10 extra person; EP. No credit cards.

OPEN: All year.

FACILITIES AND ACTIVITIES: Picnic area. Nearby: Ramsey Canyon Preserves, bird-watching, hiking trails in Huachuca Mountains, Chiricahua and Coronado National Monuments, Tombstone, and Bisbee.

Ramsey Canyon Inn sits under tall pine trees at the very entrance to the Ramsey Canyon Preserves Nature Conservancy. Innkeeper Shirlene is a member of the conservancy and of the National Audubon Society, and she says the main reason people come to Ramsey Canyon is that more species of hummingbird have been recorded here than anywhere else in the United States. "Plus two hundred other

species!" Ron adds. "This is a bird-watcher's paradise, made for people who love nature and hiking. We go through fifty pounds of sugar a week, feeding literally hundreds of hummingbirds."

All the rooms are comfortable and cool, furnished with antiques refinished by Shirlene, who is both artistic and handy. She has stenciled decorations along the walls of each room with designs she painted to match comforters, pillow shams, and bed ruffles. "I like things to match," she says. Shirlene also bakes birthday and anniversary cakes and presents flowers to birthday guests, flowers that she has cultivated in spite of the voracious forest creatures that surround her. "The javelina and the deer eat everything I plant but snapdragons!" Along with the birds, the deer, and the javelina, you may see raccoons, coatimundi, ring-tailed cats, mountain lions, foxes, and small black bears in Ramsey Canyon.

Shirlene serves a full gourmet breakfast. Individual puffed Dutch pancakes with sliced strawberries and whipped cream; cooked apples, peaches, and blueberries; sausage; and cranberry-pecan or banana muffins will fuel a lot of hours of bird-watching. And you can do it lounging on the covered porch or under the tall black walnut, chokecherry, oak, maple, and sycamore trees of the picnic area if you wish, because Shirlene brings the show to her door.

HOW TO GET THERE: From I–10 take Highway 90 south, turning onto Highway 92 south through Hereford 6¾₀ miles to Ramsey Canyon Road. Turn right and follow the trail 3½ miles to the inn, on the right just before you enter Ramsey Canyon Preserves.

Ghost City Inn
Jerome, Arizona 86331

INNKEEPER: Joy Beard

ADDRESS/TELEPHONE: 541 North Main Street (mailing address: P.O. Box 382); (888) 63–GHOST; fax (520) 634–4678.

ROOMS: 5; 1 with private bath. No smoking inn.

RATES: $75 to $95, double; $15 extra person; EPB and afternoon tea.

OPEN: All year.

FACILITIES AND ACTIVITIES: Hot tub, parking in front. Nearby: restaurants, shops, galleries, historic buildings, Jerome State Historic Park Museum.

Joy's breakfast specialty is an artichoke and salsa bake, most original. "It has seven layers," she says, but insists that it's not hard to make. And it is delicious; here are the layers: (1) salsa, (2) artichokes, (3) mushrooms, (4) Parmesan cheese, (5) Monterey Jack cheese, (6) cheddar cheese, (7) a sour cream and egg mix. It's then all baked together—and, oh, my, is it delicious. But first you'll have strawberry yogurt, assorted cereals, and granola if you want, and Joy describes her blueberry, banana-nut, lemon-poppyseed muffins or apple turnovers as "some kind of breakfast bread, depends what I'm in the mood to bake!" Breakfast is served at 8:00 A.M., "but the coffee's out by 7:30," Joy promises.

Guests enjoy two common rooms, one downstairs and one up. Downstairs the parlor is for both visiting and eating, and the Cleopatra Hill Room opens right off the parlor. The room has a queen-sized antique pineapple bed (the inn is on Cleopatra Hill, in case you are wondering who she is) and lovely stained-glass windows. A spiral staircase leads to the upstairs common room, which offers a cozy corner sofa and wing chair. The room has a television and telephone, books,  and a shelf full of the most interesting teddy bears, all in funny costumes. The hot tub is on the porch, and there's even a waterfall—the grounds of the inn are on several levels, due to the fact that Jerome is built on the mountain!

The Satin and Spurs Room is furnished in contemporary Southwest style, with a queen-sized, very high up four-poster bed, all accented with Old West charm. The room shares a bath with Hearts and Flowers, a floral hideaway with a lovely curly brass, antique queen-sized bed, a television, and a Dutch door out to the veranda for a total or partial view of the Verde Valley. Ladies of the Night Room, the smallest, has a full-sized antique brass bed that's watched over by black-and-white photos of some of the real early inhabitants, like Miz Jennie Banters, Madame Pearl, Myrtle, Trixie, and Bubbles. The "ladies" room shares a bath with the Champagne and Propane Room, with teddy bears everywhere, especially on the oak queen-sized bed. Every door is festooned with a wreath, and some of the nice amenities include baskets of towels, shampoo, and so forth; terry robes; the bed turned down at night with a chocolate on your pillow; clock radios in every room—and afternoon tea and cookies promptly at 4:00 P.M.

HOW TO GET THERE: From I–17 take exit 260 and follow this to Highway 89A to Jerome. Once in Jerome, follow curving streets to Main Street, and the inn is on the right at the last curve before the one-way street going the other way. If you pass this, you've gone too far and had better follow the innkeeper's advice, which is to "just ask anyone in Jerome; they will know. Or call 63–GHOST if you get lost!"

High on a Mountain Peak

You have to see Jerome to believe it. It sits way on top of Mingus Mountain, and in this historic Wild West copper-mining town, you can look down on the green Verde Valley and see the fantastic red-rock formations of Sedona in the distance.

For all intents and purposes, Jerome has only one street, so don't get discouraged as you follow it around to the inns; you'll get there. Along the way you'll be treated to American architecture of the early twentieth century, because although the town's booming copper mines closed in 1973 and folks thought that Jerome would become a ghost town (the population shrank to about fifty), the buildings carry on as museums, art galleries, antiques shops, and restaurants.

The Surgeon's House
Jerome, Arizona 86331

INNKEEPER: Andrea Prince

ADDRESS/TELEPHONE: 100 Hill Street (mailing address: P.O. Box 998); (520) 639–1452 or (800) 639–1452

E-MAIL: surghouse1@juno.com

WEB SITE: www.virtualcities.com

ROOMS: 4; 2 with private bath; one room available for pets at innkeeper's discretion. No smoking inn.

RATES: $95 to $125, double; $25 extra person; EPB.

OPEN: All year.

FACILITIES AND ACTIVITIES: Hot tub, three terraced gardens. Nearby: restaurants, shops, galleries, historic buildings, Jerome State Historic Park Museum.

Just driving up to this inn is an exciting adventure. The road winds round and round Mingus Mountain, higher and higher as your ears pop and your eyes pop out at the spectacular mile-high views of mountain and valley. Jerome was first a booming copper-mining town, then a ghost town; now it's a tourist's dream of the picturesque and the quaint. Here Andrea Prince has rescued and restored the Spanish stucco house that was once the home of the town's mining-camp doctor.

But Andrea says that Jerome has rescued and restored her. "I'd been on the road thirteen years (as an engineering consultant), and something was calling me to stay home. Jerome picks people, people don't pick Jerome," Andrea says. She bought the house and finished many of the interior changes and restoration in four months, for which speediness she gives Jerome craftspeople full credit.

"The floors had eighty years of wax and varnish; the windows were either nailed, glued, or painted shut; all the ceilings had to be replaced, the bathrooms gutted," Andrea relates. But when the work was finished, the result was so attractive that people began asking for tours through the historic home.

Walking people through the house is what gave Andrea the impetus for innkeeping. "They were so appreciative, and I'm neither wealthy enough nor old enough to retire," she says, and she gets a lot of pleasure from sharing her home. The house sits high on a hill, and the huge picture windows in the living and dining rooms open onto the broad expanse of Verde Valley. The atrium next to the living room has wide arched windows, letting the sunlight in for the hanging baskets and brightening up the rattan furniture and the black-and-white tile floor.

Over the mantel in the living room, there's a lovely watercolor of the inn done by an area artist. From the dining room, French doors lead out to the garden. Poppies, wisteria, and delphiniums surround the house with grace and color, and there's an herb garden out the back door. Corner cupboards hold pretty china, and the cages of Andrea's two lovebirds are in the opening into the kitchen.

Andrea's breakfasts are really special. How about getting up for this breakfast: Jerome sunshine orange juice, creamy strawberry soup, pears and cherries in yogurt, eggs Lindsay (portobello ham and chilis), potatoes Roquefort, spicy breakfast beef, and a butterscotch stickie pull-apart?

The Blue Room has deep blue walls and white furniture; in the hall there's a wreath made by Andrea's great-grandmother, and she'll ask if you know what it's made from. The Maid's Room was occupied by the doctor's servant years ago, and Andrea relates how she met her recently. "Her name is Concha Garcia, she's eighty-six years old—and she now runs a tamale factory in Avondale!"

HOW TO GET THERE: From Prescott or Sedona follow U.S. 89A into town; the highway winds through the town, forming the principal thoroughfare. On Clark Street—at the corner near the Episcopal Church, across from the Jerome Palace, which houses the Haunted Hamburger—a cobblestone driveway leads to the inn.

Maricopa Manor
Phoenix, Arizona 85011

INNKEEPERS: Mary Ellen and Paul Kelley

ADDRESS/TELEPHONE: 15 West Pasadena Avenue; (602) 274–6302 or (800) 292–6403; fax (602) 266–3904

E-MAIL: mmanor@getnet.com

WEB SITE: www.maricopamanor.com

ROOMS: 5; all with private bath, phone, and TV; wheelchair accessible. Smoking in designated areas.

RATES: $89 to $229, double; $35 extra person; continental-plus breakfast.

FACILITIES AND ACTIVITIES: Hot tub. Nearby: Camelback Road with restaurants and shops; museums; state capitol and park; botanical and Japanese gardens; golf, tennis, festivals.

*L*ife wasn't busy enough for Mary Ellen and Paul, raising twelve children; now they've opened their lovely Spanish-style home as a very luxurious inn, which they're calling an urban inn instead of a country inn. The house is a combination of surprises: Off the spacious entry hall is a very formal living room with some beautiful French antiques. In fact, two of the fragile-looking end tables are 1937 reproductions of tables that Marie Antoinette had, probably at Versailles. Two satin love seats face each other in front of the fireplace, which has a screen made of Dutch lace. "But we move it in the winter, when we want a fire," Mary Ellen assures me. There's a harp, and guests make themselves at home both here and in the large, modern Gather-

ing Room, with a cathedral ceiling, and The Pit, a sunken corner that's the television area. Amusing and entertaining is an antique slot machine that still works. "Some guests are in high heaven with that," Paul says. "If it's your nickel, you keep your winnings; if it's our nickel, we keep."

The dining room is large, and, according to Mary Ellen, "It's seen many a family celebration dinner." Three of the children they raised were their own; the others were foster boys, as well as a Salvadoran exchange student who never went home! Married now, he and his family are part of the family.

Mary Ellen serves breakfast—fresh fruit, homemade bread and jams, and gourmet coffee—in a basket and delivers it to each suite. "We've had people take it to Sedona and even the Grand Canyon!" she says. "I change the china, and every morning there's a surprise." This morning it was a delicious quiche.

The inn's five unique and luxurious suites are a delight. The Library Suite has several hundred leather-bound books to read. Well, not all at once, but "that's what they're there for," Paul says. "People should enjoy them." The Palo Verde Suite, named for the state tree, has an original Franklin stove amid green and pink Laura Ashley fabrics; the Victorian Suite is done up in satin and lace with a mirrored armoire. Reflections Past has antique mirrors and a canopied bed; Reflections Present, adjoining, is a study in black, gold, and white modernity reflected in a collection of mirrors. "Our son said, 'Let's get out of the antiques for a change'—and it just seemed like a wonderfully crazy idea," Mary Ellen says with a laugh. She's enjoyed the change, even adding her own artistic touch, painting a lacy, black tree silhouette on two of the walls and adding the perfect touch of a red, red rose in a vase.

Both the large beautiful home, with its luxurious space and lovely grounds, and the gracious innkeepers make this a wonderful place to stay. "It's our home," Mary Ellen says simply, "and we now share it with anyone who chooses to come. People," she adds, "are so interesting. They [inn guests] are a special breed."

HOW TO GET THERE: From I–17 take Camelback Road east to Third; then go left on Third to Pasadena Avenue and turn right. The inn is one house west of the intersection of Pasadena and Central.

Bartram's White Mountain Inn
Pinetop/Lakeside, Arizona 85929

INNKEEPERS: Petie and Ray Bartram

ADDRESS/TELEPHONE: Route 1, Box 1014; (520) 367–1408

ROOMS: 5; all with private bath and patio; no air-conditioning (elevation 7,000 feet); electric blankets. No smoking inn.

RATES: $85, double; $20 extra person; EPB and afternoon snacks.

OPEN: All year.

FACILITIES AND ACTIVITIES: Infant equipment, ski storage, volleyball, badminton, horseshoes. Nearby: restaurants, Woodland Lake Park, Apache Indian Reservation, fishing, hiking, biking, tennis, horseback riding, skiing, golf, and antiques shops.

"We never hear traffic noises," Petie Bartram says happily. "Instead we hear birds and see wild horses, elk, eagles, and bears. The inn overlooks the Apache Indian Reservation, and the other day a herd of wild horses was grazing in the field shared by the inn and the reservation." Petie, having decided that if she kept on the way she was going, she'd be dead, gave up a well-paying job for life here in the woods. "I'm going to be dead a long time when I die," she says, "and this is what I want to be doing now."

Ray is a long-distance truck driver, but with the inn, Petie never gets a chance to be lonely. "My guests are fun," she says. "It's such fun when you have people who are willing to be fun back!" "But Petie," her guests protest, "it's you who's fun." And indeed, Petie works hard to make the inn special; she wants it to be an affordable escape for people who can't manage an expensive getaway resort. She and Ray do things like make homemade ice cream in the summer. "We do whatever fits into someone's lifestyle," she says.

In winter guests like to curl up with an afghan on the sofa in front of the petrified-wood fireplace and take a cozy nap. The fireplace heats the entire house. On the wall above, there's a collection of Apache snowshoes that guests who want to trek in the snow can borrow.

There are notions and hand-decorated towels in the bathrooms. Rooms were decorated with great enthusiasm by Petie, and it's a hard choice between the Blue Room, the Peach Suite, and the Satin Room. The Garden Room has a queen-sized bed and a daybed, done in lovely cool green and soft flowers. The Jenny Lind Room has the same, but in here it's all antiques. Both rooms have private entrances.

Petie is proud of her seven-course breakfast—a whopper. We had juice, coffee, tea, and hot chocolate; "cheesy eggs" with mushrooms, scallions, cream, and cheese sauce; hash brown potatoes with paprika and Parmesan cheese (or sometimes potato cakes with curry and sesame seeds); two kinds of muffins (banana sour cream with walnuts and bran raisin sticky buns); bacon (sometimes smoked turkey, ham, smoked pork chops, or Italian sausage); a fruit platter with cream sauce; and (time to holler "Enough!") stuffed French toast. Everything is delicious.

The inn has delightful pets, most unusual ones like Farnsworth, the house-trained pig, and Nugget, the parrot, who lives in a cage in the back room. "Nugget can walk right out here now; he's housebroken," Petie says. "All our animals are strays. Ray was making a delivery in back of a store at 3:00 A.M., and there was this big green parrot sitting out there. Ray held out his hand and the bird jumped on. They fell madly in love. We advertised, but no one came to claim him." There are also five outdoor cats and three dogs: the poodle, Shammy; a collie named Samantha; and another collie, Yum-yum. "But we call him Yummy," say the two animal lovers.

The Meadows Inn
Pinetop/Lakeside, Arizona 85935

INNKEEPERS: Don and Ev Sandstede, Howard and Jackie Bowers

ADDRESS/TELEPHONE: 453 North Woodland Road (mailing address: P.O. Box 1110); (520) 367–8200

ROOMS: 7; all with private bath and telephones; wheelchair access to two. No smoking inn.

RATES: $85 to $125, seasonal; $20 extra person; EPB.

OPEN: All year.

FACILITIES AND ACTIVITIES: Restaurant, library, games, VCR library. Nearby: Woodland Lake Park with hiking, nature trails, water sports; Apache Indian Reservation; fishing and boating, biking, tennis, golf, horseback riding, skiing, and antique shops.

*H*ere's an interesting find—a country inn that was built to be a country inn, a charming small place in a lovely country setting between the small towns of Pinetop and Lakeside, which grew until they grew together. The inn is set in the magnificent White Mountains, the wildlife is all around, and these innkeepers had a lot to learn about nature, since elk migrate here in the spring. The local black bears already know where and how to find what they like to eat.

The Sitting Room is two stories high, and you can look down at it from the staircase. A cozy fireplace, soft cushiony sofas, an antique Victrola, an organ—and a rocker—make it a pleasant place to rest for a bit. Upstairs the Library offers more than 300 books, as well as a television with a small video library and lots of games and puzzles. It's a pleasant retreat, with white leather sofas, a colorful rug, and an old trunk.

The guest rooms are almost too pretty to describe properly, and all have unusually large and bright bathrooms. The downstairs guest rooms are sunken, which makes for nice high ceilings—you step down a step or two into the room. Bright and fresh are the pretty flower-print quilts and wainscoted decorator wallpaper.

HOW TO GET THERE: The inn is off Woodland Lake Road between the twin towns of Lakeside/Pinetop. Turn south on Woodland Lake Road and take the first road on your left; it's a gravel road, and the inn is at the end of it.

The Marks House Inn
Prescott, Arizona 86303

INNKEEPERS: Dottie and Harold Viehweg

ADDRESS/TELEPHONE: 203 East Union Street; (520) 778–4632

ROOMS: 4 suites; all with private bath; no air-conditioning (elevation 5,300 feet). No smoking inn.

RATES: $75 to $135, double; company rate for business guests, breakfast extra; EPB.

OPEN: All year.

FACILITIES AND ACTIVITIES: Nearby: Historic Prescott Courthouse Square, restaurants, shops, and museums; golf, boating, hiking, tennis, and swimming at area lakes Lynx, Walker, Goldwater, and Watson.

High on a hill overlooking Courthouse Square and Whiskey Row, the historic Marks House stands in regal splendor, a fine old dowager of a mansion built in 1894 by an early Arizonian who was reputed to be the wealthiest man in the area at the time he built the home for his bride, Josephine. Jake Marks—trader, mine owner, and general merchandiser—evidently was quite an adventurer, joining General Crook in fighting the Pitt River Indian Wars. When he wasn't off fighting Indians, he also was involved in both the liquor business and the politics of the time.

Gorgeous sunsets are on view from the veranda and the curved windows in the circular corner turret of both the parlor and the Queen Anne Suite above. The old house is on the National Register of Historic Places, and it took seven years to restore it. The spacious mansion certainly bears witness to wealth, with polished hardwood floors and beautiful wood moldings and doors. The dining room floor is inlaid with a pattern of walnut, oak, and mahogany, and there is a fireplace back to back with the parlor one. The orig-

inal wood floors creak even when lightly trod upon, and there seem to be several resident ghosts. The creakings, thumps, and bumps that generally come with an old house add to the mystery.

The two bedrooms of the Ivy Suite on the main floor are decorated in soft greens, which complement the Victorian antiques; the Princess Victoria Room has an 1890s copper tub from a bathhouse in Syracuse, New York. The Tea Rose Room has a queen-sized bed and is close to the hall bathroom. In the mornings Dottie serves a main dish of some sort

The Town That Didn't "Just Happen"

Prescott didn't just happen. No sir, unlike most Western towns, the mile-high city was carefully laid out with New England–influenced buildings of, first, log cabins and, eventually, frame buildings. They were constructed of timber from the surrounding forests—no adobe haciendas for the founders of Prescott.

The city has some interesting historical sights, not the least of which is Whiskey Row, once a lineup of maybe hundreds of bars and brothels during the days when Prescott was a wild territorial capital. Today the only relic is the Palace Bar, but it does its best to carry on the traditional of the Wild West.

About a hundred Yavapai Indians live on a 1,400-acre reservation nearby; the Smoki Museum, with a wealth of American Indian artifacts, offers exhibits of their culture.

of breakfast casserole, along with fresh or cooked fruit, homemade muffins, coffee, tea, cocoa, and juice, and a side dish of breakfast meat if there's none in the casserole.

HOW TO GET THERE: From Courthouse Square go east up the hill of Union Street to Marina. The inn is at the corner of Marina on the right.

Pleasant Street Inn
Prescott, Arizona 86303

INNKEEPER: Jean Urban

ADDRESS/TELEPHONE: 142 South Pleasant Street; (520) 445–4774

ROOMS: 4; all with private bath. No smoking inn.

RATES: $85 to $155, double; $10 extra person; EPB.

OPEN: All year.

FACILITIES AND ACTIVITIES: Nearby: historic Prescott Courthouse Square; historic Whiskey Row; Prescott Fine Arts Association Theater and Gallery; Elks Opera House; hiking trails, boating, swimming, golf, and tennis at area lakes Lynx, Goldwater, Walker, and Watson.

*I*nnkeeper Jean rescued the pleasant house on Pleasant Street. The 1906 home had been moved from another location and was going to be demolished to make room for a new police station. A local contractor said, "You can't destroy historic property!" and he moved it. If you ask Jean what had to be done, she laughs. "Everything!" It's hard to imagine that it once was rather dark and gloomy; Jean has let a lot of light in. The house evidently had a hard life, and she opened it up with windows everywhere, from the bay in front to the big ones opening onto the two terraces. Summertime breakfast is served there, and guests also gather there for afternoon and evening sociability.

In the winter they gather around the fire in the living room, enjoying hors d'oeuvres and beverages and good company. The Pine View Suite, complete with a fireplace in the sitting room, has a king-sized bed; the bright and sunny Coventry Room, with its view of Prescott's tree-covered mountains, has twin beds that can be made into a king. Jean hopes that the Garden Room, with flowered fabric and white wicker furniture, will make guests think of an English garden. Downstairs, the Terrace Suite has both a sitting room and a private covered deck. The color scheme in the living room, of soft rose, blue, and gray, is restful. The old chestnut-pegged game table was inherited from Jean's parents, while many of the other pieces are antiques.

Jean's breakfasts are delicious. She'll serve you a continental one if you insist, but "nobody's asked for that yet," she says. I had warm spiced fruit with sour cream for starters. Next came stuffed French toast, chock-full of cream cheese, cinnamon, and nuts. With it there was ham, but sometimes it's sausage or bacon, whatever I'm in the mood for. The morning-glory muffins were glorious, too. Like the French toast, they were stuffed with such goodies as apples, nuts, and raisins. Jean's pumpkin muffins are not to be sneezed at, either.

HOW TO GET THERE: From I–17 take Highway 69 into Prescott. It becomes Gurley Street in town. Go about 4¹/₁₀ mile on Gurley to Pleasant Street, turn left, and go 2 blocks.

The Inn at the Citadel
Scottsdale, Arizona 85255

INNKEEPER: Lorraine Irving

ADDRESS/TELEPHONE: 8700 East Pinnacle Peak Road; (602) 585–6133; fax (602) 585–3436

ROOMS: 11; all with private bath; wheelchair accessible. No smoking inn.

RATES: $89 to $335, double; continental breakfast.

OPEN: All year.

FACILITIES AND ACTIVITIES: Two restaurants, piano bar, limo tours of the desert, health and beauty spa facilities, boutiques. Nearby: hiking to Pinnacle Peak; golf.

This posh, family-built inn in chic Scottsdale sits at the foot of outstanding Pinnacle Peak. The inn had a propitious beginning. Built on Hopi Indian land, the Hopis were invited to a blessing of the land. It's a pretty sumptuous establishment for the casual Southwest, more like a fine European-style hotel than a country inn, set in grand country with Pinnacle Peak just overhead.

Each of the eleven rooms is decorated with careful detail, down to the smallest item. Original artwork by such artists as Jonathan Sobel and Armond Laura hang on the walls, and antiques are used extensively. The armoires in six of the rooms were painted by local Arizona artists Liz Henretta, Skip Bennett, Sherry Stewart, and Carolyn Baer. Rooms have safes, robes, hair dryers, bath amenities, and an honor bar stocked with premium liquors, wine, and champagne, and playing cards, along with the expected soft drinks, crackers, and candy bars.

Fresh hot coffee comes along with the complimentary newspaper each morning. A massage, facial, or manicure can come to your room, too, if you wish. Each room has cable television with HBO. The larger rooms are more like suites, with large sitting areas and desks. The king-sized beds are covered with quilted satiny spreads, and the pillow shams match the dust ruffles. Actually, the Citadel is not just an inn. It's a restaurant and shopping complex in a shady courtyard complete with a pond and a bubbling waterfall. The continental breakfast begins with fresh-squeezed orange juice followed by a large serving of seasonal fresh fruit and moist zucchini, bran, or corn muffins, and, of course, coffee or tea.

HOW TO GET THERE: From I–17 take Bell Road 30 miles east to Scottsdale Road, then go north 4 miles to Pinnacle Peak Road, and east 2 miles to the inn.

Apple Orchard Inn
Sedona, Arizona 86336

INNKEEPERS: Paula and Bob Glass

ADDRESS/TELEPHONE: 66 Jordan Road; (520) 282–5328 or
(800) 663–6968; fax (520) 204–0044

ROOMS: 7; all with private bath; wheelchair accessible. No smoking inn.

RATES: $135 to $195, double; $20 extra person; EPB; lunch and dinner
if the entire inn is booked by one group.

OPEN: All year.

FACILITIES AND ACTIVITIES: Massage room and masseuse on call;
private tour guide; hiking trails; VCRs and videos. Nearby: half a mile
from shops, galleries, and restaurants; Sedona Heritage Museum;
airplane, helicopter, balloon rides; tours; horseback riding, jeeps, train
rides, tennis; Grand Canyon 110 miles north.

*P*art of the Historic Jordan Apple Farm, these inn grounds cover
two acres of the great outdoors, covered with piñon pine, juniper,
and Arizona spruce. Wilson Mountain and Steamboat Rock,
orange and red, ragged and craggy, loom protectively over the back of the
inn, providing a very picturesque backdrop.

Paula and Bob say they are working hard to be an "upscale" inn. Com-
mitted to the spirit of personal hospitality, they offer such amenities as
minirefrigerators in each room,
filled with water, juice, and
sodas—and it's complimentary.
The turndown service comes
with a chocolate on your pillow;
there are bathrobes and hair
dryers in the guest rooms. Most
rooms have patios and/or fireplaces; all have showers and
whirlpool tubs.

Each guest room is different—the only thing they have in common (aside
from comfort) is imagination. The Victorian is a plush, romantic room; the
Wild Bill Room celebrates the spirit of the West; Old Barn Sides sports a

headboard and an armoire fashioned from barn wood. In Old Mission you can sleep in an authentic Mission–style Stickley queen bed, or you can hide in The Hideaway, the inn's most private room. The Sedona Room, of course, has beautiful views of those famous red rocks, as does Steamboat Rock.

The large Great Room, with a rock fireplace, is furnished with an eclectic assortment of comfortable chairs and colorful Southwest rugs on the wide-plank wood floor. Breakfast is prepared by two chefs, John Paul and Susan Etlinger, whose credentials include training at L'Auberge de Sedona, Four Seasons in Boston, and culinary school in Milan, Italy. So you might feast on cheese blintzes with a brandied peach and cherry sauce, accompanied by sausage and fresh fruit with homemade scones. Or you might enjoy eggs Florentine, Canadian bacon, baked apples with cream, and fresh banana-nut bread—the mouthwatering possibilites are endless.

HOW TO GET THERE: From Highway 89A in Sedona, go through the Uptown (shopping) area, turning onto Apple Street (Oaxaca Restaurant on the corner), and continue on to Jordan Road. Turn right on Jordan and follow the gravel drive past the Apple Orchard sign on your right. The inn is up the slight hill.

Canyon Villa
Sedona, Arizona 86336

INNKEEPER: Marion and Chuck Yadon

ADDRESS/TELEPHONE: 125 Canyon Circle Drive; (520) 284–1226 or (800) 453–1166; fax (520) 284–2114

ROOMS: 11; all with private (whirlpool) bath, 1 with wheelchair access. No smoking inn.

RATES: $135 to $225, double; $25 extra person; EPB and afternoon refreshments.

OPEN: All year.

FACILITIES AND ACTIVITIES: Heated pool. Nearby: golf, tennis, and massage at Sedona Golf Resort; Oak Creek Country Club; Sedona Racquet Club.

Instead of remodeling or rebuilding for their inn, Marion and Chuck began from scratch. "We built from the ground up," Marion says. Driving up to the Moorish arches of the entrance, it's hard to tell whether this is real or an illusion. The beautiful, pale-pink stucco villa with its Mediterranean look lies at the base of one of Sedona's fantastic red rock formations, and the ensemble looks like a movie set. The blue Arizona sky and the clear, rarified air of Sedona add to the thought that the picture is too perfect to be true.

But Canyon Villa is as real as it is beautiful, and staying here is a wonderfully refreshing adventure. The villa's tall windows and wide doors open onto exhilarating vistas. "Just open the French doors to your patio or balcony and enjoy the view," Marion points out invitingly. Beyond the pool, which is bordered by bright green grass and fenced in by ornate white grillwork, Bell Rock and Courthouse Butte tower over the scene, seeming almost close enough to touch.

Marion and Chuck have lived all over the country, and although they like the four seasons, "we're warm-weather people at heart." And, like many others, they were looking for a change. "We were tired of the same old things and wanted to find something new before we got too old." She adds with a laugh, "It turned out to be a little more than we expected!"

The pride that Marion took in decorating the villa shows in every room of the spacious inn. Her grandmother's cut glass collection is displayed in a large, mirrored breakfront along with Waterford and Svartski crystal. The fireplace in the huge, vaulted-ceilinged common room opens through to the dining room, a large room containing two dining sets. "My Mom's, and mine," Marion says. "We can seat twenty-two."

For those who like to plan ahead, tomorrow's breakfast menu is out for perusal and anticipation. Today's delicious mushroom-and-artichoke omelette and homemade cinnamon rolls just might be upstaged by tomorrow's four-cheese herb quiche and angel biscuits.

Late afternoons, from 5:00 to 6:00, there are refreshments: maybe chips and guacamole, cream-cheese chutney, crab spread, or crackers and nuts, with iced tea and punch. Complimentary soft drinks and juices are available all day long and Marion's homemade Sweet Dreams cookies every night.

Her grandparents' sofa is comfy in the library off the patio, and there's a nice collection of reading matter. "We've even sent people home with books they want to finish—and they mail them back!" Guest rooms, described by Marion and Chuck as a blend of Old World charm and Southwestern style, are wonderfully imaginative. Decorating eleven separate rooms so charmingly takes a lot of talent. "Several pieces of furniture, like the dining room sets, and art pieces have been handed down through our family," Marion explains. The rooms are named for regional flora; what a choice—and what a chance to exercise every woman's decorating dream: Indian Paintbrush (country charm), Claret Cup (traditional elegance), Evening Primrose (Victorian), Ocotillo (Southwest Santa Fe), Spanish Bayonet (Old World Spain), Desert Daisy (Americana and quilts), Strawberry Cactus (garden wicker), Manzanita (rustic antique), and Prickly Pear (Old West and brass).

HOW TO GET THERE: From Highway 89A in Sedona, go south on 179 through Oak Creek Village; turn right on Bell Rock Road, go 1 block, and then take a right on Canyon Circle Drive.

Casa Sedona
Sedona, Arizona 86336

INNKEEPERS: John and Nancy True

ADDRESS/TELEPHONE: 55 Hozoni Drive; (520) 282–2938 or (800) 525–3756; fax (520) 282–2259.

ROOMS: 16; all with private bath; 1 with wheelchair access. No smoking inn.

RATES: $125 to $205, double; $25 extra person; EPB.

OPEN: All year.

FACILITIES AND ACTIVITIES: Nearby: walking trails, golf and tennis, Indian ruins, jeep tours, hiking, hot-air ballooning.

*B*reakfast here can be served in the Sunrise Alcove, to catch the first rays of the morning sun, or outside on the deck overlooking the garden between two huge cypress trees. The delicious full breakfast will begin with fresh fruit, a Southwest-style entree or pancakes, French toast or blintzes, and always homemade granola.

Guest rooms are lovely, each one more restful and pleasing than the next. They all have a terrace, spa tub, and fireplace. The Serena Room was inspired by the wallpaper; the Kachina Room, of course, was inspired by the dolls. Juniper Shadows pays tribute to the beautiful old trees on the property on which the inn was built.

The Cowboy Room is accessible to wheelchairs, and a sidewalk around the building leads directly to a dining deck. The Hopi Room was inspired by a Hopi dance. The Sierra Room is the television and music center. The library, with its cozy fireplace, was planned for reading and relaxing—the furniture was designed with that in mind. The inn itself was designed by architect Mani Subra, a disciple of Frank Lloyd Wright. He said, "I wanted to bring the view toward Casa Sedona, to have the surrounding natural environment and sky become part of the structure so that wherever guests sit or stand, they will be able to enjoy the view."

HOW TO GET THERE: From the intersection of Highways 89A and 179 in Sedona, follow Highway 89A into West Sedona. Go 3 miles west to Southwest Drive (or Tortilla Drive, which comes next), and turn right. Follow either road around to Hozoni Drive. The inn is at the end of Hozoni.

Cathedral Rock Lodge
Sedona, Arizona 86336

INNKEEPERS: Carol and Samyo Shannon

ADDRESS/TELEPHONE: Star Route 2, Box 856; (520) 282–7603;
fax (520) 282–4505

ROOMS: 4; all with private bath; suite with kitchen and TV; cabin with
full kitchen, deck, bath, bedroom, and upstairs loft. No smoking inn.

RATES: $80 to $150, double; $10 extra person; EPB, continental break-
fast in cabin. Two-night minimum on weekends; three-night minimum
for cabin; special rates for longer stays.

OPEN: All year.

FACILITIES AND ACTIVITIES: Picnic equipment, library of local history
and videotapes of movies filmed in red rock country. Nearby: Sedona,
with restaurants and arts and crafts; shopping at Tlaquepaque; 300-acre
Red Rock State Park for environmental education; hiking, horseback
riding, Indian ruins.

Carol and her son Samyo had no problem deciding what to name
their inn—wait until you see Cathedral Rock! From almost every
window of the inn, you can see this glorious hunk of the beautiful
red rock that the Sedona area is famous for. This is the scenery you oohed
and aahed at during all those
Western movies where the bad
guys chased the good guys among
gigantic formations.

Carol, who is from Tempe,
camped here with her children for
several years before she acquired
the inn. "I wanted to live in this
gorgeous country," she says, and
she gave up her work as volunteer
coordinator among the city's museums, libraries, and senior citizens. Now
she earns a living where she once only *dreamed* of living.

"Since so many people are on cholesterol-free diets, my biggest challenge
is finding eggless dishes," she says with a laugh. One specialty is sour-cream

Belgian waffles with pecans, along with ham, fresh fruit, and fresh-ground coffee. A Mexican breakfast is a guest favorite, too; it's a Mexican soufflé, with green chilies, not too spicy unless you want it that way. "You make Mexican food *picante* (hot) with the sauce," Carol remarks. "And Mexican food stays with you," she promises—in case you're worried about going hungry! In the afternoons, she sets lemonade, iced tea, and homemade cookies out in the lounge.

The lounge has a wall of windows, and that huge Cathedral Rock outside—red, red rock against deep blue Arizona sky—looks too good to be real. "Viewing Cathedral Rock, that's our most popular local activity," Carol announced one afternoon as she served lemonade to two contented Easterners sitting at the picnic table under the huge old shade trees. "We fell in love with these monster elms. There's nothing like them in Sedona; they must have been planted when the house was built in the forties."

Both guest rooms in the main house are furnished with family antiques, and the beds sport handmade quilts. Connected in back are the Garden Room, with its own wildflower quilt and photographs of Carol's mother and sister, and the Homestead Room, with lace curtains and room for three. The Amigo Suite overhead, with a private deck, has a king-sized bed, a double-bed couch, and a kitchen. When I visited, a pair of grandparents were happily ensconced up there with a small grandchild.

The cabin is a separate building with a private deck. It's a renovated 1940s cabin, and it has a kitchen, a queen-sized bed plus a sleeping loft for two, and a garden bath. "In cold weather, guests just come down in their robes," Carol says. Informality and comfort are the rule here. The common room is packed with books and magazines, children's films for the VCR, and information on hiking, historical sites, and Indian ruins to visit—once you decide to quit loafing at this happy inn.

HOW TO GET THERE: From the traffic light at the intersection of Highways 179 and 89A, go west on 89A 4¹⁄₁₀ miles. Go through West Sedona to the traffic light at Upper Red Rock Loop Road. Turn left and go 2⁷⁄₁₀ miles to the driveway marked with a bucket of flowers on the left side of the road.

Graham Bed and Breakfast Inn
Sedona, Arizona 86336

INNKEEPERS: Carol and Roger Redenbaugh

ADDRESS/TELEPHONE: 150 Circle Canyon Drive (mailing address: P.O. Box 912); (520) 284–1425 or (800) 228–1425; fax (520) 284–0767

E-MAIL: graham@sedona.net

WEB SITE: www.sedonasfinest.com

ROOMS: 6; all with private bath. No smoking inn.

RATES: $139 to $229, double; $20 extra person; EPB.

OPEN: All year.

FACILITIES AND ACTIVITIES: Pool and spa, bicycles. Nearby: restaurants, tennis, golf, racquetball, shopping at Tlaquepaque, horseback riding, jeep rides, hiking, Indian ruins.

*G*raham Inn is located in the heart of Arizona's red rock country, surrounded by jagged strata of bright orange rock jutting dramatically against the blue, blue sky. The inn, smooth and square and white, makes a cool contrast to its surroundings.

Traveling through Sedona, Carol and Roger, like so many others, were awestruck by the beauty of the famous red rock formations. I think it's called "red rock fever"! They purchased the inn from Marni and Bill Graham, who were such wonderful innkeepers that the Redenbaughs decided to keep the inn's name. "I wouldn't trade places with anyone in the world," Carol says of Sedona. "We love every second; we really have fallen into our niche. Lovely Sedona, lovely guests, and we're close to my sister Linda and brother-in-law John" (Linda and John Steele), who own Sedona's Territorial House Inn.

The inn was decorated by the Grahams, with the help of a California-trained designer, and the results were outstanding. The common rooms are welcoming, with views of wonderful red rock formations from wide glass windows up to the vaulted ceilings. The love seat in front of the fireplace is popular. "We have about one honeymoon couple a week," Carol says, "and they love to snuggle there; it seems to get a lot of action." Each guest room has a name with a theme to match. French antiques add to the charm of the Champagne Suite, with a king-sized bed and two cozy wing chairs in front of the fireplace. The private balcony offers views of Bell Rock and Courthouse Butte. The Southwest Room brings the glorious colors of Sedona indoors: the beiges, canyon reds, and teal. There's a love seat in front of the fireplace, a queen-sized bed, a balcony, and a Jacuzzi in the bath.

The Sedona Suite, in colors of mauve, clay, and teal, has a king-sized bed with two tall posters draped in soft fabrics. There's a tile fireplace with a cozy sofa, as well as a private patio here. The San Francisco Room has kept the soft grays and peach colors of the Sedona sunset. The new Country Room is a tribute to Carol's mother, who used to be a schoolteacher in Kansas. The old ledger she kept reveals what schoolteachers in Kansas were paid in 1940: $70 a month! The room is, for Carol, a memory of her childhood on a Kansas farm. The Garden Room has kept its white wicker furniture, dark-green-and-crimson wallpaper, and deep-green carpet. There's a private balcony here, too; and televisions and VCRs in each room with a nice video collection.

When Carol is chef, breakfast is a delicious German pancake; when Roger cooks, it's a special cheese strata, although more and more they've discovered that they enjoy working together. Accompanying the fresh vegetable frittata is something called praline bacon. "I can't make enough of it," Carol says of the meat coated with chili powder, crushed pecans, and sugar. The strawberry bread pudding is special, too, as are the baked bananas, the chocolate-chip banana muffins, and the always popular *huevos rancheros*.

HOW TO GET THERE: Canyon Circle Drive circles off Bellrock Boulevard, which is in the south Sedona suburb of the Village of Oak Creek. From Highway 179 turn west at the intersection that has a convenience store and a service store on the right—that is Bellrock Boulevard. Canyon Circle Drive and the inn are on the right about a block down the road.

Lantern Light Inn
Sedona, Arizona 86336

INNKEEPERS: Kris and Ed Valjean

ADDRESS/TELEPHONE: 3085 West Highway 89A; (520) 282–3419;
fax 520–282–3419

ROOMS: 3; all with private bath. No smoking inn.

RATES: $85 to $110, double, seasonally; $15 extra person; EPB.
No credit cards.

OPEN: All year.

FACILITIES AND ACTIVITIES: On-site shiatsu and deep-muscle massage
therapist and yoga instructor. Nearby: restaurants, shops, hiking, horseback riding; access to private tennis club with courts, pool, whirlpool,
steam room, aerobic studio, and fitness equipment.

*T*his small, cozy inn is named for Kris's collection of lanterns,
which are an interesting sight, especially if you arrive after dark
and see the entrance one all lit up. Two posts at the entrance
make the inn easy to find: On one post there's the inn sign, and on the opposite post is, of course, a lantern— and a huge one at that.

The curved drive of earth-colored stones leads to an open breezeway, also
full of plants and hung with lanterns. "I've collected them from everywhere,"
Kris says. "I even have more in the garage, waiting for a place!"

The inn has a unique arrangement, in that the guests get the
downstairs and the Valjeans have
the upstairs. The well-furnished
common area is a long room
that's for both sitting and dining,
with books and brochures as well
as a television/VCR corner. Up
the stairs are the innkeepers' living quarters and the kitchen.

Two guest rooms are off the long hall in the main building: The Queen's
Room, mauve and pink, opens onto a lovely back garden with a sundeck;
the King's Room next door is done in blue with oriental rugs. The Ryan
Room across the breezeway is large, with a sofa bed and a kitchen as well as
an entrance all its own.

Breakfast includes fresh-squeezed orange juice, mixed-fruit salad with lemon yogurt sauce, and hash brown or home-fried potatoes with a Southwest casserole of chilies, egg, and three cheeses. Other specialties are cheese blintzes with raspberries, Belgian waffles, and thin blueberry hotcakes, all served with sausage—"no pork; all sausage, bacon, and ham are really turkey." Delicious, too, are Kris's pies (vanilla, yogurt, coconut, Grand Marnier) that she plies guests with in the evening.

HOW TO GET THERE: Take Highway 89A west. The inn is on the left.

The Lodge at Sedona
Sedona, Arizona 86336

INNKEEPERS: Barbara and Mark Dinunzio

ADDRESS/TELEPHONE: 125 Kallof Place; (520) 204–1942 or (800) 619–4467; fax (520) 204–2128

E-MAIL: lodge@sedona.net

WEB SITE: www.sedona.net/bb/lodge

ROOMS: 13; all with private bath, 1 for the handicapped. No smoking inn.

RATES: $120 to $225, double; $25 extra person; EPB and afternoon refreshments.

OPEN: All year.

FACILITIES AND ACTIVITIES: Boardroom, sports court, horseshoes, basketball, holiday dinners. Nearby: uptown Sedona's shops and restaurants; walking trails, golf and tennis; Indian ruins, jeep tours, hiking; access to two local health spas.

Barbara and Mark make welcoming and eager innkeepers, despite the fact that they really didn't expect to be doing this. "We weren't looking for an inn," Barbara says with great good humor, "although I'd stayed in one in Ireland and decided it's the best way to travel. We were out biking and came by to look this property [The Lodge] over for someone else, who was interested in it as a treatment center. We fell in love with the property, but what we went through to get it!"

The Lodge began life in 1959 as a home for a doctor and his family of twelve. It went on to become a home for the elderly, a minister's home and church, and finally an in-patient rehab treatment facility. The friend wasn't interested in The Lodge, but Barbara and Mark were, thereby beginning two years of frustration and tenacity. "Just as we submitted our proposal, someone else bought it," Mark says.

"We were devastated," Barbara adds. "So we began a two-year journey, searched all over Phoenix for another property, and I finally had to say, 'Oh, well, maybe we're not meant to do this.'" But eventually there was a happy ending. "This fell out of escrow, and it was wonderful the way the community welcomed us."

The Lodge is secluded, shrouded in greenery and almost hidden from the road. Friends came to help with the restoration. "They'd come to do landscaping," Mark says. Barbara laughs. "And we'd end up in a bedroom discussing decor." Innkeeping assistant Michelle says Barbara is too modest about her decorating prowess. "When I ask her how she did such a wonderful job, she always says, 'Oh, my sister came up,' or 'A friend helped out.'" She laughs. "But I've heard her family say, 'We always knew Barbara could do it.'" Seven guest rooms are downstairs; six are up above. The Nature Suite has a king-sized bed and a comfortable sofa. French doors lead to the porch, and the pink tub in the bathroom lends itself to a luxurious soak. The English Garden has an undisturbed view of the colorful Sedona sunset, while the Master Suite and the Cherokee have private entrances. So does the Susannah, cozy with a pretty quilt and wicker chairs.

Both the Renaissance Room and the Traviso have a charming Old World European air, which is only fitting, since the latter is named for the Italian town that Mark's family came from. Things have gotten so busy that the inn boasts an Italian chef for weekend cuisine: Antonio Fiznoglia, who studied his art in New York.

Besides breakfast, afternoon refreshments are served from 5:00 to 6:00 P.M. Accompanying sodas and juices on some days are homemade pizza slices or chicken *taquitos*; on other days, guacamole, salsa, and chips or crackers and cheese.

The Lodge is situated on two and a half acres of wooded land, so there's lots of room to breathe. I awakened to the fragrance of pine and went eagerly to breakfast. We began with pears simmered in port wine with cinnamon and grated orange peel; next came The Lodge's specialty of the day: layered egg, cream cheese, and roasted red and yellow peppers. Other choices (or additions) were assorted juices and Barbara's special Lodge Granola with yogurt. The grand finale was a delicious blueberry crumb cake.

HOW TO GET THERE: From the intersection of Highways 89A and 179 in Sedona, follow Highway 89A into West Sedona for 2 miles west. Kallof Place is on the left, The Lodge on the right.

Saddle Rock Ranch
Sedona, Arizona 86336

INNKEEPERS: Fran and Dan Bruno

ADDRESS/TELEPHONE: 255 Rock Ridge Drive; (520) 282–7640; fax (520) 282–6829

E-MAIL: saddlerock@sedona.net

ROOMS: 3; all with private bath and cable TV with remote. No smoking inn.

RATES: $120 to $150, double; $20 extra person; EPB and afternoon snacks. Two-night minimum stay; extended-stay specials.

OPEN: All year.

FACILITIES AND ACTIVITIES: Swimming pool and spa, concierge service, Sedona airport transportation. Nearby: restaurants, shops, hiking, fishing, horseback riding, Hopi Mesa tours.

This luxurious home is not what you would expect from a place that calls itself a ranch. Today the historic homestead, built in 1926, is on the edge of a residential area. But it sits on three acres of hillside overlooking Sedona, and it has starred in many Old West films.

"I just saw a late-night thirties movie, *Angel and the Bad Man*," Dan says, "and there was our whole house! It was a dude ranch back then, and the wife of the owner always played an Indian princess in the films," he adds with a laugh. Fran and Dan, who met while both were employed at a prestigious California hotel, are experts in providing special attention to guests. What you'll get is the same VIP treatment that they gave to many of the "rich and famous." And before that Dan had a rather adventurous career: You might recognize his name, because he played football for the Pittsburgh Steelers.

"He's lived every man's fantasy," Fran says. "He also raced with Mario Andretti on the Indy circuit." They moved to Sedona for the climate, and now Dan and Fran are having an adventurous time innkeeping. "Our guests are wonderful, outstanding, and we want them to have the same total experience throughout their visit. It's a point of pride to us that our guests get the best of not only what we have to offer but what  Sedona has to offer as well," Dan says, so you can expect full concierge service with restaurant reservations at Sedona's finest—concerts, theater, tours, and anything else you, or they, can think of.

Guest rooms are elegantly comfortable, as is the living room. Large Saddle Rock Suite has a country-French canopied bed and a rock fireplace; furniture in the Rose Garden Room was Fran's great-great-grandfather's, and the room has its own private walled rose garden. The Cottage in back, with wood-paneled walls, is surrounded by panoramic vistas as well as having its own private patio. Robes, nightly turndown, chocolates, bottled water, afternoon snacks, guest refrigerator, and microwave oven—just make yourself at home in this just-about-perfect inn.

There are cuddly teddy bears everywhere, and it's Dan who collects them! "I was born at home, and the doctor brought a bear when he delivered me. I still have it," he says. It lives in retirement with other teddy bears on a daybed that belonged to his great-great-grandfather.

Breakfast is served in the large and sunny dining room, and specialties are heart-shaped peach waffles and individual Dutch babies (pancakes) filled with apples and vanilla ice cream or yogurt. "I like to use our local Sedona apples, peaches, and pears," Fran says. Orange juice is always fresh-squeezed, and if you prefer tea to coffee, there are sixteen different ones to choose from.

Fran, a professional potter, often welcomes returning guests with individual casserole dishes and a copy of their favorite breakfast recipe. At the rear of the property, a national forest shelters wildlife; deer come to the salt lick, and quail abound.

HOW TO GET THERE: Take Highway 89A (Airport Drive) to Valley View; go south 1 block to Rock Ridge Drive, left to Forest Circle, and right to Rock Ridge Circle; continue beyond Rock Ridge Drive and take the gravel road on the left up the hill to Saddle Rock.

Territorial House
Sedona, Arizona 86336

INNKEEPER: Linda and John Steele

ADDRESS/TELEPHONE: 65 Piki Drive; (520) 204–2737; fax (520) 204–2230

E-MAIL: oldwest@sedona.net

ROOMS: 4; all with private bath. No smoking inn.

RATES: $109 to $159, double; $20 extra person; EPB.

OPEN: All year.

FACILITIES AND ACTIVITIES: Exercycle, hot tub, hiking, biking. Nearby: uptown Sedona's shops and restaurants; walking trails, golf, tennis, Indian ruins.

*L*ittle angel figures scattered around the inn illustrate Territorial House's creed: "Do not neglect to show hospitality to strangers for by this some have entertained angels unaware." Linda has been collecting the figures for more than a dozen years. They delight in showing Old West movies that were filmed in and around Sedona. Linda's late-day snack of homemade gingerbread goes quite well with this activity.

All the guest rooms are named after areas or eras of Sedona history. Red Rock Crossing, opening off the porch, has a Southwest-style canopy bed and other rugged furniture, with a lighted breakfront chock-full of Precious Moment angels for contrast. Schnebly Station consists of two rooms, the Sedona Room and Carl's Cabin, and can sleep up to four persons. Carl's, up a curving stairway, has two cozy window seats under the eaves, and out on the balcony there's a telescope for long-distance mountain and moon viewing. "You can see the lights of Jerome from here," John boasts. Jerome is an old-timey mining town sitting atop a high mountain peak on the road to Prescott. The Sedona Room boasts a king-sized bed, a fireplace—and a needlepoint angel.

Breakfast, beginning with bananas and grapes and strawberry yogurt, continues in true Southwest style with blue-corn waffles and sizzling country links. "The syrup is 'light,'" Linda promises, and there's a delicious choice of maple and boysenberry. There are homemade bran muffins, too, and an assortment of coffee; you can choose Morning Blend or Folger's regular or decaf.

HOW TO GET THERE: From the intersection of Highways 89A and 179 in Sedona, follow Highway 89A west into West Sedona 3$\frac{1}{10}$ miles to Dry Creek Road. Turn right, go $\frac{2}{10}$ of a mile, then take a left on Kachina Drive. Piki Drive is on the left, about $\frac{4}{10}$ of a mile.

Strawberry Lodge
Strawberry, Arizona 85544

INNKEEPER: Jean Turner

ADDRESS/TELEPHONE: HCR 1, Box 331; (520) 476–3333

ROOMS: 12; all with private bath; wheelchair accessible; no air-conditioning (elevation 6,000 feet). Pets permitted.

RATES: $45 to $57, double; $3 to $6 for rollaway, extra person; EP. No credit cards.

OPEN: All year.

FACILITIES AND ACTIVITIES: Restaurant, barbecue patio. Souvenir shop. Nearby: gateway to the Mongollon Ridge with fishing, hunting, horseback riding, hiking, scenic attractions.

I knew this was a happy place the minute I walked in the door. If it hadn't been the vibrations telling me so, it would have been the happy voices in the crowded restaurant, which is where everybody enters the lodge, although there's a perfectly good entrance to the inn lounge. Back when Jean's children were small and her husband, Richard, was alive, the family drove through Strawberry on a holiday. "Oh," she said then, with her wonderful enthusiasm, "wouldn't this be a heavenly place to live!" So it seemed like fate when later on they saw "a little two-line squib about a hunting lodge for sale" in that very place.

The lodge was so neglected that it was a big challenge. "My husband, who had never built a thing in his life, built all the fireplaces and did all the wood-work." Each of the newer guest rooms has a real wood-burning fireplace, and each is different. Richard used all native materials in remodeling the inn,

learning how to do it himself. Rooms are rustic but warm and comfortable, with wood-paneled walls and nice touches like coordinated print wallpaper in the bathrooms and designer linens and quilts on the beds.

I was dying to know how the town got its name. "The original settlers found this whole valley a mass of wild strawberries—at least that's the story," Jean says. Now the only strawberries are at happy Strawberry Lodge.

HOW TO GET THERE: Strawberry is on Highway 87/260, and the inn is on the left just as you drive into the town from the south.

Priscilla's Inn
Tombstone, Arizona 85638

INNKEEPERS: Barbara and Larry Gray

ADDRESS/TELEPHONE: 101 North Third Street (mailing address: P.O. Box 700); (520) 457-3844

E-MAIL: prisc@theriver.com

WEB SITE: www.priscilla@tombstone1880.com

ROOMS: 4; 1 with private bath and TV; portable phone. No smoking inn.

RATES: $39 to $69, double; $15 to $18 extra person; EPB.

OPEN: All year.

FACILITIES AND ACTIVITIES: Large gardens with paths through flowerbeds, fountains. Nearby: historic town with walking map of shops and restaurants, OK Corral, Boot Hill Cemetery, Tombstone Historama, Tombstone Epitaph, Pioneer Home Museum, and others.

Barbara Gray has named her inn after her mother, who was born in 1910. "She was a bit Victorian—there's a picture of her at nineteen, over there above the doll collection." The two-story clapboard house was built in 1904 by an affluent Tombstone attorney. Painted in authentic Victorian colors, its gardens are surrounded by the original picket fence. The living room and dining room are typical of a comfortable family-style home at the beginning of the new century.

The downstairs suite offers a choice of twin beds in one room or a double bed in the other, and there's a comfy rocker. I liked the old roller-top desk in the entry, which was opened up by removing a wall and rerouting the large old oak staircase—originally it led down to the dining room. "I think we did a good job of matching the wood," Barbara says as she strokes the smooth wood banister of the new addition. Upstairs, all three guest rooms have wash basins, set very cleverly in lovely antique dressers and bureaus, and the bath they share is large. The shower has an absolutely huge tile seat. The Violet Room has an antique brass bed, covered by a pretty print spread in soft pastels, and a wood floor.

Breakfast, served on the large oak dining table, begins with grapefruit halves, followed by bacon, sausage, scrambled eggs, and, if you're lucky, pancakes made by Larry. Thin and crisp, Larry's pancakes are out of this world. "Several couples have asked me, 'If we come back, will Larry make the pancakes?'" Barbara says with a delighted laugh. She's also delighted with the way guests enjoy her garden, the result of hours of loving care. Sometimes she serves tea, coffee, and cookies among the flower beds and fountains.

HOW TO GET THERE: From Highway 80 turn north onto Third Street and go 1 block to Safford. The inn is on the corner of Third and Safford, on your left.

Casa Alegre
Tucson, Arizona 85705

INNKEEPER: Phyllis Florek

ADDRESS/TELEPHONE: 316 East Speedway; (520) 628–1800; fax (520) 792–1880

ROOMS: 5; all with private bath. No smoking inn.

RATES: $80 to $105, double; $10 extra person; EPB. Weekly, business, and seniors' rates available.

OPEN: All year.

FACILITIES AND ACTIVITIES: Swimming pool, hot tub, exercise equipment, holiday dinners. Nearby: University of Arizona campus, University Medical Center, Tucson Community Center, Fourth Avenue businesses and restaurants.

"One of the nicest things about being near the university," Phyllis Florek says, "is the interesting people who come to stay here. Italy, Belgium, South Africa, a biologist/anthropologist from Argentina . . . " The guest books she's placed in each room make fascinating international reading.

Phyllis became an innkeeper because, she says, "people are fun." Once busily managing the service branch of a California bank, she suddenly asked herself, "What do you really want to do?" Sitting down then and there, she wrote a list of her requirements. "Sunshine, cultural action, history...and then, I had gone to high school and college here in Tucson, so it was like coming home." Casa Alegre has a great location, right between the University of Arizona and downtown Tucson. Built in 1915, it has been home to a pharmacist, a doctor, and an artist. Phyllis has furnished her inn with pieces that reflect highlights of Tucson history, from its beginnings as an Indian nation to the mining industry that figured so largely in Arizona's development.

The inn's parlor, with its white walls and shining dark woodwork, has a period look. The golden wood floor is graced by large, colorful rugs, and an upright piano is angled in a corner by the door to the sunroom. Off the formal dining room, a door opens into that bright and sunny room, furnished with yellow wrought iron and white wicker.

"Someone in California gave me the fabric, and a friend and her parents brought a sewing machine here and made the curtains," Phyllis says—how nice to have such friends! The same pretty fabric is used for the looped valances and the window-seat cover. "This is a favorite place for winter breakfasts," Phyllis adds, and I can see why.

Books and games are in the hall. "When people come in and sit down, it's fun to see what they choose to play," Phyllis says. The Arizona Room has the television set. "No television or telephone in your room to interrupt your relaxing visit with us." (Three guest rooms have phone jacks if you're serious about communicating with the outside world.) This common room opens onto the patio, a courtyard bright with Mexican morning glories and mesquite around a fountain. "Gee, you don't realize you're in the middle of town!" was one guest's surprised comment.

The furnishings of the Saguaro Room, with its own fireplace, were inspired by the cactus of the same name: The handmade armoire and the queen-sized lodgepole bed sport ribs from the sturdy desert plant. Mining memorabilia sets the theme for the Rose Quartz Room—Phyllis's father was a mining engineer. "My mother says he spent most of his life in a hole in the ground," she says jokingly. The Spanish Room's queen-sized headboard was made originally for a Mexican priest, and the Amethyst Room is decorated with early-1900s antiques.

Phyllis carries her decorating philosophy to the breakfast table. "It's the mental image," she says. "If people can say, 'Oh, that looks good!' they know it's going to *taste* good." Raisin bread French toast stuffed with cream cheese, "very health-conscious turkey sausage," sliced plums on green lettuce—yes, it tasted as good as it looked!

HOW TO GET THERE: From I–10 take Speedway Boulevard east 1 mile to Fifth Avenue. The inn is on the right, on the southeast corner of Speedway and Fifth.

El Presidio
Tucson, Arizona 85701

INNKEEPERS: Patty and Jerry Toci

ADDRESS/TELEPHONE: 297 North Main Avenue; (520) 623-6151 or (800) 349-6151

ROOMS: 3 suites; all with private bath, phone, and TV. No smoking inn.

RATES: $95 to $115, double; $25 extra person; EPB. Weekly and monthly rates available. No credit cards.

OPEN: All year.

FACILITIES AND ACTIVITIES: Courtyard garden, bicycles. Nearby: restaurants, historic district, Sonora Desert Museum, Old Town Artisans handicrafts.

Patty is strongly dedicated to two things. The first is the landmark historic district that surrounds the El Presidio Inn. The second, in my opinion, is the marvelous food she serves her guests. The Tocis have won several awards for her restoration of the old property. "My focus," Patty says, "is this landmark historical property and the entire district. This is where Tucson began, at El Presidio, when Tucson was a walled city to protect the settlers from Apache Indians."

The delightful Territorial Victorian adobe building looks deceptively small. Built on a corner, it hides a large back courtyard—the pride of Patty and Jerry's gardening talents, centered with a fountain that Jerry found in Mexico and shaded with a huge magnolia that provides greens for Christmas celebrations. "I'm a good old Southern girl," Patty says. "We always had magnolia greens back home for Christmas, and when old friends visit us here, they can't believe our big magnolia, growing right here in Tucson, Arizona!

"Innkeeping is a great lifestyle," Patty says. "It's your social club as well." Breakfasts on the glassed-in sunporch are leisurely feasts, so don't be in a hurry. Patty says she has so many repeat guests that she makes notes on what she fed them last. The long table is beautifully appointed. On my visit we began with fresh orange juice, then progressed to a magnificent fruit cup of kiwi, strawberry, orange, pineapple, and cantaloupe. Next came two kinds of French toast, one made of cinnamony raisin bread, the other stuffed with homemade peanut butter and bananas. Canadian bacon came with this, and yet I really could not resist having two of the lemon-nut muffins topped with streusel. Like every good cook, Patty was pleased as punch to see me stuff myself! "The recipe for the lemon muffins isn't original with me," she says. "But the streusel topping is."

She puts her happy touch on everything. Guest rooms are provided with fruit, juice, coffee, teas, and snacks. There are bathrobes to wrap up in. The

Victorian Suite, with a huge sitting room furnished in cool white wicker, has a photograph of Patty's grandmother, setting the period mood. The Carriage Suite combines an Eastlake lady's desk with a collection of Southwest antiques, including a trunk that held a pioneer's goods. The Gatehouse Suite has Bar Harbor–style wicker furniture. The Zaugan Room, the lovely common room, has a tile fireplace, wreaths of fragrant dried flowers, books to read, and current magazines providing information on the best of Tucson. "We've been living here long enough to know the best things to do," the Tocis say. "The Mexican and craft festivals here in our neighborhood during spring, summer, and fall have become grand affairs."

HOW TO GET THERE: From I–10 take the St. Mary's exit and go right 4 blocks to Granada. Cross Granada to the next street, which is Main. Turn right at the intersection of Main and Franklin, and the inn is on the southeast corner. Curbside parking is permitted if you get a permit from Patty to put on your windshield.

Catalina Park Inn
Tucson, Arizona 85705

INNKEEPERS: Mark Hall and Paul Richard

ADDRESS/TELEPHONE: 309 East First Street; (520)792–4541; fax (520) 792–0838

E-MAIL: cpinn@flash.net

WEB SITE: www.catalinaparkinn.com

ROOMS: 6; all with private bath and telephone. No smoking inn.

RATES: $95 to $125, double; EPB.

FACILITIES AND ACTIVITIES: Three gardens. Nearby: downtown, restaurants, Sonora Desert Museum, art and photography museums, Old Town Artisans handicrafts, University of Arizona, easy drive to Sabino Canyon and Saguaro National Monument.

*I*f you're interested in the finer details of older homes, when craftsmanship was highly valued, you'll like the beautiful woodwork and architectural details of this 1927 showcase—not to mention its being close to downtown and the University of Arizona. Two small dogs, Jackie and Pearl, will welcome you, and the full gourmet breakfast will give you energy to tour the area.

"It's an easy drive to the Sonora Desert Museum," the innkeepers say, as well as to Saguaro National Monument, with its acres of strangely shaped cacti. But you can see desert cactus much closer to home: One of the inn's three gardens is a cactus and succulent garden. The other two celebrate roses, both the East Rose Garden and the West Rose Garden. The six guest rooms have very comfortable beds, as well as robes, hair dryers, even iron and ironing board if you feel inclined to spruce up. The Oak Room has a tall four-poster, flanked by a pair of very cozy lavender easy chairs facing the television set. The  West Room has bookshelves and a pair of framed oak prints. The plushly pillowed bed is covered with a plaid that matches the drapes, and the bed's dust ruffle and nearby easy chair are matched in forest green.

The Billiard Room is Southwest, with twin beds and a sofa, as well as an easy chair to lounge on. Depending on the weather, you'll find a cheerful fire blazing away in the common room. On both sides of the fireplace, lighted cabinets display a colorful collection of china plates.

For breakfast you'll be treated to such gourmet specialties as papaya-and-lime scones, lemon ricotta pancakes, pear crisp, and lots of San Francisco coffee.

HOW TO GET THERE: From Tucson Airport take Benson Highway exit to Kino Parkway, which becomes Campbell Avenue. At Speedway Boulevard go left onto Fourth Avenue for 1 block to East First Street and turn right. Inn is at the end of the block on the right. From Highway 10 take exit 257 (University of Arizona/Speedway Boulevard) east to Fourth Avenue, turn right 1 block to East First Street and turn right. Again, the inn is at the end of the block on the right.

Hacienda Inn
Tucson, Arizona 85712

INNKEEPERS: Barbara and Frederick Shamseldin

ADDRESS/TELEPHONE: 5704 East Grant Road; (520) 290–2224 and (888) 236–4421; fax (520) 721–9066

E-MAIL: hacienda97@aol.com

WEB SITE: members.aol.com/hacienda97

ROOMS: 4; all with private bath and telephone; 1 with wheelchair access. No smoking inn.

RATES: $85 to $105, double; $25 extra person; EPB and evening treats.

FACILITIES AND ACTIVITIES: Heated outdoor spa, exercise room, secluded patio, off-street parking. Nearby: restaurants, Sonora Desert Museum, Sabino Canyon, San Xavier Mission, Saguaro National Park, Old Tucson Studios, Pima Space and Air Museum.

Relax at the pool, or work out at the exercise room—or just fall apart in one of the Great Rooms opening off the courtyard. Each has a fine sound system if you want to be soothed by music. Soft sofas, armchairs with hassocks to stretch your legs on—ah, this is the life. The downstairs common room has a hardwood floor for dancing, and the upstairs Arizona Room looks out toward the Catalina Mountains.

The Teal Room downstairs is handicap accessible and has a coffee maker and microwave. Upstairs, both the Jade Room and the Desert Rose Room share the  convenience of the Arizona common room, with TV/VCR, a small refrigerator, and table and chairs. Both the Desert Rose Room and the Turqoise Room have hide-a-beds. The solar pool is next to the heated spa, and the exercise room is equipped with Stairmaster, treadmill, and free weights. All rooms have telephones and cable television. Access to an on-line service is available for e-mailing from your home away from home in this contemporary setting.

The full breakfast includes fruit or orange juice; hot breads; eggs; and sausage, bacon, or ham. If you have special dietary needs, just give Barbara advance notice and she's pleased to accommodate you.

HOW TO GET THERE: From I–10 take Grant Road east to number 5104 to Craycroft Road. The inn is on the right just past the road.

La Posada del Valle
Tucson, Arizona 85719

INNKEEPERS: Karin and Tom Dennen

ADDRESS/TELEPHONE: 1640 Campbell Avenue; (520) 795–3840; fax same

ROOMS: 5; all with private bath; 2 with telephone. No smoking inn.

RATES: $90 to $135, double; $25 extra person; EPB.

FACILITIES AND ACTIVITIES: Lunch and dinner catered by reservation; bicycles, patio. Nearby: University of Arizona, Art District, restaurants, Sonora Desert Museum, art and photography museums, Old Town Artisans handicrafts, discount membership to Tucson Racquet Club.

La Posada del Valle occupies a lovely villa designed in 1929 by a renowned Tucson architect, Josias T. Joesler. Built of adobe and stucco, the inn is a perfect example of early Santa Fe–style architecture. Tom is a retired Air Force colonel, originally from Boston. Karin is a nurse from Germany, and they met in Cape Town, South Africa! "We lived a dream in Africa," Karin says nostalgically. "We raised our three children on an eighty-acre farm on the Crocodile River outside Johannesburg." While they were there, Tom owned various enterprises. "One of them was a chain of fast-food and ice cream parlors called Pickin Chickin–Dairy Den," Karin says. "When it was time to leave South Africa, we found our place in the sun— Tucson, Arizona."

She says that one lucky day they walked into enchanting La Posada del Valle, bought it, painted it, loved it, and "retained its charm." Rooms are named for women who were popular back when the house was built, carrying out the twenties and thirties theme. There are Pola's Room (Pola Negri, actress), Isadora's Room (Isadora Duncan, dancer), Claudette's Room (Claudette Colbert, actress), Zelda's Room (Zelda Fitzgerald, dancer and perhaps, as some claim, F. Scott's ghost writer), and Sophie's Room (Sophie Tucker, singer). All but one have a private entrance, and all are furnished with fine antiques and other period pieces.

Each room has black-and-white photographs of the women. Fresh flowers from the gardens make each room fragrant, and the innkeepers provide

personal touches such as turned-down beds, freshened rooms, candy, and mints. There's a menu basket in the living room, and the innkeepers make a point of helping with guests' plans and reservations for dinner.

The patio is certainly enchanting, with a fountain and ornamental orange trees. They were planted by nuns from a nearby church who lived in the house awhile back. I doubt that they would recognize the trees now, they have grown so. It's delightful to sit out under the orange trees and breathe in their fragrance, but the oranges there are not for eating, alas. But grapefruit and lemons from inn trees are served. Breakfast might be cream cheese blintzes with raspberries, and there are always home-baked bread, muffins, and coffee cakes.

Breakfast is served in the dining room, which overlooks the Catalina Mountains. Afternoon tea, with the beverage either hot or cold, will be served with cookies and fancy bread-and-butter scones in a living room appointed with fine Art Deco furnishings from the 1920s and 1930s or in the courtyard—in Tucson, the weather is usually very pleasing! "At tea time we either mingle with the guests or leave them alone," Karin says, sensitive to the prevailing mood.

HOW TO GET THERE: From I–10 take Speedway Boulevard exit and go east on Speedway to Campbell Avenue. Take Campbell north to Elm Street. The inn is on the corner of Campbell and Elm; the inn entrance is on Campbell, but there is guest parking on the side of the inn on Elm.

Rimrock West
Tucson, Arizona 85749

INNKEEPERS: Mae and Val Robbins

ADDRESS/TELEPHONE: 3450 North Drake Place; (520) 749–8774

ROOMS: 3; all with private bath and TV; wheelchair accessible.
No smoking inn.

RATES: $120, double; cottage $175; $40 extra person; EPB.
No credit cards.

OPEN: All year.

FACILITIES AND ACTIVITIES: Twenty acres with swimming pool; art
gallery, hiking, bird- and other wildlife watching. Nearby: Raven Golf
Course; twenty minutes from the University of Arizona, airport, and
metropolitan Tucson.

This Southwest hacienda is a haven of peace and quiet; even the
road leading to the spread-out, low pink stucco building is a private one. The Catalina Mountains sprawl across the northern
horizon, with the Rincon Mountains to the east. Terra-cotta pots spilling
over with pretty pink flowers line the portales of the entrance, and a hammock is strung under the roof in a corner. And if an artist's easel is sitting out
in front, you'll know for sure that you've come to the right place: The whole
Robbins family is artistic. Val is a sculptor and furniture maker; Mae does
enamel work, as her beautiful tiles, which enhance the blue-and-white
kitchen, proclaim. Artwork by both hosts and son Christopher beautifies the
inn. Mae and Christopher are self-taught.

Val's handiwork is evident, beginning with the cocktail table in the television room and continuing on to the chests in the dining room. He's been

Casa Grande Ruins

Casa Grande National Monument, midway between Phoenix and Tucson, preserves an important chapter of America's prehistory. For centuries, wandering groups of Native Americans survived in this desert, gathering fruits from the surprising fruitfulness the Sonoran offered: edible cacti like saguaro, cholla, hedgehog, and prickly pear. They hunted the desert's wild animals, small game like jackrabbits and bigger game like mule deer and bighorn sheep. For these Stone Age people, survival was a daily challenge—think of having no metal tools, no wheels, no horses or any other beasts of burden.

But, desert or no desert, there was water. About 2,000 years ago these desert dwellers, somehow influenced by Mexican civilizations to the south, developed a new way of life. The Gila River flowed nearby, and with only Stone Age tools, the Hohokam dug hundreds of miles of canals across the desert, irrigating it and making them the first farmers in the American Southwest. They grew corn, beans, squash, cotton, and tobacco, and they began to build permanent villages, compounds such as that at Casa Grande. But between 1300 and the mid-1400s they disappeared.

Where did they go? Although they left no written records, evidence of their lives is found at Casa Grande Ruins. Yet a few years after the building of the Big House, they abandoned this and other compounds. There is evidence that years of heavy flooding were followed by years of low river flow, possibly damaging both canals and crops, causing irrigation canals to fall into disrepair and trade routes to break down until, by the mid-1400s, the Hohokam culture disintegrated. Community building came to a halt, and the Hohokam disappeared as a people.

When the Spanish came in the 1600s, all they found were small farming villages, peopled by Pima and Papago Indians who today call themselves the O'odham. It's recorded that Spanish missionary Father Kino, who founded a mission in the area, was told by Pima Indians nearby that their ancestors were "ho-ho-KAHM," "all gone," or "all used up," and this has become the name of the ancient peoples.

making furniture for more than twenty years and some fine pieces of sculpture as well. Not everything is newly crafted; there's a lovely antique desk in the foyer and a wonderful hand-carved antique headboard in the Queen Room, brought with them from Pennsylvania.

Breakfasts are works of art, too. Strawberry waffles smothered with whipped cream, sinful! All-bran muffins, though, are healthy enough, and there are also cornbread muffins or crunchy apple streusel ones for your sweet tooth. Mae is famous for her smoothies, too. "I just throw everything from the fruit bowl into the blender and add orange juice. Everybody loves them!" What Mae loves is to garden. "It's my life," she declares passionately. The only problem is the jackrabbits. They eat everything, even the cactus. "But we're planting faster than they can eat," she says with satisfaction.

HOW TO GET THERE: From I–10 take Grant east to Wilmot (which becomes Tanque Verde) for approximately 4 miles to Catalina. Turn left and go 1 mile to Prince. Turn right on Prince; in 1 mile turn right onto North Drake Place. There is a sign on Prince; the inn is at the end of short North Drake Place.

The Suncatcher
Tucson, Arizona 85748

INNKEEPER: Shirley Ranieri

ADDRESS/TELEPHONE: 105 North Avenida Javelina; (520) 885–0883 or (800) 835–8012

ROOMS: 5; all with private bath, phone, TV, and VCR; wheelchair accessible. No smoking inn.

RATES: $140 to $165, double; $25 extra person; EPB.

OPEN: All year.

FACILITIES AND ACTIVITIES: Heated pool and spa, bicycle. Nearby: restaurants, tennis and health club, hiking, horseback riding, Saguaro National Monument; fifteen minutes to downtown Tucson.

The Suncatcher has tried to take all the qualities of a first-class hotel and put in the charm of a bed-and-breakfast," Shirley says of her luxurious inn. "I've kept everything just about the same as it was with the previous owner, David Williams." A sure clue is each guest room's name, that of one of the world's prestigious hotels. There's the Connaught, the Four Seasons, the Regent, and the Oriental.

One guest room opens off the huge airy and spacious common area, two have French doors opening off the pool, and the fourth is around the corner with its own entrance. The Connaught (London) is furnished with Chippendale-style furniture in gleaming dark mahogany; the Four Seasons with a formal canopied bed. The Regent (Hong Kong) has lovely original Oriental scrolls, and the Oriental (Bangkok), the largest, has its own Jacuzzi among other splendors. All have at least one comfortable chair, writing desks, original artwork, and fresh flowers.

Shirley has kept the inn emblem, little terra-cotta faces that are on the walls and elsewhere. "The inn was named for the desert attractions—the sun, the dry heat, the desert—and I want to keep it as a retreat, a getaway, a place to catch the sun."

She had a restaurant in New Jersey for fourteen years, "and I was ready for a change," she says. "I began thinking about other things I could do." She'd always come west for vacations, and when she began to look for a house, with plans to open another restaurant, she came across The Suncatcher for sale. With the inn, she says she has the best of both worlds: a home and looking after people. (And, she confides, she's finding innkeeping much less work than a restaurant!)

"I'm used to taking care of people," she says with a laugh. "I have a nursing degree, and I love being around people. And I love Tucson—it's absolutely beautiful." The huge common area (seventy square feet), with its soaring ceil-

ing, has several focal points. In one corner there's a large copper-hooded fireplace; in another, a mirrored mesquite bar. Display cases show off treasures from Shirley's travels to Thailand and Hong Kong, and she has also collected interesting Southwestern pieces. The entire area—sitting, dining, kitchen—is open, and you can watch the chef prepare breakfast. It's a full hot meal, with Southwestern eggs or maybe an omelette—mushroom, perhaps, or ham and mozzarella cheese—accompanied by corn muffins, blueberry muffins, cheese pastries, and bagels.

Shirley says the open space seems to lure her guests from their rooms. "People can mingle; they hang out in the main house now, since I leave the door open all the time. We sit around and talk and laugh; people talk about things in their lives. It's nice. My pleasure is sitting down and speaking with my guests."

HOW TO GET THERE: The inn is on the edge of Saguaro National Monument. From I-10 and downtown Tucson, take Broadway east, crossing, as a last landmark, Houghton. Continue on to Avenida Javelina, bearing in mind that Avenida Javelina is beyond the DEAD END sign on Broadway. Turn north on Javelina, and the inn is on the left in the middle of the block.

The Johnstonian Inn
Williams, Arizona 86046

INNKEEPERS: Pidge and Bill Johnson

ADDRESS/TELEPHONE: 321 West Sheridan; (520) 635–2178

ROOMS: 4; 1 with private bath; 1 with TV/VCR. No smoking inn.

RATES: $50 to $70, double; $10 extra person; EPB.

OPEN: All year.

FACILITIES AND ACTIVITIES: Exercycle/Health Rider. Nearby: quaint small town with walking map of shops and restaurants; Grand Canyon, Grand Canyon Railway, Grand Canyon Helicopter tours; nine-hole golf course, hiking, hunting, fishing, and skiing.

idge's name is Edwina, but when she was little her uncle called her Pigeon. And, she says good-naturedly, "it's stuck with me all my life." Pidge is just as good-natured about innkeeping. "This is our home," she says, "and if we knew we were going to be a bed-and-breakfast, we'd probably have done differently!" She's referring to the fact that they began by remodeling the home, a Victorian treasure dating from 1900, just for themselves.

The Johnstons have a lovely custom. "We take pictures of each of our guests for our guest book, and they sign it," Pidge says proudly. The house is not a large one, but it has a front porch with welcoming wicker rockers just sitting there invitingly. White shutters frame the front windows, and a white picket fence encloses it all tidily.

The living room is comfortable with a soft sofa and chairs and a huge mirrored armoire. The dining room has lace curtains and a painted matching dining room set, one of Pidge's finds: table, chairs, and buffet, all painted a soft sort of green. "I always liked antiques," she says. " The public interest in antiques started in the fifties, although it wasn't really popular until the sixties. I think the hippies got all the choice first picks!"

The Queen Room, with the private bath, has a waveless waterbed covered by a flowered quilt, Victorian chairs, and a television/VCR on an interesting gold-metal stand, one of Pidge's finds. "I rescued it from the Grand Canyon Lodge, and it's perfect for the television, don't you think?" The private bath has a tub and is pretty, with flowered wallpaper. The other three guest rooms are upstairs, and they share a hall bath, with towels color-coordinated to the rooms behind the room doors. There's a comfy upstairs sitting room, too, with a television, a desk, and games to play. Breakfast often means pancakes because, as the innkeepers say, "pancakes are an international food." One of their special kinds is apple-blueberry pancakes, served with bacon and

Ukranian potato pancakes, or scrambled eggs with applesauce and, of course, juices, coffee, and tea.

HOW TO GET THERE: From I–40 take exit 163 to Grand Canyon Boulevard (second street); turn south to Sheridan Avenue; turn right onto West Sheridan and go 2 blocks. There is a sign.

Terry Ranch Inn
Williams, Arizona 86046

INNKEEPERS: Sheryl and Del Terry

ADDRESS/TELEPHONE: 701 Quarterhorse; (520) 635–4171

E-MAIL: terryranch@workmail.com

ROOMS: 4; all with private bath and wheelchair access. No smoking inn.

RATES: $60 to $125, double, seasonally; $15 extra person; EPB.

OPEN: All year.

FACILITIES AND ACTIVITIES: Nearby: quaint small town with walking map of shops and restaurants; Grand Canyon, Grand Canyon Railway, Grand Canyon Helicopter tours, nine-hole golf course, hiking, hunting, fishing, skiing.

There's a romantic reason this inn calls itself a ranch, and it's not because it really is a working ranch. There has been a Terry Ranch in the Terry family since the 1650s, although back then the locale was Bucks County, Pennsylvania.

"Family tradition dictated that only the eldest son could inherit the family spread, so younger sons went off and created their own Terry Ranches," Del Terry says. "Since the 1600s we've had Terry ranches all across the country; I grew up on a Terry Ranch near Enterprise, Utah."

Sheryl says she always wanted a bed-and-breakfast inn, all the while they were raising Brangus cattle (still are) and six youngsters. "I knew I could build it [the inn]. I knew I could decorate—but I wasn't certain I could run it," she confesses with a laugh. "I'm a shy person basically. But I was inspired

by another Arizona innkeeper, and I've learned how wonderful it is to meet new people."

So Del and Sheryl built the inn from scratch, literally. "We built it ourselves, log by log," Sheryl says as she lovingly strokes one of the smooth wood logs that make up the walls of Terry Ranch Inn. "We try to offer the same hospitality that Terry Ranches have provided since 1670," the innkeepers say. Guest rooms and baths are exceptionally roomy. "When all of them are ready, we'll form a corporation," Del says good-humoredly. Each bath contains something wonderful, plus shelves to put things on—what a boon to travelers! And guest rooms are named for the brides who lived at Terry Ranch during the 1800s, a lovely, romantic theme. A portrait of each bride hangs in her room, and each is decorated in her favorite colors. Mary Ann's Room is named for the first Utah bride, who helped build the Utah ranch, first living in a dugout, then a stone fort. It's decorated in her favorite colors, peach and white, and the Terrys consider it their honeymoon suite. Eliza Jane, the second bride, was the youngest at age sixteen. She came west as a "child bride." Hannah Louisa's Room is named for the third bride, who, "at twenty-three, was the oldest," Del says. Charlotte Malinda helped her husband establish the town of Enterprise, Utah, just south of the Terry Ranch there. The large dining room table easily seats twelve, and it's covered with a lovely lace cloth made by Del's mother. Grandmother's wedding china reposes on the shelves on each side of the fireplace. Pretty as it is, it has to share space with Sheryl's collection of twelve individual place settings. This is what she serves breakfast on, and each place setting has a story.

"I haunted antiques stores, and whenever I saw a set I wanted to add to my collection, I'd always ask, is there a story?" Sheryl says. "I like 'firsts' particularly." Speaking of breakfast, the Terrys serve a real hearty ranch breakfast, what else? Begin with fruit topped with yogurt, cream, and sweet crumb sprinkles; then English Floddies, which are grated potato, egg, onion, and crumbled bacon pancakes; along with Amish friendship bread muffins. The Amish friendship bread has a history, too—Sheryl makes it from a starter she's had since the late seventies!

HOW TO GET THERE: Take Fourth Street north to Railroad Avenue. Turn right (east) and follow it around to Rodeo Drive. Turn left and go a short way to Quarterhorse; the inn is on the corner of Rodeo and Quarterhorse.

Select List of Other
Inns In Arizona

The Calumet & Arizona Guest House

608 Powell
Bisbee, Arizona 85603
(520) 432–4815

6 rooms; 2 with private bath; breakfast prepared to order from menu.

High Desert Inn

P.O. Box 145
8 Naco Road
Bisbee, Arizona 85603
(520) 432–1442 or (800) 281–0510

5 rooms; all with private bath; gourmet restaurant.

Main Street Inn

P.O. Box 433
26 Main Street
Bisbee, Arizona 85603
(800) 467–5237

10 guest rooms; 2 with private bath; others share 4 baths. Right downtown.

Gotland's Inn

P.O. Box 4949
Cave Creek, Arizona 85327
(604) 488–9636; fax (602) 488–6879

4 rooms; all with private bath. Desert mountain view.

Inn at Rancho Sanora

4198 North Highway 79
Florence, Arizona 85232
(520) 868–8000 or (800) 205–6817

10 rooms; all with private bath. Original 1930s adobe inn, a Southwest experience.

Taylor's

P.O. Box 63
Florence, Arizona 85232
(520) 868-4857

3 rooms; 1 with private bath. Historical setting that dates back to the 1500s.

Fountain Hills Inn

16240 Kingstree Boulevard
Fountain Hills, Arizona 85268
(602) 837-8908 or (800) 484-9746

3 rooms; 1 with private bath, 2 share. Thirty minutes from Phoenix Airport.

Casa de San Pedro

8933 South Yell Lane
Hereford, Arizona 85615
(520) 366-0701 or (800) 588-6468

10 rooms; all with private bath. San Pedro riparian area.

La Estancia

4979 East Camelback Road
Phoenix, Arizona 85018
(602) 808-9924

5 rooms; all with private bath. Golf, galleries, museums, theaters, shopping nearby.

Mount Vernon Inn

204 North Mount Vernon Avenue
Prescott, Arizona 86301
(520) 290-2224 or (888) 236-4421

7 rooms; all with private bath. In Mount Vernon Historical District, Victorian homes.

Adobe Hacienda

10 Rojo Drive
Sedona, Arizona 86351
(520) 284-2020

5 rooms; all with private bath. Among the red rocks of Sedona.

Silver Nugget

520 East Allen Street
Tombstone, Arizona 85638
(520) 457–9223

4 rooms; 2 with private bath. Whole town is National Monument.

Victoria's

211 Toughnut Street
Tombstone, Arizona 85638
(520) 457–3677 or (800) 952–8216

3 rooms; all with private bath. Daily gun reenactments, stagecoach rides.

Adobe Rose Inn

940 North Olsen Avenue
Tucson, Arizona 85719
(520) 318–4644

7 rooms; all with private bath. 2 blocks from University of Arizona, pool, hot tub.

Bienestar

10490 East Escalante Road
Tucson, Arizona 85730
(520) 290–1048 or (800) 293–0004

3 rooms; all with private bath. Adjacent to Saguaro National Park.

Car-mar's Southwest Inn

6766 West Oklahoma Street
Tucson, Arizona 85746
(520) 578–1730

4 rooms; 2 with private bath. Quiet in the Sonora Desert.

Peppertree Inn

724 East University Boulevard
Tucson, Arizona 85719
(520) 622–7168 or (800) 348–5763

6 rooms; all with private bath. Walk to the University of Arizona.

Skywatcher's Inn

420 Essex Lane
Tucson, Arizona 85711

3 rooms; all with private bath. Adjacent to the Vega-Bray Observatory.

New Mexico

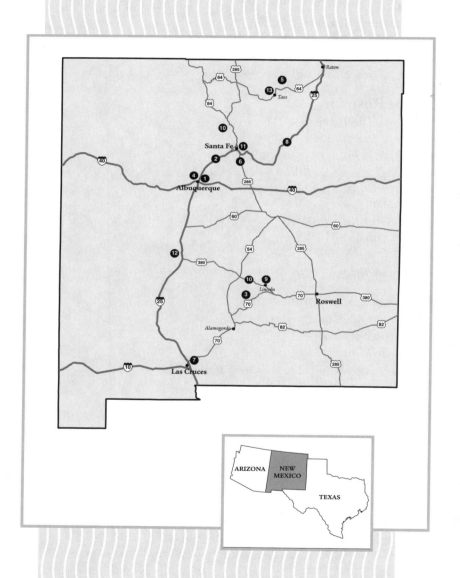

New Mexico

Numbers on map refer to towns numbered below.

*Top Pick Inn

Brittania and W. E. Mauger Estate 📱
Albuquerque, New Mexico 87102

INNKEEPERS: Keith Lewis; Mark, Matt, and Shannon Brown

ADDRESS/TELEPHONE: 701 Roma Avenue Northwest; (505) 242–8755 or (800) 719–9189; fax (505) 842–8835

E-MAIL: mark@innpoints.com

ROOMS: 8; all with private bath. Pets permitted in one room.

RATES: $89 to $179, double; pet fee $30; EPB and evening refreshments.

OPEN: All year.

FACILITIES AND ACTIVITIES: Nearby: 4 blocks to the Convention Center; historic old town, Indian Pueblo Museum, Rio Grande Zoo, museums, restaurants, shopping; Sandia Peak Tramway to Sandia Peak and the ski area; Botanical Gardens, Rio Grande Nature Center, Aquarium "BioPark," hike and bike trails.

The Mauger (pronounced "major") Residence has been on the National Register of Historic Places since 1985. The inn, once an old boardinghouse, won a blue ribbon for elegant restoration from the local Board of Realtors. Now the new owners are carrying on the inn's aim of "offering comfortable Victorian accommodations for sixteen souls in a style reminiscent of an era when graciousness, thoughtfulness, and elegance were a way of life."

The Queen Anne house was built in 1897, for the whopping sum of $1,600, by the daughter of a local tavern owner named Talbot. An unhappy marriage sent her into the arms of a New Yorker, and she left the house to be sold to William and Brittania Mauger, who were in the wool business. The Wool Room, on the second floor, was the business office.

There are three other guest rooms on the second floor. The Brittania, the original master bedroom, has three windows overlooking downtown and the beautiful Sandia Mountains. The Boston Sleeper was a screened sleeping porch for summer dog days—now it's all glassed in with an additional room for use as a suite. The Tuers Room was a bedroom/sewing room, and it, too, has a fine mountain view as well as morning sun.

The third-floor room has been completely redecorated in Victorian style, with a queen-sized bed, a matching daybed, and a trundle—perfect for traveling families. The Talbot Room, named for the original owner of the house, has a sleigh bed, a comfortable lounge chair, and a huge old desk. The Garden Room is bright with green plants. The inn is cozy, with lace curtains in the windows, and there are green plants in the two dining rooms. Breakfasts begin with fresh fruit plates and home-baked cobblers. "We go in for a mix of Southwestern and European cuisine, along with tasty Midwestern dishes," the innkeepers say. "You're more than set for the day! They also offer the option of a continental breakfast, even a "Brown Bag Business Express" for the busy business traveler.

HOW TO GET THERE: From I-25 take the Grand Street exit west to Seventh Street. Turn right on Seventh Street, go 1 block to Roma; the inn is on the northwest corner.

Casa del Granjero 📱
Albuquerque, New Mexico 87114

INNKEEPERS: Victoria and Charles (Butch) Farmer

ADDRESS/TELEPHONE: 414 C de Baca Lane Northwest; (505) 897-4144 or (800) 701-4144; fax (505) 897-9788

ROOMS: 6; all with private bath; wheelchair accessible. No smoking inn.

RATES: $79 to $159, double; $20 extra person; EPB, complimentary beverages and snacks.

OPEN: All year.

FACILITIES AND ACTIVITIES: Lunch and dinner by arrangement; hot tub, pool, bicycles, exercise equipment, rose garden, lily pond and waterfall, gazebo, horses (to pet), pygmy goats. Nearby: hiking trails, Albuquerque Old Town Plaza, Historic San Felipe Church, Museum of Natural History, Albuquerque Museum, skiing.

The name of this inn (pronounced "gran-hair-o") means "the farmer's house." When Victoria and Butch found this wonderful adobe hacienda nestled in the historic North Valley of Albuquerque, "we knew we were home." More to the point for the likes of us, right from the beginning they were encouraged to open their home to guests. "Everyone told us that this is the kind of house everyone wants to see and explore," Victoria says happily. She immediately set to work furnishing and decorating the home in a manner worthy of its size and history. The main house was 110 years old when they arrived, with beams from an 1860s bakery and bricks from the roadbed of famous old Route 66 (acquired when the highway was paved).

The first surprise at Casa del Granjero is opening the front door and walking into the huge common area, with Mexican tiles and a pool sunk in

the middle of the room. It's surrounded by soft pink brick walls, a corner fireplace, and cushy white sofas, cactus, clay pots of other green plants, a huge oriental rug in tones of soft reds and blues—and overhead, glass clerestory windows add even more dimension. For Victoria the inn has many happy memories of Butch's grandmother, now deceased. "Granny didn't know what a bed-and-breakfast was. When we told her she said, 'Oh. I can maybe make quilts!' She came across the country in a covered wagon when she was five; she died at eighty-seven," Victoria says. "She was my best buddy." Her name was Lilla Farmer, and she regaled guests with stories of old Taos (north of Albuquerque and Santa Fe). Victoria takes me out on the patio. "Those are Granny's wind chimes. There are days when there is no wind . . . yet we hear the chimes . . ." In the dining room the long Spanish mission–style table and chairs rest on another huge Oriental rug, while two breakfronts display an assortment of glass and objets d'art. The overhead dark-brown wood beams are older than the house. In Quarto del Rey the old radio actually works, handcrafted Mexican tiles accent the kiva fireplace, and the view is of not only the courtyard but also the mountains and trees. Quarto de Flores (Flowers Room) boasts great-grandmother's flower needlepoint as well as Granny's colorful quilts. French doors lead to the patio and the portale that winds around to the main courtyard.

Perfect Winds for Ballooning

Albuquerque is the place to be for hot-air ballooning, either watching or doing. There are fifteen hot-air balloon events a year here, including the largest balloon festival in the world, the Kodak Albuquerque International Balloon Festival. You won't be surprised to learn that it's also the most photographed balloon event in the world!

Between the first Saturday and second Sunday in October, more than 799 balloons light up and fill the night with a multitude of amazing shapes and colors. Just as exciting is the mass ascensions at dawn, with hundreds of balloons floating up to the sky.

There's a reason the event is so successful here: The weather is reliable, the landscape is beautiful, and the high altitude and famous "box" winds keep the balloons from wandering too far. And you don't have to be a do-it-yourselfer—you can join the crowd by chartering a balloon flight.

The Allegre Room presents an entirely different ambience: Butch made the four-poster that is hung with white satin and Battenburg lace. Breakfast is a wonderful concoction of blue-corn pancakes with sour cream and a caramelized apple topping, cool apricot-pear-pineapple frappe, a molded rice custard (a variation of the Mexican flan, with rice instead of eggs but still with the traditional, delicious baked-on caramelized sugar sauce), and crisp bacon. "I find that people don't always like breakfast meats, so I often serve chicken instead," Victoria says.

HOW TO GET THERE: From I–40 north take Alameda Boulevard west to Fourth Street. Turn left at C de Baca, then take a right to the inn, which is on the left.

Casa de Sueños Old Town Country Inn

Albuquerque, New Mexico 87104

INNKEEPER: Robert Hanna

ADDRESS/TELEPHONE: 310 Rio Grande Southwest; (505) 247–4560; fax (505) 842–8493

E-MAIL: info@casasdesuenos.com

ROOMS: 21 casitas; all with private bath, phone, and TV. No smoking inn.

RATES: $95 to $250, double, seasonal; $20 extra person; EPB.

OPEN: All year.

FACILITIES AND ACTIVITIES: Hot tubs. Nearby: Old Town Plaza with restaurants, shops, and galleries; health club, museums, zoo, festivals, golf, swimming, horseback riding, longest aerial tram in North America, skiing, Aquarium and Botanical Garden.

Be prepared for a wild surprise when you drive up to this adobe inn. Above the entrance gates looms a most unusual structure, added to the inn in 1976 by Albuquerque's famous artist, Bart Prince. "I tried to call it the Nautilus, but our neighbors call it 'the snail,'" Robert says. Nautilus or snail, whatever you call it, it's a fascinating structure, and I wasn't surprised to hear that people come knocking on the door to ask, "What is that thing?" Just as fantastic inside as it is out, it's entered by a spiral staircase, and it serves as a lounge as well as a television and meet-

ing room. The view of nearby mountains is impressive from any of the amazing structure's three levels.

You'd think it would be hard for the rest of the inn to live up to such an introduction, but not so. These "houses of dreams" (*casas de suenos*) were built in the 1930s by artist J. R. Willis, growing into a cluster of small casitas around a huge old elm in the courtyard.

The dining room was the artist's studio, and the large northern wall of windows faces the gardens. Guest rooms are furnished with antiques, heirlooms, art, Oriental and Indian rugs, goosedown comforters, bath amenities, and luxurious towels; some have kitchens, and most have fireplaces as well as adjoining sitting rooms and outdoor garden areas. Cascada even has its own waterfall. The Cupid Suite has a skylight; the Georgia O'Keeffe Suite features reproductions of her work; the Rose Room blends the romance of yesteryear with the comfort of today; Route 66 Suite is so named because it's just 1 block off the famous highway.

HOW TO GET THERE: From I–40 west take the Rio Grande exit south toward Old Town. Cross Mountain Road and Central Avenue and go 2 more blocks. The inn is on the left, facing the Albuquerque Country Club Golf Course.

Hacienda Vargas 🖤
Algodones, New Mexico 87001

INNKEEPERS: Paul and Jule De Vargas

ADDRESS/TELEPHONE: 1431 El Camino Real (mailing address: P.O. Box 307); (505) 867–9115; fax (505) 867–1902

E-MAIL: hacvar@swcp.com

ROOMS: 8; all with private bath; 1 wheelchair accessible. No smoking inn.

RATES: $69 to $139, double; $15 extra person; EPB.

OPEN: All year.

FACILITIES AND ACTIVITIES: Hot tub, barbecue area, Murder Mystery Weekends. Nearby: golfing, river and lake fishing, water sports, snow skiing. Albuquerque is about 25 miles south, Santa Fe about 30 miles north.

Algodones was a Spanish military garrison in the 1620s and '30s, and caravans crossed the Rio Grande to travel up and down the narrow road. Often there were raids by bandits and Navajos in spite of the military presence. Later the village was a stagecoach stop and trading post and eventually the site of a U.S. Post Office.

Hacienda Vargas is on that bit of El Camino Real once called the Chihuahua Trail. Paul imparts an interesting bit of history that also explains the name. "Until 1821 this territory was part of Mexico. The Spanish would not allow Mexicans to trade with Americans. They could trade only with Chihuahua [the city and state directly south of the border]."

The adobe building, more than 200 years old, has lived through a lot. "Three or four families lived in smaller areas on the one-acre site," Paul says as he points out the old bell tower and the family chapel (complete with candles, fireplace, and

Hacienda Vargas   NM

benches if you want to sit and meditate awhile). I was fascinated by the glassed-in openings that the innkeepers have installed in several places to reveal the original adobe walls.

The long, wide Delgado Sala, with an entire wall of French doors leading out to the courtyard, is both entry and art gallery. Care has been taken to combine the spirit of the Old West with the influence of the early Spanish settlers and the original Pueblo Indian culture. The furniture is all authentic New Mexico antique, and there are many fascinating pieces such as the old icebox, now used to store table linens, and the old dentist's medical cabinet in the Pena Room.

In the Pena Room you'll also find three signed pieces by famous Southwest artist Amado Pena. "He sent us them as a gift," Paul says with pleasure. The bed and headboard are of a unique design, and the innkeepers have framed and glassed in one of the openings, showing the original walls.

The Wagner Room, the largest of the guest rooms, was inspired by the composer, of whose music Paul is fond. "I lived in Austria, in Innsbruck, for a while when I was a student," he says. The room has a kiva fireplace, a separate sitting area, and a Jacuzzi tub with a skylight view—pretty luxurious! The Piñon Room, with its white wrought-iron bed, has a great view of the gardens (Lawrence's handiwork) and a 200-year-old elm tree. The old-timey bath has a claw-footed tub and a pull-chain commode.

The chef has been featured in several cookbooks, with such delights as French pancakes and waffles served with a homemade nectarine topping; a fluffy four-layer soufflé of eggs, ham, and vegetables; and such different flavors as mandarin muffins and pumpkin pancakes.

HOW TO GET THERE: North on I–25 to Algodones exit (approximately 5 miles past the Bernalillo exit), west to El Camino Real (Highway 313). Turn left on El Camino Real; Hacienda Vargas is behind the adobe wall, immediately on the right. The front door is at the second entrance.

Sierra Mesa Lodge
Alto, New Mexico 88312

INNKEEPERS: Lila and Larry Goodman

ADDRESS/TELEPHONE: Fort Stanton Road (mailing address: P.O. Box 463); (505) 336–4515

ROOMS: 5; all with private bath; no air-conditioning (elevation 7,000 feet). No smoking inn.

RATES: $95 to $100, double; single $10 less; EPB and high tea.

OPEN: All year.

FACILITIES AND ACTIVITIES: Indoor spa, games, Murder Mystery Weekends. Nearby: skiing, horseback riding, fishing in Alto Lake, Ruidoso Downs race track and golf, hiking trails in Lincoln National Forest, restaurants in Ruidoso. Spencer Theater for the Performing Arts 3 miles away.

"We'd been planning this for years," Lila says of the bright blue-and-white inn high above the Sierra Blanca range of New Mexico, just north of Ruidoso. "Larry took early retirement, and we thought of emigrating to New Zealand; we checked out the Caribbean; we went all over the world." When they saw this area, they were hooked. Larry wanted to build a small hotel, but Lila argued that "meeting people is what an inn is all about."

She enjoys her guests; she says it's like having family in the home. "We play cards and dominoes with our guests; we're good friends by the time they leave." If the guests want television, they're banished upstairs to the television room, where there's a telescope, too. "We want them to visit, we don't want the television on; that ends the conversation," she says with a laugh.

Lila has two hobbies: cooking and making delicate porcelain dolls. Each guest room has an occupant, a china doll that she created from scratch. "I walked into a paint store for some paint, and a woman was demonstrating doll making. Just like that, I was lost!"

Guest rooms are individually decorated with flair. The mirrored, black enamel queen-sized bed in the Oriental Room is an eye-catcher, and the other authentic Oriental pieces are outstanding, too. A magnificently embroidered Oriental marriage robe hangs on the wall.

Each room has a window seat, but otherwise variety reigns. There are the Victorian, French Country, Country Western, and Queen Anne rooms, each ruled over by one of Lila's dolls. Comforters, goose-down pillows, kimonos, rockers, and chaise longues may spoil you rotten.

So will the food, Lila and Larry's other area of expertise. For breakfast you are at the mercy of the cook, but not to worry—you'll manage to live through

waffles, quiches, poppyseed bread, fruit parfait with honey and sour cream, and, perhaps, Lila's blintz soufflé. Lila will even pamper you with breakfast in bed.

Afternoon tea means a special chocolate bread with cream cheese, peanut butter cream pie, and chocolate streusel. In the evenings guests gather around the cheery fire for wine and cheese and good conversation. The lodge is now offering exciting Murder Mystery Weekends if you get five friendly couples together for two evenings of fun and fine food: breakfast, afternoon tea, dinner, and late-night wine and cheese.

HOW TO GET THERE: Take Highway 48 north from Ruidoso approximately 6 miles to Fort Stanton Road on your right. Keep to the left at the fork in the road; you'll find the inn on your left about 2 miles down the road. There is a sign.

Chocolate Turtle 📱 💲
Corrales, New Mexico 87078

INNKEEPER: Carole Morgan

ADDRESS/TELEPHONE: 1098 Meadowlark Lane, (505) 898–1800; fax (505) 898–5328

E-MAIL: turtlebb@aol.com

WEB SITE: www.collectorsguide.com

ROOMS: 4; all with private bath; 1 with TV. No smoking inn.

RATES: $59 to $95, double; $5 to $10 extra person; discounts for long stays; EPB.

OPEN: All year.

FACILITIES AND ACTIVITIES: Hot tub, parking in front, boarding for horses, 1½ acres for hiking and provisions for hikers. Nearby: horses and bicycles for rent, golfing, hiking, skiing, historic pueblos, Rio Grande Petroglyphs, fifteen minutes from Albuquerque with zoo and tram; fifty minutes from Santa Fe.

Carole was an insurance underwriter and broker in Michigan when she first began to travel to New Mexico on her vacations. "I just kept coming back and started forming the idea [the inn]—people kept telling me I'd be great. I was on the way to Dallas, and I was in tears! I drove by this house . . ." She bought it, and it took her eight months to remodel, lightening all the dark wood and putting in two more bathrooms. The huge great room has a large fireplace, a high ceiling with those nice lightened beams, wall hangings, and prints of Indian pots, all very relaxing. The patio opens off the room, with wrought-iron furniture and a wonderful view of the Sandia Mountains. Carole has xeriscaped for less water usage, and nothing gets in the way of the spectacular magenta sunset—but you have to catch it quickly before the moon comes up. But that's nice, too, because at night you can see the city lights of Albuquerque in the distance.

The bright skylighted dining room has a microwave; Carole says her guests can go get pizza and bring it in; the table's always set. There's a refrigerator, an electric kettle, cereals out always, and snacks at night. The Caramel Room is bright turquoise and coral and has a queen-sized bed. The French

Mint Room, perfect for the single traveler, is like a study, with a trundle bed, a desk, and a small chest. All the inn furniture, frosted oak with pastel decorations, is made locally, making all the rooms harmonious in modern Southwestern design.

The Truffle Room has its private bath opening off the hall, but Carole very cleverly has put a screen across for privacy. "The kids in the neighborhood call this 'the Purple Room,'" she says with a laugh. "They knock on the door and ask, 'Can I see the Purple Room?' You know they want a candy!

"I started making handmade chocolates for Christmas for family, and I developed my own recipes and made delicious truffles. But—people want only turtles! I haven't made truffles in ages!" There are turtles out on a tray; it's hard to be polite and take just one! Carole also puts cookies out at night, rich ones such as butter cream with nuts. In the large and clean, well-organized kitchen, more turtles are spread out on racks, waiting for their chocolate shells.

The Turtle Suite hasn't a candy name—but then, it's turtles that are the inn's signature; happily, they are chocolate ones. There's a king-sized bed, a sleeper couch, and a door leading to a small private courtyard. Come breakfast time, you're likely to get salmon quiche and blue-corn pancakes, made with pastry flour. Carole says she likes to cook French—but light. (The better to make room for all that chocolate!)

HOW TO GET THERE: From I–25 take exit 232 (Paseo del Norte) and go west to Coors/Corrales. Turn right on Corrales, and go 2 miles to Meadowlark Lane. Turn left and go 1 mile on Meadowlark to the inn, the third house on the right past Loma Larga.

Salsa del Salto

El Prado, New Mexico 87529

INNKEEPERS: Dadou Meyer and Mary Hockett

ADDRESS/TELEPHONE: P.O. Box 1468; (505) 776–2422;
fax (505) 776–5734

E-MAIL: salsa@taos.newmex.com

ROOMS: 10; all with private bath; 4 with TV. No smoking inn.

RATES: $85 to $160, double; $20 extra person; EPB.

OPEN: All year.

FACILITIES AND ACTIVITIES: Swimming pool, hot tub, tennis court,
croquet. Nearby: hiking trails, fishing in Rio Hondo, skiing in Taos Valley, Indian pueblos; 10 miles to historic Taos with shops, restaurants,
mountain-bike rentals; eighteen-hole golf course.

El Salto is the big mountain on the horizon, and lovers of spicy food
know how lively salsa is, and that, says Dadou Mayer, is how he gave
this inn its name. To wallow in luxury beneath the rugged peaks of
the Sangre de Cristo Mountains makes for quite a contrast: outdoors, the
wild mountains, the mesas, and the high blue sky; indoors, an elegant home
with finely crafted New Mexican furniture and gourmet food prepared by a
Frenchman trained in a hotel school in Nice.

Dadou is also a skier, a former member of the Junior National French
Ski Team. In one year's Grand Marnier ski race, he won the love of his life,
a shining chrome convection-and-steam oven that he keeps polished to a
fare-thee-well.

Of innkeeping, "It's my profession; I love it," he says with a most charming smile. Past owner of the Hotel Edelweiss up in the mountains, where he
had a cooking school, he likes the change to a small inn.

"The inn is so much more personal than the hotel business," he says.
"Our guests say, 'How nice of you to welcome me into your home.'"

Both Dadou and Mary know the answers to all the questions guests
might ask—"or you can bet that if we don't, we'll find out for you!" they say.
"We can direct guests to all the 'shouldn't miss' galleries, fishing holes to cast
your fly for native trout, the Pueblo dances and ceremonies, quaint shops,

and the best restaurants. And, on cliff walks, we've found some petroglyphs that we share with our guests."

The huge square lobby and dining area, with big windows open to the far vista of mountain and mesa, is furnished with soft beige leather sofas begging you to sink into them. The room is divided by a giant fireplace made of rocks from the old Taos Ski Valley copper mine. I asked Dadou about the row of sleigh bells on the rough wood mantel, and he shook them impishly. "I just found them somewhere and I like them," he said, grinning like a little boy.

Guest rooms are large and uncluttered, with lounge chairs and tables on which to put things—a necessity, I think. Down comforters and nightly mints are nice features. There is a token television area, mostly used by hopeful amateurs to view ski and tennis tapes.

Breakfast you can bet will be grand—perhaps eggs Catalan and, on the buffet, yogurt, fresh fruit salad, cardamon-and-piñon-nut dill bread, and cereals. Special is the Chanterelle Omelette. "The chanterelle mushroom is abundant in the Southwest," Mary says. "We freeze them and love to serve these souvenirs of summer in the winter." There's a refrigerator where guests can help themselves to ice, soda, or glasses of wine.

HOW TO GET THERE: Take Highway 68 north out of Taos; at the blinking light turn right on Highway 150, the Taos Ski Valley Raod. One mile past the small town of Arroyo Seco, you'll see the inn in the right; there is a sign.

Galisteo Inn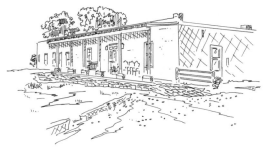

Galisteo, New Mexico 87540

INNKEEPERS: Joanna and Wayne Aarniokoski

ADDRESS/TELEPHONE: 9 La Vega; (505) 466–4000; fax (505) 466–4008

E-MAIL: galisteo@aol.com

ROOMS: 12; 8 with private bath; no air-conditioning (elevation 6,300 feet); wheelchair accessible. No smoking inn.

RATES: $65 to $195, double; $20 extra person; EPB.

OPEN: All year except last three weeks in January and first week in December.

FACILITIES AND ACTIVITIES: Picnic lunches, dinner by reservation Wednesday through Sunday; horse boarding and horseback riding, swimming pool, hot tub, sauna, trail bicycles, hiking, skiing the Turquoise Trail and the Santa Fe Ski Basin. Nearby: old pueblo, old church, old Spanish graveyard, museum, petroglyphs (Indian rock paintings) 8 miles south of town, Old Turquoise Trail mines.

O f this more-than-250-year-old classic Spanish adobe inn, Joanna says, "It looks even better than ever." Wayne is a landscape contractor, and they have beautified the inn even further to please their artistic eyes. But they have no quarrel with the pink and blue mountains that surround them.

"We fell in love with New Mexico," Wayne says. "The clean air, the serenity . . ." So these two fugitives from California gathered up young daughter Paige and headed for these hills. Centuries ago the Galisteo Inn was the hub of a Spanish trading post, a fourteen-room hacienda owned by the Ortiz y Pino family. All remodeling was done carefully so that the inn continued to fit in with its surroundings, which include some of the oldest colonial buildings in America.

(Remember that the Spanish were here long before the Pilgrims landed in the Northeast.)

The inn is situated on eight acres of land under huge old cottonwood trees. It's a long, low adobe building hidden behind a long, low stone wall, and I almost missed it. Galisteo is not much more than a mark on the map; I don't advise looking for it in the dark!

But what a wonderful place to discover, no matter if I had a little difficulty finding it. Staying here is like going on a retreat. The simple rooms have whitewashed walls with wood vigas above. Handmade furniture and handwoven rugs are the decor. Some rooms are angled, some have adobe fireplaces; all are clean, simple, and uncluttered, yet with what Joanna calls "lots of decorative upgrades. We are always redesigning and refurbishing to keep the inn pretty and fresh."

Breakfast is a refreshing eye-opener with fruit smoothies (a kind of fruit milk shake) and a fruit platter and may include waffles, breakfast breads, or quiche. "We use seasonal and local foods whenever possible," Joanna says. Dinners are superb, a heavenly feast in the wilderness (the inn is 23 miles south of Santa Fe). The food is a delicious combination of Southwest and nouvelle cuisine. Spinach-and-chorizo sausage–stuffed duck and blue-corn polenta are specialties. The innkeepers tend their own garden—they use fresh lettuce, peppers, squash, and herbs, as well as fruit from their orchards—and a vegetarian meal can be requested. "A lot of health-conscious people come here," Joanna says. They come for what I was delighted to find: a beautifully decorated Southwestern retreat, quiet and low-key. Two cozy cats, Rudy and Murphy, are still on the premises, legacies from the previous owners. Smart animals: They know the Galisteo Inn is too good a place to leave.

HOW TO GET THERE: From Albuquerque take I-40 east to Moriarty, I-41 north toward Santa Fe through Galisteo. From Santa Fe take I-25 north to 285 south toward Lamy, I-41 south to Galisteo.

Happy Trails Ranch
Las Cruces, New Mexico 88005

INNKEEPERS: Sylvia and Barry Byrnes

ADDRESS/TELEPHONE: 1857 Paisano Road; (505) 527–8471

ROOMS: 3; 1 with private bath. Pets welcome. No smoking inn.

RATES: $80 to $100, doubles; discount may apply; EPB.

OPEN: All year.

FACILITIES AND ACTIVITIES: Wet bar, microwave, swimming pool, Jacuzzi, VCR, courtyard, grill, horse stalls and dog run, horses for rent, trail rides. Nearby: tennis courts and golf courses, historic Old Mesilla, White Sands National Monument, Gila Wilderness with cave dwellings and petroglyphs; hiking and rock climbing at Organ Mountain and Desert Recreation; Cloudcroft Ski Resort.

*V*ivacious innkeeper Sylvia Byrnes has brought her enthusiasm and her outgoing personality as a dancer in New York (she danced in *West Side Story*!) all the way to a small horse ranch in New Mexico. The inn/ranch is out in the country, just minutes from town. The courtyard has lovely old trees, huge mulberry and sycamore. Surrounding the inn are locust trees, and there's an uninterrupted view of the Organ Mountains in the distance, with historic Old Mesilla barely seven minutes away.

The large common room has a brick floor and fireplace, books, television and VCR, and a large wall of glass through which at night, across the fields, you can see the lights of Las Cruces twinkling away. The Sun Room, off the courtyard behind a window wall, has a refrigerator stocked with juice and sodas. The microwave is here, too, as well as coffee, tea, milk, and cereal.

Breakfast might be egg enchiladas (made with egg substitute for the health-conscious) with red and green peppers, onions, and cheese, served with picante and green enchilada sauce; croissants and raisin bread with homemade jams. Favorites are strawberry—and jalapeño!

HOW TO GET THERE: Take the Old Mesilla turnoff from I-10 and follow Highway 28. Turn right at the Onate Plaza (Calle Del Norte), then go ½ mile to Paisano. Turn right on Paisano and go ⁹⁄₁₀ mile. The inn will be on your right, and there is a sign—look up; it's way up over the gate.

Bosque del Apache Wildlife Refuge

Along I–25 between Albuquerque and Las Cruces you'll find Bosque del Apache National Wildlife Refuge—57,191 acres of wildlife habitat. The cottonwood groves from which came the name (*Bosque del Apache* is Spanish for "Woods of the Apache") are being invaded by salt cedar bush, an ornamental shrub introduced into the United States around the turn of the century. But the Bosque provides a habitat for some 295 different bird species, and more than 400 different mammals, reptiles, and amphibians such as mule deer, rattlesnakes, soft-shelled turtles, and porcupines.

The refuge has played a major role as a protector and provider for wildlife in danger of extinction. It began with the greater sandhill crane, which in 1914 only numbered seventeen. Today they not only hold their own, they are out of danger; it's the bald eagles, peregrine falcons, and whooping cranes that need to find refuge here.

You can be pretty sure of seeing a whooping crane or, perhaps, a Cooper's hawk, skunks, snake, or skink. Whatever, you're sure to see an abundance of wildlife, especially if you come by during early morning and early evening hours.

Hilltop Hacienda 📱
Las Cruces, New Mexico 88012

INNKEEPERS: Teddi and Bob Peters

ADDRESS/TELEPHONE: 2600 Westmoreland Avenue; (505) 382–3556

ROOMS: 3; all with private bath and phone; TV and VCR available. Pets with prior approval. No smoking inn.

RATES: $65 to $85, double; $15 extra person; EPB.

OPEN: All year.

FACILITIES AND ACTIVITIES: Kitchen with refrigerator and freezer, microwave, and stove for guests' use; gas barbecue grill; small gift shop.

Hiking trails, sleds and sled boards, patios and gardens. Nearby: historic Old Mesilla, where the Gadsden Purchase was signed and Billy the Kid temporarily apprehended; White Sands National Monument; Gila Wilderness with cave dwellings and petroglyphs; hiking and rock climbing at Organ Mountain and Desert Recreation; Cloudcroft Ski Resort.

*Y*ou'll be sitting on top of the world at this inn, perched atop eighteen acres of open countryside just ten minutes from town, but wonderfully remote when you wind your way up to the hilltop. Birds sing, hummmingbirds hover, quail and roadrunners are out and about; sometimes so are giant jackrabbits. The unusual arched, two-story adobe brick dwelling is built in Spanish Moorish architectural style. There's a spacious veranda on the top floor (which is where you'll enter) and arched patios on the second floor underneath—remember, the inn is on a hilltop.

Country Rose Room has a king-sized bed, a cedar chest, and a wonderful antique "fainting couch." The pale blue bath for this room is across the hall.

The Southwest Room, with green decor, has a queen-sized bed, a desk, and a lovely city and garden view. Maggie's Room is cool and refreshing, with white wicker furniture and a white iron bed. The large common room has wide windows open to the surrounding  views of the mountains, what Bob calls a "four-cups-of-coffee" view. It's cool in summer, with white sofa and white wicker chairs, and cozy in winter, with a wood-burning fireplace.

"We accommodate special diets," Teddi says. Otherwise one of her specialties is what she calls her Dona Ana Quiche, along with homemade salsa, chorizo potatoes, and a fresh fruit compote of berries, apples, oranges, bananas, dried blueberries, and fresh pecans—all topped with vanilla yogurt, nutmeg, and fresh mint from the herb garden. You might also meet with a tray of homemade cinnamon-apple-pecan muffins, rich bran muffins, and empanadas, those little stuffed Southwestern (and Mexican) pies.

HOW TO GET THERE: From I-10 take I-25 north to Highway 70 (North Main); turn north onto Del Rey (there is a K-Mart store at the signal) and go for 3 miles to Westmoreland. Turn right; continue on Westmoreland. In 1 mile look for the Hilltop sign on the mailbox on your right. Turn right into driveway and up the hill to the inn.

Lundeen Inn of the Arts
Las Cruces, New Mexico 88005

INNKEEPERS: Linda and Gerald Lundeen

ADDRESS/TELEPHONE: 618 South Alameda Boulevard;
(505) 526–3326

WEB SITE: www.innofthearts.com

ROOMS: 20; all with private bath and phone; 19 with TV; wheelchair accessible. Pets permitted. Limited smoking permitted.

RATES: $70 to $100, double; $15 extra person; EPB.

OPEN: All year.

FACILITIES AND ACTIVITIES: Kitchen open for guest use, bicycles, garden, gazebo, exercise equipment, conference rooms. Nearby: Old Mesilla, Herschel Zohn Theater, Rio Grande, hiking in Gila Mountain Wilderness and Bosque del Apache Bird Refuge, horseback riding.

Walking in one front door of the Lundeen Inn of the Arts, you'll find yourself in an art gallery first and foremost, with wonderful paintings by such New Mexico artists as Keb Barrick, who studied with Grant Wood. A side entrance, located off the quiet, tree-shaded patio, leads directly into the Merienda Room, two stories high with enormous arched windows. This common room, also filled with art, was designed by Gerald to connect the two historic Llewellyn Houses that make up the inn.

Gerald is an architect, Linda has the gallery, and both are wide-awake, vital, energetic people who make guests feel part of the electricity in the air. Both are actively involved with the arts in Las Cruces; they print a newsletter that keeps guests informed.

"Our guests are part of the family immediately—we treat them like that," says Linda. "We have a regular guest from Bogota, Colombia, who needs a phone, so we put a jack in his room." The inn has all sorts of international guests, and you're bound to meet very interesting people, perhaps even in the kitchen! I liked having the freedom of the modern, attractively tiled kitchen, where a guest from Portugal was poaching his own eggs, an actor was fixing his health breakfast, and a vegetarian woman was preparing her own special brought-along food.

The Merienda, an afternoon social hour from 5:00 to 7:00 P.M., is complete with wine and Southwestern hors d'oeuvres: chili con queso, guacamole, perhaps shrimp soufflé. If it's an off day, there will be a basket of fruit in your room instead.

Downstairs guest rooms lead right and left off the two-story Merienda Room. A circular stairway leads up to a balcony overlooking the large room and into the upstairs guest rooms. Each room is named for an artist famous in the Southwest—such as Georgia O'Keeffe, Fritz Scholder, and Olaf Weighorst. The Weighorst Room has headboards cunningly made from antique gas-grate hoods padded with decorator fabric matching the bedspreads. I loved the bathroom's footed tub, painted bright red.

Two weeks of every month are devoted to the Elderhostel program, with the knowledgeable Lundeens holding forth on "Ancient Art and Architecture" and "Historic New Mexico Art and Architecture." Gerald has built a *horno*, an Indian oven, at the end of the garden; guests helped make the adobe bricks. Now every third morning or so, the Lundeens bake thirty-six loaves of fresh bread! While watching the oven work, you can play croquet or toss horseshoes or perhaps watch a filming. The inn was used by a film studio last year to make a movie, which gives you an idea of the vibrant atmosphere and architecture here.

"We all interact," says Linda, and it's easy to see how at the Lundeen Inn of the Arts.

HOW TO GET THERE: From I–10 west take Mesilla exit and turn east, then go left on Main Street, and left again on Alameda. The inn is 2 blocks down on Alameda Boulevard next to the First National Bank Tower, the only high-rise on the street.

Carriage House Inn
Las Vegas, New Mexico 87701

INNKEEPERS: Anne and John Bradford

ADDRESS/TELEPHONE: 925 Sixth Street; (505) 454–1784

ROOMS: 5; 3 with private bath. Smoking in common rooms only.

RATES: $59 to $75, double; $10 extra person; EPB.

OPEN: All year.

FACILITIES AND ACTIVITIES: Nearby: historic square, Plaza Bridge Street art galleries, Douglas Street shopping district, Fort Union National Monument, Rough Riders Museum, Montezuma Castle, National Wildlife Refuge, golf, Highland University.

Anne and John are from Suffolk, England, but they had been in California for quite a while. John imported British stereo equipment, and Anne worked in the hotel industry. Deciding that an inn would fulfill their urge to offer more friendly hospitality, John and Anne hoped for a location that would meet their three requirements: "a small town, a university town, and one with some historical significance."

The Carriage House is one of Las Vegas's special Victorian houses, a relic of the gracious days of long ago. The polished and well-preserved golden woodwork is lovely; some interesting gingerbread crowns the hall between the living room and the stairs. Anne and John have filled the inn with an eclectic collection of period pieces and antiques. Of course I wasn't surprised to see her choice collection of English teacups, and she serves tea in them "upon request." Guest rooms are large, ceilings are high, and baths are spacious with claw-footed tubs. The rooms are bright with flowered bedspreads and curtains, except for the Blue Room, which is rather tailored. The bedspread,  drapes, valence, and swag over the bed are done in a lovely dark paisley pattern in navy and deep red. The bedside tables are solid squares of wood, and the brass lamps are tailored, too.

Breakfast might be what Anne calls her "thingamajig" (English muffin with bacon and cheese) or orange French toast, carrot and fresh ginger muffins, pumpkin bread—and, of course, fruit and juice, coffee, and tea.

HOW TO GET THERE: Take University exit off I-25 to Sixth Street. Turn right to number 925; the inn is on the left.

Casa de Patron
Lincoln, New Mexico 88338

INNKEEPERS: Cleis and Jeremy Jordan

ADDRESS/TELEPHONE: P.O. Box 27; (505) 653–4676

ROOMS: 3, plus 2 two-room casitas; 3 rooms with private bath; casitas with private bath, hide-a-bed, and kitchen; no air-conditioning (elevation 5,700 feet). No smoking inn.

RATES: $89, double; $13 extra person; single, deduct $10; EPB for main house, continental for casitas; afternoon drinks and snacks.

OPEN: All year.

FACILITIES AND ACTIVITIES: Dinner by advance reservation. VCR, special entertainment such as German Evenings and musical Salon Evenings. Nearby: Billy the Kid country with state monuments and Heritage Trust museums, Lincoln National Forest, hiking, skiing, horse races at Ruidoso Downs, soap-making and quilting workshops.

*I*nnkeepers Cleis (pronounced Cliss) and Jeremy used to camp in nearby Lincoln National Forest, and she fell in love with the little town of Lincoln. "I told Jerry I had to live here," Cleis says with a laugh. "He thought I was bananas; this house was a wreck. But it had great charm, and after it was fixed, we decided to share it with others." The historic nineteenth-century house was the home of Juan Patron, born in 1855. The

Jordans decided to name the inn after his family, who lived in the house and kept a store there during the mid-1800s. Young Juan lost his father in an 1873 raid on Lincoln, forerunner of the Lincoln County Wars.

Billy the Kid, Sheriff Pat Garrett, murders, and rival mercantile establishments—these are the ingredients of the bloody Lincoln County Wars. I'll leave it to you to visit the museums and flesh out the story, but it was pretty wild in Lincoln back then.

Today there's peace and tranquillity in the beautiful forested country, the calm broken only by the many festivals and pageants in the tiny town and in nearby Capitan (home of Smokey Bear) and Ruidoso. Each guest room in the spanking-white adobe-and-viga house is decorated with collectibles and antiques such as the 1800s spinning wheel from Jeremy's family back in Deerfield, Illinois. The number-1 Southwestern Room has twin beds and a full bath; number-2 Southwestern Room has a queen-sized bed and wash-basin and private bath around the corner; the Old Store has a queen-sized bed, private bath, and outside entry to a patio. The casitas are completely private, and the Jordans are understandably proud of the fact that they built them from scratch. Casa Bonita has a cathedral ceiling in the living area and a spiral staircase winding up to the loft bedroom.

Breakfast might be Cleis's baked egg soufflé, strawberry-walnut muffins, home-fried potatoes, and fresh fruit—in the clear mountain air, appetites are hearty. The huge kitchen has a wonderful collection of washboards, those old-fashioned thingamajigs for scrubbing clothes. Hot or cold drinks in the evening are enhanced by music, with Cleis at the baby grand in the parlor or

Legend of Billy the Kid

Southern New Mexico is Billy the Kid country. His name was really Henry McCarty—it wasn't until 1877 that, as a young itin-erant ranch horse turned horse thief, he picked up the alias "Kid" Antrim. He'd grown up with a sketchy past: Born back East, per-haps in New York City, he moved with his mother and older brother, first to Indianapolis, then to Wichita, then to Silver City.

When his mother died of tuberculosis, he was placed in foster homes and soon got into trouble. Arrested for theft in 1875 and jailed, he shimmied up a chimney and ran away. Although some say he killed twenty-one men, he was responsible for killing four on his own; he merely helped dispatch some others. He didn't become "Billy the Kid" until a Las Vagas newspaper named him that in 1880. By the time rancher Pat Garrett shot and killed him in 1881, he was already receiving lots of recognition.

His sudden and violent death at such a young age (twenty-one), combined with his daring exploits and his good and evil traits, seems to have captured the imagination of writers and musicians, movie makers, and even ballet, thanks to Aaron Copeland (*Billy the Kid* ballet), creating a legend.

at the real live pipe organ in the dining room. You can be sure the music is professional—Cleis has a master's degree in organ music.

As for dinner, you can drive to La Lorraine in Ruidoso, Chango in Capitan, or Tinnie's Silver Dollar in Tinnie; but, says Cleis with a laugh, "that's one of the reasons we went into the dinner business [by prior arrangement only]. People said, 'What, you mean we have to get in the car and drive 12 miles?'"

A Salon Evening might be a night of ragtime and American cuisine or German specialties accompanied by suitable music. "But it's the people that are the fun part," says Jeremy.

HOW TO GET THERE: Casa de Patron is located at the east end of Lincoln on the south side of Highway 380, which runs between Roswell and I-25. The highway is the main and only road through the tiny town.

Orange Street Inn
Los Alamos, New Mexico 87544

INNKEEPERS: Margaret Fraser and Valerie Miller

ADDRESS/TELEPHONE: 3496 Orange Street; (505) 662-2651; fax (505) 661-1538

ROOMS: 8; 4 with private bath; wheelchair accessible; no air-conditioning (elevation 7,500 feet). No smoking inn. Pets can be accommodated outside.

RATES: $46 to $75, double; EPB.

OPEN: All year.

FACILITIES AND ACTIVITIES: Bicycles, golf clubs, tennis racquets, skis and assorted boots available; laundry facilities. Nearby: restaurants, Aquatic Center, golf, tennis, hiking, skiing, canoeing, rafting, Indian pueblos and prehistoric ruins, shops, Bradbury Science Museum.

You have to wind your way up the mountain to reach this homey inn on a mountaintop. And there's only one way down, too. But you'll be glad you made the climb when you linger over the table at Orange Street breakfasts. In addition to fresh fruit and juices, there may be homemade pot cheese to spread on homemade granola breads and muffins and, perhaps, chicken soufflé, or delicious Southwestern specialties such as breakfast quesadillas or sopaipillas. "We certainly emphasize our good food," the innkeepers say, sometimes adding oven puff pancakes, Ital-

ian frittata, oatmeal soufflé, French breakfast sandwiches, and huevos los Alamos
with corn crepes to the menu.

I could emphasize their other objec-
tives: to provide nicely decorated rooms
(not large but comfortable, in country or
New Mexican motifs) as well as unusually
good food. "And cleanliness is important
to us." Guests can make themselves at home in the kitchen, make popcorn,
use the microwave or the dishwasher, and check the refrigerator for beverages, frozen yogurt, and other good snacks. "People can bring food in if they
want," Michael says. There's also access to a copier (some of their scientists
are busy with laptop computers) as well as such homey things as sewing and
ironing needs, shampoo, conditioner, or anything else you might have forgotten. "I've even fixed people's cars," Michael says with a laugh.

There are books, a dartboard, and games of checkers. There's a lot to do
nearby, too, from the Larry Walkup Aquatic Center a few streets away to
more rugged outdoor activity. "If you're any kind of outdoors person, you
can do anything," Michael promises. "Great biking, ice skating, rock climbing at Bandolier National Monument, great trout fishing. . . ." What a grand
place for an all-around vacation!

HOW TO GET THERE: From Central Street (in center of town) go west to
Canyon Street. Turn left to Diamond Street (next signal), right on Diamond
to Orange Street (next signal), right on Orange, and down the hill. The inn is
on the left.

Alexander's Inn
Santa Fe, New Mexico 87501

INNKEEPER: Carolyn Lee

ADDRESS/TELEPHONE: 529 East Palace Avenue; (505) 986–1431;
fax (505) 982–8572

E-MAIL: alexandinn@aol.com

ROOMS: 16; 14 with private bath; no air-conditioning (elevation
7,000 feet). No smoking inn.

RATES: $75 to $160, double; $20 additional person; continental
breakfast and afternoon tea.

OPEN: All year.

FACILITIES AND ACTIVITIES: Hot tub, sundeck, patio, mountain bikes; guest privileges at El Gaucho Health Club. Nearby: Santa Fe Plaza, with shops, art galleries, museums, and historic buildings, is within walking distance.

Alexander's Inn is a surprise in New Mexico; it's not an adobe hacienda. The two-story American country–style house is located in a residential area on Santa Fe's historic east side. Built in 1903, it has retained the cozy feeling of a family dwelling (although there are adobe haciendas in the rear courtyard). At Alexander's Inn guests are encouraged to make themselves at home, make themselves coffee or tea, put food in the refrigerator, have friends over and visit in the cozy living room/dining area. The roomy entry, too, has a corner by a window where guests can relax.

The quaint inn is full of nooks and crannies, skylights and eaves. The Master Bedroom has a four-poster king-sized bed, a skylight, a large bricked bath, and a sitting area in front of the fireplace. Rooms 3 and 4 have four-poster queen beds and private baths. Up the narrow stairs, two guest rooms share a large bath; one has twin beds and the other an iron-and-brass queen bed. Just down the lane, the two-bed-room house has queen-sized beds; a living room with kiva fireplace, cable television, and VCR; as well as a dining room and kitchen in pretty Mexican tile. Seven new rooms are in adobe haciendas around the courtyard, and there's The Madeleine, a historic adobe house.

Check-in brings tea and cookies, a nice afternoon pick-me-up. Both breakfast and afternoon tea are often as not served outside on the patio to take advantage of Santa Fe's lovely weather.

Homemade granola, blueberry muffins, cereals, and fruit, such as a melange of pineapple, strawberries, and kiwi, are served for breakfast. Alexander's Inn guests can snack with impunity—they can work it off with swimming, indoor or outdoor tennis, exercise classes, and machines at the El Gaucho Health Club.

HOW TO GET THERE: Exit I–25 at Old Pecos Trail, which turns into the Old Santa Fe Trail. Turn right at Paseo de Peralta and follow around curve to Palace Avenue. Turn right and go 3 blocks. Alexander's Inn is the old brick-and-wood building on the left. There is a sign.

Adobe Abode
Santa Fe, New Mexico 87501

INNKEEPER: Pat Harbour

ADDRESS/TELEPHONE: 202 Chapelle; (505) 983–3133;
fax (505) 986–0972

E-MAIL: adobebnb@sprynet.com

ROOMS: 6; all with private bath; 1 with wheelchair access.
No smoking inn.

RATES: $105 to $155, double; $15 extra person; EPB.

OPEN: All year.

FACILITIES AND ACTIVITIES: Nearby: Palace of the Governors; Santa
Fe Plaza with shops, galleries, and restaurants; Fine Arts Museum;
St. Francis Cathedral; Mission of San Miguel; Santa Fe Opera;
Indian pueblos.

"*I*'m a collector of all types of things," Pat says, and wherever your eyes alight they rest on something beautiful, interesting, fascinating. I loved the colorful Mexican *animalitos* (little animals) and the Philippine overseer's chair. "I go off to the flea markets and come back with treasures," she says. Could be because Pat and her daughter, Allison Harbour, both have an artist's eye: Pat's background is fashion and advertising, and Allison studied at New York's Parson School of Design. It was she who cre-

ated the inn's award-winning logo: a colorful, stylized bed-and-fried-egg combo. The inn is hung with many fine paintings; a painting by Allison takes pride of place over the living room fireplace. The room is Southwestern-style, complete with Indian artifacts, vigas, a fireplace—and cable television. The seventy-year-old small adobe

Adobe Abode Santa Fe NM

house, pink with blue trim, is just 4 blocks from the Plaza. Set on a corner, it's bounded by a low stone fence, with a narrow sitting area on the side of the house and a lovely garden hidden behind high walls in the back. There's comfortable wicker furniture in which to relax and enjoy the blue skies and fresh Santa Fe air, which Pat says "has been polluted by nothing more than the Indian smoke signals of ages past."

The room called Bronco has its own private walled patio, and the wall beside the Southwestern-style four-poster is hung with a collection of western hats, typical of the originality with which Pat has decorated her inn. A departure is the Provence Suite, decorated in the bright and sunny colors of Southern France—yellows and blues. Pat's artistry hasn't stopped with decorating; every meal boasts a different menu and place setting. Two guests stayed for fourteen days and returned for a sixteen-day stay. "It was a challenge to come up with breakfast menus and place settings for their entire stay, but we did it!" Pat says. I got to sample only one menu, but it was delicious. Fresh orange juice and pineapple were followed by caramelized French toast (which I had to agree with Pat was absolutely decadent) and crusty cinnamon muffins. I hope to return for Pat's famous Santa Fe Cheese Casserole, Apple Skillet Cake, and Fiesta Baked Tomatoes, all of which have been selected for inclusion in a regional cookbook. But of her blueberry muffins, Pat says, "Unfortunately, that's a family recipe I have sworn not to divulge."

I love the questionnaire that Pat hopes each guest will fill out. It includes requests for such information as "What I like best about AA's breakfast" (muffins, entrees, etc.) and "What I like least about AA's breakfast." Pat keeps adding things "to make your visit a little nicer," she says. There are Adobe Abode terry-cloth robes embroidered with the inn's crest, special Adobe Abode soap, shampoo, conditioner, and lotion in little Adobe Abode bottles; morning newspapers; and Santa Fe cookies. These last were new to me, so I had to taste each flavor; I have to recommend chocolate piñon nut.

As for seeing the sights of Santa Fe, "My guests tell me I'm the best travel guide in the area," Pat boasts.

HOW TO GET THERE: From I–25 north take the St. Francis exit and go 3 miles north to Cerrillos. Turn right onto Guadalupe, crossing Alameda. Go 3 more blocks on Guadalupe to McKenzie, and turn right to Chapelle. The inn is on the left-hand corner.

Dos Casas Viejas
Santa Fe, New Mexico 87501

INNKEEPERS: Susan and Michael Strijak

ADDRESS/TELEPHONE: 610 Agua Fria Street; (505) 983–1636; fax (505) 983–1749

ROOMS: 8; all with private bath, phone, and TV; 1 with wheelchair access. No smoking inn.

RATES: $165 to $245, double; $15 extra person; EPB.

OPEN: All year.

FACILITIES AND ACTIVITIES: Lap pool. Nearby: Governor's Palace; Santa Fe Plaza with shops, galleries, and restaurants, Fine Arts Museum, St. Francis Cathedral, Mission of San Miguel, Santa Fe Opera; Institute of American Indian Arts Museum, Santuario de Guadalupe, Loretto Chapel, Cross of the Martyrs, Indian pueblos.

A pair of 1860s adobe buildings make up Dos Casas Viejas: The name means "two old houses." There are strict regulations in Santa Fe when it comes to historic property. "You keep everything the way it is" is the edict, which presents quite a challenge. The historic buildings lie within a half-acre compound enclosed by walls 18 inches thick. Passing through the gate into the courtyard is like driving into the narrow street of a pueblo in Old Mexico. The walls of the courtyard blend into the thick walls of the buildings, and you're surrounded by pink adobe; the only thing missing is the cobblestones.

To the right is the main house, with its long, shaded portale. It contains the lobby/library and dining room. Straight ahead and a little to the left is the second house, which houses the guest rooms. Each one has a private entrance off the secluded courtyard, and the deluxe suite has a living room, bedroom, two fireplaces, and two patios. Guest rooms are furnished with authentic Southwestern antiques. All have original vigas and great lighting; the mirrors are flattering. There are also flowers, bath sheets, and wood-burning kiva fireplaces for chilly days and nights. On warm, sunny days guests like to sit outside by the heated lap pool (and exercise in it, of course) and listen to the fountain cascading into the far end of the pool.

Breakfast can be served there or in the dining room, or, if you like, you can carry a basket back to the privacy of your room. It's a continental breakfast, but more than just coffee and doughnuts—fresh-squeezed orange juice, fresh raspberries or blackberries, chocolate yogurt coffeecake, or maybe pistachio yeast bread.

HOW TO GET THERE: From I–25 north take the St. Francis exit, and go 3‰ miles into town. At Agua Fria Street, turn right. The inn is 2 blocks on the right, next to Guadalupe Inn. There is a sign.

Four Kachinas
Santa Fe, New Mexico 87501

INNKEEPERS: Andrew Beckerman and John Daw

ADDRESS/TELEPHONE: 512 Webber Street; (505) 982–2550 or (800) 397–2564; fax (505) 989–1323

E-MAIL: info@fourkachinas.com

WEB SITE: www.fourkachinas.com

ROOMS: 6; all with private bath, phone, and TV; 1 with wheelchair access. No smoking inn.

RATES: $70 to $149, double; continental breakfast and afternoon tea.

OPEN: Closed mid-January.

FACILITIES AND ACTIVITIES: Nearby: Santa Fe Plaza with shops, galleries, and restaurants; Governor's Palace, Fine Arts Museum, St. Francis Cathedral, Mission of San Miguel, Santa Fe Opera, Institute of American Indian Arts Museum, Santuario de Guadalupe, Loretto Chapel; Cross of the Martyrs; Indian pueblos.

Kachinas are Hopi dolls, but they're not toys. They are sacred objects for Hopi children to study. Bright and elaborate, they represent a variety of gods, spirits, departed ancestors, and such. They make a wonderful theme for this inn: Each room represents one of these supernatural beings, with the decor reflecting the kachina's persona.

Tawa represents the Hopi Sun God; it's the only room on the second floor. It has a window seat with a view of the Sangre de Cristo Mountains. Each of the other three rooms, downstairs, has a small private garden patio. As for the kachinas, they're from John's collection; you might have Poko the Dog, Hon the White Bear, or Koyemsi the Mudhead Clown. All six rooms are decorated with custom-made furniture, colorful Navajo rugs, and lovely antiques.

Andrew is an architect, and in California John was a combination of caterer and social services worker. "He's used to soothing people," Andrew says. "This is a people business, too," John answers. "We're very much in people's lives. Sometimes they show up late, are cranky; we help them get oriented, give them a soothing cup of tea. . . ." Sounds great to me! Being pampered is a large part of the charm of staying at an inn, and John and Andrew have made a serious study of this. Having been to Japan three times, they were very impressed with Japanese hospitality. They've patterned Four Kachinas after an inn in Kyoto. "We like the Japanese style of hospitality, the personal contact, the bringing of breakfast."

Consequently, your continental breakfast can be brought to your door if you like. You're presented with a form ready to be filled out with your selections of juice, fresh fruit, yogurt, and homemade pastries, as well as the time you'd like to have your breakfast. "I've never been keen on waking up on my travels and facing a bunch of strangers," John says. "I want to have my coffee in my room."

Four Kachinas Inn Santa Fe N.M.

But if you prefer to be sociable, the old adobe garage in the courtyard has been converted into a guest lounge. You can shop there, too, if you like: There are a variety of travel books, maps, and guidebooks, as well as a nice collection of art, silver jewelry, and Indian crafts for sale.

John is the pastry chef, and he's good. A lot of noses were out of joint when his coconut pound cake took "Best of Show" at the 1992 Santa Fe County Fair. John laughs. "Yes, I won the prize. People are still bitter about it! Especially since I won again in 1995 and 1997!"

Kachinas are not the only history connected with this interesting inn. Andrew and John built it from scratch, but the land it's on has an interesting history. It belonged originally to the Digneo family, who came from back East to build Santa Fe's St. Francis Cathedral. The family was sponsored by the very archbishop, Jean Baptiste Lamy, who is the central figure in Willa Cather's novel *Death Comes to the Archbishop*.

Grant Corner Inn
Santa Fe, New Mexico 87501

INNKEEPER: Louise Stewart

ADDRESS/TELEPHONE: 122 Grant Avenue; (505) 983–6678;
fax (505) 983–1526

ROOMS: 12; 10 with private bath, all with phone and TV, 1 with wheelchair access. No smoking inn.

RATES: 85 to $155, double; $20 extra person; EPB and evening refreshments.

OPEN: All year except January.

FACILITIES AND ACTIVITIES: Picnic, lunch, and dinner for twelve or
more by reservation; afternoon tea, open to public; yearly bazaar
between Thanksgiving and Christmas. Nearby: historic Santa Fe Plaza
1 block away, Anthropological Museum, Georgia O'Keeffe Museum.

On each guest-room door of this handsome Santa Fe Colonial home hangs a red-velvet-and-lace heart that says WELCOME. This should give you a hint of the cordiality of this inn. But there's a sense of humor at work here, too. The reverse side of the stuffed velvet heart on your door will say BEWARE OF OCCUPANT.

"We can't really pamper our guests, but we can come pretty close," says Louise. Close—like cookies and chocolates in your room, plus a terry robe if you're sharing a bath. Like a personal welcome card. Like warm, personal care not only from the family but also from all the inn staff.

Begin with this truly outstanding, tall blue-and-white house on the cor-ner of Grant Avenue. It's surrounded by a spanking-white picket fence and absolutely draped in weeping willows. Inside, blue-and-white walls, white drapes, and the warm woods of antique furniture meld with the large antique Oriental rugs covering polished wood floors. There's a convenient rest room on the first floor.

Guest rooms have antique pine and brass beds, and you can have twin, double, queen, or king (some of them four-poster), depending on which room you choose. Double Deluxe rooms—numbers 7 and 8—have their own porch, and four rooms have space for a rollaway.

Louise is an interior designer with a background in the hotel business, so you can see why Grant Corner Inn is pretty much a masterpiece. The Sunday Brunch is special, but not to worry. Every day is tasty, too, with dishes such as eggs Florentine, banana waffles, and a special New Mexican soufflé. Louise compiled the *Grant Corner Inn Breakfast and Brunch Cookbook.*

Need I say more? In the winter, breakfast is served in front of the blazing dining room fire. In the summer you can have it on the front veranda, under the willows. Louise is eager to provide guests with information on local events, such as the Indian pueblos and their dances and music and art festivals, as well as the renowned Santa Fe Opera, with a July/August season. Santa Fe

Shopping in Santa Fe

Santa Fe's Plaza is bound on the north side by the Palace of the Governors, and you can fnd vendors of turquoise jewelry, pottery, leather goods, and other handicrafts settled and waiting for you under the palace's block-long porch. Indians from the nearby pueblos make it a picturesque scene, with their traditional clothing and braids. It's almost an obligation to bargain over the articles that catch your fancy, but if you want to take photos, be sure to ask first.

The Plaza is 6,999 feet above sea level, and all building must conform to the city's traditional "pueblo" or "territorial" architecture, which means plenty of picturesque pink adobe.

Most of the town's interesting shops and tourist attractions are within a block or two of the Plaza or are strung along Canyon Road, a few blocks up the Sante Fe River, which runs through town.

Plaza, practically on the inn doorstep, is lined with shops and restaurants, art galleries, and curio shops. Don't miss the art museum, housed in one more of Santa Fe's pink adobe buildings.

HOW TO GET THERE: The inn is on the corner of Grant and Johnson just south of Santa Fe Plaza. Grant is the street that borders the Plaza on the west.

The Guadalupe Inn
Santa Fe, New Mexico 87501

INNKEEPERS: Henrietta Quintana, Dolores Quintana Myers, and Pete Quintana

ADDRESS/TELEPHONE: 604 Agua Fria; (505) 989–7422; fax (505) 989–7422

WEB SITE: www.guadelupeinn.com

ROOMS: 12, including 2-bedroom suite; all with private bath, phone, and TV; some with Jacuzzi, 1 with wheelchair access. No smoking inn.

RATES: $125 to $175, double; $15 extra person; EPB.

OPEN: All year.

FACILITIES AND ACTIVITIES: Hot tub. Nearby: Santa Fe Plaza with shops, galleries, and restaurants; Palace of the Governors, Fine Arts Museum, St. Francis Cathedral, Mission of San Miguel, Santa Fe Opera, Institute of American Indian Arts Museum, Loretto Chapel, Indian pueblos, Santa Fe Ski Basin, Georgia O'Keeffe Museum.

Don't be put off by the deserted-looking, old-fashioned store to the right of the entrance into The Guadalupe Inn's courtyard. The inn is a family business, built by two sisters and their brother on family property, and that little store was their grandfather's. That makes this a family business in the best sense of the term.

The street in front of the inn, Agua Fria, was once the famous Camino Real, connecting what is now northern New Mexico with Mexico. First Indian, then Hispanic, traders traced the route. This is the historic Guadalupe District, less than a mile from Santa Fe Plaza.

"We used to work in the store," Dolores says, "since I was eight and Henrietta was seven. The front buildings were our grandparents' home and store. When they died the family said if anybody wanted it, they'd listen. So we bought it from the estate, but we couldn't decide what to do with it."

They let it sit for four or five years, until inspiration struck. Pete is in heating and air-conditioning and metal roofing, and in New Mexico, Dolores says, you can construct your own building. So, eureka! They decided to build an inn. "We each got three rooms to decorate," Dolores says. "I never decorated anything in my life!" But wait until you see the rooms—each is more delightful than the next. Guest rooms have no names, just numbers, and number 3 is one of Dolores's creations. She carved the back of the wooden luggage rack in the room, and it's amazing. "Henrietta carves," she notes, "and I wanted to see if I could do it, too."

The rooms, off galleries or balconies with views of the Sangre de Cristo and Jemez Mountains, are furnished with wonderful Southwestern pieces, and a surprising number were made by these artistic innkeepers.

I loved Henrietta's multicolored bed in number 11. The room also has an old-fashioned bathtub, surrounded by mirrors. Number 5 has a colorful sunburst bed and a desk in an alcove. Number 8, one of Pete's rooms, has blue-covered beds. Colors are all soft Southwestern blues and pinks and grays, warmed by the golden tones of the wood and cooled by the white adobe walls.

And—I did say it was a family business, didn't I?—nephew Chris Quintana made the beautiful metal sconces covering the gallery lights, and a little niece even decorated one of the rooms for the guests' enjoyment.

Breakfast is a feast. We had our choice of *huevos rancheros*, burritos, or a western omelette, finishing off with turnovers of cherry, strawberry, apple, apricot, or peach. "Our turnovers are terrific," Dolores says as she hands me a peach one—and, oh, my, are they ever!

HOW TO GET THERE: From I-25 north take the St. Francis exit 3⁹⁄₁₀ miles into town, to Agua Fria. Turn right; the inn is 2 blocks on the right, next to Dos Casas Viejas Inn.

Preston House
Santa Fe, New Mexico 87501

INNKEEPERS: Signe Bergman and Ann Leighton

ADDRESS/TELEPHONE: 106 Faithway; (505) 982–3465; fax (505) 988–2397

E-MAIL: prstonhse@aol.com

WEB SITE: www.prestonhouse.com/santafe

ROOMS: 8; 6 with private bath; all with TV. No smoking inn.

RATES: $75 to $165, double; $20 extra person; generous continental breakfast and afternoon tea.

OPEN: All year.

FACILITIES AND ACTIVITIES: Nearby: historic Santa Fe Plaza with restaurants, shops, art galleries, and the Palace of the Governors; Indian dances, hiking, tennis, museums, Santa Fe opera.

*T*his charming house is the only Queen Anne in New Mexico, Signe told me. It was built in 1886 and has some wonderful features. The large arched window halfway up the stairs faces west, and the window seat on the large landing is a favored spot for afternoon refreshment. The staircase itself, all gold and black lacquer, is very unusual. "It looks Oriental," I said to the innkeeper. "It is," she replied. "It was built by Chinese workmen who came to build the railroad. This is the only way they knew to build."

Room number 1 has a tile fireplace with a built-in wood cupboard. The

flowered wallpaper, high ceilings, and lacquered oval Oriental nightstands on each side of the king-sized bed were a hit with me. From the third-floor room, another favorite, there's a wonderful view and an outside spiral staircase to the garden below. The parlor has a communal television in case you want company, as well as an antique armoire, furniture upholstered in cool white, and a tile fireplace.

Breakfast is served in the large dining room, and it's generous. Pear streusel, bread pudding, sour-cream coffeecake, four cold cereals, yogurt, and fruit salad are accompanied by homemade jams and jellies. New bread recipes are being added, alternating with standbys, continuously. An afternoon tea is also served between 4:30 and 6:30. "This is a place where you get to know people instead of merely serving them," says Signe, pretty much summing up the spirit of innkeeping, I think.

HOW TO GET THERE: Take Palace Avenue 4 blocks east of the Plaza. Turn left on Faithway, just 1 block long; the inn is on the right, and Holy Faith Episcopal Church is on the corner.

Spencer House Inn
Santa Fe, New Mexico 87501

INNKEEPER: Jan McConnell

ADDRESS/TELEPHONE: 222 McKenzie Street, (505) 988–3024 or (800) 647–0530; fax (505) 984–9862

WEB SITE: www.spencerhse-santafe.com

ROOMS: 5; all with private bath. No smoking inn.

RATES: $95 to $190, double; $15 extra person; EPB.

OPEN: All year.

FACILITIES AND ACTIVITIES: Nearby: Santa Fe Plaza with shops, galleries, and restaurants; Palace of the Governors, Fine Arts Museum, St. Francis Cathedral, Mission of San Miguel, Santa Fe Opera, Institute of American Indian Arts Museum, Santuario de Guadalupe, Loretto Chapel, Indian pueblos.

This lovely old adobe house was a fine private residence from a bygone era, and the decor is simple, clean, uncluttered. Guest rooms have pine or brass beds, brown wicker chairs, small wooden armoires, bedside tables, and lamps for reading. Linens are stylish and chic, adding just the right touch to the white walls and wood floors. Other nice touches include a plaid rug and a matching plaid chair cushion, old painted chests, and gas lamps (electrified). The cottage has a fireplace and its own private patio.

Common rooms have rich antiques,

kilim rugs, and artwork from some of the galleries Santa Fe is known for. The breakfast room has a wall of windows on two sides and a wooden ceiling bisected by a skylight; you can imagine how sunny and light it is. The outdoors is very near; the birdfeeder attracts hummingbirds and sometimes in summer purple finches and house finches, too.

A tidy adobe fence encloses the property; there are two white picket gates to enter from the sidewalk, the front double windows have shutters and a windowbox, and there is a white sign on a white signpost in the corner of the yard of this tidy inn. Breakfast is filling, with such fare as blue-corn piñon pancakes with pure maple syrup and eggs; smoked chicken or sausage with sun dried tomato, corn and tomato salsa fresca, and savory corn cakes.

HOW TO GET THERE: The inn is located 4 blocks from Santa Fe Plaza. From the Plaza drive west on Palace Avenue to Grant, turn right on Grant to Griffen and left onto McKenzie. The inn is on the southeast corner of McKenzie and Chapelle, and there is a sign.

Eaton House
Socorro, New Mexico 87801

INNKEEPERS: Anna Appleby and Tom Harper

ADDRESS/TELEPHONE: 403 Eaton Avenue; (505) 835–1067 or (800) 383–CRANE

E-MAIL: crane@eatonhouse.com

WEB SITE: www.eatonhouse.com

ROOMS: 7; 3 plus 4 casitas; all with private bath. No smoking inn.

RATES: $85 to $135, September 1 through May 1; $70 to $110, June 1 through August 31; $20 extra person; continental breakfast or Birding Basket for bird-watchers.

OPEN: All year.

FACILITIES AND ACTIVITIES: Nearby: Historic town walking tour, Mineral Museum, New Mexico Tech Golf Course, petroglyphs, observatory, Bosque del Apache Wildlife Refuge, Alamo Indian Reservation.

The inn, on the New Mexico Historical Register, was built in 1881 and is a cross between eastern Victorian and New Mexican Territorial—there's even a widow's walk on the roof! It was built by

Colonel Ethan W. Eaton, who was an important figure in the $30-million Magdalene Kelly Mine back in the 1880s. The area is rich in silver, lead, zinc, and copper, as well as more ancient points of interest, such as the Piro Indian petroglyphs in nearby San Acacia.

Socorro in Spanish means "aid" or "help," and it got its name back in 1598 when Spanish explorers received aid from the Piro Indians, who are believed to have been the area's first inhabitants. The climate, typical of high desert, is a great bird-watching area, and many Eaton House guests have come for just that. "We have hundreds of hummingbirds from April to September, as well as dozens of other species," Anna says.

Guest rooms, bright and comfortable, contain Southwestern furniture, much of it made by a local artisan. In spacious Colonel Eaton's Room, though, there's a four-poster from Santa Fe and an antique 1859 desk and old liquor cabinet. A closet wall in Daughters Room is all mirrors, and the twin beds were hand carved for twin daughters.

"We've had great-granddaughters and -sons [of the original family] stay here," Anna says. The *trastero* (combined bench and armoire) in the Vigilante Room is an interesting piece. There's luxury in the down comforters and the huge bath sheets, but the iron bars in the windows of the hallway are a reminder of a 1906 earthquake—that's when the colonel put them in. The only thing changed of the original house are the added portales (covered walkways) so that each room could have its own entrance.

HOW TO GET THERE: From I–25 in Socorro take Manzanares west to California. Turn south on California for 2 blocks to Church, west on Church 4 blocks to Eaton Avenue, south on Eaton to 403.

Adobe & Pines Inn
Taos, New Mexico 87557

INNKEEPERS: Charil and Chuck Fulkerson

ADDRESS/TELEPHONE: P.O. Box 837, Rancho de Taos, 87557;
(800) 723–8267; fax (505) 758–8423

E-MAIL: adobepines@taos.newmex.com

WEB SITE: www.taosnet.com/adobepines

ROOMS: 8; all with private bath; 2 with TV. No smoking inn.

RATES: $95 to $185, double; $20 extra person; EPB.

OPEN: All year.

FACILITIES AND ACTIVITIES: Jet tub. Nearby: historic St. Francis de
Assisi Church; shopping; art galleries; seven minutes from Taos with its
historic Plaza, galleries, shops, and restaurants; historic Taos Pueblo; Kit
Carson Home and Museum; Rio Grande Gorge; Taos Ski Valley.

Even the innkeepers admit that if you're not watching for the orange,
blue, and turquoise poles that mark the road to the inn, you'll miss
the turnoff. But, like me, you can always turn around and look
again. And once you find it, you'll get a friendly welcome from Rascal, the
cocker-terrier, who, says Charil, "along with our horse, Desi, requests no
other pets at the inn."

And what an inn; it's full of beauty, beginning with the lovely mural at the
end of the 80-foot-long portale, a 1950s scene of the famous Taos Pueblo.
"We didn't come into this blind," Charil says. "We even hired a consultant
who told us what to expect from innkeeping." She laughs. "We've had our
eyes opened more ever since."

Like so many happy innkeepers, they were looking for a lifestyle different
from their hectic one in San Diego. They sold everything they owned and
traveled in Europe for a year. "We didn't know we were doing our homework," Chuck says. They landed in Taos because Chuck had a birthday and
Charil surprised him with tickets to the balloon festival in Albuquerque.
While there they chanced to look at an advertisement on business opportunities. "Taos was not a plan, but we fell in love, made an offer.

"Then we had three-and-a-half months of intense renovation," Chuck
says ruefully of the 150-year-old adobe home on four acres of fruit and pine

Adobe & Pine Inn Rancho de Taos NM
(1991)

trees. He brightens up. "But it's all Charil's decor. She does a dynamite gourmet breakfast, too!"

This was true. It was so gorgeous that guests left the table to get cameras for photos before we destroyed the 4-inch-tall puff pastry hiding banana yogurt and the German pancakes smothered with fresh raspberries and golden raisins. Chuck is no slouch, either, when it comes to muffins. Lemon poppyseed, apple cinnamon . . . "Guests dub them Chuck's killer muffins," Charil says. They've had so many requests for recipes that Chuck has compiled their own Southwest cookbook.

Rooms are beautiful, too. Two open off the portale: Puerta Azul, a blue room with an antique writing desk and a hand-painted kiva fireplace; and Puerta Verde, with green and rust colors and a romantic canopy bed and sitting area by the fireplace. "We utilized the one-hundred-year-old 'Dutch' doors," Charil says. They open at the top for a view outside without opening the entire door. Puerta Rosa, off the courtyard, conceals a surprise under vaulted ceilings: an oversize, sunken bathroom with Mexican tiles surrounding a large cedar sauna (and a separate shower). There's a fireplace to warm the room and another in the bedroom by the sitting area. Puerta Turquesa, a separate guest cottage off the courtyard, has a jet whirlpool bath as well as two fireplaces. There's a kitchen here, too, if you want to stay awhile and make yourself at home.

HOW TO GET THERE: The inn is off Highway 68, 4 miles south of Taos. The turnoff to the inn, which is on the east side of the road, is marked by orange, blue, and turquoise poles ³⁄₁₀ mile south of St. Francis Plaza and 4 miles north of the Stakeout Grill and Bar. Both landmarks are on the east side of the road.

American Artists Gallery House
Taos, New Mexico 87571

INNKEEPERS: LeAn and Charles Clamurro

ADDRESS/TELEPHONE: 132 Frontier Road (mailing address: P.O. Box 584); (505) 758-4446 or (800) 532-2041; fax (505) 758-0497

E-MAIL: aagh@taosnm.com

WEB SITE: taoswebb.com/hotel/artistshouse

ROOMS: 10; all with private bath; no air-conditioning (elevation 7,000 feet); limited wheelchair access. No smoking inn.

RATES: $75 to $150, double; $25 extra person; EPB and afternoon snacks.

OPEN: All year.

FACILITIES AND ACTIVITIES: Hot tub. Nearby: Van Vechten Lineberry Museum, hiking, horseback riding, skiing, tours, Taos Indian Pueblo and museums, historic Taos Plaza with restaurants, shops, and art galleries.

American Artists Gallery House was one of the first fine inns in these parts, with bright, comfortable guest rooms decorated in pleasing Southwestern style and hung with art. New innkeepers LeAn and Charles, with Charles's past experience as a hotel manager "coming up through the food and beverage ranks," are carrying on the tradition of the inn. As Charles says, his food and beverage experience has added to the creativity of the inn's breakfasts.

The living room windows overlook the inn's famous outdoor garden, and the hot tub on the outdoor deck is wonderful after a winter's day of skiing, in any season in the mountains, or after taking in Taos's museums, shops, and galleries.

The main house continues to live up to the inn's name with ever-changing exhibits of handmade Southwestern artwork: paintings, photographs, sculpture, jewelry, and metalwork. An enchanting piece of metal sculpture, a sort of stylized kachina figure, stands in the front yard. "That's our 'bed-and-breakfast goddess,'" LeAn says, "to watch over your stay to ensure that you have a very special visit to Taos." The adjoining ¾ acre now forms part of the inn, adding three deluxe suites, complete with Jacuzzis. The landscaping between the newly dubbed East and West Compounds brings the separate areas together to form a lovely whole.

HOW TO GET THERE: Coming into Taos from the south on Old Santa Fe Road (the main highway through Taos), turn right on Frontier, located by the Ramada Inn. American Artists Gallery House, surrounded by a low adobe wall, will be on your right a short way down the road.

Casa de las Chimeneas
Taos, New Mexico 87571

INNKEEPERS: Susan Vernon Rios and David Rios

ADDRESS/TELEPHONE: 405 Cordoba Road, Box 5303; (505) 758–4777; fax (505)758–3976

E-MAIL: casa@newmex.com

ROOMS: 6, all with private bath; 1 wheelchair accessible. No smoking inn.

RATES: $125 to $170, double; $15 extra person; EBP.

OPEN: All year.

FACILITIES AND ACTIVITIES: Hot tub; fitness/spa facility, sauna, massage, guest laundry, trolley to Taos Plaza with shops, galleries, and restaurants; Taos Pueblo; museums and seasonal events; skiing.

Chimeneas is Spanish for "chimneys," and the inn is named for the traditional New Mexico kiva fireplaces in each room. Guest rooms have French doors opening onto a walled and grassy courtyard where fountains play and flowers bloom. Inside, designer linens (Ralph Lauren), down pillows, Evelyn and Crabtree toiletries, skylights, and hand-carved furniture make for a luxurious stay. Unexpected are the color, cable television sets and the ice makers concealed behind carved *trasteros*.

The large common area is light, bright, and sunny; local artists' work enhances the thick adobe walls. Sodas and juices are complimentary, and so is the homespun treatment of guests, typical of the warmth of Taos.

For breakfast you might be fed warm bread pudding with blueberry sauce and incredible apple-oatmeal muffins, as well as a fruit parfait with oranges and yogurt sauced in a cream-cheese orange sauce, beautifully layered in a parfait glass. Pre-dinner treats are served between 5:00 and 6:30 and are well worth waiting for: tomato bisque with cheese biscuits, green-chili corn chowder, vegetable quesadillas, alternating with soups and stews in cold weather.

HOW TO GET THERE: Going north on the South Santa Fe Road, turn right on Los Pandos (between the Shell Station and Pueblo Motors) for a short way, keeping a lookout for Cordoba, a small unpaved road to your right. The inn is behind an adobe wall to your left almost as soon as you turn the corner.

Casa Encantada 📱
Taos, New Mexico 87571

INNKEEPERS: Susan, Paul, and Larry Ruffino

ADDRESS/TELEPHONE: 416 Liebert Street (mailing address: P.O. Box 6460); (800) 223–TAOS; fax (505) 737–5085

ROOMS: 10, 5 plus 5 suites; all with private bath; all with TV; some with kitchen; children and pets welcome. No smoking inn.

RATES: $95 to $135; EPB.

OPEN: All year.

FACILITIES AND ACTIVITIES: Nearby: within walking distance of historic Taos Plaza with shops, galleries, and restaurants; historic Taos Pueblo; Kit Carson House; Millicent Rogers Museum; Rio Grande Gorge; Taos Ski Valley; hiking; fishing; white-water rafting on Rio Grande.

Casa Encantada means "enchanted house," and behind the all-encompassing pink adobe wall there's an interesting combination of peace and quiet—in the garden—and activity around the portales, with children playing and guests mingling happily and busily.

The old hacienda imparts a feeling of history, of generations of family and friends who lived and visited here. And the Ruffino family has been in the hospitality service business for more than 200 years. In the garden there's the scent of sage and piñon; the fresh mountain air is exhilarating, and chirping songbirds greet each new day. The inn's lounge is a spacious, warm, and welcoming area, tastefully decorated in Southwest style. Comfortable sofas are grouped around the large fireplace that divides the lounge from the dining room.

Casa Encantada Taos NM.

Under the skylight in the dining room, the long Mission-style table is prettily set. Sunlight pours in, and puffy white clouds drift through the deep blue New Mexico sky above. Breakfast dishes include an offering of one egg entree and one eggless, as well as cereal and fresh fruit smoothies and espresso.

All guest rooms have private entrances—they open off the long portale along the side of the house facing the garden, and all have been upgraded with antiques and design pieces.

HOW TO GET THERE: From the traffic light on Highway 68 at the Plaza, turn right on Kit Carson Road (Highway 64) and go 5 blocks east to Liebert Street. Turn right and make a jog; the inn is behind the large adobe-walled property on the right.

Casa Europa
Taos, New Mexico 87571

INNKEEPERS: Marcia and Rudi Zwicker

ADDRESS/TELEPHONE: 840 Upper Ranchitos Road; (888) 758–9798

ROOMS: 7; all with private bath; several have built-in bancos that convert to a twin bed; no air-conditioning (elevation 7,000 feet); children welcome. Smoking permitted in public areas.

RATES: $95 to $165, double; $20 extra person; EBP and afternoon tea.

OPEN: All year.

FACILITIES AND ACTIVITIES: Sauna and hot tub; three private courtyards for play; a special clubhouse; hiking, horseback riding, and winter skiing. Nearby: Taos Indian Pueblo and museums; historic Taos Plaza with restaurants, shops, and art galleries.

Rudi and Marcia both are used to the public and enjoy entertaining: They were proprietors of a fine restaurant in Boulder, Colorado, for many years before coming to Taos. But idleness was not for Rudi. "I needed to do something with people again," he says. "He needs to work about eighteen hours a day," Marcia adds with a fond laugh.

"Well, we get our guests started, we introduce them, and then they are fine," Rudi says. I certainly was fine, my only problem being one of indecision at teatime; should I choose the chocolate-mousse-filled meringue or the raspberry Bavarian? Or perhaps the Black Forest torte or one of the fresh fruit tarts? (I really wanted one of each, all made by Chef Rudi, who was trained at the Grand Hotel in Nuremberg, Germany.)

Breakfast is another such feast prepared by Chef Rudi: fresh fruit salad, a mushroom-and-asparagus quiche, lean bacon edged in black pepper, home-fried potatoes, and fresh homemade Danish that absolutely melted in my mouth. Wonderful, too, are the blue-corn waffles with piñon nuts.

The house itself is a treasure, with fourteen skylights and a circular staircase to the gallery above the main salon. Appearing deceptively small from the outside, the large common rooms (but very uncommon!), both upstairs and down, lead to six exceptionally spacious and elegant guest rooms. But it's also very comfortable, and, as Marcia observes, "Children nowadays appreciate the fine things as well as their parents do—like our son, Maxi, who is also well traveled." The wood floors are graced with Oriental rugs; the white stucco walls are hung with original art by such New Mexican artists as Veloy Vigil and Danny Escalante, artists who can be seen in the museums and the galleries on the Plaza.

HOW TO GET THERE: Driving into Taos from the south on Highway 68, take a left onto Lower Ranchitos Road at the blinking-light intersection just north of McDonald's and south of Taos Plaza. Go 1½ miles southwest to the intersection of Upper Ranchitos Road, which will be on your right.

Hacienda del Sol
Taos, New Mexico 87571

INNKEEPERS: Marcine and John Landon

ADDRESS/TELEPHONE: 109 Mabel Dodge Lane (mailing address: P.O. Box 177); (505) 758–0287; fax (505) 758–5895

E-MAIL: sunhouse@newmex.com

ROOMS: 9; all with private bath; no air-conditioning (elevation 7,000 feet). No smoking inn.

RATES: $75 to $135; $22 extra person; EBP.

OPEN: All year.

FACILITIES AND ACTIVITIES: Brown-bag lunches on requesst; hot tub; beautiful flower garden. Nearby: Taos Indian Pueblo; Taos Plaza with art galleries, shops, and restaurants; Kit Carson Home and Museum; Millicent Rogers Museum; Martinez Hacienda.

"I was in education for thirty years," Marcine says, "and John was a traveling salesman. A long time ago, we decided we'd retire at age fifty-five and do something together!" They used to visit Taos twice a year at least, and, like so many happy innkeepers, once they saw this inn they fell in love with it. "It's our home," Marcine says, "and that's how we treat it. We don't come in in the morning, we're already here."

The inn's story is part of Taos history. Mabel Dodge Luhan, the wealthy arts patron who brought Georgia O'Keeffe and D. H. Lawrence to Taos, bought the home as a hideaway for her Taos Indian husband, Tony, so he wouldn't feel like a fenced-in bear. What's more, Georgia O'Keeffe painted her "Sunflowers" here.

The inn, like so many New Mexico homes, is an old adobe building hidden behind a wall. But it backs up to 95,000 acres of Indian land, with a beautiful view of Taos Mountain, the Magic Mountain of the Taos Indians. "Now I can't imagine living any farther from that mountain than I have to," Marcine says.

Each of Hacienda del Sol's rooms is equipped with a cassette player and tape selections; a "help" basket with needle and thread, safety pins, Band-Aids, corkscrew, hair dryer, and hand mirror; and a library with current magazines.

Luxurious, too, is the outdoor hot tub, where you can loll back and let the magic of the mountains work on you. The Casita, a separate little adobe house, has two guest rooms, two baths, and fireplaces. It can be used as a suite or as two separate rooms, each with a bath.

"We both are people oriented," John says. "This is pretty much a continuation of what we were doing." Marcine adds with a laugh, "Except that I'm cooking for more!" A guest convinced them of the joy of a bread machine, and you can imagine how delicious the inn smells in the morning. As for which one is the chef, "If it comes out of the oven, I do it," Marcine says. "From the top, John does." Guests rave about John's "elegant" stuffed French toast or Marcine's porridge topped with vanilla ice cream—how's that to start the day? Or eggs tostada served on a blue-corn tortilla with fresh salsa or blue-corn pancakes with blueberry sauce. And for you coffee hounds, know that the brew is their own special blend, Cafe del Sol.

HOW TO GET THERE: The inn is 1 mile north of Taos Plaza, on Highway 64/Paseo del Pueblo Norte. Turn right on an unpaved road immediately alongside the Southwest Drum and Moccasin Company; the inn is on the left, hidden behind a tall "latilla" fence that surrounds the inn's one-and-two-tenths acres.

Inn on La Loma Plaza 📱
Taos, New Mexico 87571

INNKEEPERS: Peggy and Jerry Davis

ADDRESS/TELEPHONE: 315 Ranchitos Road, Box 4159; (505) 758–1717 or (800) 530–3040; fax (505) 751–0155

E-MAIL: laloma@taoswebb.com

WEB SITE: taoswebb.com/laloma

ROOMS: 9; all with private bath, telephones, and television; 1 wheelchair accessible. Children welcome. No smoking inn.

RATES: $95 to $195; $10 to $20 extra person; EPB.

OPEN: All year.

FACILITIES AND ACTIVITIES: Hot tub; Athletic Club privileges. Nearby: historic Taos Plaza with shops, galleries, and restaurants; historic Taos Pueblo; Kit Carson Home and Museum; Millicent Rogers Museum; Rio Grande Gorge; Taos Ski Valley; hiking; fishing; white-water rafting on Rio Grande.

The L-shaped building is between Ranchitos Road and the southwest corner of La Loma Plaza, a historic residential square. Some of the thick adobe walls were built as far back as 1800 and served as part of the fortifications of the plaza. (Things were not as restful back then as they are now!)

Now there's a beautiful garden, with a fishpond in which several koi, the large Japanese goldfish, swim lazily. The front lawn, shaded with towering old cottonwoods, has a fine view of the Sangre de Cristos Mountains. The front entrance opens into a bright glassed-in sunroom with a fountain.

Breakfast is a fulsome buffet of various fresh fruits, cereals, pastries, breads, juices, yogurt, and a special entree each day, like breakfast burritos, basil strata, eggs Olé, eggs Florentine, green chile strata, granola peaches, or French toast a l'orange.

There are four rooms in the main house, with three more opening off the building's bendings and archways. The inn once contained the studios of several artists, and two outside suites are complete with kitchenettes and fireplaces and can sleep up to four persons.

The inn furniture is handmade from New Mexican wood: there are lots of books, pottery, and art. The art and pottery are for sale; the inn doubles as a showroom for Taos artists. Guest rooms are luxurious, each with individually designed tiles in the baths. The Sky Room has a window seat and steps up to a small deck. Happy Trails is happy-making indeed, with such faithfulness to Western motif as chaps and spurs on paneled walls, a mirror framed in a horse collar, furniture painted with Western scenes, and even a rocking horse—with a saddle, no less!

HOW TO GET THERE: From Highway 68 into town take La Placita Road (just past McDonald's on the right) left to Ranchitos Road (Highway 240). Then left to Valdez and either left again to La Loma Plaza at the end of the block, where there's parking and an entrance off the Plaza, or straight ahead to another entrance to the inn on Ranchitos Road.

La Posada de Taos
Taos, New Mexico 87571

INNKEEPERS: Nancy and Bill Swan

ADDRESS/TELEPHONE: 309 Juanita Lane (mailing address: P.O. Box 1118); (505) 758–8164 or (800) 645–4803; fax (505) 751–3294

E-MAIL: laposada@newmex.com

ROOMS: 6; all with private bath; 1 wheelchair accessible. No smoking inn.

RATES: $65 to $115; $15 extra person; EPB. No credit cards.

OPEN: All year.

FACILITIES AND ACTIVITIES: Complimentary twenty-four-hour tea/coffee/soda service. Nearby: historic Taos Plaza with shops, art galleries, and restaurants; historic Taos Pueblo; Kit Carson Home and Museum; Millicent Rogers Museum; Rio Grande Gorge; Taos Ski Valley; hiking; fishing; white-water rafting on Rio Grande; horseback riding; golf.

*N*ancy and Bill fell in love with Taos twenty years ago when they used to come to New Mexico to visit her brother, who lived in Albuquerque. As for becoming innkeepers, Nancy says, "We've had that dream since 1981. Bill was stationed in Suffolk (England) until 1984, and ever since that day I've been collecting furniture, especially English furniture." Bill laughs. "It all started when we were having lunch in a pub with friends. In a shop window across the street there was a cupboard. . . ."

"It was an old food cupboard," Nancy says. "I told our friends, 'That thing is really calling to me.' That was the beginning of the inn."

Bill grins. "That was the most expensive pub lunch we ever had."

As for Bill, Taos really spoke to him. "Wow!" he says he told Nancy. "We gotta find something to do in this great town." Bill was a fighter pilot in the Air Force Reserves, and acting as a consultant with the admissions process at the Air Force Academy is what brought them home from England.

"I know lots of people think they're going to do it, have an inn, but we really have done it!" Nancy says exultantly. "Bill went off for a walk, looked at this inn, and that was it." La Posada de Taos had been the dream of long-time innkeeper Sue Smoot, who has retired happily to Albuquerque. She could hardly have turned over her lovely inn to a more enthusiastic couple.

The result is a cozy mix of Southwest style and English pine Nancy and Bill brought from England. They have a photograph of the house they lived in while in England, built from 1560 to 1620—and we think *we* have historical homes! "It was fascinating," Nancy says. "It was two houses together."

Of the twenty-drawer corn chandler's chest in the entry, "Oh, it's modern," says Nancy. "It can't be over 150 years old." Each of the merchant's drawers held a different grain: barley, rice, oats, etc. On the shelves at the top, there's a lovely collection of Blue Willow china that Nancy acquired "one piece at a time." Bookshelves in the common room are stacked for a good read before the tile fireplace. Several of the rooms have wood-burning stoves or fireplaces.

The long dining room faces French doors onto the east garden and sunshine. Nancy and Bill cook breakfast with zest, especially since they like to eat with their guests. First we began with a canteloupe half filled with blue-berry yogurt and topped with a sprig of mint. Next came an aromatic frittata of eggs, potatoes, and leeks, which blended deliciously with tomato slices and spicy sausage. For dessert, a rich bread pudding with whipped cream kept us talking for an hour and a half, enjoying one another's company. Nancy says she likes this part almost the best; "it's amazing."

HOW TO GET THERE: From the traffic light at the Plaza and Kit Carson, go west on Don Fernando for 2 blocks; go left on Manzanares, and take the first right, onto Juanita Lane. The inn is on your right at the end of the street.

Neon Cactus Hotel
Taos, New Mexico 87571

INNKEEPER: Sharon Winder

ADDRESS/TELEPHONE: 1523 Paseo del Pueblo Sur, Box 5702; (505) 751–1258 or (800) 299–1258

ROOMS: 4; all with private bath. No smoking inn.

RATES: $65 to $125; $10 extra person; EPB.

OPEN: All year.

FACILITIES AND ACTIVITIES: Hot tub; Taos Spa and Court Club. Nearby: historic Taos Plaza with shops, galleries, and restaurants; historic Taos Pueblo; Kit Carson Home and Museum; Millicent Rogers Museum; Rio Grande Gorge; Taos Ski Valley; hiking; fishing; white-water rafting on Rio Grande.

Who among us hasn't dreamed at some time or other of the glamorous life of an old-time movie star? Sharon surrounds herself—and her guests—with all the luxurious trappings of Hollywood in the good old days when stars were stars. The Marilyn Monroe Suite, the Rita Hayworth, the James Dean—oh, what a fun getaway place this is! Sharon has been collecting movie memorabilia from the '30s, '40s, and '50s, and her inn, with its art deco decor, is a perfect foil for the collection of rare movie photographs and posters of those times.

In the Marilyn Monroe Suite, a large photograph of the star hangs above the black satin-tufted headboard, and other pictures of Marilyn are placed around the remaining walls. The queen-sized bed is covered with a black quilted spread; there are art deco lamps on the art deco bedside tables. It's all glamorously set off by a pink carpet and soft-pink walls. The James Dean Room, on the other hand, is suitably masculine, with a crouched black leopard poised atop the headboard of the queen-sized bed; another on the tailored desk; another, a little smaller, on one of the tailored bedside tables.

This room has its own deck, with a wonderful view of the mountains to the east. And all the while James is smiling down on you from the photograph above the bed.

Neon Cactus Hotel Taos NM

As for the Billie Holiday Room, "I like to think she wouldn't be singing the blues in her room," Sharon says with a laugh. This cheerful room is all pink and soft green, with a small mirror—and an opened pink Japanese parasol—over the bed. Billie has her photos here and her own private deck. The common area is tiled with warm Saltillo tile, and the clerestory windows over the living room bring in lots of bright New Mexico light. A softly quilted mauve sofa is accented by pillows of Native American weavings. Some hang on the walls, along with colorful Southwestern paintings. Sharon likes Japanese parasols and fans and has used several here, too. Magazines, plants, and a fireplace make this a most pleasant room.

Breakfast—a bountiful continental with fresh fruit, yogurt, homemade baked goodies, croissants, and bagels and cream cheese—is served in the adjoining dining room. It has a wall of windows as well as a skylight to let in even more light—I think the stars would really have shone here! Feather boas, peacock feathers, pink flamingoes, snaky white lamps with black-and-gold shades—shades of Hollywood of the past are everywhere. The climax is the Hall of Stars photo gallery; what a show!

HOW TO GET THERE: Highway 68 in town is Paseo del Pueblo Sur, and the Neon Cactus is on the east side of the road between Dona Ana Drive and Paseo del Canon (Highway 64). The inn is the square pink adobe with the red Spanish-tile roof. Although the left front part of the building has a sign saying LAW OFFICES, ignore that and take the walk to the right, past the Neon Cactus sign.

Old Taos Guesthouse
Taos, New Mexico 87571

INNKEEPERS: Tim and Leslie Reeves

ADDRESS/TELEPHONE: 1028 Witt Road (mailing address: P.O. Box 6652); (505) 758-5448 or (800) 758-5448

ROOMS: 9; all with private bath; no air-conditioning (high altitude); children welcome. No smoking inn.

RATES: $70 to $125; $10 extra person; continental breakfast.

OPEN: All year.

FACILITIES AND ACTIVITIES: Hot tub. Nearby: historic Taos Plaza with shops and restaurants, Indian pueblos, museums, hiking, fishing, skiing area, mountain bike and horseback rentals.

The moment you walk through the extra-wide front door, late of the old Taos post office, you'll be caught up in Tim's enthusiasm for anything and everything Southwestern. "We just want to accomplish what we set out to do," he says: "renovate this wonderful 150-year-old adobe hacienda using imagination—but retaining the old Southwest flavor." He and Leslie (and daughter Malia, although she's a little small to contribute much yet!) are renovating the house at the same time they're running the inn, but you'd never know everything wasn't already completed. Each guest room is different, and Tim loves to tell of the stern professor who unbent enough to say upon departure: "I have to tell you I've traveled this world, and this is one of the neatest places I've been to."

Neat is right, and Tim's enthusiasm is contagious. "Look!" he says of Room 6. "Everything everybody wants in the Southwest—stained glass, vigas, sculptured posts, adobe showers, Mexican tile, kiva fireplace, log furniture. . . ." I had to holler "halt!" and he laughed. "It's so great when you complete a project and people ooh and ah," he confessed. "And we take it per-

Historic Taos

Taos was founded in 1615, and there are lots of interesting historical spots to visit. Begin with the Plaza, where Kit Carson defied Confederate sympathizers during the Civil War by flying Old Glory. He nailed the U.S. flag to the flagpole and guarded it day and night.

In 1898 two artists, Bert Phillips and Ernest Blumenschein, stopped by to have a broken wagon wheel repaired, and they liked it so much they never left. So began the art scene that Taos is famous for. When socialite Mabel Dodge arrived in 1917 (and married native Tony Luhan), she brought Ansel Adams, Willa Cather, D. H. Lawrence, Georgia O'Keeffe, and Thomas Wolfe, among other luminaries.

About fifty years later the second highest suspension bridge in the U.S. highway system was begun over nearby Rio Grande Gorge. The only problem was that there was no funding to continue the road on the other side, and the span was dubbed "the bridge to nowhere." But not to worry—that was back in 1965. You can cross the gorge today, while taking a look way down below.

sonally when someone's not happy." It would be difficult to be unhappy in such congenial circumstances and in such well-thought-out and complete guest rooms. It's a casual, homey, comfortable kind of place, where you can do your own thing or mingle with the other guests. A group of doctors was staying while I was there. As soon as they came back from their happy outdoor pursuits, they began to plan an evening barbecue on the patio.

The split-level traditional hacienda with territorial windows was a guest house back in the 1940s. Situated on a rise over Taos, it presents a fabulous mountain scene. "Our view makes our hot tub the best in the Rockies," Tim says with his usual verve. Their next project is to enlarge the kitchen because "the kitchen is the place where people get together. So we want to build an even larger one."

While Tim is busy being the master builder, Leslie is the cook, quite a change from her previous life with the ski patrol in Santa Fe. "My freshly baked breads and muffins are always different," she says, "but always healthy." She also serves hot cereal and fresh fruit.

Surrounded by lovely trees so old they almost hide the inn, and on seven and a half acres of land with fabulous vistas, the Old Taos Guesthouse is already so delightful I can't imagine what future improvements Tim and Leslie have in mind. It'll be interesting to see what they come up with next!

HOW TO GET THERE: Take Kit Carson Road east for 1¾₀ miles to Witt Road. Turn right on Witt Road and go ⁷⁄₁₀ of a mile. The inn is on your right, and there is a sign.

Touchstone Inn
Taos, New Mexico 87571

INNKEEPER: Bren Price

ADDRESS/TELEPHONE: 110 Mabel Dodge Lane; (505) 758–0192 or (800) 758–0192; fax (505) 758–3498

ROOMS: 8; all with private bath, telephones, and TV; no air-conditioning (elevation 7,000 feet). No smoking inn.

RATES: $75 to $135; $10 more in ski season; $10 extra person; EPB.

OPEN: All year.

FACILITIES AND ACTIVITIES: Dinner by resevation, hot tub, hammock, access to river for wading, fishing for trout. Nearby: Taos with its Plaza of shops, art galleries, and restaurants; historic Taos Pueblo; Kit Carson Home and Museum; Millicent Rogers Museum; Rio Grande Gorge; Taos Ski Valley; hiking; fishing; white-water rafting on Rio Grande; horseback riding; golf.

Bren is an artist, and the inn is filled with her work—Western scenes reflecting what this portion of the world means to her. "I've been coming to Taos since I was three years old, but I never knew what my 'touchstone' was until I found this place," Bren says, speaking of how magical she feels the place is. It certainly has inspired a good deal of prose: Taos patron Mabel Dodge Luhan bought the house and wrote about it in her book, *Winter in Taos*. She also filled it with famous people, D. H. Lawrence among them, who described it as "a gay little adobe house . . . in a light, clear air. . . ."

The inn is situated on about two acres with a clear view of famous Taos Mountain, and the grounds reach all the way to Taos Indian Pueblo land. It

was owned by a Spanish family, and part of the inn, what is now the common room, dates from the 1600s. The large common room, in the original building, has cheerful Indian rugs, a kiva fireplace, comfortable sofas, a piano, a TV/VCR, and a chess set.

Guest rooms have lots of privacy—and a place for your suitcases: a black bench just for that purpose, such a treat! The Lawrence Room has a kiva fireplace and a queen-sized bed; the bathroom has a Jacuzzi and lovely tiles by New Mexican artist Gorman. The O'Keeffe Room has a luxury bath, too, and a pretty etched-glass window. The Hapgood Room is small but cozy, with a double bed; the Ciello Room, with a green tile bath, also has a Jacuzzi—and a sundeck. The Crumbo Suite is practically an apartment, with a king-sized bed and a sofa that becomes a queen-sized bed, a fully equipped kitchen, a washer/dryer, and its own covered patio.

Mabel's Room and Tony's Room connect (their story is part of the Taos legend); Tony's is mainly black and red with Moroccan rugs on the parquet floor. Mabel's Room has a green print sofa facing the kiva fireplace, a brass bed—and a pink Jacuzzi bath. And for breakfast, how about Touchstone Frittata, Belgian waffles, blueberry pancakes with lemon sauce, or Bandido Bake (a sort of Spanish lasagna).

HOW TO GET THERE: From the stoplight at Kit Carson Road go north on Highway 68 for 1 mile, and turn right onto Mabel Dodge Lane; there is a sign.

Willows Inn

Taos, New Mexico 87571

INNKEEPERS: Janet and Doug Camp

ADDRESS/TELEPHONE: 412 Kit Carson at Dolan, Box 6560 NDCBU; (505) 758–2558 or (800) 525–8267; fax (505) 758–5445

E-MAIL: willows@newmwx.com

ROOMS: 5; all with private bath; limited wheelchair access; children welcome; pets boarded down the street. No smoking inn.

RATES: $90 to $140; $15 extra person; EPB.

OPEN: All year.

FACILITIES AND ACTIVITIES: Guided fly-fishing service. Nearby: historic Taos Plaza with restaurants, shops, and art galleries; Taos Indian Pueblo, Van Vechten–Lineberry Taos Art Museum, hiking, horseback riding, skiing, tours.

This lovely inn is on a corner, hidden behind high pink adobe walls. Once the home of artist E. Martin Hemmings (one of his paintings hangs in the White House, others are on exhibit in the Taos Art Museum), the inn is now a quiet retreat for innkeepers Janet and Doug and their guests. The Willows is named for the two massive trees on the front lawn. "They're registered as two of the largest willow trees in North America," Doug says. They are magnificent. Doug is an avid fisherman, "after his breakfast duties are complete, of course," Janet says, and he often guides guests who share the same interest, taking them to local streams and lakes where he knows they're biting the best, right?

The inn is listed on the National and State Historic Registries, and all sorts of exciting activities take place here. In addition to Doug's excursions, the Orvis Flyfishing School meets and takes trips in the summer. Painting classes are offered on the grounds periodically, and tours of the home and Robert Henning's Studio are given during Taos Institute of the Arts tours hosted by Henning's biographer. There's more: "We've been on the annual tour of artists' homes hosted by the Taos Garden Club," Janet is pleased to say.

The main house was built in 1926 by Taos Indians for Hemmings, with his studio a large, light room at the back of the courtyard. Four guest rooms in a courtyard setting were added to turn the home into an inn. A local architect was engaged to do the work. Guest rooms reflect the culture of the area. The Cowboy Room reflects the spirit of the Old West, and the Anasazi Room honors the Indians who lived in the area in ancient times. The Conquistador Room, with its Old World charm, reflects the roots of the Spanish explorers who tried to conquer the Southwest, and the Santa Fe Room is decorated in the ever-popular contemporary Southwestern style.

Guests feel really welcome during Complimentary Hospitality Time from 4:30 to 6:30 every afternoon. Hot apple cider or mint lemonade, depending upon the weather, joins beer, wines, and sodas to go with the fresh-baked desserts and appetizers. "We love to cook and eat here!" Janet says, and it's easy to believe, seeing the strawberry-rhubarb cobbler and the juicy cherry pie being served out on the flagstone courtyard. (In winter it's indoors in front of a cozy fire.) There are also fresh veggies spiced with herbs, in case your sweet tooth isn't operating at that hour.

Breakfast can be either the family-style complete meal served at 8:30, or you can partake of the extended continental breakfast the Camps serve at 7:30 or 9:30. Janet revels in the full breakfast, making everything from scratch, including her famous sourdough bread. Hot entrees can be anything from apricot-stuffed French toast with pineapple-apricot sauce, praline sauce, and Bavarian whipped cream, to a Taos strata with New Mexico green chilis, sausage, and cheese. Or it may be blueberry–wheat germ pancakes or Belgian waffles with blackberry/raspberry sauce.

Very special is Janet's Breakfast-in-a-Loaf—layers of egg, ham, peppers, mushrooms, cheeses, and tomatoes baked inside a loaf of bread. Or, a strata of sun-dried tomatoes, carmelized onions, and basil, served with peasant-fried potatoes and a fruit parfait. "I could go on for days," Janet says dreamily, dreaming up the next breakfast, and the next. . . .

HOW TO GET THERE: From U.S. 68 turn east onto Kit Carson Road (the traffic light just east of the Plaza) to Dolan. The inn is on your right.

Select List of Other Inns
in New Mexico

Adobe & Roses

1011 Ortega Road Northwest
Albuquerque, New Mexico 87114
(505) 898–0654

3 rooms; all with private bath. Inn pets: 2 cats, 1 dog, chickens, and golden pheasants.

Bottger-Koch Mansion

110 San Felipe Northwest
Albuquerque, New Mexico 87104
(505) 243–3639

7 rooms; all with private bath. On the edge of Albuquerque's Old Town.

Casa del Cocinero

P.O. Box 835
Alto, New Mexico 88312
(505) 336–7815 or (800) 360–3500

4 guest rooms; all with private bath. Southwest culture and worldly cuisine.

La Hacienda Grande

21 Baros Lane
Bernalillo, New Mexico 87004
(505) 867–1887 or (800) 353–1887

6 guest rooms; 3 with private bath. Midway between Santa Fe and Albuquerque.

Casa de Gavilan

P.O. Box 518
Cimmaron, New Mexico 87714
(505) 376–2246

6 rooms; 4 with private bath, 2 share. Historic inn in the foothills of the Sangre de Cristo Mountains.

Raymond Gilmer Lodge

321 Smokey Bear Boulevard
Capitan, New Mexico 88316
(505) 354–2583 or (888) 81-LODGE

3 guest rooms; all with private bath. On Billy the Kid Scenic Byway.

Elaine's

Box 444, 72 Snowline Estates
Cedar Crest, New Mexico 87008
(505) 281-2467 or (800) 821-3092

3 guest rooms in a rustic log and stone house next to Cibola National Forest.

The Lodge

1 Corona Place, Box 497
Cloudcroft, New Mexico 88317
(505) 682-2566 or (800) 395-6343

61 guest rooms; all with private bath. With a view of White Sands from afar.

Burro Street Boardinghouse

608 Burro Street
P.O. Box 462
Cloudcroft, New Mexico 88317
(505) 682-3601

3 guest rooms; all with private bath. Webster's says that a boardinghouse is "a lodging house at which meals are served."

The Crofting

300 Swallow Place
Cloudcroft, New Mexico 88317
(505) 682-2288

8 guest rooms; all with private bath. An eighty-year-old house up in the clouds.

Little Tree

226 Honda Seco Road, Box 960
El Prado, New Mexico 97529
(505) 776-8467 or (800) 334-8467

4 guest rooms; all with private bath. Most authentic adobe in Taos.

T. R. H. Smith Mansion

909 North Alameda Boulevard
Las Cruces, New Mexico 88005
(505) 525-2525 or (800) 526-1914

4 rooms; 2 with private bath, 2 share. In a stately 1914 mansion.

Meson de Mesilla

1803 Avenida de Mesilla
Mesilla, New Mexico 88046
(505) 525-9212

15 guest rooms; all with private bath. Old Mesilla, where Billy the Kid was sentenced to hang for murder and got away.

Monjeau Shadows

HC 67, Box 87
Nogal, New Mexico 88341
(505) 336-4191

6 guest rooms; 4 with private bath. Close to Ruidoso Downs.

Casa Blanca

13 Montoya Street
P.O. Box 31
San Antonio, New Mexico 87832
(505) 835-3027

3 guest rooms; all with private bath. Victorian farmhouse built in 1880.

Bear Mountain Guest Ranch

P.O. Box 1163
Silver City, New Mexico 88062
(505) 538-2538 or (800) 880-2538

15 guest rooms; all with private bath. Bird-watching par excellence.

Brooks Street Inn

Box 4954
Taos, New Mexico 87571
(505) 758-1489 or (800) 758-1489

6 rooms; all with private bath. Relax in the garden swing and watch the birds.

Orinda

461 Valverde, Box 4451
Taos, New Mexico 87571
(505) 758-8581 or (800) 847-1387

3 guest rooms; all with private bath. Peaceful and restful on four acres.

The Pecan Tree

802 Old Mescalero Road
Tularosa, New Mexico 88352
(505) 585-2238

3 guest rooms; all with private bath. Close to White Sands National Monument.

North Texas

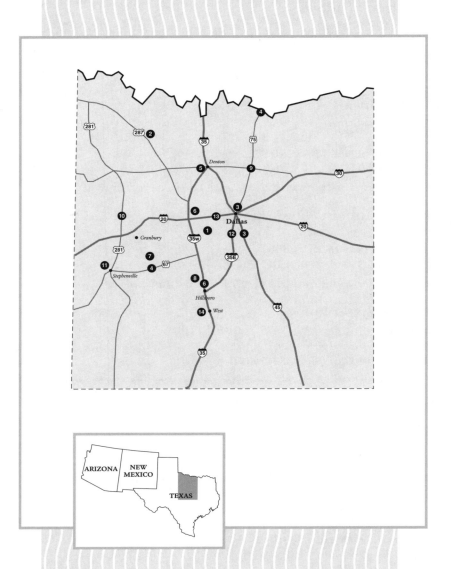

North Texas

Numbers on map refer to towns numbered below.

*Top Pick Inn

Sanford House
Arlington, Texas 76011

INNKEEPERS: Sharon and Leonard Bergstrom

ADDRESS/TELEPHONE: 506 North Center Street; (871) 861–2129

ROOMS: 11; all with private bath and TV; wheelchair accessible.

RATES: $100 to $250, double; EPB.

OPEN: All year.

FACILITIES AND ACTIVITIES: Swimming pool. Nearby: Six Flags Over Texas, Texas Rangers Baseball Museum, close to Dallas and Fort Worth activities.

There's a gazebo in the gardens of Sanford House, and a fountain, and Sharon and Leonard hope guests relax here in what they've planned as a quiet French-country garden. Inside the inn, the decor is French-country with antiques. The library at the top of the winding staircase offers lots of good reading material, and the cupola provides lots of bright light.

Four of the guest rooms have Jacuzzis, one has a fireplace, and, with the exception of one room with twin beds, they all have either king- or queen-size beds. Tapestries cover the windows, and bedspreads are coordinated to match.

Breakfast in the dining room usually includes lively conversation with other guests.

HOW TO GET THERE: Off I–30 south take the Cooper exit to Sanford Street. Go north on Sanford to Center Street. The inn is on the northwest corner of Sanford and Center Streets.

The Gazebo
Bowie, Texas 76230

INNKEEPERS: Clyde and Janet McMurray

ADDRESS/TELEPHONE: 906 Sessions Street; (940) 872–4852 or (877) 269–4389

ROOMS: 4; 2 with private bath.

RATES: $80 to $90, double; EPB.

OPEN: All year.

FACILITIES AND ACTIVITIES: Dinner Tuesday through Saturday by reservation only. Outdoor hot tub, stationary bicycle, rowing machine. Nearby: Amon Carter Lake, golf, Fort Worth (60 miles), Trade Days and festivals, Main Street Town.

Gazebos, say Clyde and Janet, serve as resting places to enjoy the solitude and beauty of nature. Their Georgian-style home is situated on three-quarters of an acre amid a canopy of oak trees, a perfect setting for enjoying nature. Indoors mahogany, cherry, and walnut period furniture reflect both Empire and Victorian periods.

In Susan's Room, Janet says you can wake up feeling like Scarlett O'Hara in a queen-size tester bed, while in Tom's Room you might be able to feel Rhett's presence amid the tailored Federal-style furnishings. Both rooms have private baths; Mattie Belle's Room and Lillie's Room share a large bath with shower/tub and a Victorian vanity just down the hall.

Breakfast might be stuffed strawberry cream-cheese French toast topped with apricot drizzle, Cajun puffed eggs, sausage soufflé, baked eggs with cheese, or waffles and crepes. If you stay awhile, you can sample them all!

HOW TO GET THERE: Take Highway 287 from either Fort Worth or Wichita Falls to Bowie and take Highway 59 north to Sessions Street.

Hotel St. Germain
Dallas, Texas 75201

INNKEEPER: Claire Heymann

ADDRESS/TELEPHONE: 2516 Maple Avenue; (214) 871–2516; fax (214) 871–0740

ROOMS: 7; all with private bath, TV, and radio. Smoking permitted except in dining room.

RATES: $245 to $600, double; continental breakfast.

OPEN: All year.

FACILITIES AND ACTIVITIES: Dinner Tuesday through Saturday by reservation only; bar service, room service, valet parking; guest privileges at the Centrum Health Club. Nearby: downtown Dallas, with Dallas Museum of Art, Kennedy Memorial, Old City Park, Reunion Tower, West End Historic District, Farmers' Market, and more.

For sheer luxury, unabashed, unashamed sybaritic living, the small and elegant Hotel St. Germain takes the prize. Well, it's already taken several prizes, such as the *Inn Business Review*'s naming the St. Germain "one of the outstanding inns of 1992."

The inn, a beautiful residence built in 1906, is architecturally imposing. The white, three-story structure has two balconies on the left and two curved porches on the right, with black wrought-iron railings, which also frame two sets of stairs to the curved driveway in front. French doors lead out, and in the stairwell, a huge twenty-four-pane window is crowned with a glass arch.

With its impressive foyer, 14-foot ceilings, sumptuous parlor, stately library, and lavish suites, it takes all the adjectives in *Roget's Thesaurus* to describe this inn adequately. The antique pieces alone are a feast for the eyes. "My mom was an antiques dealer," Claire says, pointing out the Aubusson carpets, the Mallard beds, and huge armoires. "We serve on antique Limoges—my grandmother's heavy gold china, and sterling." She alternates eight different sets of china, which are stored in the china cabinet in the small dining room.

Hotel St Germaine Dallas Tx. (sw)

The large dining room has bay windows of decorative glass, topped with an extravagant valence over Austrian shades. The crystal chandelier is palatial. Beyond is a romantic New Orleans–style walled courtyard. Breakfast here takes on another dimension: The chive-and-cheese quiche and blueberry muffins taste like nectar and ambrosia.

Soft classical music plays in the library, and there is a grand buffet piano for more personalized music. The original wallpaper is charming, and it's a treat to study the before-and-after renovation photographs in the hall. Suite One, a huge room decorated in rose and gray, has a rose spread and a high canopy over the bed. Suite Three has what appears to be a larger-than-life king-sized bed, which can be divided into two twins. The sitting room has a lovely antique Belgian sofa, and there's a separate dressing room. Suite Four boasts a Jacuzzi as well as a Mallard bed, a huge armoire, and a sitting area with a sofa and fireplace.

The Dangerous Liaison Suite is 600 square feet of blue, green, and gold. Besides the bed there's a bed-lounge in the wall, a Cheval mirror, and antique Mallard furniture. In the sitting area are a fireplace and a sparkling chandelier. The Smith Suite, on the third floor, overlooks downtown Dallas. The Napoleon sleigh bed has a crown canopy, and there is a Victorian sitting area, complete with fireplace. The padded-cloth walls are another example of sheer luxury, an atmosphere that the Jacuzzi in the bath does nothing to dispel. Hotel St. Germain is really a taste of another world!

HOW TO GET THERE: From Central Expressway exit at Hall Street; turn right to Cole. At Cole turn left onto Cedar Springs, take a left onto Maple Avenue, and go half a block. From North Dallas Toll Road, heading south, pass the

Wycliff exit and veer to the left as you curve around to the first traffic light, which is Wolf Street. Turn left and go 2½ blocks to Maple Avenue, turn right, crossing Cedar Springs to the inn, the large white mansion with a curved driveway.

Ivy Blue
Denison, Texas 75020

INNKEEPERS: Lane and Tammy Segerstrom

ADDRESS/TELEPHONE: 1100 West Sears; (903) 463–2479 or (888) IVY–BLUE

ROOMS: 6 guest rooms; all with private bath.

RATES: $65 to $150, double; $35 extra person; EPB.

OPEN: All year.

FACILITIES AND ACTIVITIES: Swimming pool; European massages by appointment. Nearby: Lake Texoma, horseback riding, Sunset Cruises on Lake Texoma, Eisenhower's birthplace, antiques shopping.

Here's a carefully restored Victorian home, with three guest rooms in the main house and two private suites in the carriage house across the pool. There are several lovely stained-glass windows as well as historical reproductions of wall coverings and fabrics. The Stein Room, brightly furnished in blue and yellow, is named for the original owners who restored the house. The Tobin Room is decorated with a French motif, and the Harwell Room boasts a 10-foot-tall Eastlake half-tester bed decorated in the sheerest lace from an antique wedding dress.

Breakfast is served in the formal dining room, and Lane and Tammy will regale you with the story of Ivy Blue's history while you feast on banana-almond waffles or mango-coconut pancakes.

Then, if you want to really relax, seat yourself on the inviting swing out on the large sweeping porch or on the three-tiered deck around the pool.

HOW TO GET THERE: From Dallas go north on Highway 75 to Denison exit, and go east on Highway 120 (Morton Street). Travel 1⁷⁄₁₀ miles; turn south on Highway 91 (Tone Avenue) and go 1 block to Sears. Ivy Blue is on the corner of Tone and Sears.

Molly Cherry Inn
Denison, Texas 75020

INNKEEPERS: Regina and Jim Widener

ADDRESS/TELEPHONE: 200 West Molly Cherry Lane; (903) 465–0575

ROOMS: 7 guest rooms; all with private bath.

RATES: $79 to $179, double; $15 extra person; EPB.

OPEN: All year.

FACILITIES AND ACTIVITIES: Sport pool, Jacuzzi, gazebo, walking trails. Nearby: Lake Texoma, horseback riding, Eisenhower's birthplace, antiques shopping, arts district, Hagerman Wildlife Refuge.

On six wooded acres practically in the middle of town, the Molly Cherry is a lavish Queen Anne Victorian built at the turn of the century. In 1872 the M. K. T., known as the Katy Railroad, needed a railhead across the Red River into Indian Territory. Along came J. J. Fairbanks, real estate tycoon and gambler, who built this mansion for his wife, Edith, in 1890.

The J. J. Fairbanks is a two-room suite with an Eastlake double bed; the Gandy Dancer boasts a French flair; the Katy has a 6-foot-tall oak bed. There's also the Presidential Suite, the Crown Suite, Ashburn, and Sugar Bottom, with antique French twin beds. The whole estate has beautiful grounds around the large pool with decks, walking trails, hammocks, and even a place to park boats and trailers in case you're towing any.

The full Plantation Breakfast in the Main Dining Room might start with a chilled peach soup and go on to peach cream French toast; ham and eggs or sausage casseroles; home fries, and homemade breads, biscuits, and muffins.

HOW TO GET THERE: From Dallas take Highway 75 north 75 miles to Denison. In Denison take exit 66 onto Highway 503 as it curves north. Turn left onto Molly Cherry Lane just past Garcia's.

Savior of France's Vineyards

The home of Thomas Volney Munson in Denison has a state marker on it. Not a lot of people have heard of Volney, but he's the man who many think saved the vineyards of France. He moved to Denison from Kentucky in 1876 with some grapevine cuttings, which he began crossing with the wild grapes he found growing along the creeks.

Meanwhile, French vineyards were being devasted by phylloxera: Lo and behold, Munson's Texas strain was resistant to the insect. He sent French grape growers some of his vines, they crossed the Texas vines with their own, and the vineyards were saved. This earned Munson the French Legion of Honor.

Grayson County College at Denison has a vineyard you can visit—a memorial to T. V. Munson boasting the world's largest collection of hybrid grapes as well as a Viticulture and Enology Center where you can learn all about growing grapes for wine.

The Redbud Inn
Denton, Texas 76201

INNKEEPERS: Donna and John Morris

ADDRESS/TELEPHONE: 815 North Locust Street; (817) 565–6414 or (940) 565–6414; fax: (940) 565–6515

E-MAIL: redbudbb@gte.net

WEB SITE: www.BBHost.com/redbudbb

ROOMS: 7; all with private bath, telephones, and TV.

RATES: $56 to $105; $10 extra person; EPB; 2 large suites in Magnolia House next door, rates $105 to $125; no smoking inn.

OPEN: All year.

FACILITIES AND ACTIVITIES: Restaurant in the Morrises' Magnolia House, part of the inn, next door. Nearby: Courthouse Square with shops and restaurants.

*R*usty, the friendly dachshund who greets us, is introduced by Donna Morris, an innkeeper with a sense of humor, as "our used dog." This requires an explanation: "Everything else is used," Donna says, motioning to the lovely antique furniture in the living room, "so we had to have a used dog. We got him at the pound."

While visiting pets are not welcome among the lovely antique furniture, visiting children most heartily are; there's even an antique cradle for babies. Says Donna, "I saw all these beautiful antiques as piles of wood and piles of junk [before restoring and refinishing], and if some child tears them apart, well, I can just put them together again."

With young guests in the inn, she offers spontaneous tea parties, takes them to the park, even invites them into the kitchen to help make cookies. Donna and John did a lot of planning and research before opening the Redbud Inn. Busy in the nursing profession for thirty-three years, Donna always dreamed of being an innkeeper. Traveling, the couple stayed in bed-and-breakfast inns all over England and Scotland. "They really added to our dreams." From their travels around the world, they brought not only antiques but all sorts of decorations as well. In the Walnut Suite, the Eastlake walnut bed has been converted into a comfortable queen size, and there's a small hall leading to a comfortable sitting area with sofa and lots of books before you come to the bathroom.

The Oak Room has warm oak antiques, and in the bathroom there's what lots of people call a "soaking tub," large and claw-footed. There's another in the bath of the Country Suite, where the windows look out back over the treetops. The Wicker Room is all navy blue and white, the wicker furniture set off with dark-blue cushions. There are windows on two sides of this room, too, and although the half bath is in what was once a closet, the tub (another "soaking" one) is right inside the room.

The house was built sometime between 1902 and 1910 and had been vacant for five years when the Morrises found it. They had to tear it apart and put it back together again, and the renovation took a lot of work; the now-open stairwell had been closed up in order to turn the house into four apartments.

"John is a scrounge," Donna says. "That wormy chestnut wood around the dining room doorway is from a barn in Pennsylvania, and these banisters up the stairs are from the First Methodist Church—they gave them to John just to haul away." As for breakfast, "I love to titillate taste buds with Texas cuisine and homemade breads," says Donna. One specialty is French toast stuffed with Muenster cheese, accompanied by sausage patties and some of her homemade breads. Of course there's fresh fruit in season: a lovely mix of cantaloupe, kiwi, honeydew, strawberries, and bananas.

HOW TO GET THERE: From I–35 east take Dallas Drive (exit 464) and go north, taking a left on Eagle and making a quick right on Locust Street. Continue on Locust past Courthouse Square and continue north to 815 Locust. The inn is on your left, and there is a sign.

Godfrey's Place
Denton, Texas 76201

INNKEEPERS: Marjorie and Dick Waters

ADDRESS/TELEPHONE: 1513 North Locust Street; (940) 381–1118; fax (940) 387–2805

E-MAIL: godfrey@Iglobal.net

ROOMS: 4; all with private bath.

RATES: $79 to $119; $10 extra person; EPB. No smoking inn.

OPEN: All year.

FACILITIES AND ACTIVITIES: Exercise room, greeenhouse, organic garden. Nearby: Courthouse Square with shops and restaurants, Texas Women's University (across the street), Lake Roy Roberts (minutes away).

his inn is no stranger to guests. It was built in the 1920s by Dr. Jesse Louise Herrick, who lived downstairs and rented the upstairs rooms to female students.

Today one of the downstairs rooms, the Herrick Room, is for guests, with a view through French doors of the inn gardens. Upstairs the Bluebonnet Room features Texas memorabilia and shares a balcony with the

Heritage Room. The Prairie Room has a sleigh bed of loblolly pine and its own private balcony.

Coffee and tea are available early in the morning and, perhaps, Texas wine and munchies in the late afternoon in the Keeping Room. Breakfast is served on the downstairs north porch, with a view of the always-blooming organic garden, the fruits of which add color and interest to the inn's special heart-healthy meals.

HOW TO GET THERE: From I-35 take Dallas Drive (exit 464) and go north, taking a left on Eagle and making a quick right on Locust Street. Continue on Locust past Courthouse Square and continue north past Ferguson. The inn is across from Texas Women's University between Ferguson and College Streets.

The Texas White House
Fort Worth, Texas 76104

INNKEEPERS: Jamie and Grover McMains

ADDRESS/TELEPHONE: 1417 Eighth Avenue; (817) 923–3597 or (800) 279–6491; fax (817) 923–0410

ROOMS: 3; all with private bath, TV, and radio. No smoking inn.

RATES: $80 to $115, double; $15 extra person; continental breakfast on weekdays, EPB on weekends.

OPEN: All year.

FACILITIES AND ACTIVITIES: Membership in health club. Nearby: Texas Christian University, bocce ball, horseshoes, zoo, four museums, Botanic Gardens, Water Gardens, Trinity Park, golf.

The Texas White House has been collecting awards, such as the Historic Preservation Council Pedestal Award and the City of Fort Worth Historic Landmark. Decorated in unelaborate but elegant country style, the downstairs has both a parlor and a living room with fireplace as well as a formal dining room and a half bath for the convenience of guests.

Upstairs the Land of Contrast Room has a brass bed; Lone Star is brown and gold, and Tejas provides a drop-leaf desk. Soaps, lotions, bubble bath, thick plush towels—even a feather bed (upon request)—add to guests' comfort, as do afternoon snacks and beverages.

You can have breakfast privately in your room or join the gang in the dining room. Either way, you're in for a treat of a baked fruit compote and baked egg casserole served with homemade breads and muffins. This is served on antique china with sterling silver and crystal, and is offered anytime during the morning. "Vegetarian? Diabetic? Food restrictions? Just let us know," say these innkeepers, "and we'll meet your needs."

HOW TO GET THERE: From I–30 take the Summit exit and turn left (south) at the Ballinger stop sign. Ballinger dead-ends at Pennsylvania; turn right. Go 2 blocks west and turn left (south) on Eight Avenue. The inn is 1½ blocks pass the fourth light (Magnolia).

Doyle House on the Lake
Granbury, Texas 76048

INNKEEPER: Linda Stoll

ADDRESS/TELEPHONE: 205 West Doyle; (817) 573–6492

ROOMS: 3; all with private bath, TV, and radio. No smoking inn.

RATES: $80 to $115, double; $15 extra person; continental breakfast on weekdays, EPB on weekends.

OPEN: All year.

FACILITIES AND ACTIVITIES: Swimming pool, barbecue pit, fishing dock, boat tie-ups, basketball, volleyball, bocce ball, horseshoes. Nearby: historic Granbury Square with shops, restaurants, and Opera House; Railroad Depot Museum; Hood County Jail; Acton State Historical Site; Lake Granbury, with boating, fishing, water sports, and cruising on the *Granbury Queen*; The Gulch at Granbury; Fort Worth (25 miles); Dallas (50 miles).

*D*riving up the residential street to the Doyle House, you wonder how it can live up to its name of "on the lake." But although the view from the front parlor window is of the house across the street, from the back there's a sweep of shade trees and green lawn that does indeed go all the way down to Lake Granbury.

Linda kept moving between Texas and Illinois. In Illinois she worked in a gourmet kitchen shop and loved it. "This is a business I've always been intrigued by," Linda says. "Looking for roots, I came to the right place at the right time. I bought the house empty and in very good shape and added all my own furnishings. The house is just the right size; it's like having guests in your home."

It's definitely like visiting friends when you step into the living room with its pink walls and mauve carpet, the baby grand in front of the picture window, and the wing chair pulled up to the flowered sofa. Plants fill the corners and the hearth in front of the white fireplace.

Emily Doyle once lived here with her doctor father, who built the house sometime around 1880 on the bank of the lake. The room named after her

Where the West Begins

Fort Worth's motto is "Where the West begins," and you can believe it when you visit the Stockyards National Historic District, especially if you have time to attend a cattle auction. At one time the stockyards were the largest in the world, and in an effort to avoid being annexed by Fort Worth, the meat packers claimed that the 1-mile area was a separate enclave known as Niles City.

Called the richest town per capita in the country, with a population of 650 and a property valuation of $25 million, it lost the annexation battle in 1922—but not after a lengthy court fight.

More than seventy million head of livestock have been processed here in the past, but today work is on a much smaller scale. The area is now a major tourist attraction, with mounted police, restaurants and bars, lots of shops selling western gear, and rodeos in Cowtown Coliseum. You can still hang over the fence and see pens full of cattle near the coliseum.

Doyle House on the Lake Granbury Tx

has a pretty pink spread on the four-poster king-sized bed, and the pale-green carpet makes a pleasing contrast. The Jacuzzi in the bath is sunken, and there's a separate sitting room with bookshelves and furniture of cherry and mahogany. It has a separate entrance, as do all the guest quarters.

The Carriage House is a paneled two-room suite with a queen-sized bed plus a trundle and a refrigerator, microwave, and coffeemaker. There are books here, too, and the decor is Shaker. The outside deck has a lovely old tree smack in the middle.

The Pool Cottage also offers kitchen privileges, with a "microkitchen" in a closet. Large, the Cottage has a second door opening right onto the pool and a covered deck for lounging. Decor here is Mission-style. Books and games are handy, and the futon sofa becomes a double bed.

During the week breakfast is continental, with fresh fruit and juice and apricot bread or sour-cream coffeecake, but on weekends Linda serves specialties such as stuffed French toast with apricot sauce and ham cakes with fresh fruit garnish. Of course, there's always juice and coffee. And honeymooners rate breakfast in their room.

It's just a short stroll to Granbury's historic town square—the whole square is on the National Register of Historic Places. Plays and musicals are presented at the Granbury Opera House most weekends. If your tastes run to the macabre, the Hood County Jail just off the square, built in 1885, still has the original cell block and hanging tower. Nearby Acton State Park is the smallest state park in Texas. It contains the grave of Elizabeth Crockett, Davy Crockett's second wife.

HOW TO GET THERE: From I–20 west take either Highway 171 south to FM (Farm Road) 51 or Highway 377 to Granbury to Historic Square. Go 1 block west to Lambert and 2 blocks south to Doyle. The inn is on the right, behind a white picket fence.

Park House of 1908
Itasca, Texas 76055

INNKEEPERS: Jo and Dick Williams

ADDRESS/TELEPHONE: P.O. Box 564; (254) 687–2968

ROOMS: 5; all with private bath and television.

RATES: $75 to $95, double; EPB.

OPEN: All year.

FACILITIES AND ACTIVITIES: Nearby outlet mall with one hundred stores; antiques shops.

Here's another Texas Medallion Home, listed with the Texas Historical Commission. The three-story classic Greek Revival/Victorian house in this quiet country town has massive Corinthian columns supporting porches and verandas.

The Blue Room has a king-size bed, sitting area, dressing area, and a private entrance with a porch. The Green Room has floor-to-ceiling windows under the sculptured tin ceiling, looking out to a side view. Rose Room is a corner one, bright with six windows, as is the Gold Room.

There's an Entertainment Room on the second floor, with cable television, a VCR, and videos. Breakfast includes fresh fruit juice and fruit dishes, breads, and one of Jo and Dick's special entrees—or you might want to have your breakfast made to order!

HOW TO GET THERE: From I–35 West take exit 8 (Farm Road 66 west); turn right at the Clayton Funeral Home, and the inn is 2 blocks on your right.

Dowell House 📱
McKinney, Texas 75069

INNKEEPERS: Diane and Fred Mueller

ADDRESS/TELEPHONE: 1104 South Tennessee; (972) 562–2456 or (800) 373–0551

E-MAIL: ABnB@aol.com

ROOMS: 3; 2 with private bath, all share the one Hollywood bath (which opens both into the master bedroom and the hall); all with phone. No smoking inn.

RATES: $85 to $155, double; $25 extra person; EPB.

OPEN: All year.

FACILITIES AND ACTIVITIES: Gardens, and the "whole house except for the kitchen," says Diane. Nearby: historic courthouse, shops and restaurants and walk/drive tour of historic places; the Heard Natural Science Museum and Wildlife Sanctuary; Bolin Wildlife Exhibit.

he Dowell House has quite a claim to fame—at least for those old enough to remember the 1970s film *Benjie*, because this is the very house where the movie was filmed. But never fear, it certainly does not look anything like it did then! The movie producer described it at the time as a huge old graying two-story, once-impressive mansion, weathered and paintless, overgrown with weeds and vines and crawling shadows—every kid's idea of a real haunted house.

You certainly won't recognize it as such today, thanks to a series of home improvers who set the scene for Diane and Fred Mueller. Diane wanted an inn. She and Fred were newlyweds (with their respective grown children out of the house), and when they saw the house, Fred agreeably went along with Diane's dream. In fact, he's so enthusiastic, he'll even crawl underneath the house if something needs fixing.

"There's an old *bois d'arc* foundation of an even earlier house under there, but I kind of have claustrophobia," she explains. As to how they got the house, "Fred and I were out for a Sunday drive—you know, where you don't want to be doing any work. Just for a lark we asked an agent to show us the house—and it just grabbed us. But, we thought, what can two oldies like us want with a 4,000-square-foot house?" Clever Diane had the answer ready, and their enthusiasm carried them through the two years they had to wait for the zoning okay.

The white-picket-fenced veranda wraps around the front corners of the house, with the great entry a striking introduction to the old house. Built in 1870 by James Patterson Dowell, who came to McKinney from Tennessee in 1856, the house was home to his bride, Ida Blanche Sparks from Waco, and their eleven children. The great L-shaped entry hall was used as a living room; the parlor around the corner was only for special occasions. Today the parlor is the living room, and it features comfortable period furniture, a baby grand piano, and a huge French window opening to the veranda. The fireplace, decorative only, is still lovely with a white marble hearth, and all the first-floor chandeliers are of solid brass and Czechoslovakian crystal.

Robes, toiletries, and other amenities offer hospitality; the 13-foot-long, 9-foot-tall antique cherry armoire in the master bedroom offers amazement. Lined in cedar, it's a wonder to behold. The yellow-and-white guest room has its own armoire, a bleached pine antique made in England around the turn of the century, and nothing like the size of the one across the hall! The third guest room is painted a soft peach, very pleasant with the strips of white molding crisscrossing it. The white marble fireplace is pretty but nonfunctional, and there are all sorts of collectibles around the room.

For breakfast there's baked French toast with cheese and sausage (or sometimes bacon) with delicious hot breads and muffins, an assortment of orange-nut, bran, and banana.

HOW TO GET THERE: From U.S. Highway 75 take Louisiana east to the town square. At the southwest corner (Kentucky and Louisiana) turn right. Go 1 block to Davis and turn left; go 1 block on Davis, then turn right on Tennessee and go 11 blocks to Graham. The inn is on the northwest corner of Tennessee and Graham.

Silk Stocking Row
Mineral Wells, Texas 76067

INNKEEPERS: Bob Tyson and Ken Saxton

ADDRESS/TELEPHONE: 415 Northwest Fourth Street; (940) 325–4101

E-MAIL: silkrowbb@aol.com.

ROOMS: 3; all with private bath, phone, and TV. No smoking inn.

RATES: $69 to $96, double; EPB.

OPEN: All year.

FACILITIES AND ACTIVITIES: Library, wraparound porch. Nearby: Bat World Bat Sanctuary, historic downtown, three lakes within minutes, antiques shows.

amed for the 1904 area of prestigious homes in which the inn is located, the house is a fine example of an Eastlake Queen Anne mansion. The Turret Room has great bay windows; the South Chamber's queen-sized iron bed is draped with lace valances; the Baker Room contains a unique four-poster rice bed draped with flowing fabric; the Brazos Room is big and roomy with a brass bed; and the Tygrette Suite has its own comfortable sitting room.

Extra pillows and thick, oversize towels, a turndown "treat," all make guests feel pampered. Waiting for you will be a bottle of Crazy Water along with a bucket of ice, and every room has access to both main- and second-floor wraparound verandas.

Freshly ground coffee awaits the early birds who need their coffee fix before breakfast is served in the dining room. Breakfast is served in courses: juices, fruit plate, cereals, and fresh breads on weekdays, with such specialties as eggs Monterey on weekends.

HOW TO GET THERE: From I–20 take U.S. 281 north about 12 miles into Mineral Wells. Turn left onto Northwest Fourth Street and go 4 blocks to number 415.

The Oxford House
Stephenville, Texas 76401

INNKEEPERS: Paula Oxford, Karen and Pete Payne

ADDRESS/TELEPHONE: 563 North Graham Street; (254) 965–6885; fax (254) 965–7555

ROOMS: 4; all with private bath. No smoking inn.

RATES: $65 to $95, double; $15 extra person; EPB.

OPEN: All year.

Lunch, dinner, and afternoon tea by reservation; gazebo; use of the Oxfords' swimming pool five minutes across town. Nearby: golf and horseback riding; bronzing factory; Fossil Rim Wildlife Preserve and Glen Rose dinosaur tracks forty-five minutes away; local festivals.

*W*hen Judge W. J. Oxford, Sr., was paid the sum of $3,000 in silver coins for trying a case back in the 1890s, he knew just what to do with such a treasure. Between 1890 and 1898, he built the Oxford House. The judge's third wife told stories of how it took 1,000 loads of fill dirt, at 75 cents a load, to make even a start on the foundation and how the lumber was brought from Fort Worth across the Bosque River.

It was a busy time at the judge's back then, and you'll still find a busy whirl at the Oxford House, what with weddings, receptions, luncheons, and dinners, as well as breakfast for inn guests. "We even do an English tea," Paula Oxford says. "Three courses: dainty savory sandwiches; then piping hot scones and nut breads topped with butter, jam, and lemon curd; finishing with a dessert course of moist cakes, strawberry tarts, truffles, and pastries."

Paula says, "Nobody was using the old house, so it was my idea to make it into a bed-and-breakfast inn." There's much family history bound up in the tall Victorian manor. Marie's Suite, named for a child who grew up in the house in its early days, contains an antique seven-piece

bedroom suite from the 1890s. Aunt Mandy's Room is decorated with photographs of an aunt who was "a real pill," Paula says. "She expected to be waited on hand and foot, so they always put her in the room that was hot with sun in the summer and cold in the winter, hoping she wouldn't stay long!"

Each guest room has a private bath with antique claw-footed tub. Bubble bath and special soaps encourage you to soak and meditate—very relaxing. The Victorian charm of the inn includes a sleigh bed built in the 1890s, beveled glass mirrors, and antique armoires. Porches, reaching three-quarters of the way around the house, are made of cypress with hand-turned gingerbread trim.

Good food keeps the inn humming, like pears in brandy with crumbles on top, sausage yeast biscuits, German cinnamon rolls, or fruit-swirl coffeecake. They start the day out just fine. Other meals are by reservation; if you order dinner, possibilities are chicken breast in wine sauce or seafood crepes, perhaps served with rice/apricot pilaf, mandarin orange salad, and cheesecake with praline sauce.

If you park in the back, you'll enter under an arbor. The wide back lawn has a big old swing, and there are white chairs and tables under the trees.

HOW TO GET THERE: Highway 108 becomes Graham through town. The inn is 2 blocks north of the town square, on the east side of the street. There's a sign out front.

Bonnynook Inn ⬚
Waxahachie, Texas 75165

INNKEEPERS: Bonnie and Vaughn Franks

ADDRESS/TELEPHONE: 414 West Main; (972) 938–7207; fax (972) 937–7700

ROOMS: 5; all with private bath; children welcome. No smoking inn.

RATES: $85 to $125; EPB.

OPEN: All year.

FACILITIES AND ACTIVITIES: Two guest rooms with Jacuzzi, coffee nook with small refrigerator, lunch and dinner by reservation. Nearby: historic square with famous courthouse; downtown with restaurants, shops, antiques and craft malls.

*D*riving up to the Bonnynook, you'll see this plaque: HISTORIC WAX-AHACHIE INCORPORATED RECOGNIZES THIS PROPERTY BUILT IN 1895 AS WORTHY OF PRESERVATION. Bonnie says both she and Vaughn were brought up in old houses. "We had old furniture that didn't work in modern houses, so we said, 'Why don't we look for an old home that needs restoration? If nothing else, we'll have a home.' As soon as we walked into this house, Vaughn and I turned to each other and said, 'I think we're home.'"

The first thing that caught my eye in the double parlor was what Bonnie says is an Austrian cozy corner, a huge piece of furniture that seems to be a sofa encased in a bookshelf above a chest of drawers, with a pullout table/desk alongside. All sorts of interesting collectibles surround the cozy upholstering, and it fits beautifully in a corner of the room, a cozy corner indeed.

The antique claw-foot table in the Sterling Room was rescued from Bonnie's grandmother. "She was folding linen on it!" Bonnie says in amused dismay while explaining that the room is named for her favorite nephew. The Morrow Room has her grandad's trunk, still with its labels from Wales and with Uncle Wiggly books spilling from its bottom drawer. "I grew up on Uncle Wiggly books," Bonnie says nostalgically. "As for the trunk, it's been to college five times."

Candy, fresh flowers, and evening snacks from cheese and crackers to cookies and brownies encourage guests to comment "in the comment book, which is a lot of fun." Breakfast is a combined effort because Vaughn loves to cook as much as Bonnie does, except that he has his recipes written down while Bonnie's are in her head. "When we get in the kitchen, anything goes!" they confess. Anything, as in special crepes, shoofly pie, applesauce pancakes, ginger pears. . . .

HOW TO GET THERE: From I-35 take Business Route 287 (West Main) east; from I-45 at Ennis take 287 west 11 miles to Waxahachie.

The Chaska House
Waxahachie, Texas 75165

INNKEEPERS: Linda and Louis Brown

ADDRESS/TELEPHONE: 716 West Main Street; (800) 931-3390

ROOMS: 5; all with private bath, TV, and telephone jacks. No smoking inn.

RATES: $90 to $130; $20 extra person; EPB.

OPEN: All year.

FACILITIES AND ACTIVITIES: Porches, gardens, bicycles. Nearby: the Ellis County Courthouse, with its fancy carved stone faces representing a legend of disappointed love; shops, boutiques, and restaurants around the courthouse square.

*L*ike most innkeepers of inns in lovely old homes, Linda and Louis Brown love old houses. It was quite an asset, too, to have lots of wonderful old furniture. "Our families go way back in antiquing," Louis says happily, and they were delighted to discover the Chaska House in 1980.

The 6,000-square-foot house is furnished with eclectic American and English "with some French thrown in," the innkeepers say. Linda loves silver and she has quite a collection, as well as a collection of old Victorian purses.

"We have lots of things to look at, and people seem to like to look at them," John tells me as he catches me admiring several framed needlepoint pieces above the living room fireplace.

Do you know what Tussie Mussies are? Well, I didn't either—and they're another one of Linda's collections. They are little Victorian Posey Holders, and of course a posey is a small bouquet of flowers. "The first one I ever saw was in the Smithsonian," Linda says, and that was enough to set her off collecting them. She also "collected" the smaller-than-usual church pew in the same back hall that houses the posey holder collection. "It's from the back of a church, put there for mothers to use when nursing their babies."

Linda's not the only collector; Louis has been collecting antique firearms for thirty years of more, so it's quite an assortment to examine.

The gracious two-story Chaska House is just a few blocks from the site of the once-prosperous Emporium of Fashion (now the Marchman Building) belonging to William and Marie Chaska. When the house was built by the Waxahachie merchant, America had just been the victors of the Spanish-American War, William McKinley was president, and "Teddy" Roosevelt was his vice president.

This was 1900, and although brass bands paraded in victory and literary societies flourished, West Main Street was still a dirt cul-de-sac. But Chaska and Jolesch's dry goods emporium flourished along with literature, as mule-

drawn trolleys rumbled back and forth between the square and the shaded Chautauqua Society campgrounds along Waxahachie Creek.

Greek Revival was the style, and the Browns' eclectic antiques are right at home. "I like to think this is the sort of four-poster Rhett and Scarlett slept in," romantic Linda says of the queen-size bed, circa 1850, from an antebellum plantation in Alabama. It's in the romantic Plantation Room on the first floor; there's a comfortable sitting area there as well, and the bath has a large claw-foot tub.

The French Room's furniture was their son's when he was little—imagine sleeping in an ornate Louis XIV double bed! It's also the room that had space for the player piano. Breakfast is what the Browns like to call "Texas Chic," served formally on china and fine linen. But "it's really laid-back formal," Louis assures his guests. It's usually either a tasty frittata with salsa and jalapeño or a French toast strata rich with cream cheese, served with fresh biscuits, orange juice, and coffee.

HOW TO GET THERE: From I-35 east take Brookside Road (exit 401A) east to West Main Street. Go south on West Main to number 716 on the southeast corner of West Main and Gibson.

A Spurned Swain's Revenge

There's an interesting story about the Ellis County Courthouse in Waxahachie. Incidentally, each of the three *a*s in the name is pronounced differently: the first as in "ah," the second as in "uh," the third as in "hatchet." It's an Indian name meaning Buffalo Creek.

But about the courthouse: Three stonecarvers were brought from Italy to carve male and female faces atop the columns. One of the stonecutters fell in love with his landlady's daughter. He supposedly carved a pretty face as her likeness, but she married someone else. The story is that one of the ugly faces gracing the building is also his work, expressing his disappointment and anger at being spurned.

The Rose of Sharon
Waxahachie, Texas 75165

INNKEEPER: Sharon Shawn

ADDRESS/TELEPHONE: 205 Bryson Street; (972) 938–8833

ROOMS: 3; all with private bath, 2 with Jacuzzi. No smoking inn.

RATES: $75 to $125, double; $25 extra person; EPB and afternoon refreshments.

OPEN: All year.

FACILITIES AND ACTIVITIES: Porches with swings. Nearby: the Ellis County Courthouse, with its fancy carved stone faces representing a legend of disappointed love; shops, boutiques, and restaurants around the courthouse square.

The entire house is furnished with antiques, and, not to worry, the antique beds have been converted to queen-size. Baths have claw-foot tubs to soak in, and Sharon provides lots of bubble bath. You'll enjoy the beautiful stained-glass windows, and there are books all over the place if you want to lose yourself in one of them.

Breakfast in this haven of Country Victorian (Sharon's inn is mentioned in *Antique Almanac*) might be Sharon's special orange-almond pancakes or a breakfast quiche, served with homemade biscuits and muffins—and Fat Apple Dumplings.

HOW TO GET THERE: From I–35 south take the Waxahachie Business exit, Highway 287, and go to the first red light. Go left on Grand Street and across the railroad tracks. The first street to the right is Marvin. Take Marvin to Bryson Street, turn left and go to 205.

St. Botolph Inn 💙
Weatherford, Texas 76086

INNKEEPERS: Shay and Dan Buttolph

ADDRESS/TELEPHONE: 808 South Lamar Street; (800) 868–6520

ROOMS: 5; all with private bath, 2 with Jacuzzi. No smoking inn.

RATES: $75 to $125, double; $25 extra person; EPB and afternoon refreshments.

OPEN: All year.

FACILITIES AND ACTIVITIES: Swimming pool, lawn games, small prayer chapel, children's playground, pet kennel. Nearby: First Monday Trades Day; Weatherford Junior College; Fort Worth (26 miles); Dallas (35 miles).

*D*an and Shay have named their inn after a seventh-century saint Dan claims to have had in his family. The spelling of Dan's family name has changed over time, but only slightly, from Botolph to Buttolph. Dan researched the priest's life and was inspired by what he found.

"We lived in England for fourteen years," he says, "and we visited all the sites." He says that St. Botolph founded a monastery in 654 in Boston, Lincolnshire, which was known as Botolph's Town back then. His church still stands there. With such a saintly background, it's no wonder that the inn's motto is "As for me and my house, we will serve the Lord."

The inn brochure also points out, "Come, let us pamper you." They do it very well. This large, classic Queen Anne was built in 1897, and Dan and Shay

have painted the house. "She's now a Victorian painted lady of nine colors!" Dan brags. It is distinctive for its size and its gingerbread molding decorating the two large eaves and the pointed turret. The first floor is beautifully symmetrical, with matching wraparound porches on both sides of the front door.

But first you march up the red stone steps and pass under a rugged red brick arch leading up the rise to the inn. There you're greeted on the day of your arrival with a Victorian high tea of scones and cucumber sandwiches, Victorian cookies, and Victorian blueberry-walnut cake.

Dan was in the U.S. Army for thirty-five years, and Shay was a Red Cross nurse. Besides England, they have lived in Korea, the Netherlands, Hawaii, Turkey, Liberia, and Vietnam; the inn furnishings reflect the furniture, art, and artifacts they have collected from what seems like all over the world.

I loved the King David Room. It has a Philippine wicker bed with half-canopy, a white-marble-and-wood washstand from England, and, best of all,

Weatherford's Peter Pan

Entertainer Mary Martin, who became famous playing in the musical *South Pacific*, was born here. Her childhood home is at 314 West Oak Street. It's not open to the public, but you can go see a life-size, 5-foot-4-inch statue of her in one of her more famous roles, Peter Pan, on a pedestal outside the public library (1214 Charles Street). The library also has a small collection of Martin memorabilia.

Another of Weatherford's claims to fame is as the site of the first Texas cattle drive to northern markets, organized by Oliver Loving back in 1858. After the Civil War he was joined by friend Charles Goodnight, the famous ex–Texas Ranger who had established the first ranch in Palo Duro Canyon in West Texas after the Indians had been cleared out. They established the Goodnight-Loving Trail from Texas to New Mexico. Loving, fatally wounded in an Indian attack in New Mexico, asked Goodnight to bury him in Texas. His grave is in Greenwood Cemetery on the 200 block of Seward.

a small private stairway up to a private turret room, where a breakfast table is set in case you want your own private breakfast. So cozy, with the walls of the stairway and the room covered with the same paisley cloth as the drapes in the bedroom, and the four tall, narrow, curved windows of the turret offering a rounded view below.

The St. Mark and St. Luke rooms share a large blue bath with glass tiles set in the 1950s, when that was chic. St. Mark has an antique walnut double bed. St. Luke has twin pink-covered beds, cloth wallpaper, and a wonderful Italian mirror over a very handsome Korean chest.

Breakfast can be served in your room, on the porch, around the pool, or in the formal dining room. You get to order breakfast the evening before, and there's a choice of the full Victorian breakfast, continental, or the St. Botolph Inn special of the day, which on this day was Texas pecan–buttermilk pancakes served with sausage or bacon. The full meal begins with fruit juice or honey-broiled grapefruit, offers a choice of eggs (I had a hard time deciding between the coddled and the shirred with cream, so British) served with sausage or bacon and a basket of assorted homemade breads and muffins. The continental comes with a mixed-fruit compote and orange marmalade for the contents of the bread basket.

HOW TO GET THERE: From I–10 take exit 407 to the third traffic light and turn left on Russell Street. Go to the fourth stop sign and turn right onto Lamar. The inn is up the hill to the right; parking is in the rear.

Victorian House
Weatherford, Texas 76086

INNKEEPER: Candice Dyer

ADDRESS/TELEPHONE: 1105 Palo Pinto Street; (817) 599–9600; fax (817) 817–8295

ROOMS: 9; all with private bath, TV; 5 with stereo. No smoking inn.

RATES: $99 to $269, double; $50 extra person; EPB.

OPEN: All year.

FACILITIES AND ACTIVITIES: Three acres of landscaped grounds; horseshoes; badminton; two game rooms for chess, cards, etc. Nearby: First Monday Trades Day; Peter Pan Statue of Weatherford native Mary Martin; Weatherford Junior College; Fort Worth (26 miles); Dallas (35 miles).

hat a wonderful home this Victorian beauty is, all 10,000 square feet of it! Three stories tall, it commands an eye-catching view of the entire city. "We claim to have the best view in town," Candice says, and it would be hard to gainsay her. Built in 1896 by C. D. Hartnett, a local banker, high on its own hill and surrounded by several old oak trees—and one hackberry—the inn is a sensational reminder of an extravagant age. All three acres are terraced, with a bright green lawn up the front walk. The gabled home, surrounded by wraparound porches and with a three-story round corner turret topped by a steep, pointed roof, is spruced up with soft taupe paint, white trim, and a dark roof that appears to be lighter on the turret.

Born and raised in the hospitality industry, Candice is an expert in the food business. Her family had a motel in nearby Granbury in the 1950s and 1960s. It took six long years to restore the Victorian House. The 10-foot pocket doors, the transoms over them, the original millwork, the stained-glass windows in the entry, and especially the stained glass in the big bay window make this house outstanding.

Victorian House
N. TX

The single-panel front door hardly prepares you for the space immediately inside: a wide hallway that stretches from front to back. The staircase is to the right, leading from the turret room and an open, adjoining parlor. It makes a turn up to the second floor and a second wide hall, past the second-floor game room, and on up to another game room in the turret, with a view out over the expanse of green lawn to the skyline of Weatherford.

Candice had been collecting antiques over the years, and here she found the perfect setting for her many beautiful pieces. All the downstairs guest rooms, with their outstanding antique furniture, have a private sitting porch (for people who want to smoke) and a private entrance. The rug and rocker in room number 1 were purchased from an estate sale and supposedly once belonged to President Lyndon B. Johnson. Room number 6 is huge, made all the more so by its mirrored armoire. All the rooms have comfortable sitting areas, monogrammed bathrobes, and bath amenities. Breakfast is filling, with frothy whipped orange juice, a medley of fresh fruit, a ham-and-cheese quiche, and homemade biscuits topped with homemade apricot jam.

HOW TO GET THERE: Take exit 414 (Highway 180), which in town is Palo Pinto. Go west for 6 miles and turn right into the driveway of the inn, which is on the hill immediately to your right; there's a big sign on the front lawn.

The Zachary Davis House
West, Texas 76691

INNKEEPER: Marjorie E. Devlin

ADDRESS/TELEPHONE: 400 North Roberts; (254) 826–3953

ROOMS: 8; all with private bath. No smoking inn.

RATES: $59 to $65, double; $12 extra person; EPB.

OPEN: All year.

FACILITIES AND ACTIVITIES: Nearby: historic town with restaurants and bakeries, antiques and craft shops; Playdium Swimming Pool; festivals; hunting and fishing at Lake Whitney; West Station Train Depot Museum; Waco (15 miles).

In her youth, Marjorie says, she was bitten by the hotel bug, going to school mornings and working afternoons in the largest hotel in her home town of Laredo. She went on to bigger and better things in the hotel industry, and you can be sure she knows how to take good care of her guests. Turndown service, sweets on your pillow, complimentary wine, all combined with a lovely old home decorated with perfectly color-coordinated bed linens, towels, and comforters. "We had a lot of fun picking out the linens," Marjorie says of the family, who lured her back to her home state after years in California.

"They all wanted me to move back to Texas, for one thing, but I didn't want to just sit around." Marjorie, beginning such a new career, has eight grandchildren and twelve great-grandchildren, and it was a granddaughter who said, "Grannie, there's a nine-bedroom house here in West that would make a wonderful bed-and-breakfast—and we really need it!" They convinced her that with all her hotel experience, having an inn should be right up her alley.

In remodeling the house, which was built in 1890 for an early settler of West (originally named Bold Springs), Marjorie at first was baffled by the problem of adding a bath to each room. But it was solved very cleverly: Each room has fixtures concealed behind an attractive screen. (All except two have showers rather than bathtubs.)

There's a sense of humor here. The Quack Room has a border of wallpaper ducks around the ceiling, ducky linens, and a wooden duck: "I have several doctors who ask for this room," Marjorie says with a twinkle. The Southwest Room, the smallest (a single), has the largest bathroom in the house, and the Downstairs Room, with Oriental furnishings, is called that not only because that's where it is, but also, says Marjorie, "because I couldn't decide whether to call it the Chinese Room or the Emperor's."

Each room is different, and it's hard to make a choice, especially since she keeps changing the decor, adding new linens, comforters, and knickknacks. The Poppy Room has white wicker furniture to set off the bright poppy linens; the blue-and-white Bluebonnet Room celebrates the Texas state flower. Mary's Room is named after a previous owner's daughter, who said, "Oh, Mrs. Devlin, I would love to have it named after me!" Breakfast usually features Nemecek bacon or sausage—they've been in business in West since 1896—as well as all kinds of eggs, in casserole or out. The full country breakfast also alternates with French toast, chicken or beef fajitas (sautéed meat wrapped in flour tortillas), and hotcakes. West, known for its Czech heritage, also is famous for kolaches, and Marjorie is sure to serve them, but you'll probably want more from some of the town's good bakeries!

"I like to be part of the community," Marjorie says. She sponsors two Little League teams on the three back acres of her land she calls her "back forty." In the entry just beside the door is an authentic Czech costume. "It's what everybody wears, come Westfest over the Labor Day weekend."

HOW TO GET THERE: From I-35 take exit 353 in West and go east on Oak Street to Roberts. Turn north 1½ blocks. The inn is on the right.

Select List of Other Inns
in North Texas

The Carleton House

803 North Main
Bonham, Texas 76240
(903) 583-2779

3 guest rooms; all with private bath. Historic home in Sam Rayburn's territory.

Alexander Acres

Route 7, Box 788
Gainsville, Texas 76240
(903) 564-7440 or (800) 887-8794

4 guest rooms; all with private bath. Nestled on sixty-five acres of meadow and wood near Lake Texoma.

Inn on the River

205 Southwest Barnard Street
Glen Rose, Texas 76043
(254) 897-7729 or (800) 575-7729

22 guest rooms; all with private bath. Along the Paluxy River among the "singing trees."

Arbor House

530 East Pearl Street
Granbury, Texas 76048
(817) 573-0073

7 guest rooms; all with private bath; 4 blocks from Historic Granbury Square.

The Captain's House

123 West Doyle Street
Granbury, Texas 76048
(817) 579-6664

3 guest rooms, all with private bath. Overlooking Lake Granbury.

Elizabeth Crockett

201 Pearl Street
Granbury, Texas 76048
(817) 573-7208

4 guest rooms; all with private bath. Historical landmark named for the wife of Davy Crockett.

The Iron Horse Inn

616 Thorp Spring Road
Granbury, Texas 76048
(817) 579-5535

7 guest rooms; all with private bath. Largest historic home in town.

Windmill Inn

Route 2, Box 448
Hillsboro, Texas 76645
(254) 582-7373 or (800) 951-0033

3 guest rooms; all with private bath. Among pecan and oak trees on twenty-one acres.

The Harrison

717 West Main Street
Waxahachie Texas 75165
(214) 938-1922

3 guest rooms; all with private bath. Relax and unwind in English-country elegance.

East Texas

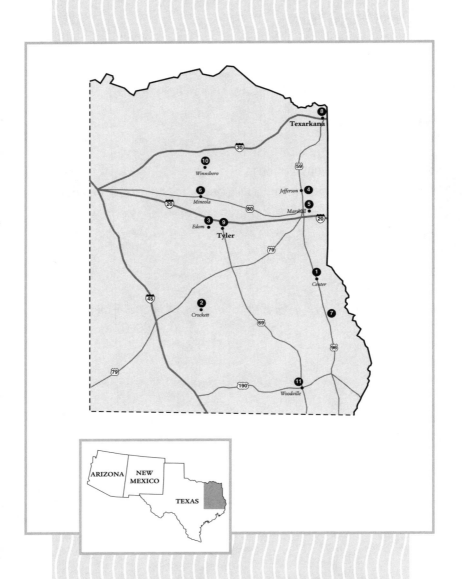

Texarkana

Winnsboro

Jefferson

Mineola

Marshall

Edom

Tyler

Crockett

Center

Woodville

ARIZONA

NEW MEXICO

TEXAS

East Texas

Numbers on map refer to towns numbered below.

Top Pick Inn

Pine Colony Inn
Center, Texas 75935

INNKEEPER: Regina Wright

ADDRESS/TELEPHONE: 500 Shelbyville Street; (409) 598–7700;
fax (409) 598–8060

ROOMS: 8; all with private bath, TV, and phone. No smoking inn.

RATES: $45 to $65, double; $10 extra person; EPB.

OPEN: All year.

FACILITIES AND ACTIVITIES: Art shows, antiques, art gallery, and
custom frame shop; yearly quilt show. Nearby: nineteenth-century
courthouse; swimming pool, fishing, hiking, and hunting at family's
Caddo Pass Lodge; Sabine National Forest; Toledo Bend Reservoir
and Pinkston Lake.

This old hotel was lovingly restored by daughter Regina Wright and
parents Marcille and Pershing, who prided themselves on being
natives of Shelby County, one of the oldest in Texas. "At first people want to make sure they have their
room key," Regina says. "Then they
realize there's no need." If the front
door is locked, guests can come and
go at will up the side stairs to the
front balcony and into the large sitting room, complete with overstuffed
sofas and a television set.

Breakfast is on request because
Regina finds that most business travelers don't want it. But if you do, it
might be pancakes with homemade ribbon cane or blueberry syrup, eggs
"any way," bacon, or sausage, or you might be asked, "What can you eat?"

Rooms are small and simple but comfortable, with touches that make each
one individual. Miss Barnhart's Room honors the woman whose bedroom
suite furnishes it. The Indian Room has both pottery and paintings done by
Regina. An old spinning wheel decorates the entrance hall, and a bank of old-
fashioned brass mailboxes, one for each room, is set into the wall by the front
door. If guests stay long enough to receive mail, they get to use one.

HOW TO GET THERE: Highway 87 becomes Shelbyville Street, and the inn is
on the corner of Pine Street.

Warfield House 📱
Crockett, Texas 75835

INNKEEPERS: Judy and James Ostler

ADDRESS/TELEPHONE: 712 East Houston Avenue; (409) 544–4037; fax (409) 544–4037

ROOMS: 4; all with private bath. No smoking inn.

RATES: $75 to $100, double; $15 extra person; EPB. Corporate rates available.

OPEN: All year.

FACILITIES AND ACTIVITIES: Swimming pool and hot tub; dinner by reservation. Nearby: Davy Crockett Memorial Park, Visitor Center–Museum, Fiddler's Festival, Davy Crockett National Forest, and Mission Tejas State Historic Park.

Crockett is a delightful small town (about 7,000) "filled with friendly people, unique shops and restaurants, and many historic sites," Judy says in her bubbling, enthusiastic way. "Being the fifth oldest town in Texas, it has a special place for history buffs. We're certainly a visitor-friendly town and enjoy the opportunity to show off!"

Well, showing off is a Texas trait, and I, for one, enjoy it. The Warfield House is one of Crockett's lovely older homes, built by a Minnesotan who came to town in 1897. He took three years to complete the house, built Minnesota-style with twelve rooms, a third-floor attic, and a three-room cellar. Put together of rough-cut heart of pine and square-head nails, it was built to last.

Warfield House, Crockett Tx (sw)

"I moved here from Houston when I was nine, and Jerry moved here with the General Telephone Company, and with these perfect old homes, we thought Crockett needed an inn," Judy says. "Jerry and I had this dream for four years." The town didn't think so at first and resisted, but Judy was aided and abetted by her friend, Alma Turner Sevier, who served as Judy's contractor, decorator, plumber, and designer. "She was 86 when she did the house," Judy says. "She made the drapes, made and covered the benches at the foot of the beds, and did the magnolia paintings on the walls."

We had what Judy calls a "historical" egg casserole, with bacon, biscuits, homemade asphodel bread, strawberry muffins, and fruit compote. Morning coffee and tea are placed on a window seat so that guests can help themselves when they wake up. "And we have Diet Coke—a lot of people want that," it being a Texas tradition to have a Coke even before coffee in the morning. Of course there's an Alma Room, "named in honor, too, of all the ladies who really cared about the house," says Judy. A violet-and-green color scheme and a four-poster bed make it both regal and romantic. Ruth and Leela's Room, named for the Warfield daughters, has twin beds covered in periwinkle blue. The walls are sunny yellow, and the songbirds along the ceiling border and on the drapes are planned to invite the outdoors in. Marlene's Room, decorated so that you feel it's "your friend's home," Judy says, is in honor of another friend who helped make the inn dream come true. "My friend and her husband wanted to sell their home—this one—but didn't want to put it on the market until they consulted us. 'We want you to have it,' they said, so Jerry and I figured this was meant to be our inn."

People like to come and stay in this homey place. "I had a bank examiner who stayed a week," Judy says. Other long-term guests include two New

Davy Crockett

Davy Crockett is believed to have camped at Crockett overnight on his way to a date with fate at the Alamo in San Antonio. The campsite is marked with a plaque, which you'll find at the underpass at the intersection of State Highways 7 and 21. Crockett's friend, A. E. Gossett, donated the town site, and the town was named for the Alamo hero.

The town is on the Old San Antonio Road, also known as El Camino Real, the Royal Road. The trail was blazed by order of the king of Spain in 1691 by Domingo Teran de Los Rios, the first provincial governor of Texas. Today State Highway 21 follows the road from San Antonio to the Louisiana border.

Yorkers who stay here every year and commute the 34 miles to Centerville for business. Judy is proud of the nineteen quilts she has inherited from her mother and grandmother. The needlework in the inn is her mother's, too. She found some photographs of her great-great-grandfather and his twin in an old trunk and learned that they fought barefoot in the snow at Shiloh—an interesting note for Civil War buffs.

HOW TO GET THERE: Entering town on Highway 287 or Highway 21 (Old Camino Real), follow the road into downtown. From downtown Courthouse Square, the inn is 3 blocks east on Houston.

Wild Briar Inn,
The Country Inn at Edom
Edom, Texas 75764

INNKEEPERS: Mary and Max Scott

ADDRESS/TELEPHONE: P.O. Box 21; (903) 852–3975

E-MAIL: mscotexas@aol.com

ROOMS: 6; all with private bath. Smoking permitted in public room ("the snug").

RATES: $120; per room; MAP. No credit cards.

OPEN: All year, except for Tuesdays and Wednesdays when holidays fall on those days.

FACILITIES AND ACTIVITIES: Dinner by reservation; gift shop of East Texas crafts. Nearby: hiking paths, craftspeople, East Texas antiques stores, Canton First Mondays Trade Days.

Wild Briar is a two-story, manor-style brick house almost completely hidden in the trees surrounding it: oaks, sweet gum, pines, cedars, and holly. Although the inn is named for the wild berry vines on its twenty-three acres, indoors it's as British as Mary and Max can make it.

"We travel in England, and when we go we like to visit many of the inns our rooms are named for, as well as seek out new places. We want to be a true country inn, where people can stay and feel welcome." The "snug," where

smoking is permitted, copies the coziness the Scotts enjoy in British pubs. There are videos of old movies, and dinner orders are taken here.

Mary taught junior high school for twenty years, and she'll teach you a great deal about England and its inns. The Wild Briar presents a mix of English, Welsh, and Scottish country inns the Scotts have stayed at. Each room is named for one of their favorites. Whether you stay in Sturminster Newton, Bonthddu, Harrogate, Glebe, Thakeham, or Tresanton, you'll be glad you did.

"What do most people come and do?" I asked Mary. "Nothing!" was her mirthful answer. The morning begins with a mug of coffee in the kitchen or on the patio, but at breakfast you'll have to exchange the mug for a cup in Mary's Spode Summer Palace pattern to match the breakfast china. Juices, fruit such as grapefruit and strawberries or the huge Edom blueberries, strawberry bread, zucchini muffins, all go with "any eggs to order" and bacon or sausage. Mary often makes quiche ahead so that Max won't have a problem feeding guests if it's her turn to teach Sunday school. On weekends Max makes gravy for biscuits, "his forte, not mine," Mary said.

Dinners are delicious, full-course meals, perhaps starting with gumbo or broccoli-cheese soup; next comes a green or fruit salad, followed by rolled tenderloin with cornbread dressing or buttermilk-pecan breast of chicken. Family-style vegetables might be a selection of green beans, new potatoes, corn on the cob, squash, sliced fresh tomatoes, all "from our farmer friends down the road." Dessert? How about profiteroles, or mystery pie, so called because you can't tell which fruit is in it.

The Scotts are civic-minded folk; Mary serves on the city council of Edom (with a population of 300), and Max is on the water board.

HOW TO GET THERE: Take Highway 314 south off I–20 (Van exit) to Edom. Turn right on FM (Farm Road) 279 to FM 2339 on your left. Wild Briar is the first driveway on the left on FM 2339.

The Captain's Castle
Jefferson, Texas 75657

INNKEEPERS: Barbara and Buck Hooker

ADDRESS/TELEPHONE: 403 East Walker; phone and fax (903) 665–2330

ROOMS: 7, in 3 buildings; all with private bath and TV. No smoking inn.

RATES: $90 to $110, double; $20 extra person; EPB.

OPEN: All year.

FACILITIES AND ACTIVITIES: Sundeck, gazebo. Nearby: restaurants, antiques shops, historic homes, Jefferson Museum, riverboat ride, surrey ride, Mardi Gras, Springtime Pilgrimage, Christmas Candlelight Tour, Caddo Lake, Lake o' the Pines.

*I*n the early 1870s Captain Thomas J. Rogers combined two houses: one of Texas Planters Architecture, which he had oxen roll on logs across town from down on the riverfront, and one already on this site. The more imposing one he attached to the front, and this is what you'll see.

"He was trying to make his house antebellum," Barbara explains. Well, I don't know how antebellum The Captain's Castle is, but it certainly is impressive, with its tall white columns and spacious grounds. It's mighty impressive on the inside, too, and it was a popular feature on the Jefferson Historic Home Tour even before the Hookers acquired it.

"I'd been on the road as a manu-facturer's rep for years," Buck says. "I got tired of traveling. Some of our friends retired around here, and this is as close to Virginia as we could get without going back." Barbara and Buck are from the Tidewater section of Virginia, and they love the country around Jefferson because it reminds them of Virginia. "The rolling hills, the trees, the green—they're a lot alike." There was no sense in going back to Virginia when he retired, he says, because "I've been in Texas since 1960 and everybody's gone back there. All my friends are here."

As for Barbara, she spent those "best years of her life" raising three children, and she admits she must be one in a million, because she likes to have her retired husband home. "Buck traveled three weeks out of every month, so now when he's home it's mighty nice."

The guest rooms in the main house are named for daughters and a granddaughter. Katherine's Room, painted a deep, almost hot pink, has a four-poster bed of solid mahogany, hand carved and from Indonesia. Elizabeth's Room is a light pink. It has a pretty, king-sized four-poster carved bed in a rice design as well as a copy of Thomas Jefferson's desk. Other furniture recalls Carter Braxton, and Buck was a little surprised when I asked, "Carter Who?"

"Why, he signed the Declaration of Independence! If you look, you'll see his name, right at the bottom in the center!" Teri's Room is pale blue, with a queen-sized Eastlake bed, Victorian marble-topped tables, and a flowered love seat. Breakfast is served on an impressive claw-footed table. It's always something good, like a Panhandle Casserole of eggs and cheese and meat, with stewed cinnamon apples, homemade biscuits, and more fruit—a compote of three to five fruits, depending on what's in season.

What's more, it's served on elegant Minton china, and Buck even knows the pattern. "It's Cockatrice." An hour before breakfast is served, coffee arrives at your door along with strawberry, blueberry, or apple-cinnamon muffins, always homemade. "I like being at home, I like to cook and bake," Barbara says. When I say I'd prefer tea, Buck jumps right in. "Coffee, tea, orange juice, whatever you like," he says. "I've even got Coke if you want.

"I try to get people away from work, from the stuff they have to fight," he adds. "I used to do that, so when I could get away I sure did. After a while, all that traveling isn't so great!"

HOW TO GET THERE: Go east at the intersection of Highways 59 and 49, then go 2 blocks to Alley Street. Turn right and go 2 blocks. The Captain's Castle is on the right, on the corner of Alley and Walker.

Falling Leaves Inn ▢ ♥
Jefferson, Texas 75657

INNKEEPERS: Joe and Barbara Bell

ADDRESS/TELEPHONE: 304 Jefferson Street; (903) 665–8803

E-MAIL: falling leaves@tyler.net

ROOMS: 4; all with private bath. No smoking inn.

RATES: $90 to $100; EPB.

OPEN: All year.

FACILITIES AND ACTIVITIES: Screened porch with rockers. Nearby: restaurants, antiques shops, historic homes, Jefferson Museum, riverboat ride, surrey ride, Mardi Gras, Springtime Pilgrimage, Christmas Candlelight Tour, Caddo Lake, Lake o' the Pines.

This antebellum Greek Revival mansion is listed in the National Register of Historic Places, and each of the four guest rooms is filled with antiques to match the spirit of the place. Some of the namesake leaves come from the huge magnolia tree planted around 1855 by the original owners; others, from what must be the largest crepe myrtle tree in all of East Texas, planted in 1875.

The Magnolia Room is romantic. At least Eloise Amoss thought so back in 1867 when she etched her name in the window pane with her diamond engagement ring. The Dogwood Room sports a curly pine fireplace mantel from an Alabama plantation, as well as a Victorian white-wrought-iron bed. The Pine Room's romantic decor is lighted by a chandelier illuminating the solid cherry Windsor bed and other family antiques, while the Cypress Room's Great Estate bed is complemented by a beautiful armoire.

Coffee and newspapers are available at 7:00 A.M., to hold you until Barbara's gourmet breakfast at 9:00, with daily surprises. While you wait, relax and rock away on the screened-in porch.

HOW TO GET THERE: From I–20 north take Highway 59 to Jefferson. After entering the city limits, go right (east) on Jefferson Street to the second house on the right. There is a sign.

Pride House 📱 💟
Jefferson, Texas 75657

INNKEEPERS: Carol Abernathy and Christel Frederick

ADDRESS/TELEPHONE: 409 Broadway; (800) 894–3526;
fax (903) 665–3901

E-MAIL: jeff@mind.net

WEB SITE: www.jeffersontexas.com

ROOMS: 10, including 1 suite (6 in main house, 4 in annex); all
with private bath; 1 room for handicapped; wheelchair accessible.

RATES: $85 to $110, double; $15 extra person; EPB.

OPEN: All year.

FACILITIES AND ACTIVITIES: Front porches, swings, rocking chairs,
and reading material everywhere. Nearby: historic homes to tour,
Jefferson Museum, railroad baron Jay Gould's railroad car.

*J*efferson is the part of Texas that seems most like the Deep South,
and the hospitality of the Old South is what comes naturally to the
innkeepers of the very first bed-and-breakfast inn in Jefferson—and
probably Texas!

A national magazine has called it "one of the twenty-three most romantic
spots in America." Stained-glass
windows in every room of the
house—red, blue, and amber fram-
ing the clear-glass centers—together
with ornate woodwork, long halls,
and gingerbread trim on the porch
make this house a treasure.

The parlor has an antique piano
that the Historical Society asked
permission to keep there. Over it
hangs a wonderful old gilt mirror from a riverboat family; riverboating was
big business on Jefferson's Big Cypress Bayou until the Civil War.

The main house has six guest rooms. The Golden Era Room next to the
parlor commemorates the era of the town when more than 30,000 people
lived here instead of today's 2,300. It's a lovely golden room with a roman-

tic 9-foot half-tester bed and a large stained-glass bay window. I was equally happy in the large Blue Room with its Victorian slipper chairs and king-sized bed. The Green Room has antique white wicker furniture; the West Room is imposing with rich Victorian-red walls and an Eastlake walnut full-sized bed. The Bay Room is furnished with Eastlake Victorian furniture and has gold stars twinkling on the ceiling.

The other four guest rooms are at the rear in the saltbox house, called Dependency—because it was the servant's quarters, and the folks in the main house were dependent on their work. A refreshing contrast to the Victoriana of Pride House is the common room at the rear, large and bright, with a window wall lighting up the chic black-and-white tile floor and the plants all around. It's the most popular gathering place in the inn. Breakfast includes Texas bluebonnet muffins with lemon zest, and the eggs Olé with picante sauce, ham, and sour cream may make you cry "Ay! Chihuahua!" And there are complimentary hot and cold drinks and other "stuff" the innkeepers know you want to nibble on, like chips, crackers, and candy bars. After all, they say, "it *is* your vacation!"

HOW TO GET THERE: Highway 59 becomes Broadway as it heads east into town. The Pride House is on the northwest corner of Broadway and Alley Street.

Jefferson's Railroad Car

Jefferson began as a riverport, and it was so satisfied with itself that it spurned the railroads when they began to spread all over Texas. Eastern railroad tycoon Jay Gould wanted to bring a rail line to the city, but the city fathers declared that grass would grow in the streets of their town before railroad tracks would.

Gould was furious (you can read where he cursed the town in the guest register of the Excelsior Hotel), and it pretty much happened: Jefferson became a ghost town for quite a few years while the trains went to nearby Marshall, which prospered mightily.

Jefferson rallied as a tourist destination, and one of the attractions is Gould's palatial private railroad car, Atalanta. Gould used it to travel around his railroad empire in the 1880s, but the city has the last word. The car is parked on a lot across the street from the hotel on Austin Street, and tourists can tour it for a song.

McKay House
Jefferson, Texas 75657

INNKEEPERS: Lisa and Roger Cantrell

ADDRESS/TELEPHONE: 306 East Delta Street; (903) 665–7322;
fax (903) 665–8551

E-MAIL: McKAYhsebb@aol.com

ROOMS: 7; all with private bath. No smoking inn.

RATES: $99 to $135, double; $20 extra person; EPB.

OPEN: All year.

FACILITIES AND ACTIVITIES: Special romantic packages and Murder
Mystery weekends are individualized by Lisa. Nearby: Jefferson restaurants and antiques shops, museums, historic homes, horse-and-carriage
rides, riverboat rides, Mardi Gras, Jefferson Historic Pilgrimage in May,
Candlelight Tour at Christmas.

*T*he McKay House has undergone all sorts of changes and enlarge-
ments. For starters, the roof was raised to make two lovely suites.
Still imbued with the spirit of old times, Lisa dresses in period
costume to serve breakfast, and Roger wields hammer and nails to continue
refurbishing the historic house. The dining area has been restored, and a
conservatory designed for both
dining and relaxing now overlooks the lovely garden.

"McKay House is one of the
oldest houses in Jefferson," Lisa
says, "and one of the oldest operating as a bed-and-breakfast, so
we want to be as authentic as possible; we want things to be as they
were back then."

The inn offers things like
designer linens, Crabtree & Evelyn toiletries, fresh flowers in the rooms, and
custom-made Amish quilts on the beds—wallpaper samples were sent to
Indiana to have them made to match. The Cantrell imagination and sense of
fun are at work everywhere. The Keeping Room in the rear guest cottage is
patterned after the room where Lisa says pioneers did everything—cooking,

eating, sleeping, bathing. The footed tub is in the dormer, the dresser is an old icebox, a chopping block is an end table, and the commode is enclosed like an outdoor privy in a little house of original wood shingles, complete with half-moon peephole. The cottage's other room is a Sunday Room, like the parlor used when farmers cleaned up and went to town for the Sabbath.

When I opened the clothes cupboard in my room and found two garments hanging there, I thought the last guests had forgotten them. But no, each guest room is complete with Victorian nightwear: a woman's nightgown and a man's sleep shirt. Lisa hopes they are used.

"We want our guests to know how it was back in the 1850s," she says. They have fun wearing the vintage hats at the full sit-down breakfast in the conservatory. "When all the ladies wear their hats, you've never seen so much picture taking," she says with a laugh. And what a conversation starter to get people acquainted!

Lisa's "Gentleman's Breakfast" of Chicken a la McKay or honey-cured ham, cheese biscuits, and homemade strawberry bread with cream cheese and strawberry preserves is something to write home about, as are the cheese blintz soufflé and zucchini muffins. Hospitality is the hallmark of McKay House, and you may be called to breakfast with a tune on the old Packard pump organ. "Or better yet, just pull a few stops yourself," says Lisa.

HOW TO GET THERE: The McKay House is located 2 blocks east of U.S. 59 and 4 blocks south of Highway 49 (Broadway).

Old Mulberry Inn
Jefferson, Texas 75657

INNKEEPERS: Gloria and Douglas Dehn

ADDRESS/TELEPHONE: 209 Jefferson Street; (903) 665-1945 or (800) 263-5319; fax (903) 665-9123

ROOMS: 5; all with private bath. No smoking inn.

RATES: $110 to $125, double; $25 extra person; EPB.

OPEN: All year.

FACILITIES AND ACTIVITIES: Bicycles. Nearby: Jefferson restaurants and antiques shops, museums, historic homes, horse-and-carriage rides, riverboat rides, Mardi Gras, Jefferson Historic Pilgrimage in May, Candlelight Tour at Christmas.

*T*he Old Mulberry Inn is rather a misnomer: the local folk call it "the new house that looks old." Built in 1997, its columns and porches reflect nineteenth-century ambience, but the owners pride themselves on having everything new and crisp.

The Front Room is Southern, but without frills, with a king-sized rice bed, a comfortable wing chair, and California posters by artist David Lance Goines. A collection of ceramic Victorian houses add to the charm of Sophie's Room, crisp in white and cornflower blue and furnished in both antiques and handcrafted pieces. In the Leaf Room grandmother's needlework adorns the bed and the window, and the recliner tempts total relax-ation. A tribute to the Lone Star State from the California-transplant owners is the Star Room, with handcrafted star quilt and twinkling stars on the bathroom walls.

Having lived in California for two decades, Gloria and Donald say, "We eschew the Southern Plantation Breakfast." Their offerings are lighter, including quiches, homemade breads and fresh fruit; a popular specialty is the delicious cranberry bread.

HOW TO GET THERE: From Highway 59 turn east on Jefferson Street to 209, 2 blocks from the highway.

The Steamboat Inn
Jefferson, Texas 75657

INNKEEPERS: Marian and Pete Sorensen

ADDRESS/TELEPHONE: 114 North Marshall; (903) 665–8946

ROOMS: 4; all with private bath and TV; wheelchair accessible. No smoking inn.

RATES: $95, double; $25 extra person; EPB.

OPEN: All year.

FACILITIES AND ACTIVITIES: New sunroom overlooking the garden. Nearby: restaurants, antiques shops, historic homes, Jefferson Museum and Texas Heritage Archives Museum, riverboat ride, surrey ride, Mardi Gras, Springtime Pilgrimage, Christmas Candlelight Tour, fishing and boating on Caddo Lake and Lake o' the Pines.

*M*arian and Pete have built themselves a new-old inn, completely from scratch. "It's just like an old Greek Revival, and Pete's done it from all old materials. He went knocking on doors and old storage places to find old doors and windows." The flooring is heart of pine, and the house is so authentically antique that it's hard to believe it's new.

Marian and Pete are veteran innkeepers, but their last inn became too much for them. "We love the business," Marian says, "but our other place just grew too big." They got started in the inn business by accident, you might say. "We were on our way to a wedding in Longview," Pete says, "and just on impulse we walked into the Chamber [of Commerce] office and asked, 'Do you know of a business for sale? We are bored to tears.' I had retired from the oil business and we were looking for something to take up the slack time." The Sorensens are from Louisiana Cajun country. Pete looks more like a Danish sea captain—white beard, tattoo, and all—than a retired oil man. Even more surprising is that he is quite artistic; he paints—or rather, he did before he became a busy innkeeper.

Steamboat Inn

Both Pete and Marian are delighted with this "impulsive" turn in their lives. "What's nice about it," says Marian, "is that you get into the mainstream, even though you're retired." People, she says, bring the world to them. As for Pete, he roars, "We pamper the daylights out of them!"

Breakfast is delicious, and Pete is the chef. Scrambled eggs, bacon and sausage, cheese grits or hash browns, are one specialty combination. Lately he's been making a tasty ham-and–Swiss cheese soufflé, crowned with hollandaise sauce. Add homemade sesame biscuits as well as fruit and orange juice, and the morning is complete. Especially since an hour before breakfast you'll find coffee (or tea if you prefer) and muffins at your door. Pete learned to cook when he was pretty young, and he found it was something he really enjoyed. "I was next to the youngest of twelve children, and I would go to Cajun restaurants in New Orleans to learn how," he says.

Guest rooms at The Steamboat Inn are named for the steamboats that came to Jefferson when it was a wild and raucous riverboat town before the Civil War. (Today things are more sedate.) The Golden Era Room (yes, that was a steamboat) has twin antique sleigh beds, and the old tub in the bath is something new to me. "It's skirted," Marian says as she shows it to me. "These came before the claw-footed ones." The Starlight Room has another of the interesting old tubs—and here I thought claw-footed was as old as they got!

The Runaway is pretty, with a beige lace canopy over the four-poster old rice bed, now a queen. As for the Mittie Stephens, well, it's named for a steamboat that caught fire and sank in Caddo Lake. They've recently found her, or what's left of her. "They've just been able to bring up parts of it so far," Marian says. "You can see some of the relics in the Jefferson Museum."

Each of the guest rooms has an English coal-burning fireplace. "You would not know they're really gas," Marian says, and I was almost sorry she told me.

HOW TO GET THERE: Follow Highway 59 into town where it becomes Jefferson Street. Go east for about 2 blocks, past Lion Street Park, and the road veers to the right and becomes Marshall. The inn is just past the stop sign, almost immediately beyond the park.

Twin Oaks Country Inn
Jefferson, Texas 75657

INNKEEPERS: Carol and Vernon Randle

ADDRESS/TELEPHONE: Highway 134 South (mailing address: P.O. Box 859); (903) 665–3535; fax (903) 665–1800

WEB SITE: www.twinoaksinn.com

ROOMS: 6; all with private bath, telephone, and TV. No smoking inn.

RATES: $80 to $100, double; EPB.

OPEN: All year.

FACILITIES AND ACTIVITIES: Swimming pool, horseshoes, croquet, old-fashioned tree swings, hammock for two, gazebo, rose arbor, seven acres to explore. Nearby: restaurants, antiques shops, historic homes, Jefferson Museum and Texas Heritage Archives Museum, riverboat ride, surrey ride, Mardi Gras, Springtime Pilgrimage, Christmas Candlelight Tour, fishing and boating on Caddo Lake and Lake o' the Pines.

There's so much to do here, you'll be busy getting it all in. Begin with a tour of the plantation (the 104-year-old home was moved to this pre–Civil War plantation site) before relaxing in the pool. Then it's time for badminton, croquet, or horseshoes, and sometimes there are special Saturday evening events planned. "There's so much going on, sometimes it looks like the YMCA," says Vernon. "We have people in the pool around the clock, and people playing croquet, badminton, and horseshoes.

"People ask us how can we keep this up. Heck, we say it's just like having a party—and getting paid for it!"

Each of the guest rooms in this more-than-one-hundred-year-old Victorian home is different, and there's quite a choice. Harrison-Lee is inspired by both tradition and heritage of days gone by, inspired by Carol's family, one of the oldest in Jefferson. Georgianna, light and airy in pastel blue, is Victorian, with a king-sized bed set against lace curtains in a bay window; the  furniture is mahogany. Delia is charming French-country with red-and-white French wallpaper setting off handpainted and wicker furnishings. There's a private porch as well.

Caroline has a queen-sized tester bed and a bath with a stained-glass window, while in Taylor you can step back to early American times in Williamsburg. Then there's the Bungalow by the Pool, with warm yellows and floral patterns setting off the king-sized white-iron bed and the wicker furniture.

The Gathering Room is the place for early morning coffee. Breakfast is all made from scratch, and you can feast on homemade apple dumplings, Dutch waffles, thick-sliced bacon, homemade biscuits, and fresh fruit. "Carol and I have never worked together before like this," Vernon says, "and it's been incredible—don't know why we waited so long!"

HOW TO GET THERE: Follow Highway 59 north and go 1 mile east on Highway 2208 to Highway 134. Head south (toward Karnack) for 1 mile to Twin Oaks Country Inn.

The Fry-Barry House
Marshall, Texas 75670

INNKEEPERS: Cymber and Tim Morin

ADDRESS/TELEPHONE: 314 West Austin; (903) 938–4848

ROOMS: 3; 1 with private bath. No smoking inn.

RATES: $65 to $75, double; $10 extra person; EPB.

OPEN: All year.

FACILITIES AND ACTIVITIES: Game room, pool table, electonic dart board, video games, treadmill and weights, bicycles. Nearby: Marshall Pottery, Ginocchio National Historical District, Harrison County Historical Society Museum, Michelson-Reves Art Museum, Starr Family Historical Site.

his Texas medallion home has been in the family since 1872; Cymber is the great-great-grandaughter of Major and Mrs. Edwin James Fry. The house was built in 1853–1860, and it was renovated in the 1980s. So it has all the modern conveniences while losing none of the unique charm of the 1850s.

Aunt Pammie's Room, in light blue and ivory, has a canopied maple bed and its own bathroom. The Isabel Raguet is decorated in cream with a floral border, and has a full-size walnut tester bed. It shares a bath with The Major's Quarters, with furniture original to the house. Both the Major Quarters and the Isabel Raguet can be rented as a suite with a shared bath.

For breakfast you'll be treated to homemade buttermilk pancakes or Chili Relleños Casserole, a bit spicy and quite cheesy, or, maybe, the "No-Tellin' Casserole" of sausage, eggs, and cheese. "Can't tell the recipe," says Cymber, because she's been threatened with her life by a good family friend if she ever gives it away!

HOW TO GET THERE: Take I–20 to Highway 59 north to Highway 80, then left on 80 through four traffic lights and turn left onto Fulton Street. Go past two stop signs; the inn is on the left on the corner of Fulton and Austin.

Heart's Hill
Marshall, Texas 75670

INNKEEPERS: Linda and Richard Spruill

ADDRESS/TELEPHONE: 512 East Austin; (903) 935–6628;
fax (903) 935–6932

E-MAIL: heartshill@internetwork.net

ROOMS: 4; 3 with private bath. No smoking inn.

RATES: $85 to $100, double; $10 extra person; EPB.

OPEN: All year.

FACILITIES AND ACTIVITIES: Exercise equipment, sunporch and other numerous porches, patio and garden. Nearby: Marshall Pottery, Ginocchio National Historical District, Harrison County Historical Society Museum, Michelson-Reves Art Museum, Starr Family Historical Site.

*T*his large, lovely Victorian mansion was constructed in 1900 by a local doctor for his wife, Sally. The semicircular turret has a pillared gallery overlooking the garden. The landing in the upstairs hall is a perfect place for coffee, soft drinks, and either conversation or television, while the sunporch is great for contemplating the surrounding treetops or curling up with a book.

Three spacious guest rooms, all with fireplaces, open off the second-floor hall. The fourth is a private retreat in a carriage house on the grounds, with a kitchette downstairs, a loft bedroom and sitting area above.

Breakfast is dependent upon the chef's whimsy. "Menus are always changing," says Linda. "But it's always beautifully presented," she promises.

HOW TO GET THERE: Take I–20 to Highway 59 north into Marshall. Take a left onto Highway 80 and go west. Go to Alamo Street and turn left and left again onto Austin Street.

The Solomon House
Marshall, Texas 75670

INNKEEPERS: Shannon and David Howard

ADDRESS/TELEPHONE: 207 North Grove Street; (903) 927–1368

E-MAIL: dhoward@etbu

WEB SITE: www.marshalltxchamber.com

ROOMS: 3; 1 with private bath. No smoking inn.

RATES: $90 to $100, double; business discount; EPB.

OPEN: All year.

FACILITIES AND ACTIVITIES: Dinner by reservation, veranda and garden. Nearby: Marshall Pottery, Ginocchio National Historical District, Harrison County Historical Society Museum, Michelson-Reves Art Museum, Starr Family Historical Site.

The Howards chose the pineapple as a symbol of hospitality, so you'll see the motif on their logo. Once Victorian, now Colonial, the home was built in 1894 by the Harle family. You'll enjoy the beautifully carved staircase as well as the four fireplaces, the veranda, and the back garden.

The Library not only contains a selection of books, but there's also an antique claw-foot tub right next to the fireplace and French doors that open onto the veranda. The Grace Room is named for a long-ago lady of the house, and in addition to a queen-sized white-iron bed and sitting area, there's an antique tub behind a privacy screen. Antoinette's Room is luxurious indeed, with a whirlpool tub as well as an antique bed and dresser from the 1800s.

Breakfast might be frittata with cheese and sausage, delicious pecan muffins, and hot fruit with cream, or, maybe, American/Norwegian pancakes, a treat with Blackburn's syrup.

HOW TO GET THERE: Take I–20 to Highway 59 north into Marshall. Take a left onto Highway 80 and go west. Go to North Grove Street, south on North Grove to 207.

Marshall Sights

The clay found in Marshall is perfect for pottery, and as far back as 400 B.C., the Caddo Indians discovered this—you can see their work in the Harrison County Historical Society in the remodeled former courthouse.

And visitors make tracks to Marshall Pottery Factory's huge store on Farm Road 31. The pottery factory, established in 1895, has been operated by the same family since 1905, making the city a serious major pottery center.

Another sight to see in Marshall is the old Ginocchio Hotel, listed on the National Register of Historic Places. Built by an Italian immigrant in 1896 near the Marshall railroad station, it boasted a roster of distinguished guests who lodged and dined here. One was actor Maurice Barrymore, who was actually wounded in a shooting scrape here in the wild early days. The building is considered the finest example of Victorian architecture in Texas.

Three Oaks Inn
Marshall, Texas 75670

INNKEEPERS: Laurie and Tony Overhultz

ADDRESS/TELEPHONE: 609 North Washington; (903) 935–6777

E-MAIL: clyde123@prysm.net

ROOMS: 4; all with private bath. No smoking inn.

RATES: $75 to $85, double; $15 extra person; weekdays continental-plus, weekends EPB.

OPEN: All year.

FACILITIES AND ACTIVITIES: Dinner by reservation. Nearby: fitness center, Marshall Pottery, Ginocchio National Historical District, Harrison County Historical Society Museum, Michelson-Reves Art Museum, Starr Family Historical Site.

*L*ocated in the Ginocchio National Historic District, this fully restored Victorian home boasts twenty-four rooms in all, with original leaded-glass transoms, seven hand-carved fireplaces, cut-glass French doors, polished oak flooring, and beamed ceilings. Down the block trains arrive at the T&P historic train depot, and you can watch them from the porch.

The Victorian Room is spacious, with a king bed and a double bed as well as a sitting area with rocker and a television set. The Magnolia includes a sunroom as a relaxing retreat. The Eastlake is named for the imposing antique furniture, and the inn offers a view of both the home and historic hotel of Charles Ginocchio and the T&P depot just beyond.

During the week a continental-plus breakfast of fruit, breads, and cereals is served. If you stay for the weekend, you'll be treated to a hot breakfast entree with grits, sausage, and muffins as well.

HOW TO GET THERE: Take I–20 to Highway 59 north into Marshall. Take a left onto Highway 80, and turn left onto Highway 80 east and onto North Washington; turn right. The inn is in the second block on the left.

Munzesheimer Manor
Mineola, Texas 75773

INNKEEPERS: Sherry and Bob Murray

ADDRESS/TELEPHONE: 202 North Newsom Street; (903) 569–6634 or (888) 569–6634; fax (903) 569–9940

E-MAIL: rwmurray@prodigy.net

ROOMS: 7; 3 in Country Cottage; all with private bath; first-floor room wheelchair accessible. No smoking inn.

RATES: $85 to $95, per room; $15 extra person; EPB.

OPEN: All year.

FACILITIES AND ACTIVITIES: Access to Mineola Country Club for dinner and golf. Nearby: Texas Forest; Azalea and Dogwood Trails; Mineola Junction with antiques, gifts, and arts and crafts; Canton Trade Days; Tyler (25 miles); Amtrak stop in Mineola.

"We tried to create the atmosphere of when the house was built," Sherry and Bob say of the 1898 manor house they bought, completely gutted, and put back together again. The photo album in the parlor chronicles the horrendous task they set for themselves. When they began the project, Bob says, their entire family thought they were crazy. "That's nothing," Sherry chimes in. "All our friends did, too." They even got comments from strangers such as: "It is amazing that your marriage seems to be still intact!" "But," Bob says, "we've always liked to entertain and have people in the house . . . and Sherry always wanted an old house."

The large house has two parlors, a huge dining room, and guest rooms named in honor of former owners. I was in the Blasingame Room, which had both English and American antiques; the bath had a footed tub; and my armoire had a bullet embedded down low inside the door. Bob said he's darned if he knows where it came from—it came with the armoire. A Victorian nightgown and nightshirt were provided, in case I really wanted to get into the turn-of-the-century mode. Each guest room comes so equipped, which is one of the things that makes staying at this inn an adventure. I also found a tray with a bottle of St. Regis Blanc (wine without the alcohol) cooling in my room when I returned from dinner, as well as after-dinner mints.

For breakfast you'll have a full feast: perhaps a fruit cup (for the Fourth of July it was red raspberries, white pear, and some of the area's huge blueberries), Bob's special scrambled eggs, pepper-cured lean bacon, and peach and blackberry jam to spread on fresh biscuits. Also on the menu are chilled blueberry soup, German pancakes, almond French toast, and a chili egg puff served with picante sour cream and hot biscuits. It was fascinating to hear the story of how the house was reborn; Bob spoke the truth when he said, "We'll wind up sitting in the parlor and talking about it till all hours." The Cowan Room, named after Dr. Cowan, the dentist, has his black leather dental chair as an entertaining point of interest. Bob collects all sorts of memorabilia such as shoe lasts and dinner bells. Other interesting features are the stained-glass windows, the seven fireplaces, and the wraparound porch, where morning coffee and the Sunday paper made it perfect to be outdoors.

Added to the inn are three more charming rooms, which have not changed the exterior of the historic house. The Engineer's Room and the

Conductor's Room foster memories of Mineola's great railroad days, and the Tack Room, built where the stable used to be, is complete with a hayloft and a "two-holer" (indoors, for modern guests; old documents indicate that back in the good old days, the house had "a two-holer in the alley").

HOW TO GET THERE: Mineola is located approximately 70 miles from Dallas and 80 miles from Shreveport at the intersection of U.S. 80 and U.S. 69 (it is also midway between Houston and Tulsa, Oklahoma).

The Wade House
San Augustine, Texas 75972

INNKEEPERS: Julia and Nelsyn Wade

ADDRESS/TELEPHONE: 202 East Livingston Street; (409) 275-5489 or (409) 275-2553; fax (409) 275-9188

ROOMS: 6; 3 with private bath; 1 room wheelchair accessible. No smoking inn.

RATES: $50 to $99, per room; continental breakfast.

OPEN: All year.

FACILITIES AND ACTIVITIES: Nearby: Angelina National Forest, El Camino Real (Royal Highway), Ezekiel W. Cullen Home, San Rayburn and Toledo Bend Lakes, Mission Senora de las Dolores de los Ais.

*Y*ou may have to get hold of Julia and Nelsyn at Nelsyn's Furniture Store down the block. The Wade House was the boyhood home of Nelsyn Wade, and he still lives there. Built before World War II by Will and Atheniar Wade, the house is noted for the large reception rooms on the first floor and the spacious bedrooms. Unusual for the time are the many shelves and closets in the house.

The Guest Room downstairs has a private entrance as well as a private bath. The Master Suite upstairs also has a private bath, as well as a sitting area. The Patriot Pine Room and Nelsyn's Room share a hall bath. The Servants' Quarters, downstairs, also has a private entrance.

An interesting display all throughout the house is the collection of hats worn by Mrs. Athenair Wade from the 1930s to the 1970s. Breakfast is continental, and patio breakfasts or suppers can be catered.

HOW TO GET THERE: San Augustine is located at the intersection of Highways 147, 96, and 21. The Wade House is 2 blocks east of the Courthouse, on the corner of Montgomery Street and Livingston Street, 1 block north of Nelsyn's Furniture Store.

The Mansion on Main
Texarkana, Texas 75501

INNKEEPERS: Inez and Lee Hayden

ADDRESS/TELEPHONE: 802 Main Street; (903) 792–1835; fax (903) 793–0878

E-MAIL: mansionBnB@aol.com

ROOMS: 6; all with private bath, phone, and TV; wheelchair access to first-floor rooms. No smoking inn.

RATES: $60 to $109, double; $20 extra person; EPB.

OPEN: All year.

FACILITIES AND ACTIVITIES: Guest kitchen privileges, off-street parking. Nearby: Perot Theater, Regional Arts Center, Texarkana Historical Society and Museum, Union Station, Scott Joplin Mural.

*I*f you see the Scott Joplin mural and you're wondering what Scott Joplin has to do with Texarkana, the Pulitzer Prize–winning musician was from here. And the city has another reason for fame: It is two separate municipalities, one in Texas, the other in Arkansas. Squarely on the Texas-Arkansas line, you'll find the nation's only Justice Building serving two states. Same with the U.S. Post Office. The Mansion on Main is near both.

The mansion was built in 1895 and has a Texas Historic Marker. The fourteen white, two-story-tall columns salvaged from the St. Louis World's Fair are spectacular. "Inez has always had a fascination with columns," Lee says. "Out of the blue, we got this flyer about the house saying, 'Every old house is a great bed-and-breakfast inn.' We were headed to Arkansas [from Dallas] to see family and stopped by."

The inn provides guests with Victorian nightgowns for the ladies and sleep shirts for the gentlemen, following the lead of their sister inn in Jefferson, the McKay House. Both places believe in people getting into the spirit of the thing, and that includes providing fancy Victorian hats for the ladies to wear at breakfast.

The fourteen columns are a perfect foil for the pretty pink-painted mansion. If you enter by the front door, there's handsome hand-carved wood filigree work over the entrance; from the back parking lot you'll "register" at an old post office desk. The kitchen is open, and, Inez says, "Come on in! Everybody comes into the kitchen."

The dining room, with a lovely small-block parquet floor, fireplace, and black oak furniture, displays Lee's collection of syrup pitchers. Inez and Lee find all sorts of interesting articles, and you never know what you'll see next (the sink in the powder room is from an old railroad car).

There's a piano in the parlor, and a paneled foyer leads upstairs to six guest rooms, from the Butler's Garret to the Governor's Suite, all furnished with period antiques. In the upstairs hall the telephone stand and a stereoscopic viewer vie for interest with a section of the wall that's framed and covered with glass like a picture to reveal how the house was constructed of lathes and sisal-and-pig-hair plaster.

Mansion on Main ... Tx

The Lone Star Room has a cozy reading corner by the fireplace and a Family Album to enjoy. Ragland Room has a famous bed: Both Lady Bird Johnson and Alex Haley slept there (at different times, of course). The art deco Butler's Pantry, with chestnut furniture, is at the head of the back stairs, a perfect place not to disturb the rest of the house. The inn is famous for the Gentleman's Breakfast (which ladies get to eat, too), orange-pecan French toast with pure maple syrup or fresh strawberries; shirred eggs with ham, and Israeli melon; or, perhaps, granola parfait and Chicken a la Mansion on sourdough biscuits. Chimes pleasantly call guests to table.

There's always a fireside cup of coffee or a cool lemonade on the veranda after a long day's sightseeing or attending to business.

HOW TO GET THERE: Take the State Line exit off I-30 to Eighth and turn right to Main Street. The inn is on the left at the end of the street. Turn left into the parking lot at the rear of the inn.

Charnwood Hill Inn
Tyler, Texas 75701

INNKEEPER: Judy Richardson

ADDRESS/TELEPHONE: 223 East Charnwood; (903) 597–3980;
fax (903) 592–6473

ROOMS: 8; including 1 suite; all with private bath and telephone,
5 with TV. No smoking inn.

RATES: $95 to $270, double; $30 extra person; corporate rates
Sunday through Thursday, $70 per person; EPB.

OPEN: All year.

FACILITIES AND ACTIVITIES: Elevator, gift shop. Nearby: Municipal
Rose Garden and Museum, Brookshire's World of Wildlife Museum
and Country Store, Hudnall Planetarium, Caldwell Zoo, Azalea Trail,
Texas Rose Festival, East Texas State Fair.

*I*f you'd like to experience the style of living enjoyed by an old-time
Texas oilman, Charnwood Hill Inn is the place to be. Built around
1860 by a Professor Hand, who was headmaster of a school for girls,
the mansion passed through several hands until it was purchased by H. L.
Hunt in the early 1930s. Judy Richardson became the innkeeper in 1998.

This is a mansion, all right. Common areas of the inn include the formal
living room, library, television
room, the Great Hall on the first
floor and the Lodge on the second
floor, the Garden Room, the Gathering Hall, the front and east balconies, screened swing porch, front
porches, the arbor, and the beautiful east and west gardens. Tyler's
famous Azalea Trail starts right
outside this house.

Tyler also considers itself "Rose
Capital of the World," and the annual Texas Rose Festival is an important
local event. Margaret Hunt was Rose Queen in 1935; and JoAnne Miller,
daughter of the then-owner of the home, was Rose Queen in 1954. Both times
the Queen's Tea was held in the gardens.

A pair of curved steps leads up to the white-columned entrance. The large foyer and living room are stately. The dining room is impressive, with a handmade table and ten chairs of solid pecan, a Chinoiserie breakfront displaying antique Meissen china, an Oriental rug, and a delicate chandelier. It makes a contrast to the bright breakfast room, although even that, in its way, is formal, with its glass tables, chairs covered with summery floral fabric, brick floor, and branch chandelier.

The 1,500-square-foot Art Deco Suite on the third floor was constructed for the two Hunt daughters; the gray carpet makes a perfect foil for the Chinoiserie pieces and the print fabric on a black background. The second-floor sleeping porch and one bedroom were converted into what is now called The Lodge, which has a bar, television, and lots of room for meetings.

Breakfast on weekends is a full gourmet feast. Eggs Benedict is served with an inn specialty—a tasty breakfast potato casserole—and a melange of mixed fruits and juices, coffee, and tea.

HOW TO GET THERE: From I–20 take Highway 69 south to North Broadway, which becomes South Broadway at Tyler Square. Continue south 4 blocks to Charnwood and turn left. The inn is on the right, and there's a sign.

The Rose Capital of the World

Tyler is synonymous with roses. They began to be cultivated commercially here in the early 1900s, and the city has laid claim to the title of "Rose Capital of the World" ever since, shipping stock to the entire nation and to twenty-five foreign countries.

The biggest rose garden in the United States is here, the Tyler Municipal Rose Garden and Museum, and in the twenty-two-acre garden there are 38,000 rosebushes representing some 500 varieties. Roses bloom almost all year, and there is no charge to wander through the garden and smell the flowers.

The museum features educational exhibits, in case you want to try some rose growing on your own. There's a Rose Festival every October, and the museum displays memorabilia, including dresses of the Rose Queens of former years.

Chilton Grand 🎔
Tyler, Texas 75702

INNKEEPERS: Carole and Jerry Glazebrook

ADDRESS/TELEPHONE: 433 South Chilton Avenue; phone and fax (903) 595–3270

E-MAIL: cglaze5302@aol.com

ROOMS: 4; all with private bath, telephone, and TV. No smoking inn.

RATES: $65 to $150, double; $15 extra person; EPB.

OPEN: All year.

FACILITIES AND ACTIVITIES: Hot tub, game room. Nearby: Tyler Rose Gardens, Brick Street Shoppes, Carnegie History Center, Caldwell Zoo, Rose Festival, Azalea Trails, Historic Homes Tours.

This elegant Greek Revival mansion is surrounded by oak, maple, magnolia, and pecan trees. The street, of brick, is in what was historically known as Silk Stocking Row. The innkeepers pride themselves on pampering their guests with true Southern hospitality as well as attentive service. Guest rooms are filled with antiques, and unusual are the many examples of trompe l'oeil hand-painted artwork such as stencils, faux finishes, and stained and etched glass. In Ivy Cottage you'll not only find a two-person Jacuzzi, but there's also a big surprise: an ivy-and-wisteria–draped gazebo inside.

For breakfast you'll be served a hearty baked dish with eggs, cheese, and vegetables, as well as home-baked breads and fresh fruit "delights."

HOW TO GET THERE: Tyler is the crossroads for many highways. From I–20 take Highway 31 to Chilton Avenue and go 1 block south.

Rosevine Inn
Tyler, Texas 75702

INNKEEPERS: Bert and Rebecca Powell

ADDRESS/TELEPHONE: 415 South Vine Street; (903) 592–2221;
fax (903) 593–9500

E-MAIL: Rosevine@uamerica.net

ROOMS: 7; all with private bath. No smoking inn.

RATES: $75 to $150, double; $15 extra person; EPB.

OPEN: All year.

FACILITIES AND ACTIVITIES: Hot tub, game room. Nearby: Tyler
Rose Gardens, Brick Street Shoppes, Carnegie History Center, Caldwell
Zoo, Rose Festival, Azalea Trails, Historic Homes Tours.

Tyler is the "Rose Capital of the World," and Rosevine Inn is named
both for the famous roses, which are shipped all over the world,
and the street it's located on. Bert is in real estate and was eager to
snap up the half acre where the Pope House burned down long ago, leaving
something most unusual for Tyler (and the rest of Texas): a basement. "Back
in the '30s they must have built basements. I designed the house, Becca and I
both decorated it, and we built it right on top of the basement of the Popes'
English Tudor house, which had been vacant for a long time." Bert has turned
the basement into a game room with shuffleboard, backgammon, and many
a hotly contested board game.

The guest rooms are named for
the flora of the area, beginning
with the Rose Room, which has a
high-backed antique bed, a cozy
rocker, and its own small fireplace.
The Bluebonnet Room, named for
the Texas state flower, has a white-
iron bedstead and a comfy blue
couch. The Azalea Room, peachy
like the flowers, has a brass bed.
The Sunshine Room? "Well," says Bert, "it's named for the daughter of the
man who built the house that burned down, what else?" I'm not sure I follow his logic!

The other exception is the new Sherlock Holmes Suite, in a separate cottage on the grounds. The living area has a television and stereo, the dining room is furnished with furniture in the style of the 1890s, and the bedroom has a queen-sized bed.

Becca and Bert had a great time combing the small towns of East Texas—Canton, Quitman, Tyler—to furnish the inn. Canton, 30 miles away, is famous for its First Mondays, a huge country flea-and-produce market spread out under the trees outside the small town.

Breakfast at Rosevine is hearty and delicious. There's always a hot entree such as sausage quiche or French toast or omelettes, served with toast and, perhaps, both blueberry coffeecake and applesauce muffins, along with a fruit-of-the-season cup, orange juice, and coffee and tea. Between the welcome with wine and cheese and the delicious morning odor of fresh-brewed coffee outside in the hallway, Rosevine gives you a happy, pampered feeling. "We try; what more can we say?" Bert asks with a smile. I say that the landscaped grounds of Rosevine are so lovely that it's a difficult choice whether to laze in the hot tub under the pavilion or to play volleyball and croquet on the velvet lawn beyond the fountain in the back courtyard. Bert is the hardworking gardener. The inn is set on a slight rise of smooth green lawn; nine steps lead up to the flowerpots that mark the opening in the arched white picket fence. The path then winds across more green lawn to the front door of this charming red brick house with its backdrop of leafy trees.

HOW TO GET THERE: Tyler is the crossroads for many highways. Follow Highway 31 east into town to Vine Street, turn right, and the inn is the house on the right.

The Seasons Inn
Tyler, Texas 75701

INNKEEPERS: Myra and Jim Brown

ADDRESS/TELEPHONE: 313 East Charnwood; (903) 533–0803; fax (903) 555–8870

E-MAIL: Theseasons@worldnet.att.net

ROOMS: 4; all with private bath. No smoking inn.

RATES: $85 to $125, double; EPB.

OPEN: All year.

*B*uilt in 1911 by a county lumber mill owner, the house was remodeled and bricked in 1930 into a Southern Colonial mansion. But many reminders of its wooden past have been preserved, such as the curly-pine woodwork in the parlor, music room and dining room, and the original tiger oak floors.

The theme for the Seasons was inspired by the seasonal rose and azalea flower festivals that make Tyler famous. Windows of the Spring Room, with its outdoor garden theme, look out onto lovely grounds with azaleas among the pecan and oak trees. The Summer Room contrasts brilliant red geraniums with black and white fabrics; the morning sun shines through a red tulip stained-glass window, and there's an interesting collection of purses decorating one wall. The Winter Room has Victorian furnishings, with a queen-size sleigh bed in tune with a Currier and Ives painted wallscape of an ice skating scene.

A wall in the Autumn Room in the carriage house suite is painted with a fall tree and fence scene to match the four-poster bed made of old fence posts and ironwork. And every morning breakfast is a full gourmet feast of something special to match the season.

HOW TO GET THERE: From I–20 take Highway 69 south to North Broadway, which becomes South Broadway at Tyler Square. Continue south 4 blocks to Charnwood and turn east. The inn is on the right, and there's a sign.

Oaklea Mansion
Winnsboro, Texas 75494

INNKEEPER: Norma Wilkerson

ADDRESS/TELEPHONE: 407 South Main Street; (903) 342–6051; fax (903) 342–5013

E-MAIL: oaklea@bluebonnet.net

ROOMS: 12; all with private bath; wheelchair accessible. No smoking inn.

RATES: $100 to $250, double; $50 extra person; EPB.

OPEN: All year.

FACILITIES AND ACTIVITIES: Spa house with hot tub. Nearby: Lake Bob Sandlin, Cypress Springs Lake, and twenty-two other lakes within a 20- to 30-mile radius; Autumn Trails Festival, Christmas Festival, spring and summer festivals.

*E*specially interesting in this Victorian mansion are the original Civil War–era furnishings brought to Texas by the original owners, the Carlocks, who built the home in 1903. The staircase is of rare curly pine, the chandeliers are stunning, and the Wilkersons have filled the twenty-two rooms with antique details.

The O'Hare Room features an English Hare motif; the Oak Room glows in the light from a round window facing west; La Paloma Room has a huge gothic stained-glass window and is accented by images of doves. The Angel Suite is named for its cherubs; Miss Ima Hogg Suite honors the state governor of 1891's daughter, who stayed at Oaklea; the Mariposa Room is as light as a butterfly.

After your formal breakfast of breakfast casseroles, egg dishes, or turnovers, with muffins and fruit, stroll through four acres of land dotted with a Victorian gazebo and bridge, a wishing well, ponds of koi goldfish, dovecotes, and other wonders under the canopys of old oaks.

HOW TO GET THERE: Winnsboro is on Highway 37 between I–30 and I–80. Highway 37 becomes Main Street. The inn is at number 407.

Thee Hubbell House
Winnsboro, Texas 75494

INNKEEPERS: Laurel and Dan Hubbell

ADDRESS/TELEPHONE: 307 West Elm Street; (800) 227–0639;
fax (903) 342–6627

E-MAIL: hubhouse@bluebonnet.net

WEB SITE: www.bluebonnet.net/hubhouse

ROOMS: 11; all with private bath; wheelchair accessible. No
smoking inn.

RATES: $75 to $175, double; $15 extra person; EPB; corporate rate
with or without breakfast, $65 to $75.

OPEN: All year.

FACILITIES AND ACTIVITIES: Dinner by reservation, hot tub house,
massage, exercise gym, carriage ride by reservation. Nearby: Lake Bob
Sandlin, Cypress Springs Lake, and twenty-two other lakes within a
20- to 30-mile radius; Autumn Trails Festival, Christmas Festival,
spring and summer festivals.

*E*ast Texas was more pro-Confederate than not back in Civil War days, and quite a few mansions testify to the antebellum influence. A true East Texas Southern belle is Thee Hubbell House, its white Georgian Colonial facade catching your eye as you drive down the street. The porches and upstairs gallery sport swings and rockers, and, as Dan Hubbell says, "It's amazing how people love to sit out and rock.

"If they're my age or older, they remember what it was like to sit out on the porch and rock. Our guests seem to enjoy staying around, and we enjoy it, too," Dan continues. Part of the pleasure stems from the fact that Dan is the mayor of Winnsboro. "We meet and greet our guests on a kind of official level," he says with a chuckle. "It seems to add a sort of prestige to our guests, to have the mayor serve them coffee."

The Hubbells chose *Thee* instead of *The* for their inn name because "it sounds cozier," they say. The inn has eleven charming guest rooms. There are some lovely English antiques, and Dan's grandmother's sewing chair and

Laurel's grandmother's washstand testify to their native Texas roots. Two of the guest rooms are suites: the Magnolia Suite and the Master Suite, which is the inn's largest guest room, with a dining room and its own veranda.

Nostalgia reigns at Thee Hubbell House, where you can walk the 2½ blocks downtown to antiques shops and at least three churches. The front door is open so that guests can come and go as they please. The Hubbells take their peace and safety for granted and are amused when guests ask, "Is it safe to walk?"

"We tell them, of course you can walk here, even at night. Then they take off like little school kids, giggling," Dan says. The century-old mansion has pine floors, square handmade nails, and the original wavy-glass window panes. Cabinets now surround a solid oak pie safe that was so heavy it took three men to lift it. The banister posts were made at one-time owner Colonel Stinson's sawmill; his daughter, Sallie, married Texas's first governor, Jim Hogg.

Breakfast is bountiful, to say the least. Begin with a baked apple stuffed with mincemeat. Next have shirred eggs, baked ham, buttermilk biscuits, grits and cream gravy, wheat raisin muffins, coffee, and juice. "We call it a Plantation Breakfast," says Laurel. "We serve in the dining room at 8:30, and sometimes our guests don't rise from the table until 11:00!" They join their guests if there are fewer than eight; if there are "more than we can handle, we don't eat at all, but we have coffee with them."

Talk about Southern hospitality: Mondays all Winnsboro restaurants are closed, so the Hubbells may say, "If you enjoy a good stew, with just crackers and a glass of milk, well, come and sit down."

HOW TO GET THERE: Winnsboro is on Highway 37 between I–30 and I–80. Highway 37 becomes Main Street. Turn west on Elm to number 307.

The Antique Rose
Woodville, Texas 75979

INNKEEPERS: Denice and Jerry Morrison

ADDRESS/TELEPHONE: 612 Nellius Street; (409) 283–8926

ROOMS: 3; all with private bath. No smoking inn.

RATES: $75 per room; EPB.

OPEN: All year.

FACILITIES AND ACTIVITIES: Nearby: antiques and gift shops, several restaurants, Big Thicket National Preserve, Shivers Library and Museum, Alabama-Coushatta Indian Reservation, Heritage Village Museum.

The Southern Plantation Federal–style Antique Rose was built in 1862 by S. P. McAllister, and it's pretty elegant to this day. The tidy walk bisecting the green lawn leads up to red-brick steps and four square white columns on the front porch.

Denice and Jerry moved from Houston to Woodville to retire, but, Denice says, "Jerry still works full-time—and the inn is full-time." They used to come up to East Texas to get away on weekends. "We saw this house advertised in the little Crackerbarrel newspaper," Denice says. "It was just like, 'This is it.' We both looked at each other, and called the Chamber [of Commerce] to see if it would be feasible."

It was not only feasible, it's been a delight. Once the hard work was finished, of course. "For the next two years we worked very hard pulling up floors, painting—all the things that come with renovating a house. Slowly it began to be not just a house, but our home."

Jerry and Denice moved to Texas from out of state more than twenty-five years ago, and it was a surprise. "Texas people are so different," they still say, "so much friendlier." Back where they came from, says Denice, you don't talk to strangers. "When I moved down here and went shopping, here was this man opening a door for me—I don't think I ever had someone open a door for me before."

As for small towns like Woodville, where you know everyone, while they were restoring the house, family and friends kept saying, "I can't believe you know so many people in just two years!" They have planted 150 antique rose bushes in the garden, and the three guest rooms are decorated and furnished with antiques. Walls are in pastels, and the woodwork is white. "Do you know the *Victoria* magazine?" Denice asks. She laughs. "I don't mind giving them a plug—every time I saw something I liked, even if it was just a bowl, I

Indians Among the East Texas Pines

Between Woodville and Livingston to the west you'll find the Alabama-Coushatta Indian Reservation. When the Republic of Texas was established in 1836, the white settlers expelled the Cherokees, but the Alabama-Couchatta who were there managed to fare better with the settlers, and after 1845 the State of Texas bought 1,200 acres for a reservation.

Around 1967 the Indians had the brilliant idea of turning the reservation into a tourist attraction. They revived Indian crafts and tribal dances, and they've added a petting zoo and a fishing lake. During the summer months they stage programs; there is a museum and a gift shop. So this makes an interesting stop in the midst of the Piney Woods of East Texas.

tore the page out. I'd say, 'See this picture, that's how I want it done here.'" Although she chose all the wallpaper and the pretty borders and the rugs, she also gives a plug to two of her sisters from Arizona.

"They came to Texas four times and spent many long hours decorating. We couldn't have done this without them." Ashley has a high canopy bed, the kind you need steps to get into. Jessica's decor is peaches and cream, and there's a fireplace and a spectacular sunset view. Rebecca, blue and white, is off the upstairs porch; its wrought-iron bed is an antique.

Each guest room awaits with homemade bread, coffee, tea, and hot chocolate. "We put a little pumpkin, applesauce, or fresh apple bread in the room for a snack." Breakfast might be individual quiches or breakfast pizza: "I make it out of crescent rolls, with browned sausage, hash browns piled on, then egg and cheddar and mild green chilies." It is yummy, and if you prefer vegetarian, Denice will leave out the sausage.

Jerry is in charge of the fresh fruit bowl, and he dresses up the kiwi and strawberries (or warmed canned apricots in winter) with whipped cream and nuts on top.

HOW TO GET THERE: From Highway 190 turn north onto Nellius Street and cross four small streets. The inn is on your right, across the street from Magnolia Cemetery. From Highway 287 turn south onto Nellius Street; the inn is on your left, across from Magnolia Cemetery.

Select List of Other Inns
in East Texas

Avonlea
410 East Corsiana Street
Athens, Texas 75751
(903) 675-5770

5 guest rooms; 1 with private bath. An elegant 1800s mansion, with or without breakfast.

The Carriage House
Route 2, Box 2153
Athens, Texas 75751
(903) 677-3939 or (800) 808-BEDS

3 guest rooms; all with private bath. Amid fifty acres of pastureland.

The Tree House
501 El Paso Street
Jacksonville, Texas 75766
(903) 589-2958 or (888) TREE-555

4 guest rooms; lovingly preserved 1909 home.

Charles House
209 East Clarksville Street
Jefferson, Texas 75657
(903) 665-1773

3 guest rooms; all with private bath; welcomes children and pets.

The Daniel House
502 East Taylor Street
Jefferson, Texas 75667
(903) 665-7840

4 guest rooms; 3 with private bath. Stay in main house, carriage house, or guest house.

Gingerbread House

601 East Jefferson Street
Jefferson, Texas 75657
(903) 665–8994

3 guest rooms; all with private bath. Breakfast in the house; sleep in Honey-Do Inn at rear.

The Terry-McKinnon House

109 West Henderson
Jefferson, Texas 75657
(903) 665–1933

4 guest rooms; all with private bath. Gothic Revival built in the 1870s.

Wisteria Garden

215 East Rusk
Marshall, Texas 75670
(903) 938–7611

6 guest rooms; all with private bath. Play the upright Baldwin piano in the parlor.

Hardeman Guest House

316 North Church Street
Nacogdoches, Texas 75961
(409) 569–1947

4 guest rooms; all with private bath. On Old Washington Square, once staked out by Caddo Indians.

Mound Street Inn

408 North Mound
Nacogdoches, Texas 75961
(409) 569–2211

5 guest rooms; 3 with private bath. No sign; look for a periwinkle-blue house.

The Gables on Main

212 Main Street
Rusk, Texas 75785
(903) 683-5641

3 guest rooms; all with private bath. Victorian home 2 blocks from downtown square.

Main Street Inn

409 East Main Street
San Augustine, Texas 75972
(409) 275-5013

3 guest rooms; 1 with private bath. Sam Houston rode by and watered his horse here.

Hart's Country Inn

601 North Garland
Sherman, Texas 75090
(903) 892-2271

6 guest rooms; 5 with private bath. Site of town's first hospital, built by three doctors in 1898.

Central Texas

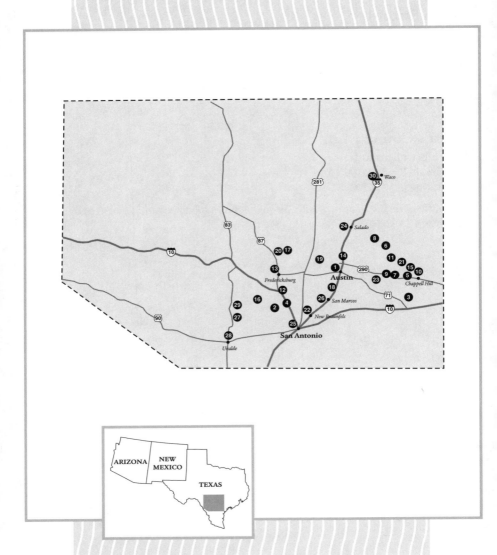

Central Texas

Numbers on map refer to towns numbered below.

*Top Pick Inn

Top Pick Inn

Austin's Wildflower Inn
Austin, Texas 78705

INNKEEPER: Kay Jackson

ADDRESS/TELEPHONE: 1200 West Twenty-second-and-one-half Street;
(512) 477–9639; fax (512) 474–4188

E-MAIL: kjackson@io.com

WEB SITE: www.io.com/~k/jackson/

ROOMS: 4; 2 with private bath. No smoking inn.

RATES: $74 to $89, double; EPB.

OPEN: All year.

FACILITIES AND ACTIVITIES: Nearby: restaurants, shops, Caswell
Tennis Courts, Shoal Creek Hike and Bike Trail, University of Texas
campus and LBJ Library.

Bright flowers lead up to this spic-and-span square, white-clap-board house, with flowers lining the flagstone path and blooming in containers on the green lawn. Indoors fresh flowers bloom in pots, and painted flowers bloom in the stencils Kay and her crew painted on walls and up the stairs. The effect is of light and air, of sunshine pouring in.

"I used lace curtains because I didn't want to close us in," Kay says. "I wanted to bring the outdoors in." She also likes to show her guests the out-doors; one guest from Czecho-slovakia wanted to see farm and ranch land, and Kay said, "Well, get in the car." They covered about 100 miles to see Central Texas's famous wildflowers. "Heavens, so many miles!" he exclaimed. "At home we'd be in Bohemia already!"

Kay is a rather rare thing, a native Austinite, and from an old Texas family to boot. Rooms are named for members of her family: The David G. Burnet Room is named for her great-great-grandfather, and I loved the white-iron half-canopied bedstead. Dodie's Room contains the furniture of a great-aunt, and the Carolyn Pearl Walker Room is furnished with pieces given to Kay's grandmother for her thirtieth anniversary. Unusual is the old daybed; there's a four-poster, too. White stenciled flowers march along the pale-blue walls under the ceiling.

Kay has set some sort of record—she's gone for five and a half weeks without repeating a breakfast menu! It became a challenge, she says, when she overheard a British guest bragging to a newcomer that Kay had not served the same thing twice in the two weeks she'd been at the Wildflower. "She stayed for almost six weeks, and I didn't repeat." So, of course, I had to ask how on earth . . . ? "I alternate sweet and savory, for one thing," she says, "and always with juice, coffee, tea, and fresh-baked bread or muffins." A favorite is eggs Goldenrod, white sauce with hard-boiled egg whites over a croissant, the yellow yolk crumbled on top—that's a savory. A sweet might be French toast stuffed with ricotta cheese with a syrup of zest of orange, orange marmalade, and brown sugar.

The house, on a quiet tree-lined street near the University of Texas campus, was built in 1936 for a professor. It's a dead-end street, so there's no through traffic. "Restoring it, we did the work ourselves," Kay says, making it sound easy as daughter Angela, home from college, laughs. "Easy! We moved walls," Angela says. "We discovered a covered-up inside staircase (there's an outside one up to the small porch outside the Texas Country Room), took a kitchenette out of the upstairs. . . ." She helped in between her college studies, as did son Jay.

"I stayed at an inn on a business trip," says Kay. "I had a woodcrafts shop, and when I went back to work, I told her, 'I'm going to open a bed-and-breakfast.' And I have to say, it all just came together." New is an impressive bi-level wood deck overlooking the pretty back yard, perfect for one of Kay's breakfasts or for sipping afternoon tea or coffee.

HOW TO GET THERE: From I–35 take Martin Luther King Boulevard (Nineteenth Street) west to the end at Lamar; turn right and go to the first traffic light (Twenty-fourth Street) and turn right again, staying in the right-hand lane. Turn right at the second street (Longview) to Twenty-second-and-one-half Street. The inn is on the right, on the corner of Longview and Twenty-second-and-one-half.

The Chequered Shade
Austin, Texas 78730

INNKEEPER: Millie Scott

ADDRESS/TELEPHONE: 2530 Pearce Road; (512) 346–8318;
fax (512) 346–7830

ROOMS: 3; all with private bath. No smoking inn.

RATES: $89, double; $15 extra person; EPB.

OPEN: All year.

FACILITIES AND ACTIVITIES: Wildlife viewing from porches and patios,
hiking and biking, fishing, boating, swimming. Nearby: pet boarding,
Emma Long City Park on Lake Austin, several restaurants, downtown
Austin (thirty minutes) and the University of Texas, LBJ Library.

*M*illie offers a warning to her guests: "When you leave our lovely
area, expect some difficulty in readjusting to everyday life!"
Here you're pretty much out in the country. The inn is just
down the hill from bucolic Emma Long City Park on Lake Austin, just on
the edge of Austin's renowned Texas Hill Country. The park offers boating,
swimming, and picnic spots, and Turkey Creek just down the road apiece is
the place for fishing.

The inn name applies to the
wonderful old oaks shading the
property: Millie was inspired by a
couplet by Milton: "To many a
youth, and many a maid, dancing in the chequered shade. And
young and old come forth to
play, on a sunshine holiday." So
it's not the window shades that
are chequered, it's the entire
property.

But Millie confesses that inspiration failed her when it came to naming
her guest rooms, so you'll have to be satisfied with choosing yours by the
beds: one king room, one queen room, and one twin room. There is a nice
mix of antique and modern furnishings throughout.

Before you set out hiking, fishing, swimming, or just viewing the wildlife from patio or porch, you'll be well fortified with one of Millie's Gourmet Breakfasts. Perhaps a ripe avocado half filled with the half of a boiled egg, quite a new taste treat. Top this with a sauce of Gorgonzola cheese and yogurt sprinkled with chives and garnished with quartered cherry tomatoes, all served with slivered ham and toasted onion bagels.

HOW TO GET THERE: Go west on RR 2222 (Bull Creek Road), crossing under Loop 360 (Capital of Texas Highway) and turning left onto City Park Road. Stay on the road until you come to a fork in the road, marked by a yellow flashing light. Turn left here and go about 7/10 mile to the bottom of the hill. The inn is on the left-hand corner, identified by 2530 on the mailbox.

Fairview Inn 📱
Austin, Texas 78704

INNKEEPERS: Nancy and Duke Waggoner

ADDRESS/TELEPHONE: 1304 Newning Avenue; (512) 444–4746; fax (512) 444–3494

E-MAIL: fairview@io.com

WEB SITE: www.fairview-bnb.com

ROOMS: 4 in main house, 2 suites with kitchens in carriage house; all with private bath, phone, and TV. No smoking inn.

RATES: $99 to $149, double; $15 extra person; EPB.

OPEN: All year.

FACILITIES AND ACTIVITIES: Nearby: University of Texas campus and the LBJ Library, State Capitol, Zilker Park with Barton Springs and Japanese Garden, Austin Art Museum, Elisabet Ney Museum, Umlauf Sculpture Garden, and more.

*W*hat a surprise this beautiful huge white-columned mansion is, barely a mile from busy downtown Austin. Surrounded by meticulous landscaping, sheltered by huge old oaks, it seems miles away in the country. "Travis Heights is a good old neighborhood,"

Duke says. "People are out walking their dogs even at 10:00, 10:30 at night. We sit on the porch and wave at the neighbors as they go by."

Both he and Nancy, native Texans, confess to having always harbored a burning desire to restore an old house, curbed for years—at least by Nancy—by the wonderful dollhouse in the Sun Parlor. Duke laughs. "It was supposed to take away the itch to restore." But he's bitten too, and plans to make a full-scale model of Fairview one day.

The large foyer and the spacious Great Room are perfect for guests who want to entertain. "You don't have to entertain in your bedroom," they say. The piano, a golden oldie from St. Louis in 1903, was "just in time for the 1904 World's Fair," Duke says, intimating that maybe Scott Joplin played on it. Then he laughs. "I never let facts stand in the way of a good story." The six-legged dining room table, though, was Nancy's great-grandfather's, for a fact.

Another piece of furniture turned out to be from Nancy's family, and she had no idea of that when they bought it. The Eastlake half-tester bed in the Ambassador Room was found in Crockett (East Texas), and putting it together was rather a puzzle. A great-aunt came to visit. "Why that's great-grandmother Littlefield's bed!" she said, and told them how to put it together. "Turns out, it's been in my family more than a hundred years," Nancy says. "It had just kinda left for a while!"

The Texas Colonial Revival mansion was built in 1910. Duke points out that most of the paneling and trim is of rare heart of longleaf pine from Calcasieu Parish in Louisiana. The house has an Austin Historic Landmark designation and a 1993 award from the Austin Heritage Society for Historic Preservation. All rooms are extraordinarily spacious, but the Governor's Suite is truly Texan in scope—the Victorian Renaissance bed (now king-sized) is dwarfed in the huge room, which has a dressing room in addition to a bath. In the large enclosed sunporch there's a sofa bed and a gigantic work table. "This setup provides an excellent setting for a small business meeting," Duke says.

"We bought the house from Ima Gullett, an elderly lady who tells us stories about famous people who were entertained in the house in the past. Names I learned about in seventh-grade Texas history—it makes my hair stand on end!" At breakfast, Belgian waffles are served with Texas pecan-peach syrup; the black-bean salsa dip is served with Texas-shaped corn chips; you can slather your biscuits with "Hill Country Mud" (don't ask, just enjoy!), and the *migas* have hot sauce—you'll know you're in Texas, all right.

HOW TO GET THERE: From I-35 take the Riverside exit west to Congress Avenue. Turn left, pass the Texas State School for the Deaf on the right, and turn left on Academy. Drive 3¹⁄₁₀ miles to Newning and turn right. The inn is the sixth house on the right. Turn into the driveway and park at the rear of the inn.

Governor's Inn
Austin, Texas 78705

INNKEEPERS: Lisa and Ed Mugford

ADDRESS/TELEPHONE: 611 West Twenty-second Street; (800) 871-8908; fax (512) 476-4769

E-MAIL: governorsinn@earthlink.net

ROOMS: 10; all with private bath, 4 with TV; 1 room wheelchair accessible. No smoking inn.

RATES: $59 to $119, double; $15 extra person; EPB.

OPEN: All year.

FACILITIES AND ACTIVITIES: Nearby: University of Texas campus and the LBJ Library, State Capitol, Zilker Park with Barton Springs and Japanese Garden, Austin Art Museum, Elisabet Ney Museum, Umlauf Sculpture Gardens, many fine restaurants.

his historical mansion was built in 1897 and for years was known as the Kenny-Lomax House before it began another life as a fraternity house. (It's 2 blocks from the University of Texas campus.) Lisa and Ed enjoy the history of their inn.

"Lisa liked the governor theme," Ed says. "She visited the Governor's Mansion [which is practically around the corner, on Eleventh Street] and learned all the names." Each room is named for a Texas governor from way back, beginning with Sam Houston.

The mansion is impressive, with high ceilings, lots of white paneling—all original—and many porches, all surrounded by a low stone wall. Wrought-iron gates lead to the inn's many entrances, but guests use the side door off the parking lot. The happy voices of university students laughing and calling to one another as they pass to and from class strike a warm and youthful note.

The parlor has a lovely rug over the polished wood floor, partially covering an interesting stencil whose shape is echoed by the white molding overhead. There are three dining rooms, each with a fireplace and more white-painted molding; the built-in cupboard of the center dining room is magnificent. Surrounding every doorway are moldings topped by a two-dimensional Corinthian pediment, like a miniature Grecian column—everywhere you'll see such unusual details, and all original. The owners did a wonderful job of restoring the home. "Rescued," Ed emphasizes. "After all, it was a fraternity house. . . ."

Lisa and Ed like their job, and for good reason. "People really are grateful for what you do, they recognize that you're working for their pleasure." They

Governor's Inn Austin Tx

are particularly pleased when they are asked for recipes. And no wonder, when breakfasts include dishes such as sausage-and-chili quiche or Eggs Governor and strawberry cream-cheese bread, not to mention a full candlelit and musical breakfast featuring the sounds of Nat King Cole, classical, and jazz. The Governor Hamilton Room is off the parlor; all the others are on the second floor, except Ma and Pa Ferguson's Suite up on the third. As you march up the stairs, on the right wall there's an interesting lineup of prints of old shoes. At the top of the flight, hanging on the wall to the left is a huge and gorgeous hand-made quilt.

Ed says a guest from Salem, Massachusetts, sent it to them. "I know," he says, pleased at my amazement. "She said she had no place to hang it and she wanted us to have it, we made her feel so welcome!"

HOW TO GET THERE: From I–35 take the MLK (Nineteenth Street) exit west to Rio Grande. Turn right and go 3 blocks to Twenty-second Street. Turn right, and right again in the middle of the block into the driveway of the inn.

The McCallum House
Austin, Texas 78705

INNKEEPERS: Nancy and Roger Danley

ADDRESS/TELEPHONE: 613 West Thirty-second Street; (512) 451-6744; fax (512) 451-4752

E-MAIL: McCallum@AustinTX.net

ROOMS: 5, including 2 suites; all with private bath and kitchen, 4 with private porch; TDD for deaf and hearing impaired. No smoking inn.

RATES: $80 to $149, double; $15 extra person (lower rates are for three nights or more and for any night Monday through Thursday); EPB. Monthly rates available. Visa and MasterCard to secure deposit only.

OPEN: All year.

FACILITIES AND ACTIVITIES: Nearby: many fine restaurants, University of Texas campus, LBJ Library, State Capitol, Zilker Park with Barton Springs and Japanese Garden, other Austin sights.

The McCallum House was built in 1907 as the home of Jane Y. McCallum, an early suffragist, her husband, Arthur, and her five children. The Danleys now have a marker from the Texas Historical Commission to authenticate the building's history. McCallum was careful to make the distinction—she was not a militant suffragette—but she had definite ideas all the same. Some of the inn furniture, such as the Blue Room set with the oval-mirrored dressing table, came with the house and reflects her taste. In the attic Nancy found the big yellow suffragette banner that now hangs in the hall: 8,000,000 WORKING WOMEN NEED TO VOTE!

The Danleys took the old house and turned it into a charming inn. Roger is a remodeling contractor, and Nancy has done some construction, too. Wait until you see the dollhouse in the entry, just below the stairs. "We did that in moments of insanity," both the Danleys say with a laugh. I would call it artistry, not insanity. It's perfectly beautiful, with downstairs ceilings decorated with molding, a hearth of real brick, and even tiny rugs needlepointed by the talented builders and decorators.

Roger's life-size triumph is Jane's Loft, a beautiful attic room with 12½-foot ceilings and wonderful etched-glass doors. A Victorian pattern done by hand by the Danleys decorates both the huge triangular window in the gable and the long, etched panels on either side of the door leading to the big, open porch.

Many guests, especially long-term ones (the Danleys often have professors visiting the University of Texas who stay for several weeks), are pleased as punch with the Garden Apartment in the back. This suite, decorated in deep rose and blue, with white wicker and a white-iron daybed in the living room, has a bedroom with queen-sized beds and a kitchen equipped for real cooking. "We've had lots of families, physicists doing research and lecturing at the university; it's a lot of fun," the Danleys say.

Now all accommodations have kitchen facilities, irons and ironing boards, hair dryers, and decks or verandas. It's a house of porches. Adjoining the Blue Room and running along the entire side of the house is a screened porch fitted with white wicker and blue chintz furniture; "I can see why folks

want just to sit here and enjoy the breeze. There's a lot of sitting around the breakfast table too—that's one of the high spots of innkeeping," Nancy says. "We sit around the table and talk for hours."

Or you can have a full breakfast tray delivered to your refrigerator the night before if you want to sleep in or work instead of joining others in the dining room. Nancy's special dish of scrambled eggs with shaved ham, sharp cheddar, onions, and parsley is served with streusel-topped blueberry-bran muffins and a fruit cup of black cherries, bananas, and peaches. Roger's specialty is a quiche with a crunchy shredded-potato crust. The filling can be ham or sausage, spinach, or mushrooms, depending on the whim of the resident chef. Also on the menu are some wonderful low-fat and no-cholesterol muffins, sweet breads, and coffee cakes.

HOW TO GET THERE: Exit I-35 at Thirty-eighth Street and go west to Guadalupe. Turn south for 6 blocks to Thirty-second; turn west on Thirty-second. The inn is on the left.

Woodburn House
Austin, Texas 78751

INNKEEPERS: Sandra and Herb Dickson

ADDRESS/TELEPHONE: 4401 Avenue D; (512) 458–4335;
fax (512) 458–4319

E-MAIL: woodburn@iamerica.net

ROOMS: 4; all with private bath; devices for hearing impaired
with advance notice. No smoking inn.

RATES: $85 to $95, double; $13 extra person; EPB.

OPEN: All year.

FACILITIES AND ACTIVITIES: Exercycle; massage by registered
therapist on site, with appointment. Nearby: restaurants, shops;
Shipe Park with pool, tennis, basketball; Elisabet Ney Museum,
many other museums; Hyde Park Walking Tour.

Woodburn House, built in 1909, has earned Austin City Landmark status for its architectural features. "Besides the Governor's Mansion, there's only one other home in Austin like
ours," Sandra says. "The double-wrapped gallery, the woodwork of the
Craftsman style, which evolved from Victorian. . . ." I was convinced the
moment I saw the beautiful old house, with its wide flagstone path flanked

with flowering shrubs and
neatly bisected at the curb
by a huge, old elm tree. The
name comes from Bessie
Hamilton Woodburn, who
lived in the house for many
years. Her father, Alexander
Hamilton (not the Found-
ing Father), was Texas's pro-
visional governor after the
Civil War.

Although the Dicksons are relatively new to Austin, Herb is a Texan, and they have wasted no time becoming active in the community. "We like to belong where we belong," Sandra says, and guests have the feeling of belonging right from the start.

The inn, as promised from the exterior, is very spacious, with 12-foot ceilings and beautiful woodwork. There are two common rooms. One, the living room, has two large maroon leather sofas and a matching chair, which you absolutely sink into, lace curtains at the windows, polished dark woodwork, oak floors, an armoire, and a bookshelf—as tall as the room—that extends around a corner and up to the ceiling. It's a lovely room. On the dining room's built-in corner cupboard sits an old clock that has been in Herb's family for generations. The home is filled with antiques from the Dickson family. I especially admired the dozens of handmade quilts left to the family by Grandmother Dickson. "Guests love to bundle up in them if it gets chilly while they're enjoying the upstairs gallery," Sandra says. It was a delight to curl up on the old glider, surrounded by huge old oak and pecan trees, and watch the squirrels, the woodpeckers, the jays, and the mourning doves go about their business.

Sandra, whose family was from Guadalajara, Mexico, likes to serve a Mexican breakfast. "Real Mexican, not Tex-Mex," she says. She makes her own salsa and grows her own Mexican spices. "We bake our own breakfast breads and alternate Mexican cuisine with Belgian waffles, quiches, and fluffy French toast, which are more Herb's specialties. He does all the cutting and chopping—I do all the baking," she adds.

One of the nicest things about the guest rooms, aside from their spaciousness, is the tall lace-covered windows opening off the gallery in front and shaded by old trees in the back. The wide halls, the front and back stairs, the butler's pantry, the large kitchen—everything about this inn is bright and gleaming.

HOW TO GET THERE: From I-35 exit Airport Boulevard and turn north to Forty-fifth Street west to Avenue D. Turn left, and the inn is on the left at the corner of Avenue D and West Forty-Fourth Street.

Ziller House
Austin, Texas 78704

INNKEEPERS: Royce Wilson and Scotty Roberts

ADDRESS/TELEPHONE: 800 Edgecliff Terrace; (512) 462–0100 or (800) 949–5446; fax (512) 462–9166

WEB SITE: www.austin.citysearch.com

ROOMS: 5; all with private bath, telephone, and TV. No smoking inn.

RATES: $120 to $200; EPB.

OPEN: All year.

FACILITIES AND ACTIVITIES: Jacuzzi; gardens. Nearby: downtown Austin; Convention Center; University of Texas campus and the LBJ Library; State Capitol; Zilker Park with Barton Springs and Japanese Garden; Austin Art Museum; Elisabet Ney Museum; Umlauf Sculpture Garden.

*Z*iller House's street is aptly named: The estate sits on the rock cliff overhanging Town Lake and facing the lights of downtown Austin; at night they seem close enough to touch. The white 1938 Mediterranean-style home is enclosed by greenery both cultivated and wild on two and a half acres.

The entire house has been recently redecorated; the living room has a lodge-like feeling, with Ralph Lauren touches and a grand piano. There's even a billiard room in the basement, in Austin a rarity, and oak paneled at that.

The breakfast room is cheery with cafe seating for eight guests, with a full meal being served between 8:00 and 10:00 A.M. Or you can have a continental beakfast in your room if you prefer.

HOW TO GET THERE: From I–35 exit at Riverside Drive and go west 1 short block to Travis Heights Avenue. Turn right, then left onto Edgecliff, which ends at the gates of the inn estate. There is parking to the left inside the gates.

Abundare River Ranch
Bandera, Texas 78003

INNKEEPER: Lynne Sims

ADDRESS/TELEPHONE: Bottle Springs Road, (830) 796-4076 or (800) 706-6712; fax (830) 796-4011

E-MAIL: info@abundare.com

WEB SITE: www.abundare.com

ROOMS: 12; 10 with private bath. No smoking inn.

RATES: $110 to $275, double; $65 extra person. Meals not included; most rooms have a kitchen or access to one.

OPEN: All year.

FACILITIES AND ACTIVITIES: Swimming pool, hot tub, bicycles, exercise equipment, tennis, outdoor games, grills, hiking, exotic wildlife: zebra, bison, llama, antelope, birds. Nearby: Medina River tubing and fishing; Bandera (Cowboy Capital of the World), shopping, numerous events.

*H*ow about an exotic mixture of zebras, bison, llamas, and other "pets" at a country inn? And the inn is a luxurious 1906 antibellum-style mansion with guest rooms both in the house and in a cabana by the pool?

The house is decorated in what Lynne terms "country elegant," and you need to call ahead to get the magic numbers to be admitted to this wonderful animal kingdom at the coded entry gate. Rooms of course have names like the Zebra Room, with African motif; Bison Room and Peacock Suite of colorful country decor; the Bandera Suite and Walker Room are of course Southwestern; and the Stables Suite includes stalls for four guest horses—so you know you're in cowboy country!

Just about every room has a kitchen, or access to one, so you're on your own foodwise. But not to worry—if you're not up to cooking, Bandera has marvelous cowboy cuisine!

HOW TO GET THERE: From the intersection of Highway 16 and Highway 173 south go south on 173 about a mile. Turn left on Bottle Springs Road, and it's 2½ miles to the inn entrance on your left.

High Cotton Inn
Bellville, Texas 77418

INNKEEPERS: Anna and George Horton

ADDRESS/TELEPHONE: 214 Live Oak Street; (409) 865–9796; fax (409) 865–5588

E-MAIL: hicotton@phoenix.net

ROOMS: 4; all share 2½ baths. No smoking inn.

RATES: $75, double; $10 extra person; EPB.

OPEN: All year.

FACILITIES AND ACTIVITIES: Small swimming pool. Nearby: boarding facilities for pets, spring and fall festivals, Historic Home Tour (April), Antiques Show (October), Austin County Fair.

*A*nna Horton says, "We're not pretentious," but the house itself is a grande dame, a beautiful home in the best Victorian manner. It's the largest house in town and was built by a very successful cotton broker back in 1906, when cotton was king. (The name High Cotton comes from a Southern expression meaning "everything's rosy.") There's a lovely formal parlor downstairs and, by the door to the upstairs wraparound porch (there's one downstairs, too), a cheerful sitting area.

The furniture is all family antiques, and I love Anna's sense of humor. "Lots of it is dead relatives," she says. "George and I got married just when all the aunts started dying, and they're all upstairs waiting to scare any guests who get out of line." The dining room table, however, is a back-East piece from Lancaster, Pennsylvania, a real conversation piece 66 inches wide, with twelve leaves. It vies for atten-

tion with the built-in china cabinet, whose huge plate-glass door slides up the wall.

Breakfast might be real country, with grits, bacon, scrambled eggs, bran muffins, and biscuits. Then again, there might be a sophisticated rum-soaked cake and Anna's new whole-wheat "Zen" pancakes with homemade syrup—and always Anna's special blackberry preserves, which she puts up herself.

HOW TO GET THERE: The inn is on Highway 36 south, on the edge of Bellville.

Ye Kendall Inn
Boerne, Texas 78006

INNKEEPER: Manny Garcia

ADDRESS/TELEPHONE: 128 West Blanco; (830) 249–2138 or (800) 364–2138

ROOMS: 13; all with private bath and TV; 1 with wheelchair access. No smoking inn.

RATES: $80 to $125, double; $10 extra person; continental breakfast.

OPEN: All year.

FACILITIES AND ACTIVITIES: Restaurant, bar, boutiques. Nearby: Agricultural Heritage Center; Cascade Caverns; Cave Without a Name; Guadalupe River State Park; San Antonio (15 miles).

*B*ack in the early days of Texas, there was no hotel for travelers to these parts until Erastus and Sarah Reed bought a parcel of land for $200 in 1859. They began renting out their spare rooms to horsemen and stagecoach travelers, and from being known as The Reed House, the building changed its name through the years to The King Place and the Boerne Hotel. It wasn't called Ye Kendall Inn until 1909. Today the old two-story building, of Hill Country stone fronted by white-railed porches 200 feet along its length on both upper and lower floors, is alive again as an inn, facing the large open spaces and white gazebo of the town square.

The old place is full of mysteries. "The cellar goes into a tunnel," says Manny. "It goes to the building way down on the corner; I guess it was for stagecoach passengers to hide from the Indians." (Too bad, it's not open to the public. Never mind, there's another mystery.) "I've been told we have a ghost who lives here," Manny says. "I haven't seen it, but there are reports of

people who say they have." Perhaps it's the quiet that leads to fanciful—or real?—visions. "Guests like us mainly because it's so quiet," Manny says. "It's the Hill Country quiet—there aren't even dances here on Saturday night." But there's plenty to do all the same, with quite a few festivals held in Main Plaza out front, such as a yearly Fun Fair with arts and craft shows, dances and pig races in town, and famous Hill Country caverns nearby.

High up along the walls in the upstairs rear of the building are what Manny calls "shootout" windows, possibly used to defend against those same Indians the stagecoach passengers were hiding from in the tunnel. The entire lobby and rooms opening off it contain boutiques with antiques and designer clothing, but the huge upstairs hall is for inn guests, with comfortable lounge chairs, a large dining table, and double doors opening off the long porches both front and back. The view to the front is of the green square; in the back there's a large courtyard with white tables and chairs.

Guest rooms are furnished with English and American antiques, and each room has a unique personality. The Erastus Reed Room is masculine, with trophy heads mounted on the wall; the Sarah Reed Room is feminine, in soft yellow and white. Fascinating are the old-fashioned bathroom fixtures, right there in the rooms, although the footed tubs and the commodes are screened off; Sarah Reed's screen is of white lace.

Breakfast is juice and coffee, fresh fruit, sweet rolls, and quiche, so it's more than plain continental. And the Cafe at Ye Kendall Inn has more gourmet fare, from fettucine Alfredo to chicken cordon bleu. (Or try the Boerne Special, chicken-fried steak with country gravy.)

HOW TO GET THERE: I–87 goes right down the middle of Boerne, and the inn is at the west end of Main Square, on Blanco, which crosses the highway.

Cool and Underground, with Room to Spare

Central Texas, situated on the Llano Uplift, the Edwards Plateau, and the beautiful Hill Country, has some surprising underground formations worthy of the most dedicated cavers. Cave Without a Name, 11 miles north of Boerne, is one of Texas's best-kept secrets of the Hill Country. The cave is off the beaten track with almost nothing to tell you it's there. But when you descend the steps underground to a chain of six huge cathedral rooms, each opening into the next, you can understand the meaning of the word "cavernous."

Nearby Cascade Caverns, 16 miles southeast of Boerne, are long and narrow, requiring some stooping under still-dripping diamond-formation ceilings, but this offers an intimate look at many formations not usually seen so closely. Grand finale is the Cathedral Room, containing one of the largest waterfalls in Texas, plunging 100 feet down the cavern walls into a 20-foot-deep pool.

Natural Bridge Caverns, on Natural Bridge Cavern Road (FM 3009) 8 miles west of I–35 between San Antonio and New Braunfels, are named for a 60-foot natural limestone bridge that spans the entrance. One of the great show caves of the world, with wonderful stalagmites and stalactites, its different minerals cause colors comparable to melting rainbow sherbet.

Longhorn Cavern at Longhorn Cavern State Park, Park Road 4 near Burnet, is another beauty in this Central Texas chain formed eons ago, when the land was raised above primordial seas. Longhorn was the home of prehistoric cave dwellers, the refuge of beasts of prey, the site of secret gunpowder for the Confederate Army, a hideout for outlaws, and a dancehall! Around the turn of the century the Burnet-Llano County folks put down a plywood floor and held dances.

The Indian Council Chamber, the largest in the cavern, was chosen by the Indians because it was warmer in the winter and cooler in the summer than the outdoors overhead. It's always around 60 degrees in the cavern, so you might want a wrap. The Hall of Gems, the Queen's Throne and the Queen's Watchdog, a Giant Icicle, and a Frozen Waterfall are some of the formations to be seen along the 1½-mile trail.

Ant Street Inn ☎ ♥
Brenham, Texas 77833

INNKEEPERS: Pam and Tommy Traylor

ADDRESS/TELEPHONE: 107 West Commerce; (409) 836-7393 or
(800) 481-1951; fax (409) 836-7595

E-MAIL: stay@antstreetinn.com

ROOMS: 13; all with private bath, telephone, TV, and VCR.
No smoking inn.

RATES: $85 to $165, double; EPB.

OPEN: All year.

FACILITIES AND ACTIVITIES: Tubs for two, back porch with rocking
chairs. Nearby: Blue Bell Creameries, Antique Rose Emporium, antiques
shops, Brenham Heritage Museum, Monastery of St. Clare Miniature
Horse Farm, Texas Baseball Hall of Fame Museum.

*T*he innkeepers call this inn "a gloriously self-indulgent Historic
Hotel," which should give you an idea of the treat in store for you.
The one-hundred-year-old building has been restored, preserving
its 12-foot ceilings, fine wood floors, and nineteenth-century antiques.

What a choice there is, what with thirteen guest rooms. What fun to take
your pick by name or number, of
201 Mobile, 202 Richmond, 203
Savannah, 204 St. Louis, 205 New
Orleans, 206 Charleston, 207 Charlotte, 208 Louisville, 209 Memphis,
210 Galveston, 211 Atlanta, 212
Austin, or 214 Natchez, and see if
the name matches the decor.

The full, delicious breakfast
usually consists of fruit in season: a
main dish of casserole, pancakes or
French toast; breakfast meat and
breads; and "a yummy breakfast dessert," promises Pam.

HOW TO GET THERE: From Highway 290 take Business Highway 290 and
head into town; go to Commerce, 1 block south of the courthouse in Brenham's historic downtown.

Bonnie Gambrel
Bryan, Texas 77803

INNKEEPERS: Dorothy and Blocker Trant

ADDRESS/TELEPHONE: 600 East Twenty-seventh Street;
(409) 779–1022; fax (409) 779–1040

ROOMS: 4; 3 with private bath. No smoking inn.

RATES: $50 to $125, double; $20 to $25 extra person; EPB.

OPEN: All year.

FACILITIES AND ACTIVITIES: Swimming pool, hot tub, exercise room,
grill. Nearby: Bush Library, Brazos Valley Museum, Children's Museum,
Carnegie Library with dollhouse collection, Reed Arena, restaurants.

*Y*ou'll find the Bonnie Gambrel in the historical area of town, which
was the original location of the township of Bryan. The home was
built by a widow from Scotland in 1913, and its social debut was
the wedding of her daughter. The first house in town to be restored and put
on the National Registry of Historic Places, the house has more than a hundred square feet of leaded glass.

Dorothy and Blocker have been collecting antiques for some forty years,
and these, plus carefully chosen reproductions, furnish the inn. The Sitting
Room has its own wet bar and
refrigerator, the Yellow Room has
twin four-posters, the Douglas
Room has a single four-poster, and
the Gregorian Suite is furnished
with Queen Anne antiques.

If you want to be up and out
early, Dorothy will serve you a continental breakfast, but most guests
opt for the full treatment of Scotch
eggs, pumpkin waffles, and such.

HOW TO GET THERE: From Highway 6 Business (South Texas Avenue) turn
into East Twenty-seventh Street at the First American Bank and go 2 blocks
to South Preston Avenue. The inn is on the corner of East Twenty-seventh
and South Preston.

The Knittel Homestead 📠
Burton, Texas 77835

INNKEEPERS: Cindy and Steve Miller

ADDRESS/TELEPHONE: 520 Main Street; phone and fax (409) 289–5102

ROOMS: 3; all with private bath. No smoking inn.

RATES: $80 to $90, double; $15 extra person; EPB.

OPEN: All year.

FACILITIES AND ACTIVITIES: Restaurant, TV in sitting room. Nearby: National Archive Center for Cotton Ginning, tours of historic cotton gin, oldest operating Texaco Station in the United States, National Bike Trail; gateway to Bluebonnet Trails; Lake Somerville for fishing, boating, and picnicking; antiques shops in Burton and nearby Brenham, Carmine, and Round Top.

This old house with a rounded bulge on the outside was built in three stages. The first was in 1870, by Herman Knittel, a Confederate soldier and Texas senator who was the little town's first postmaster and merchant; today's inn kitchen and utility area were once the post office and mercantile store.

The front wing was added in 1870 as the family's residence. Herman Knittel, Jr., added the dining room, the upstairs bedrooms, and the first indoor plumbing in Burton. "But what this house is really known for," Steve says, "is the circular staircase." That accounts for the bulge, but that's not all. The staircase was transported from Germany and took several years to get here. "It finally arrived by oxcart—and the wrong stair risers had been shipped. It had to be put in backwards!" We went to take a look, and I found it imposing all the same. "I tell people the house looks like a Mississippi steamboat," Cindy says. Would you say it's painted cream and white? "No, that's chickpea," she says with a laugh.

Two of the upstairs guest rooms open onto the wraparound porch, and the back room has its own back stairs. Bath fixtures are the original ones, and Cindy stocks all baths with specialty soaps and bubble bath. "In these old-fashioned tubs, a bubble bath is a must," she says.

The Millers are originally from Houston. They came to Burton for the Burton Cotton Gin Festival, which was the 1993 winner of the Texas Down-

town Association's award for the best festival in the state. The cotton gin itself won an award for the best restoration in the state.

"We stayed at the inn, and we loved it," Steve says. "Cindy got kinda tired of banking, and I got tired of city living." They liked what they saw, and they decided to stay. Now they are the proud owners not only of the inn but also of the cafe on the corner, which has been listed as number eight in the top ten Texas cafes.

"This is your opportunity to country dine in the historic Burton Cafe and mingle with the locals," Steve says. For breakfast, how about Bananas Foster French Toast? Or thick country-style buttermilk flannel cakes, the Knittel House egg casserole, homemade muffins filled with fruit from the Knittle orchard, Burton fresh-ground sausage, or country-cured bacon? Had enough? Save room for the mile-high biscuits. Steve had years of experience in the restaurant business in Houston. The cafe was built in 1937 after the OK Saloon burned down and, he says, "When I saw the cafe, it was perfect, I loved it, all the locals—I like to say the cafe belongs to the local citizens. The folks need a place to communicate and eat."

He's so right: "It's the kind of place where I'll get a call asking, 'Is Chester there? When he comes in, have him call me.' People have packages dropped off. . . ." Steve beams.

HOW TO GET THERE: From Highway 290 take the Burton exit 12 miles west of Brenham. Go to Main Street; the inn is on the corner of Main and Washington, opposite the post office.

Long Point Inn
Burton, Texas 77835

INNKEEPERS: Jeannine and Bill Neinast

ADDRESS/TELEPHONE: 3800 FM 390 West; (409) 289–3171

E-MAIL: neins1@aol.com

ROOMS: 4; all with private bath; children welcome.

RATES: $75 to $125, double; $25 extra person over age six; EPB. Deposit required to hold reservation. American Express only.

OPEN: All year.

FACILITIES AND ACTIVITIES: Hide-a-beds, cribs, playpen, high chair, and booster chair; fishing in five ponds stocked with catfish and bass; 175 acres of cattle ranchland; swimming; hiking. Nearby: restaurants, Miniature Horse Farm at Monastery of St. Clare, Star of the Republic Museum at Washington-on-the-Brazos State Park.

"We're so pleased. We never expected to be so busy and to have so many happy guests," says Jeannine. The Neinasts opened their lovely chalet-style home to guests because they wanted to share the wonderful lifestyle they have created for themselves out on the land.

"Come and feed the cows, fish the ponds, traipse the woods, listen to the quiet," they say enticingly. They especially welcome families with children. "After all," Bill says with a laugh, "we have nine grandchildren." And when you return from the cows, the ponds, and the woods, you'll find yourself in the lap of luxury in the form of a large story-and-a-half house that is completely and wholeheartedly turned over to guests. There's a piano in the parlor—may guests play it? But of course. "In fact, we would love it if they would come and play. But so far nobody has," mourns Jeannine.

She compensates by lavishing on her guests such marvelous breakfasts as eggs Newport (with sour cream and bacon) or a casserole of cottage cheese, spiced ham, Monterey Jack cheese, mushrooms, and chili peppers—all with biscuits and homemade wild plum jam. The fruit compote is always a hit with children, "and of course we have cereal for the youngsters who want it," Bill says.

Exciting for city kids is a hike on the land and a chance to spot the deer, raccoons, possums, fox, and armadillos that live at Long Point Inn; rabbits,

too, both jackrabbits and cottontail. Birds are there aplenty: bluebirds and jays, hawks and crows, robins and hummingbirds. "Kids especially like it when I take them down to feed the cattle," Bill says. "They're so gentle, they come and stick their heads in the truck for ranch cubes—that's like candy to them, and they'll take it from your hand." (They don't bite, he adds reassuringly. "They don't have the right teeth for it even if they wanted to, which they don't.")

Other country doings include swimming in an old-fashioned swimming hole beneath a waterfall and fishing with a string and pole (or bring your own more sophisticated equipment) in the farm ponds. Outings include a visit to the miniature horses raised nearby. "The little folks, often that's the high point of their trip, especially if they get to see a little foal."

Pie, cookies, coffee, and always Texas's great Blue Bell Ice Cream are served in the evening. The Neinasts believe in Texas hospitality with a capital *H*. Long Point Inn is an ideal hideaway from the hectic pace of city living—and, for youngsters, a wonderful introduction to the joys of the countryside.

And a wonderful introduction to life in Texas's past is a night spent in the log cabin, a cabin that was built in 1860 by Bill's great-grandfather. It has an intriguing story. "Back in the sixties it was slated for an Early Texas Village at Washington-on-the-Brazos State Park," Bill says. "But they never got around to doing anything, and meanwhile it was deteriorating." So the Neinasts have restored it in all its original cedar beauty.

HOW TO GET THERE: From U.S. Highway 290 take FM (Farm Road) 2679 to FM 390. Turn right; Long Point Inn is on the left on a hill not far from the intersection.

The Proctor House
Calvert, Texas 77837

INNKEEPERS: Margaret and Louis Mabry

ADDRESS/TELEPHONE: 508 East Gregg (mailing address: P.O. Box 778); (409) 364–3702 or (800) 856–5157

ROOMS: 4; 1 with private bath. No smoking inn.

RATES: $85 to $95, double; $15 extra person; EPB.

OPEN: All year.

FACILITIES AND ACTIVITIES: Nearby: historic Buildings, Virginia Field Park.

*I*n the 1800s Calvert was the third largest city in Texas, but you'd never think so nowadays. So this town of some 1,000 residents is a great place to get away from it all. The Proctor House was built in 1880 and was restored in 1991. You'll enjoy the stained-glass windows, the lovely staircase, the seven coal-burning fireplaces, and the wraparound porch with its swing and rocking chairs.

The Hunt Room features a king-size bed and romantic gas logs in the fireplace; the Annie Rose Room, with a queen-size iron bed, a daybed, and a trundle bed, can sleep four. In the Blue Boy Room you'll see an impressive antique bed and an old trunk, while the Plantation Room boasts a massive Victorian bed. In fact "Victorian" describes all of Calvert's business buildings as well as its residences.

Breakfast usually is delicious with quiches, blueberry pancakes, or pecan waffles and muffins and fresh fruit. Then enjoy this grand old town lost in time, full of spacious oak trees and beautiful antiques.

HOW TO GET THERE: Calvert is located approximately 60 miles south of Waco (on I–35) on Highway 6. Turn left on Gregg Street, crossing the railroad tracks, and go 3 blocks to 508 Gregg.

Sugar Hill Retreat
Carmine, Texas 78932

INNKEEPERS: Diana and Reuben Wunderlich

ADDRESS/TELEPHONE: 325 Sugar Hill Lane (mailing address: P.O. Box 9); (409) 278–3039

WEB SITE: www.virtualcities.com

ROOMS: 4; none with private bath, share 3; children welcome. No smoking inn.

RATES: $65 to $75, double; $15 extra person; EPB; no credit cards.

OPEN: All year.

FACILITIES AND ACTIVITIES: Walking trails, pond fishing, porch swing, hammock in big oak tree. Nearby: more than fifteen antiques shops, Lake Somerville, Round Top with the International Festival-Institute concerts, and University of Texas Winedale Historical Center and Shakespeare Festival.

*T*his restored 1900s farmhouse was moved from a nearby farming community to this charming small town. "Even though the population is small," Diane says, "the city park, local stores and services, and numerous antiques shops are outstanding."

Each of the four spacious guest rooms is decorated in themes from the early part of the century. Family heirlooms add to the interesting historical accents of Central Texas. Each room has a full-size bed and a roll-away, and the three baths that guests share offer a choice of a shower or a soak in a claw-foot tub.

The full country breakfast includes eggs, breakfast meat, breads, and fresh fruit as well as coffee, tea, and hot chocolate. Snacks and cold drinks are also provided for guests' enjoyment.

HOW TO GET THERE: Carmine is located on Highway 290 between Brenham and Giddings. The inn is north of 290 with an entrance on Thigpen Street running parallel to the highway.

The Mulberry House
Chappell Hill, Texas 77426

INNKEEPERS: Katie and Myrv Cron

ADDRESS/TELEPHONE: Farm Road 2447 (P.O. Box 5); (409) 830–1311

ROOMS: 5, in main house and guest cottage; all with private bath and phone; 2 with TV. No smoking inn.

RATES: $75 to $85, double, weekends; discount during week; EPB and evening snacks. No credit cards.

OPEN: All year.

FACILITIES AND ACTIVITIES: Large backyard, croquet. Nearby: Brenham restaurants and shops; historic Chappell Hill with restaurants, Bluebonnet Festival (April), Fourth of July parade, Scarecrow Festival (October); Washington-on-the-Brazos (capital of the Republic of Texas), Star of the Republic Museum, miniature horses at Monastery of St. Clare.

Mulberry House was the home of prosperous cotton farmer John Sterling Smith and his wife, Marie, and their descendants from 1874 to 1983. Innkeepers Katie and Myrv bought the house as a country retreat from the hustle and bustle of Houston, an hour and a half away. First they built the "barn," a suite of two bedrooms, living room, and kitchen, and lived there three years while they restored the house. Now the barn serves as both lovely guest quarters and Myrv's woodworking shop on the first floor.

Myrv is a consummate woodworking artist; examples of his fine bird carvings decorate the inn. There are hooded merganser and bobwhite families, all perched on wonderful pieces of driftwood, all detailed down to the last feather.

I wondered how Katie and Myrv had gotten into innkeeping. "Myrv was always working in the yard or in his shop, and I was always in the house," says

Katie with a laugh, "and one day I was in a gift shop (on nearby Brenham's square) and a young couple was looking for a place to stay. I said, 'Come home with me,' and they did, and we had a wonderful time!"

In Miss Marie's Room, named for the lady who lived there fifty years, you'll find two wonderful Jenny Lind beds that Katie hunted down expressly for that room. The huge armoire is a find, too, and the clutch of teddy bears sitting in a corner look most pleased with their quarters. The inn is filled with unusual antique pieces—some from the Smith family, who lived in the house 110 years.

Katie makes delicious breakfasts in the large sunny kitchen: egg and cheese soufflé, or ham, bacon, and egg puff, with grits and cranberry-orange muffins. At 6:00 in the evening, before guests go out to dinner at one of Brenham's fine restaurants, there's an informal cocktail hour, with neighbors sometimes joining in. "We come and go," says Katie, "and expect our guests to make themselves at home."

"Lots of people bring their bicycles," says Myrv. "They ride from here to Washington-on-the-Brazos." A round-trip of 32 miles is a good day's outing.

Chappell Hill was founded in 1847 and named for an early Texas hunter. Before the Civil War it was beginning to grow into a prominent educational and agricultural center. Today it's a charming, small village, with several annual festivals to remind the rest of Texas it's still there.

HOW TO GET THERE: Turn north off U.S. Highway 290 onto FM (Farm Road) 1155 (Chappell Hill's Main Street) and drive to FM 2447 (Chestnut Street). Mulberry House is ⁹⁄₁₀ mile east of the intersection.

Stagecoach Inn
Chappell Hill, Texas 77426

INNKEEPER: Elizabeth Moore

ADDRESS/TELEPHONE: Main at Chestnut (mailing address: P.O. Box 339); (409) 836–9515

ROOMS: 6; 4 with private bath; handicapped accessible. No smoking inn.

RATES: $90, double; EPB. No credit cards.

FACILITIES AND ACTIVITIES: Beautiful grounds and garden. Nearby: good restaurants; Chappell Hill, in the heart of early Texas history; Washington-on-the-Brazos; Star of the Republic Museum; St. Clare Monastery, which raises miniature horses.

"We want to excel in hospitality," says Elizabeth, who is carrying on the tradition of this historic inn. The Stagecoach Inn was built in 1850 and was once a major stop for the coaches it was named for. The gorgeous grounds, like a small estate, are on a corner surrounded by a white picket fence and are ablaze with color overflowing from beds and pots of flowers. All summer long, flowerpots are bursting with red, white, and pink geraniums; the flower beds are bordered in scarlet begonias; and the crepe myrtle trees shower blossoms all around. There are four separate terraces from which to drink in all this beauty. "People enjoy them so much. It gets more beautiful all the time," says this hardworking and proud innkeeper-gardener.

"We start the bulbs in the middle of December, especially the bearded iris," Elizabeth says of the flowers that appear at each place on the breakfast table. If it's not iris time, perhaps a sprig of rosemary will be at your place, but it will always be something from this fabulous garden.

Chappell Hill

The inn fronts the road, and both the Coach House and Weems Cottage are on the grounds in the rear, all part of the three-acre historic site. Breakfast can be short-order, like soft-boiled or scrambled eggs, or maybe eggs Charlotte instead, along with apple strudel, whiskey coffee cake, homemade muffins, croissants, or zucchini bread. Add grape jelly, juice of your choice, and fresh fruit in season, and you have a feast.

Whether you stay in Weems Cottage, Lottie's, or the Coach House, you have the run of the place. Weems Cottage, with two rooms and a bath, was built in 1866, and the front and back porches are full of rocking chairs, just like in the good old days. Lottie's is a 133-year-old Greek Revival house across the road from the inn, and its five rooms include two living room areas as well as the guest rooms, all furnished with authentic Texas heirlooms and antiques. The Coach House, newly remodeled into a one-bedroom suite, is way in the back under spreading old trees. "We're flexible," says Elizabeth. "We've slept an entire bridge club, an antiques group, a football weekend—as many as fifteen to twenty guests."

Whenever you spend the night, you can have a tour of the inn, which is listed on the National Register of Historic Places.

HOW TO GET THERE: Turn north off U.S. Highway 290 onto Farm Road 1155 (Chappell Hill's Main Street) and drive to FM 2447 (Chestnut Street). Stagecoach Inn is across the corner to the left, and Lottie's is on the right.

The Flippen Place 📱
College Station, Texas 77845

INNKEEPER: Susan Flippen

ADDRESS/TELEPHONE: 1199 Haywood Drive; (888) 696–7930; fax (409) 693–8458

ROOMS: 3; all with private bath and telephone. No smoking inn.

RATES: $80 to $115, double; $20 extra person; EPB.

OPEN: All year.

FACILITIES AND ACTIVITIES: Bicycles, two gardens, fifty heavily wooded acres with hiking trails and two stocked fishing ponds. Nearby: George Bush Presidential Library and Museum, Texas A&M University, Messina Hof Vineyards, antiques shops, restaurants.

*G*uests here have the freedom of fifty acres of solitude among the cattle as well as the Great Room and the Loft indoors. "Our goal was to create a warm and inviting place where you could *really* relax," Susan says. The inn is in a 170-year-old Amish barn transported from Ohio, twenty-two tons of 40-foot timbers to reassemble with wooden pegs!

But Susan and husband Flip ("who occasionally enjoys coffee with guests") were equal to it, and now the "barn" has three guest rooms upstairs with baths, a Great Room with 30-foot ceiling and huge windows looking out into the woods, and antique furnishings "that are meant to be used," says Susan.

While Susan does her best to serve a full breakfast daily, the Flippen Place is so relaxing that not only are guests permitted to select their own dining times, they can elect breakfast outdoors—or breakfast in bed!

HOW TO GET THERE: From College Station travel south on Highway 6. Exit Rock Prairie Road and go ⁹⁄₁₀ miles east. Take the second left onto Bird Pond and travel ½ mile and turn left onto Frost. Go to the first right, which is Haywood. Cross the cattle guard at the end of Haywood Drive and you're on the inn grounds.

Haven River Inn
Comfort, Texas 78013

INNKEEPERS: Danese Ofsdahl and Libby Ellison

ADDRESS/TELEPHONE: Farm Road 473 (P.O. Box 899); (830) 995–3834 or (888) 995–3834; fax (830) 995–4335

ROOMS: 10; all with private bath. No smoking inn.

RATES: $95, double; $10 extra person; EPB.

OPEN: All year.

FACILITIES AND ACTIVITIES: Recreation Room with Ping-Pong and pool table, swimming pool, hiking, fishing. Nearby: Monument to Union soldiers in a Confederate town, many structures on National Register of Historic Places, shops, and art galleries.

*B*uilt in 1911 as a family summer home on the lovely Guadalupe River, the inn is just east of the town of Comfort, a quiet farming community settled by German immigrants in 1854. This refuge sits on twenty-three acres of trees and rollling meadows on the edge of the cypress-lined river. The rambling yellow house is surrounded by porches, and there's a fascinating petrified-wood gazebo on the grounds, built by Dionicio Rodriques in the 1940s.

The huge house contains ten guest rooms (that lumber tycoon builder must have had a very large family!), and you have a choice of rooms decorated with fresh country charm or more rustic style, with hewn-wood bedposts on king-size or twin beds. The

Rose Parlor offers a cool deep-pink-and-white retreat, with bookshelves on each side of the fireplace.

The innkeepers promise you an "elegant breakfast with variety," so every morning the meal will be a surprise. A specialty is orange marsala French toast with freshly whipped cream, and there's always homemade granola with yogurt and fruit.

HOW TO GET THERE: From I–10 take exit 524 (FM 473) and go right at the fork onto Highway 87 north. Take a right at the blinking light and go east on FM 473. The inn gates are on the right a mile or so up the road, just beyond the overpass.

The Delforge Place 📱
Fredericksburg, Texas 78624

INNKEEPERS: Betsy, Pete, and George Delforge

ADDRESS/TELEPHONE: 710 Ettie Street; (800) 997–0462; fax (830) 990–8230

E-MAIL: delplace@speakez.net

WEB SITE: www.speakez.net/delforgeplace

ROOMS: 4; all with private bath, telephone, and TV. No smoking inn.

RATES: $90 to $95, double; $15 extra person; EPB.

OPEN: All year.

FACILITIES AND ACTIVITIES: Picnic baskets, patio with fountain, Ping-Pong, pool table, croquet, horseshoes, archery, sandbox. Nearby: Fredericksburg's famous Main Street (7 blocks away), with German restaurants and *biergartens*, Admiral Nimitz Museum, other historical museums, and antiques shops; Wildflower Farms; LBJ Ranch (approximately 15 miles east), Enchanted Rock State Park (18 miles north).

"We get some of the most interesting people," Betsy says. "That's why we settled here; this is such a vibrant, international little town, what with the Nimitz Museum and the LBJ Ranch." The Delforge Place is interesting and international itself, what with the front Map Room and the Quebec Room sporting ancient maps and other mementos from Betsy's sea-captain ancestor, head of the first merchant fleet that opened the Harbor of Yokohama to American sailing ships.

Guest room decor is ever changing, since Betsy lets her antique furniture and paintings go out on exhibit to museums on the East Coast. It follows that Oriental pieces join with the American, European, and family heirlooms in furnishing the old house, once a one-room "Sunday house"— you'll have to go to Fredericksburg to find out what a Sunday house is. This one was built in 1898 by German pioneer Ferdinand Koeppen on a tract of land set aside by the German Emigration Company as a communal garden. The house was moved to its present location in 1975 and during restoration was made considerably larger.

Guests relax in one of the two *versamel,* or gathering rooms, with coffee and tea, quiet games, or books off the shelves (or television, if they insist!). The Delforges stress that guests are welcome to come and go as they please: There's a lot to see and do in town.

And guests are sent off with a good start—one of Betsy's famous breakfasts. She has always featured her specialties of German Sour Cream Twists and San Saba French Toast (which is marinated in orange brandy and thick and crusty with orange peel and San Saba pecans. Delicious!). Now she's having fun varying them with no fewer than seven different breakfast menus. I hope you're lucky enough to catch her seven-course gourmet Fredericksburg Breakfast, a sampling of all the wonderful fruits, meats, breads, and pastries of the historical town.

"Food and fashion go together for me," Betsy says, and her past includes both food testing and fabric design. She grows her own herbs in hanging baskets over the flagstone patio. "When the apples come in the fall, we have sausage and apple crepes," which sounds to me like a great reason for an autumn visit.

The Upper Deck is named for Betsy's seafaring interests. It has its own outside staircase up to the deck, bright with nautical flags flying in the breeze. Skylights and an octagonal window brighten the spacious guest room, which has such original touches as weathered wooden barrels set on end as nightstands and a globe of the world on a stand, for the sailors.

HOW TO GET THERE: From Main Street (U.S. Highway 290) turn south on South Adams to Walnut, then left on Walnut for 3 blocks to Ettie Street. The inn, at 710 Ettie, is the Victorian house on the corner to your left.

Magnolia House
Fredericksburg, Texas 78624

INNKEEPERS: Joyce and Patrick Kennard

ADDRESS/TELEPHONE: 101 East Hackberry; (800) 880–4374; fax (830) 997–0766

E-MAIL: magnolia@hctc.net

WEB SITE: www.magnolia-house.com

ROOMS: 5; all with private bath and TV. No smoking inn.

RATES: $85 to $125 double; $25 extra person; EPB.

OPEN: All year.

FACILITIES AND ACTIVITIES: Porches, large patio with fountain, waterfall and fish pond; access to swimming and tennis club. Nearby: restaurants, antiques shops, Admiral Nimitz Museum and Walk of the Pacific War, Pioneer Museum, historic Sunday houses, Enchanted Rock State Park (18 miles north).

*T*his lovely home was built in 1923 for Edward Stein and his family. He was the architect for the Gillespie County Courthouse (Fredericksburg is the seat of Gillespie County), so it stands to reason that he would do a fine job for his own home, too! He handpicked every piece of lumber that went into building the home, making it one of the most carefully constructed houses in town. Now Magnolia House is a bona fide Recorded Texas Historic Landmark, so designated by the Texas Historical Commission. And it's also a very lovely inn.

Although Joyce and Patrick are new owners of the inn, they've made sure that beautiful antiques and family heirlooms continue to create the inn's charming atmosphere. The inn is light and bright and welcoming, with large, comfortable guest rooms and the kind of parlor and dining room that you'd like to call your own.

"We know that little things mean a lot when you choose an inn," Joyce says, "so we pay a lot of attention to details," such as fresh flowers, home-brewed coffee and other beverages in the evenings, monogrammed terry robes. . . . And their famous Southern Breakfast includes fresh fruit, home-made muffins, and juice—and that's only for starters. Breakfast is a buffet, and it changes every day. Maybe there will be waffles or crepes with fruit and whipped cream. Usually, too, there's an egg entree with bacon or sausage, biscuits and gravy—and always sweet rolls for that little touch of extra energy.

"It's all prepared from scratch," Joyce says as she brings out the antique china and silver on which to serve it all. Both the Magnolia Suite and the Bluebonnet Suite have private entrances; the Magnolia has a huge living room with fireplace; the Bluebonnet has a kitchen, complete with an antique refrigerator—that's still working! The Lilli Marleen Room, also on the ground floor, is a grand room with longleaf yellow pine flooring, a king-sized bed, and a triple dresser with a double mirror.

The American Beauty Room has a king-sized bed and a beautiful view of the waterfall and fish pond in the garden. The Peach Blossom Room's ceiling is decorated with a stenciled trim, and the room is furnished with a queen-sized bed and an antique dressing table.

Although the house has been remodeled, something special is still there: an unusual and delightful pass-through sort of small walkway, with a built-in small basin equipped with a genuine old hand pump. "All our guests have to try it," Joyce says. I certainly did, and although it took some pressure, I finally got water gurgling into the basin.

Built into the wall opposite this fun "toy" is the house's original icebox. Now, of course, it's been electrified. It opens on both sides of the wall (on the other side is a second comfortable common room), and guests can help themselves to the complimentary beverages therein.

Cady, the Kennards' beautiful golden retriever, isn't allowed in the house, so you'll have to pet the friendly dog outdoors.

HOW TO GET THERE: From Main Street (Highway 290 east) turn north on Adams Street to Hackberry, which runs parallel to Main. The inn is on the southeast corner of Adams and Hackberry.

River View Inn and Farm
Fredericksburg, Texas 78624

INNKEEPER: Helen K. Taylor

ADDRESS/TELEPHONE: Highway 16 South, HC 12 Box 49C;
(830) 997–8555 or (800) 364–8555

ROOMS: 6; 4 with private bath, 2 with phone, 1 with TV; wheelchair
accessible. Pets permitted.

RATES: $90 to $110; $10 to $20 extra person; EPB.

OPEN: All year.

FACILITIES AND ACTIVITIES: Farm acres to wander over, river to
fish in, cattle to visit, vegetable garden, books, and games. Nearby: Lady
Bird Johnson Municipal Park, with swimming pool, tennis, and nine-
hole golf course is 1³/10 miles away; Fredericksburg has Admiral Nimitz
Museum and German heritage museums; Enchanted Rock State Park
(18 miles north).

reezy is the word for River View Inn and Farm. It's set on a hill in
the Hill Country and has a breezeway that catches a round-the-
clock cool wind. I could just sit there for hours, taking in the
sweep of the green hills and listening to the lowing of the longhorns that
Helen's neighbors raise and that sometimes graze in Helen's fields.

Helen's guests have the run of
the house. The kitchen, the large
and comfortably furnished living
room with its big stone fireplace,
the glass-enclosed sunporch, the
breakfast room with its china cabinet full of heirloom china, the
framed German mottoes, and the

collection of framed bird pictures (mostly hummingbirds, which are Helen's
favorite) all conspire to make guests feel truly at home. Helen's breakfast is
hearty enough for a rancher, too: fresh local German sausage ("turkey
instead of German sausage for the fat-conscious"), scrambled eggs with
jalapeños (but not too hot, says Helen), cheese, biscuits, fresh peach and
cherry cobbler, jellies, and jams. She caters to vegeterians, as well.

HOW TO GET THERE: Inn is 4½ miles south of Fredericksburg on Highway 16;
1 mile south of Lady Bird Johnson Municipal Park. To the left you'll see a
fence and a cattle guard. Drive over it and there you are.

The Legend of Enchanted Rock

Enchanted Rock State Park encompasses a massive dome of solid Precambrian pink granite, covering more than 600 acres and rising more than 300 feet in height. Today the delight of hikers, climbers, and rappelers, it was famed in Indian legend. Some believed that it was haunted; others feared to even set foot on it, believing it to be the site of human sacrifices, while others used its height as a rallying point.

All held it in awe and reverence, believing it both a holy place and, perhaps, a place housing evil spirits. Some believed that ghost fires flickered on the crest on moonlit nights. Enchanted Rock is considered among the oldest exposed rocks in North America, one billion years old. The trail that leads to the top is worth the rather strenuous effort when you take a look at the view.

Ranch House Bed and Breakfast
Georgetown, Texas 78628

INNKEEPERS: Millie and Ed Pastor

ADDRESS/TELEPHONE: 95 Redbird Trail; (512) 863–2331

ROOMS: 4; 2 with private bath, telephone, and TV. Children welcome. Small pets permitted.

RATES: $50 to $75; EPB. No credit cards.

OPEN: All year.

FACILITIES AND ACTIVITIES: Swings, basketball and Ping-Pong, country walks, deer, cows. Nearby: Lake Georgetown Swimming Beach, Sun City Retirement Village, Georgetown and Southwestern University, Inner Space Caverns, Candle Factory.

*E*njoy the country quiet in an early Texas-style house with the quilts and the cows, says the invitation from Millie and Ed. They offer you ranch-style enjoyment, and on their twelve acres of land you can pick some fresh vegetables from the garden, feed the cows, fish in the lake, or hike the "back twelve" acres. Children are welcome at this country place just outside busy Georgetown, and they can experience old-time country living among the deer and the cattle.

In the guest bedrooms you'll find Millie's handmade quilts among the antiques, and you're even invited to put a few stitches in her current one—if you dare.

The continental breakfast includes fresh fruit salad, juices, homemade breads and muffins, cereal, yogurt, and herb teas among the beverages.

HOW TO GET THERE: From I-35 go west on FM 2338 (Andice Road) 6 miles to FM 3405. Turn left and make the first right turn (Redbird Trail); the inn is the first house on your right.

Tacitus T. Clay House
Independence, Texas

INNKEEPER: Thelma Zwiener

ADDRESS/TELEPHONE: Mailing address: 9445 FM 390, East Brenham, Texas 77833; (409) 836–1916

ROOMS: 4; 3 with private bath, telephone, and TV. Children welcome.

RATES: $45 to $75; extra adult $35, child $15; EPB. No credit cards.

OPEN: All year.

FACILITIES AND ACTIVITIES: Hot tub in gazebo. Nearby: antique Rose Emporium, Lake Somerville, Blue Bell Creamery, Washington-on-the-Brazos State Park.

aptain Clay's House may be located in a tiny town of 140 citizens, but it looms large in Texas history (see sidebar). The one-and-a-half-story frame house was built by Clay in the 1850s, and a sitting room, dining hall, and two bedrooms open off a grand hallway. After he finished the downstairs he planned to make the upper floor a ballroom! But the Civil War got in the way: He lost a leg and could never dance again.

The guest rooms in the main house are furnished with Victorian antiques, some of which are original to the house. They offer a choice of king or twin four-posters, and, although the beds are antique, the comfortable mattresses are new, custom-made ones. The original Cistern House, small but cozy, has twin beds and its own bath, as does the Gate House.

In the morning you'll sit down to a country breakfast with fresh eggs from the inn's henhouse. From 5:00 to 7:00 P.M., wine and cheeses, soft drinks and tea are served.

HOW TO GET THERE: From I–35 go west on FM 2338 (Andice Road) 6 miles to FM 3405. Turn left and make the first right turn (Redbird Trail); the inn is the first on your right.

A Red-White-and-Blue Town

The town of Independence began life as Coles Settlement when it was settled in 1824 by John P. Coles. He was one of Stephen F. Austin's 300 original families, brought from "back East" to settle Texas under the Mexican Empresario system. (Washington, known sometimes as Washington-on-the Brazos or Old Washington, about 15 miles due east, was the original site of the 300.) The village name was changed to Independence in 1836 to commemorate the independence of Texas from Mexico after the Texas Revolution.

The town square was laid out to be the Washington County courthouse, but Brenham, 10 miles south, won by two votes in a heated county-seat election. Today the small village takes pride in its links with the past and treasures the historical sites to be seen in the town, such as the cemetery where Sam Houston, Jr., Moses Austin Bryan, and veterans from all U.S. wars—from the Revolution through World War II—are buried.

River Run Inn 📱
Kerrville, Texas 78028

INNKEEPERS: Jean and Ron Williamson

ADDRESS/TELEPHONE: 120 Francisco Lemos Street; (800) 460-7170;
fax (830) 896-5402

E-MAIL: riverrun@ktc.com

ROOMS: 6; all with private bath and telephone, 4 with TV; wheelchair
accessible.

RATES: $95 to $135; $10 extra person; EPB.

OPEN: All year.

FACILITIES AND ACTIVITIES: Parlor with board games and TV. Nearby:
Riverside Nature Center, Cowboy Artists of America Museum, Hill
Country Museum, Kerrville Camera Safari, Texas Heritage Music
Museum, Kerrville Folk Festival.

*E*verybody loves to love the Texas Hill Country, and this inn, built of
native stone reminiscent of the area's early German settlers, who
adapted their traditional architecture to the terrain, has a romantic
history. The first recorded owner of the property was none other than
famous Texas Ranger "Captain Jack" Hays. The land was granted to him in
1847 by the first governor of the
Republic of Texas for his services to the Republic.

The inn is filled with turn-
of-the-century Texas memorabilia; it also reflects the German
and Mexican influence of this
part of Texas. Choose from
Colonel "Jack" Hays (Captain
Jack), Captain McNelly, "Shang-
hai" Pierce, Walter Prescott
Webb, J. Frank Dobie, and
Elmer Kelton, and Ron will tell you all about them. Each room has a queen-
size bed, and the bath includes a whirlpool tub as well as a shower.

Breakfast favorites are the Guadalupe River Fries, the Southwest Quiche,
and River Run Royale (baked in a bundt pan and loaded with pecans and
cranberries).

HOW TO GET THERE: From I–10 take the Kerrville exit (508) and turn left under the overpass, which puts you on Sidney Baker Street. Follow this into downtown and turn right on Water Street to Francisco Lemos Street. Turn left; the inn is on the right. The innkeepers say please note that the circular drive is marked ENTRANCE and EXIT.

The Antlers Hotel 📱
Kingsland, Texas 78639

INNKEEPERS: Lori and Anthony Mayfield

ADDRESS/TELEPHONE: 1001 King Street; (800) 383–0007; fax (915) 388–6488

ROOMS: 10; all with private bath and telephone; TV in cabins; wheelchair accessible. Children welcome in cabins.

RATES: $120 to $150; $10 extra person; continental breakfast, hotel only.

OPEN: All year.

FACILITIES AND ACTIVITIES: Game room in hotel basement with pool table, TV and VCR; treadmill, keyboard and guitar, card table, checker table, board games; fifteen acres of woodlands, water activities on 1,500 feet of Lake LBJ with three docks for boating, fishing, congregating; two boat slips available. Nearby: golf, Longhorn Caverns.

he Antlers Hotel began life as a railroad resort, built when the railroad came to the Hill Country's Highland Lakes, a chain of lakes built by damming the Lower Colorado River. Opening its doors in 1901, it welcomed fishermen and vacationers from Austin until 1923, when it was sold by the Austin & Northwestern Railroad and closed to the public. It's open and running again today, with six suites and four cabins on fifteen acres of Lake LBJ. The Railroad Suite, Antlers' Suite, Cattleman's Suite, Victorian Suite, Drummer's Suite, and the 1901 Room all have private entrances off wide porches. They're furnished with antiques from the hotel's early days. The cabins are complete with kitchens and porches.

Breakfast is for hotel guests only—in the cabins you're on your own, which is what the kitchens are for, naturally! The hotel breakfast is a full continental, served buffet style in the hotel.

HOW TO GET THERE: Kingsland is on Highway 281 between Highway 71 and Burnet. Once in town, turn onto Chamberlain Street; go 1 block to King Street and number 1001.

Colts a - Blazing

Apache and Comanche raids were the bane of early settlers in this part of the Hill County (after all, it was *their* land!)—until along came Texas Ranger John Coffee (Captain Jack) Hays. As one of Stephen F. Austin's band, his job was to protect those pioneers. But the rangers were at a disadvantage because a Comanche could charge, shooting off maybe half a dozen arrows in the time it took a ranger to reload his single-shot sidearm.

The army had scoffed at Samuel Colt's new-fangled invention, the five-shot repeater. Not Captain Jack: He quickly saw the advantage of the gun against a Comanche rain of arrows. He got a chance to test the new weapon in 1840, when a party of seventy Comanches surprised Hays and fourteen other rangers along the Pedernales River.

Instead of running for cover to reload their rifles, the rangers charged, Colt pistols blazing. The baffled Indians, used to empty guns after one round, were driven off by these seemingly inexhaustible guns, and they soon gave up on this part of Texas.

Inn above Onion Creek
Kyle, Texas 78640

INNKEEPER: Janie Orr

ADDRESS/TELEPHONE: 4444 Highway 150 West; (800) 579–7686;
fax (512) 268–1090

E-MAIL: onioncrk@Freewwweb.com

ROOMS: 9; all with private bath, telephone, and TV; wheelchair
accessible. No smoking inn.

RATES: $150 to $250; $30 extra person; EPB, lunch and dinner
included.

OPEN: All year.

FACILITIES AND ACTIVITIES: Swimming pool, 5 miles of trails in the
Hill Country, leading to an overlook of Onion Creek; cooking, art
class, and musical weekends. Nearby: San Marcos, with outlet shopping mall; canoeing, tubing, and swimming on the San Marcos River;
galleries, restaurants, and shops in Wimberley and Gruene.

The inn is a true retreat, set on 500 acres of the Texas Hill Country
5 miles away from the nearest town: tiny Kyle, once the home of
novelist Katherine Ann Porter. Janie knew exactly what she
wanted. It took longer to find than she expected, but "looking at land was a
lot of fun," Janie says. "We wanted to be no more than 30 miles from Austin,
yet off a picturesque road that made you feel you were going back in time."

While the setting is rural, the accommodations are not. Each room is
large, with room for a sitting area of sofa, loveseat, or chaise in front of a
stone fireplace. Shelves to put things on are built on one side of each fireplace, and there is room to move around the bed and bedside tables. And the
bathrooms are to rave about. Four of them have huge Jacuzzis, several have
large two-party showers enclosed in glass bricks, and for light several have
French doors opening onto small wrought-iron balconies.

The exterior is rustic. "We were really trying to find an old ranch house to
save, but they turned out to be scarce," Janie says. So they built their own old
ranch house out of cedar and Hill Country stone; upstairs porch railings, of
rough cedar posts, are very early-homestead evoking!

Breakfast is a delicious torta of venison sausage ("My son is a mighty hunter," Janie says), eggs Parmesan and cheddar cheese, with O'Brien potatoes and homemade biscuits, all prefaced by Rio Star grapefruit, the crème de la crème of the famous Texas Ruby Red. One dinner—"supper" in these parts—was chicken enchilada *suizas*, black beans, corn dip Olé and Oreo cheesecake. Janie is generous with recipes.

The wide porches in the rear look out over miles and miles of Hill Country, with not a sign of civilization in sight. The Captain Fergus Kyle Room, downstairs, is both wheelchair accessible and wheelchair prepared, with railings and a wheel-in shower.

The Jack Hayes Room, upstairs, in a rust-and-gray color scheme, has a king-size bed and a chaise longue in front of its stone fireplace. Both the Hayes Room and the Michaelis Room next door open onto a porch with a wonderful north view. "People like to stay up late on the porch and talk and rock," Janie says. It sure is restful! Convenient, too: There are back stairs leading down to the swimming pool.

The Michaelis Room's accent wall is a medium blue, very pleasant. All rooms have wonderful huge armoires, and I wondered how Janie had found so many. "I haunted antiques and garage sales—and watched the ads like crazy!" She also found an artisan who could build some of the rustic-look pieces she wanted, like the tables and chairs in the large dining room.

HOW TO GET THERE: From I–35 take exit 213, Kyle, and go west on Kyle's main Center Street to the stop sign at FM 150 (Highway 150). Take FM 150 and go 5³/₁₀ miles to the inn gate on the right; there is a sign. Turn in at the gate and go 1 mile, slowly, on a narrow, curved road until you reach the inn.

Trail's End Inn
Leander, Texas 78641

INNKEEPERS: JoAnn and Tom Patty

ADDRESS/TELEPHONE: 12223 Trail's End Road #7; (512) 267–2901 or (800) 850–2901

ROOMS: 4; 2 with private bath and TV. Children welcome. No smoking inn.

RATES: $85 to $125, double; $20 extra person; children under ten free; EPB.

OPEN: All year.

FACILITIES AND ACTIVITIES: Swimming pool, bicycles, toys and games, gift shop. Nearby: Hill Country Flyer (steam train), Lake Travis, bird sanctuary, shops and restaurants in Lakeline Mall.

Trail's End Inn is really, really out in the country—on six acres of land overlooking the Hill Country. From the Observation Deck (like a widow's walk) on top of the house, you can catch a glimpse of Lake Travis as well as lots of the Travis County Audubon Society Bird Sanctuary. The entry is large and open, two stories high.

The living room walls are cranberry red with white molding, and there's a 1930s leather rocker the same color. "One of my guests said she used to rock in one like that," which pleased JoAnn no end. She loves things from the '30s and '40s, and she designed the house to reflect that period. The Blue Room upstairs has a mahogany sleigh bed and a formal sofa to lounge on. So does the Pink Room (its walls are really pink, with flowered wallpaper on the ceiling for a change), which opens off the porch. Both rooms have unusually spacious baths.

JoAnn's delicious banana pancakes—the batter poured over sautéed banana slices—are a breakfast specialty. For omelettes she adds crisp bacon, bell pepper, onions, and cheddar cheese, asking guests, "What do you want me to leave out?" to make sure she's not serving anything someone cannot eat. With that she serves hash browns—"from scratch"—crisp and brown and biscuits either plain or with bacon and cheese. She also make delicious orange-buttermilk English muffins.

HOW TO GET THERE: From I–35 take Highway 183 north, crossing Highway 620. From 620 go 4⁷⁄₁₀ miles, through Cedar Park, to FM 1431. Turn left and go 3⁵⁄₁₀ miles to Trail's End Road (on the left). Turn left and go ⁷⁄₁₀ mile until you come to a cluster of about ten mailboxes on the left. Turn left here onto the gravel road (there's an inn sign) and follow it around past a blue house on the right. The inn is just ahead on the left, a gray house with white trim.

The Badu House
Llano, Texas 78643

INNKEEPERS: Rhonda Schneider, Brenda and Bill Schneider

ADDRESS/TELEPHONE: 601 Bessemer; (915) 247–1207

ROOMS: 8; 7 with private bath.

RATES: $65 to $95, double; $10 extra person; EPB.

OPEN: All year.

FACILITIES AND ACTIVITIES: Bar and lounge; lunch and dinner daily. Nearby: hunting (the "Deer Capital of Texas"), fishing, gem and rock collecting, hiking, golf, swimming; County Museum; art, gift, and antiques shops; Highland Lake, Longhorn Caverns, Vanishing Texas River Cruises, Falls Creek Vineyard, Highland Lakes Bluebonnet Trail (spring).

The Badu House is an inn in a million, because it began life as a small-town bank. Built in 1891 for the First National of Llano, this Italian Renaissance palace housed the bank handsomely, until it failed in 1898. Then it was bought at an auction by Professor N. J. Badu, a French minerologist who installed his family in the imposing red-brick-and-checkerboard-gray-granite building. It was occupied by the Badu family for more than eighty years.

Guest rooms are not large but are filled with antiques, and each bath has Victorian brass fixtures, including pull-chain commodes, pedestal sinks, and claw-footed tubs. Back downstairs I found the Llanite Club on the left, which is the bar and lounge where everyone gathers when not dining or sleeping. There I was welcomed heartily and invited to inspect the bar itself, a huge slab of llanite, the rare opaline stone discovered by Professor Badu and found

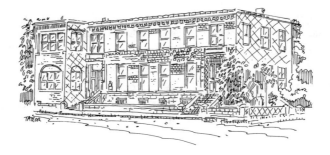

nowhere else in the world. Beyond the club a lovely brick patio faces the nicely landscaped grounds.

The restaurant floors are the white marble of the bank. Solid-brass hardware is decorated with an intricate flower motif. A full country breakfast is served, and the restaurant has a reputation for fine dining.

HOW TO GET THERE: Llano is on Highway 29 where Highways 16 and 21 meet. Drive through town past the square and the courthouse, across the bridge over the Llano River. The inn is on the left, at the corner of Highway 16 and Bessemer.

Boom, Bust, Whitetails

Llano once dreamed of becoming "the Pittsburgh of the west." That was back in the 1880s when iron was discovered. Streets were named Bessemer and Pittsburgh but in vain: Coal is needed to turn iron into steel. There was no iron in them thar hills, and the small town boom quickly went bust.

But Llano rallied to become "Deer Capital of Texas," hosting hunters of the white-tailed deer found in abundance around this Hill Country town. A bonus is the entire downtown square, designated a National Historic District.

Castle Inn
Navasota, Texas 77868

INNKEEPERS: Joyce and Gene Daniel

ADDRESS/TELEPHONE: 1403 East Washington; (409) 825–8051 or (800) 661–4346.

ROOMS: 4; all with private bath. No smoking inn.

RATES: $95 to $115; $25 extra person; EPB.

OPEN: All year.

FACILITIES AND ACTIVITIES: Porches, garden with fountain, large glassed-in sunporch, English High Tea every second and fourth Thursday afternoon. Nearby: historic town with 14-foot statue of French explorer La Salle, who came to an untimely end near here in 1687, 150 years before the town was formed; Texas Star of the Republic Museum.

This majestic Queen Anne house is well named the Castle. Local craftsmen built the mansion in 1893 as a wedding present from a local businessman to his bride. Of now-extinct curly pine, decorated with ornamental brass and beveled glass, its sunporch enclosed by one hundred beveled-glass panes, the house is outstanding.

I love the tall turret in one corner, a tower that makes the house stand out among the leafy trees outside and provides circular window seats inside on almost room-size stair landings. There's also a wonderful 20-foot stained-glass window in the stairwell.

The inn is furnished with antiques collected over years of service overseas by Joyce and Gene. He is a retired major general, and a sentimental one at that—he bought the inn as a Valentine present for Joyce! Inside the antique hand-painted Bodansee wedding cupboard in the living room, Joyce keeps the card that accompanied this magnificent present.

"We traveled and entertained extensively, and I always wanted to have a gorgeously huge Victorian home," she says as she takes out the card. The cards says on the front: "I thought a bed-and-breakfast would be romantic for Valentine's Day." Open the card, and there's a color photograph of the Castle, and below it reads: "And so—I bought you one!"

And so—they shipped 18,000 pounds of furniture to Navasota, 13,000 of it from Europe alone (the rest was in storage), and the inn has many beauti-

ful pieces to admire. The antique Normandy cupboard in the library houses the television, and lots else—it practically covers an entire wall.

The huge dining room has plenty of room for those wanting to be sociable, and there are lots of interesting things to be seen there. Up high on the plate rack are several intriguing collections: There are nine colorful Russian Storybook plates; another group of plates were hand-painted by Gene's mother and grandmother.

Breakfast begins with a fruit compote of, perhaps, grapefruit and oranges enhanced by cinnamon, sauterne, and Weaver's Honey. "Grimes County is called the 'Land of Milk and Honey,'" Joyce explains. "There are two bee-keepers here." This is followed by eggs scrambled with cream cheese, spiced oven-roasted potatoes, Canadian bacon, praline-banana muffins, and maybe even scones with clotted cream.

Joyce is the principal chef, but "Gene helps with the omelettes and crepes," she says. "I serve English High Tea every other Thursday," she says, describing the menu with relish: "five courses, beginning with Welsh rarebit." Next there are finger sandwiches of cucumber and red salmon.

The Templeman Suite, named for the family of the original builder, has a wonderful Victorian fainting couch, and Cathy's Room has antique furniture from Aachen, Germany. Framed on the wall in the Bridal Suite are the wedding certificates of Joyce's parents, and the bed is a Louisiana plantation bed; the room also has a fireplace. There are chocolates and bottled water in every room, and on special occasions there will be champagne and a snack.

HOW TO GET THERE: The inn is 4 blocks west of the Highway 6 bypass on Highway 105, which becomes Washington, Navasota's main street.

Gruene Mansion Inn
New Braunfels, Texas 78130

INNKEEPERS: Sharon and Bill McCaskell

ADDRESS/TELEPHONE: 1275 Gruene Road; (830) 629–2641;
fax (830) 629–7375

E-MAIL: gruenemansion@gruene.net

WEB SITE: www.gruene.net

ROOMS: 25, in assorted cottages on the river; all with private bath
and TV. No smoking inn.

RATES: $85 to $200, double; $20 extra person; breakfast $5 extra.
No credit cards.

OPEN: All year.

FACILITIES AND ACTIVITIES: Restaurant and bar overlooking the river,
lodge meeting facilities for 300; fax, video, computer setups available;
catering. Nearby: Grist Mill Restaurant; Gruene Dance Hall; antiques;
museums: Hummel, Sophienburg, Handmade Furniture, and Children's; Schlitterbahn Water Park; rafting, tubing, and swimming on
Guadalupe and Comal Rivers; bicycling; horseback riding; golf; tennis;
Natural Bridge Caverns and Wildlife Ranch; Canyon Lake, with fishing,
boating, swimming, and waterskiing; discount shopping malls.

"We want to become the best country inn in Texas, and we'll get
there!" Sharon says confidently. A Fort Worth native with a
background in real estate (Bill is from Gonzales, where he was in
the oil and gas pipeline business), she and Bill not only wanted a resort, they
wanted one with history. They found it in the Gruene Mansion, set on a historic cotton plantation on the banks of the Guadalupe River.

The inn is located within the Gruene (pronounced "green") Historic District on the northern edge of New Braunfels's city limits. "Bill and I really like
the history of Gruene Mansion," Sharon says. "We feel as though we're care-
takers of the property, and we try to carry on the tradition of *gemutlich*
begun by Henry Gruene back in the mid-1800s."

Gruene Dance Hall, just down the street, is the oldest dance hall in Texas.
Sharon speaks of the original owner as though she knows him. "Henry built
the hall for the closeness and warmth of his friends. He also had a little
house where travelers could come and stay; they just had to replace the logs
for the fire. He was kind to strangers, and we wanted to live that way. It's the
best way to meet people."

Wander down to Gruene Dance Hall for a beer; on weekends you can dance the Texas two-step—there's live music then. Next door, the Grist Mill Restaurant is housed in the ruins of a hundred-year-old cotton gin beneath a water tower on the banks of the Guadalupe River, with its pretty little rapids and its happy white-water rafters, many floating down from Canyon River when the water's right. You can become a river rat, too, thanks to the two outfitters on the river.

Cottages with little porches overhang the river, and they are furnished with antiques and handmade quilts; each room is different. Sharon had a great time decorating; imagine having seventeen rooms to design! Fireside Lodge #2 has a slanted ceil-

Gruene Mansion New Braunfels Tx 15 WT

ing papered with a pretty flowered wallpaper of pink and blue flowers on a black background. You can imagine the interesting contrast that makes with the rough wood paneling, made from both poplar and yellow pine. The fireplace wall is white stone; the brass bed has a colorful patchwork quilt and a crocheted afghan laid across the foot. (Feet can get chilly on cool Hill Country nights.)

Bluebonnet Lodge has huge bluebonnets painted on the walls, both bedroom and bath. The shower curtain in the bath is an old quilt (protected by a liner, of course) and dolled up with a pointed-lace valance; Sharon has many original ideas. Walls in the Grand River Lodge are painted bright blue between the wood strips and stenciled with red and yellow stylized tulips.

Newest is the "Sunday Haus" with eight rooms decorated in Victorian rustic elegance. King-sized beds, fireplaces, old Victorian bathtubs, and antiques make the *haus* (German for "house") a great addition to the inn.

HOW TO GET THERE: From I–35 take exit 191 (Canyon Lake) and go west on Highway 306 for 1 ½ miles, following the Gruene historical signs. Turn left onto Gruene and go to the end of the road. The inn is on the right.

Prince Solms Inn 📱
New Braunfels, Texas 78130

INNKEEPER: Deborah Redle

ADDRESS/TELEPHONE: 295 East San Antonio Street; (830) 625–9169;
fax (830) 625–9169

ROOMS: 10; all with private bath and phone.

RATES: $80 to $150, double; $15 extra person; continental breakfast.

OPEN: All year.

FACILITIES AND ACTIVITIES: Dinner in Wolfgang's Keller Tuesday
to Sunday. Nearby: German restaurants, antiques shops, historic
museums, Wurstfest in October, tubing and rafting on Comal River,
Hummel Museum.

*T*he Prince Solms Inn is a famous Texas landmark, having been in
continuous operation since immigrant German craftsmen built
the handsome building in 1898. Throughout its history families
of its first patrons have kept returning to this elegant yet warm and welcoming inn.

The beautifully restored building has front entry doors that are 10 feet
high, with panes of exquisitely detailed etched glass. The inn shines with
antique fittings gathered from all over the world. Bronzes are from Europe;
solid-brass doorknobs come from old Lake Shore mansions in Chicago;
doors and carriage lights, from
old San Antonio homes. Staying
here makes me feel as though I
were in a mansion back in the
days of the Astor, Rockefeller,
and Gould railroad barons.

Guest rooms are furnished
with beautiful (but sturdy)
antiques, unusual light fixtures,
and well-chosen tasteful paintings and prints. Each room is
named for the gloriously patterned wallpaper that decorates the walls. New
innkeeper Deborah is keeping up the tradition of hospitality of the inn. "It
feels as though I have the house I've always wanted," she says. Wolfgang's

Keller, the inn restaurant, is in the cellar, but what a cellar! There are old brick walls and a fireplace—and with Wolfgang Amadeus Mozart's portrait setting the tone, the atmosphere is wonderfully Old World to match the mouthwatering continental cuisine.

I had Wolfgang's wonderful Wiener schnitzel and sampled the chef's special fettucini primavera in a rich cream sauce, so I had to forgo the sinfully rich desserts until another time. Other specials include Lobster Marquis de Lafayette, shrimp a la Wolfgang's, and Scampi Fra Diablo. Mixed drinks, wine, and champagne are readily available from the bar.

The picturesque brick-paved courtyard in the rear is a delightful place to relax. I enjoyed the complimentary breakfast of banana-fruit muffins, bagels and cream cheese, and sweet rolls from one of New Braunfels's famous bakeries, all served in the dining room. Weekends, the breakfast of eggs and sausage, fine pastries, and assorted fresh fruit is satisfying. Elegant as it is, the Prince Solms Inn provides the Hill Country friendliness that makes you feel truly at home.

HOW TO GET THERE: From I–35 take exit 187 to Seguin Street, then turn right around the circle to San Antonio Street. The inn is on the left.

Heart of My Heart Ranch 📱 👪
Round Top, Texas 78954

INNKEEPERS: Frances and Bill Harris

ADDRESS/TELEPHONE: 403 Florida Chapel Road; (409) 249–3171 or (800) 327–1242; fax (409) 249–3171

ROOMS: 13; 4 in main house, 4 in Frontier House, 2 in the Carriage House, 1 in Granny's Cottage, and 2 in Log Cabin; all with private bath, color TV, and VCR. Children welcome. No smoking inn.

RATES: $85 to $125; $15 extra person; children welcome; EPB for Main House and Carriage House guests; continental breakfast for Log Cabin guests.

OPEN: All year.

FACILITIES AND ACTIVITIES: Swimming pool, game room, hot tub, Swedish massage, fishing lake, hiking, ponies, Golf Weekends, Bicycling Weekends, Duplicate Bridge Tournaments. Nearby: riding lessons and trail rides; concerts and Shakespeare at Winedale and Festival Hill; antiques shops and boutiques; Round Top Historic Museum.

"Have you had your hug today?" is Bill's morning greeting—well, to women and children guests anyway! Since he is over 6 feet tall and weighs more than 200 pounds, you can be sure his hugs are the genuine thing.

Sitting at the head of a table set with family china and crystal and surrounded by family art, he regales us with the romantic story of his love affair with Frances. This is not a first marriage for either, and his tale is very entertaining. While we are being entertained, we are feasting on a Southwest casserole of corn and ham along with smoked sausage—smoked by Bill in his smoke house—and a cinnamon-pecan coffee cake. On the buffet a Health Bar with a fresh fruit platter is spread for those who prefer granola, other cereals, and fat-free yogurt.

"Bill and I have six children and nine grandchildren between us," Frances says. "When we decided to open the house as an inn, my sister said, "Actually, you have been in training for fifty years and you didn't know it!'"

They started with only two guest rooms with shared bath. "It was like having a few friends in," Frances recalls.

"We bought this farm after three years of marriage," Bill chimes in. "As a present, I wrote Frances an IOU for ONE VICTORIAN HOUSE and I wanted to collect it. I didn't want it (the IOU) hanging out there."

In the main house, the Victorian Master Bedroom downstairs can turn into a suite when combined with a private sitting room with a queen-size sofa bed, a fireplace, and lots of books.

The Garden Room, also on the first floor, has a four-poster, a sitting area, and a view of the garden. Upstairs, a favorite is the blue-and-white Bluebonnet Room, with a brass double bed, a sitting area, and a twin brass bed in an alcove. Almeida's Room, also upstairs, has an alcove with a walnut daybed in addition to the oak double and the twin in yet another alcove—this inn has alcoves everywhere!

The Frontier House is a two-story log house built in 1828 by Jared E. Groce, one of Austin's original 300 settlers. The large entry is also a sitting area, with sofa, desk, and rocking chair. The Lone Star Room downstairs has stairs connecting it with the Harwood Room upstairs, great for families. The Brookfield Room downstairs has a king-sized canopy bed with a pretty lace edging and a cozy quilt coverlet, as well as a walnut daybed and a fireplace.

The Bride's Room has a queen-sized sleigh bed and a fireplace. The second upstairs bedroom, the Fordtran Room, has two queen-sized Shaker farm beds.

Granny's Cottage is an adorable poolside cabin with sleeping space both upstairs and down. The Log Cabin is a 150-year-old pioneer cabin in its original site and is perfect for those who long for the rustic life. The Cabine is complete with kitchen, stone fireplace, double bed, and bath downstairs and a sleeping loft with both double and trundle beds—and an outside stairway.

HOW TO GET THERE: From the blinking light in Round Top take Highway 237 south for 1¾ miles. Turn left at the airport sign on Florida Chapel Road (CR 217). Go past the Florida Chapel Cemetery for ¼ mile, and turn in at the large red gate.

Brambley Hedge Country Inn
Salado, Texas 76571

INNKEEPERS: Carol Anne and Billie Hanks

ADDRESS/TELEPHONE: 1530 Holland Road (mailing address: P.O. Box 351); (800) 407–2310; fax (254) 947–1031

WEB SITE: www.touringtexas/brambley.com

ROOMS: 4; all with private bath, phone, and TV. Children welcome. No smoking inn.

RATES: $115 to $125, double; EPB.

OPEN: All year.

FACILITIES AND ACTIVITIES: Board games and croquet. Nearby: historic Salado with shops, galleries, antiques, restaurants; golf; Gathering of the Clans; art festivals; corn festivals; Rolls Royce car meets; Christmas Strolls; Historic Home Tour.

With French-country wallpaper and hardware, brick floors, and Dutch-farmhouse roof design, Brambley Hedge has quite an international flavor. "We built the house new," Carol Anne says, "using ideas from our travels." The comfortable common rooms, friendly stone fireplace, and enclosed atrium connecting the two wings of the house make the inn an interesting and unusual building.

Each guest room has its own deck with a restful view of oak trees and the garden. The Normandy's white twin beds are crafted of old wood fences; The Garden Gate has a green queen-sized bed made from an antique iron fence; Provence has the ambience of rural France; and the bed in The Western Star is made of logs. Fresh flowers scent each room, and hot coffee and iced tea are always available.

Carol Anne is enthusiastic about breakfast, concocting treats such as Belgian waffles with berries and cream, lemon ricotta hotcakes, and crème caramel French toast, served with yogurt, cereals, assorted breakfast meats, and fresh fruit. And it doesn't end there: There's often afternoon tea to enjoy.

HOW TO GET THERE: From I-35 heading north, take exit 283 and turn left, going exactly 1 mile to the big red European Carriage House on the left.

Halley House 📱
Salado, Texas 76571

INNKEEPERS: Cathy and Larry Sands

ADDRESS/TELEPHONE: 681 North Main Street; (254) 947-1000; fax (254) 947-5508

ROOMS: 7; all with private bath; wheelchair accessible. No smoking inn.

RATES: $115 to $125, double; EPB.

OPEN: All year.

FACILITIES AND ACTIVITIES: Bicycles, horseshoes, meeting room. Nearby: historic Salado, with shops, galleries, antiques, restaurants; golf, tennis, swimming at Mill Creek Club; Gathering of the Clans; art festivals; corn festivals; Rolls Royce car meets; Christmas Strolls; Historic Home Tour, carriage rides.

he inn was built in 1860 by Captain Robert Bonner Halley, and the hospitable captain had nothing on Cathy and Larry, who are enthusiastic innkeepers. Listed on the National Register of Historic Places, the house is surrounded by oaks trees; there are swings in the trees if you want to go up, up, and away; and the pineapple symbol on their brochure stands for hospitality.

Three of the four guest rooms in the main house have fireplaces: Star of Texas Suite, The Captain's Room, and Lydia's Room. But the Capitol Suite and the three rooms in the Carriage House are just as comfortable and pleasant, with traditional and modern styles, antique and new, blended together. The comfortable seating in each room is a thoughtful touch, too.

The delicious aroma of Halley House's special blend of coffee draws guests into the dining room to the breakfast buffet, where they help themselves to quiche, homemade pastries and English muffins, cereals, and fruit along with the aromatic coffee.

HOW TO GET THERE: From I-35 heading north, take exit 283; heading south, take exit 285 and go east to Main Street. The inn is on the east side of the street next to the Old Red School House.

Inn at Salado
Salado, Texas 76571

INNKEEPERS: Suzanne and Rob Petro

ADDRESS/TELEPHONE: North Main at Pace Park Drive;
(800) 724–0027; fax (254) 947–3144

ROOMS: 9; all with private bath; wheelchair accessible. No smoking inn.

RATES: $70 to $90, double; $15 extra person; EPB.

OPEN: All year.

FACILITIES AND ACTIVITIES: Conference facilities: meeting space, VCR, monitor, projection screen, and speaker system. Nearby: historic Salado, with shops, galleries, antiques, restaurants; golf at Mill Creek Club; Gathering of the Clans; art festivals; corn festivals; Rolls Royce car meets; Christmas Strolls; Historic Home Tour; carriage rides.

*L*ocated in the heart of the town's Historical District, the inn sports both a Texas Historical Marker and a National Register of Historic Places listing. There's no difficulty relaxing here: You'll enjoy the rocking chairs, swings, and hammocks on two acres, all enclosed by a spanking-white picket fence. A hand-dug old stone well is the centerpiece for two tree-shaded and covered brick terraces.

The only thing the nine guest rooms have in common is their antique furnishings; otherwise each one is unique. Rose (Victorian) has a private porch and swing overlooking the grounds; Mary's Room shares a porch with Elli's Room; Custer has its own great porch complete with rocking chairs. Antique quilts are on display in Barton's Room; Tenney, Tyler, Norton, and Baines have sitting rooms.

Breakfast might be Belgian waffles as well as breakfast cakes, fresh fruit, and that Southern treat, bicuits and gravy.

HOW TO GET THERE: From I–35 take exit 284 and go east on Thomas Arnold Road to Main Street. Take Main Street to Pace Park Drive. The inn is on the northeast corner of Main and Pace Park Drive.

Inn on the Creek 📱 💟
Salado, Texas 76571

INNKEEPERS: Suzi and Lynn Epps, Sue and Bob Whister

ADDRESS/TELEPHONE: One Center Circle (mailing address: P.O. Box 858); (254) 947–5554; fax (254) 947–9198

WEB SITE: www.inncreek.com

ROOMS: 18; all with private bath, phone, and TV. Children welcome. No smoking inn.

RATES: $70 to $125, double; $20 extra person; EPB.

OPEN: All year.

FACILITIES AND ACTIVITIES: Dinner by reservation. Nearby: historic Salado, with shops, galleries, antiques, restaurants; golf at Mill Creek Country Club; Gathering of the Clans; art festivals; corn festivals; Rolls Royce car meets; Christmas Strolls; Historic Home Tour.

The Inn on the Creek is a collection of historic houses—Twelve Oaks, Sally's Cottage, Osage Cottage, the Holland House, and Reue House—gathered together on tree-covered land along the banks of Salado Creek. The main house, Twelve Oaks, was constructed in 1892 in nearby Cameron. After the four innkeepers moved it to the current site, they doubled the size of the building, making a total of seven guest rooms in addition to the living and dining rooms.

Sally's one-bedroom cottage is next to Twelve Oaks, as is Osage Cottage; the five-bedroom annex, Holland House, built in the 1880s, is just across the road; and Reue House, with four guest rooms, is down the road a piece. The buildings make a pleasant little compound under the old oak trees.

This parent, daughter, and son-in-law team make a great combination. "Mom and Pop moved here from Cameron, they just loved the place," Lynn says of his in-laws. "They were intrigued by the whole idea of an inn." As for Lynn, a corporate architect, he was intrigued by the challenge of the old houses.

The inn is furnished with a collection of Victorian pieces and antiques from other periods. Family photographs, antique rugs and linens, and all sorts of interesting furnishings make this a cozy getaway. Windows are hung with lace, draped with pretty valances, or covered with printed drapes to match quilted bedspreads.

"We've named the guest rooms after people who have made a significant contribution to the local community," Suzi says. In Twelve Oaks, the Rose Room, with its Victorian walnut bed covered with an antique pillowcase collection, honors Colonel Rose, who developed land in Salado. The Baines Room has warm oak furniture, the Anderson Room a gleaming brass bed and walnut accent pieces. The McKie Room, on the third floor, has its own library nook with a daybed that overlooks Salado Creek at the rear of the property.

In Holland House, the five-bedroom annex just across from Twelve Oaks, the Fletcher Room commemorates an old family name. The Alexander Room, with a four-poster bed, is named for a Salado couple. "She was an architect, and he was in construction," Suzi explains.

In the Reue House, also restored from the 1880s, the Van Bibber Room has an antique walnut four-poster and a fireplace with a limestone hearth. Not antiques but interesting all the same are the nutcrackers that Lynn and Suzi have collected. "We started with the nutcrackers back in 1993 when we

were in Rothenburg, Germany," Lynn says. The inn also has a nice collection of Audubon prints.

Breakfast is a treat, with a German apple puff pancake, ham/sausage loaf, sour-cream coffee cake, homemade carrot muffins and cinnamon rolls, fruit, juice, and coffee. As for weekend dinners, here's a sample menu: black bean and corn salad, lime-seasoned salmon with salsa, brandy-glazed carrots, zesty lemon rice, and mixed-berry tart. Pretty cosmopolitan for a town of 1,500!

HOW TO GET THERE: From I–35 heading north, take exit 283 and go north on Main Street. Turn right on Royal Street and go on to Center Circle on the left. From I–35 going south take exit 285 and go south on Main Street, past Mill Creek Drive, and over Salado Creek to Royal Street; turn left to Center Circle on the left.

Adams House Inn
San Antonio, Texas 78210

INNKEEPERS: Nora Peterson and Richard Green

ADDRESS/TELEPHONE: 231 Adams; (800) 666–4810;
fax (210) 223–5125

E-MAIL: innkeeper@san-antonio-texas.com

WEB SITE: www.san-antonio-texas.com

ROOMS: 4; all with private bath, telephone, and TV. No smoking inn.

RATES: $75 to $140, double; $10 to $15 extra person; EPB.

OPEN: All year.

FACILITIES AND ACTIVITIES: Nearby: The Alamo, La Villita, Convention Center, Institute of Texan Cultures, RiverCenter Mall, El Mercado, Seaworld, and Fiesta Texas.

The Adams House is one of several beautiful old homes in San Antonio's historic King William District. Built in 1902, the inn is filled with antiques and antique reproductions. The original owners were in the milling and woodwork business and the finely crafted red-pine woodwork has held up beautifully.
Walls in the entry, parlor, and dining room are covered with a creamy satin striped paper, and so are the ceilings in between the beautiful wood beams.

Guest rooms are also furnished in both period antiques and reproductions. The Texas Room opens on a private veranda; the O'Henry Room appeals to writers. In the Veranda Room you can wallow in an antique 6-foot bathtub, and in the 1902 Carriage House you can have total privacy, since it includes a kitchenette.

You'll enjoy a full gourmet breakfast of such delicious entrees as Texian pie, caramel French toast or French toast strata, cheesy eggs, or Feta-calamata frittata, served with fresh fruit, homemade pies—and good coffee.

HOW TO GET THERE: From I–35 take 281 south to Durango. Go west to Alamo; turn left on Adams. From I-10 take Alamo exit 155A; go east to Adams and turn right to 231.

Beckmann Inn and Carriage House
San Antonio, Texas 78204

INNKEEPERS: Betty Jo and Don Schwartz

ADDRESS/TELEPHONE: 222 East Guenther Street; (210) 229–1449
or (800) 945–1449; fax (210) 229–1061

WEB SITE: www.saweb.com/beckbb

ROOMS: 5; all with private bath. No smoking inn.

RATES: $90 to $130, double.

OPEN: All year.

FACILITIES AND ACTIVITIES: Parking. Nearby: downtown with
The Alamo, La Villita, Convention Center, museums, RiverCenter
Mall, El Mercado.

One of the many fascinating things about the Beckmann Inn is the
beds with unusual tall, pointed headboards. Betty Jo and Don are
from Bellville, Illinois, and they brought the beds with them. The 9-
foot-tall chestnut headboard in The Suite is one they bought in St. Louis.
"The original owner couldn't fit it into his house, so for twenty years it was
stored in his garage," Don marvels.

The matching (as in a
set, not in height!) dressing
table has the maker's signature underneath the marble
top and two little pullout
glove drawers on each side
of the mirror. And there is a
tiny lamp shelf above each
drawer. The adjoining sunroom, in green and pink,
has a wall full of wedding
portraits. "That's our fam-
ily," Betty Jo says. "We can't live without them." I don't think they can live
without Betty Jo's unusual collection of Anri music boxes and figurines,
either. There are two shelves in The Suite and several in the Library Room,
chock-full. "I hadn't realized she'd collected so many until we began to do

the inn," Don says with a laugh. The pink-and-pale-green bathroom in the Library Room is the "California bath," with fixtures Betty Jo says you probably can't get in those colors nowadays. "We researched this for three years," she says. "We were looking for a job change, and we stayed at inns and talked with innkeepers; we attended a conference in Santa Fe. We wanted to learn the ups and downs." It's hard to imagine any downs for this personable pair of innkeepers.

The parquet living room floor has an unusual decorative border, and when I admire it, Betty Jo says it came from Paris. "Paris, Texas?" is my little joke, because of course it's from the one in France. The inn is listed on the National Register of Historic Places and is within the City of San Antonio's King William Historical District—how's that for historic credentials? And the listing happens to mention a rating: Exceptional.

The house was built in 1886 by Alfred Beckmann for his bride, Marie Dorothea, daughter of the Guenther flour-mill family. Albert's father, Johan, died in 1907; his funeral was held here in the living room. Back then the address was 529 Madison, with the front door facing that street. But around 1913 the home's Victorian style was converted to Greek Revival, and the porch was circled around to the Guenther side. "It was so the front door could be moved, because there was a brothel on that street and they didn't want to have the same address!"

The Schwartzes were lucky to find the kitchen all up to date and very workable. Breakfast's first course is a glazed cranberry pear with mint and "matching" cranberry bread. "I like to make things that go together," Betty Jo says. Next comes cinnamon pecan-stuffed French toast with an apricot glaze, topped with strawberries and cream, almost too pretty to eat.

"The inn, it's us," Betty Jo and Don say. "It's what we're comfortable with, our guests coming in, it's an adventure. We have people coming from coast to coast, Canadians, British. . . ."

HOW TO GET THERE: From Loop 410 take 281 south and exit at Durango. Go west to St. Mary's and turn left for a short jog onto King William Street. Go 5 blocks to Guenther Street; turn left. The inn is at the corner on the left.

Bonner Garden
San Antonio, Texas 78212

INNKEEPERS: Jan and Noel Stenoien

ADDRESS/TELEPHONE: 145 East Agarita; (800) 396–4222;
fax (210) 733–6129

E-MAIL: noels@onr.com

ROOMS: 5; all with private bath and TV. No smoking inn.

RATES: $85 to $115, double; $10 extra person; EPB. Weekly rates
available.

OPEN: All year.

FACILITIES AND ACTIVITIES: Lap pool, hot tub, rooftop patio,
Nordic Track, and stationary bicycle; rooftop terrace, parking. Nearby:
downtown, with The Alamo, La Villita, Convention Center, museums,
RiverCenter Mall, El Mercado.

*B*onner Garden is named for artist Mary Bonner, who, although she achieved some prominence locally for her etching and print-making skills, probably was "a big fish in a small pond," says son Randy. Born in 1887 in Louisiana, she moved with her family to San Antonio. In 1910 they built a house that made history: It was one of the first residences in the Southwest to use concrete. They had a pretty good reason: "Their homes in Louisiana had burned down four times," Noel says. "They wanted one that wouldn't!"

The family name is Norwegian, and Noel explains his name jokingly. "I was born on Easter," he says, "but my mother thought it was Christmas. I was her seventh, and she had run out of names."

The Palladian-style house may be a fortress of concrete reinforced with steel and cast iron, but it's softened with creamy stucco and surrounded by a lovely garden. The pretty pool, in front behind fence and foliage, looks purely decorative, but Randy says it's perfect for swimming laps.

The hot tub, atop the house in the roof garden, is wonderful for lolling while admiring the view of downtown San Antonio in the distance.

"The house was definitely a find," Jan says. The gardens alone won it a Conservation Award in 1986. She is collecting Bonner's prints, and quite a few hang on the inn walls. "In her day she was better known in the Paris of the 1920s and 1930s than she was here."

The walls of the mansion are painted in varying shades of faux marble; the common rooms downstairs are a sort of terra-cotta. Upstairs, some of the marbling is in soft pastels, and furniture pieces are fascinating. The Portico Room has a painted ceiling of pale blue with puffy white clouds, and a door leads out to the pool. The Ivy Room's walls are decorated with ivy on the walls; the Bridal Suite has a Jacuzzi and old tapestries; and The Studio, where Mary Bonner worked, contains an assortment of interesting pieces of Mexican furniture and an old iron four-poster bed.

The portrait over the dining room mantel and the tiles of the fireplace were brought from Italy. The portrait makes for a fun breakfast game: Everybody gets a guess as to who or what it was. Conquistador? Soldier of fortune? Priest ? Someone's ancestor? Whatever, it adds spice to Jan's delicious breakfasts of oven omelette with crumbled bacon, cheese, and mushrooms; breakfast tacos of eggs and sausage; or Belgian waffles. French toast is topped with apricot sauce, and there are always fresh cinnamon rolls or a nice sticky pull-apart or sour-cream coffee cake.

We sat around till noon, visiting. Jan was a high school registrar, Noel a real estate broker. "It's been a partnership for years," Jan says.

HOW TO GET THERE: From I–10 take the Woodlawn exit and go east to Main. Turn right (south) onto Agarita and go to number 145, which is the last house on the street. It is on the left.

Brackenridge House
San Antonio, Texas 78204

INNKEEPERS: Sue and Bennie Blansett

ADDRESS/TELEPHONE: 230 Madison; (210) 271–3442 or
(800) 221–1412; fax (210) 226–3139

E-MAIL: benniesueb@aol.com

WEB SITE: www.brackenridgehouse.com

ROOMS: 6; all with private bath, telephone, and TV. Children and
pets welcome in Carriage House. No smoking inn.

RATES: $89 to $175, double; $15 to $25 extra person; EPB.

OPEN: All year.

FACILITIES AND ACTIVITIES: Parking. Nearby: downtown San
Antonio, with The Alamo, La Villita, Convention Center, museums,
RiverCenter Mall, El Mercado.

*H*ere is another beautifully restored turn-of-the-century home in
the heart of the historic King William District conveniently close
to downtown San Antonio. The original pine floors, double-
hung windows, and high ceilings are complemented by antique furnishings
and brought up to date with minirefrigerators, coffeemakers, and cable TV.

The decor is Country Victorian, with handmade quilts and crocheted bedspreads in Monica's Suite, Karla's
Room, Sue's Room, Benet's Suite,
and the Bride's Room. Blansett
Barn is a carriage house with two
bedrooms and bath, kitchen, and
living and dining areas, perfect
for family groups with children
and/or pets.

Breakfast can be coffee and
pastry at 8:00 A.M. or full and
gourmet at 9:00, and if you're a
real early bird, well, that's why there's that refrigerator in your room!

HOW TO GET THERE: From I–35 take 281 south and exit at Durango. Turn
right and go through three traffic lights to St. Mary's. Go south on St. Mary's
to Madison and turn left.

The Ogé House 📱 💟
San Antonio, Texas 78204

INNKEEPERS: Sharrie and Patrick Magatagan

ADDRESS/TELEPHONE: 209 Washington; (210) 223–2353 or
(800) 242–2770; fax (210) 226–5812

E-MAIL: ogeinn@swbell.net

ROOMS: 9; all with private bath, telephone, and TV. No smoking inn.

RATES: $135 to $195, double; EPB.

OPEN: All year.

FACILITIES AND ACTIVITIES: Parking. Nearby: downtown San
Antonio, with The Alamo, La Villita, Convention Center, museums,
RiverCenter Mall, El Mercado.

*I*f you're looking for a proper mansion, you have found it. A tall,
three-story building squared off by a set of porches top and bottom,
the Ogé House looms ahead at the end of the street, looking almost
like a misplaced plantation house. But not too misplaced, because it's set on
large, lovely grounds ending only at San Antonio's famous river.

The Ogé House (pronounced "oh-jhay"—it's French) is one of the most
magnificent homes to be found in San Antonio's historic King William District of fine homes. It was built in 1857 for Louis Ogé, a pioneer cattle
rancher and Texas Ranger.

Like many old beauties, the home had become an apartment house, but
it was just waiting for Sharrie and Patrick to find it. They had been looking,
driving up the East Coast for six weeks, before they realized that this was
where they wanted to be.

"I used to redo old houses back East," Sharrie says. "And we'd been collecting antiques for ten, twelve years." Visiting her father here, they heard
that the old house might be available. "We were interviewed by a member of
one of the first San Antonio families, who came originally from the Canary
Islands, before they decided they would sell us the house."

The house is huge, with two guest rooms opening off the majestic lobby,
which is actually the second floor, since you climb eleven steps up to the

front door. Once there you'll admire the antique French set of two settees and two chairs. "They're from a private suite in the Waldorf Astoria in New York," Patrick says.

The Library, at the rear of the house, is relaxing, with soft-yellow walls, white woodwork, satin-striped sofas, and books (although "there are books all over the house," as Sharrie says). The brass bucket in The Library is filled with menus from the city's many fine eating places.

Upstairs (third floor) the Giles and Mathis suites both open onto the porch across the front of the house, while Riverview, off the landing by the back stairs, is intensely private, with its own porch and view of the river. Down below, on the main level, the Mitchell Suite has a platform canopy bed and a daybed—perfect, Patrick says, "for three ladies traveling together." The Bluebonnet Room is done in Texas antiques, with a four-poster rolling-pin bed and the desk of an old Texas judge. But that's all you'll find of Texas.

"We're not a Texas country inn," Sharrie says. "We have more of the flavor of a small European hotel or an English country manor house." Sharrie's Deluxe Continental Breakfast begins with poached pears and goes on to such delicacies as pecan log roll, apple torte, cherry cheesecake, and fruit pasties. You can join everyone for breakfast in the dining room, take it out on the front veranda, or go out on the grounds and sit overlooking the river. "We're on one and a half acres, and when all the trees leaf out in the summer, you can't see any of the neighbors. You can't believe you're in downtown San Antonio!"

HOW TO GET THERE: From I–35 take 281 south and exit at Durango. Turn right and go through three traffic lights to St. Mary's. Take the first left to Pancoast; the inn is head-on at the end of the street.

Riverwalk Inn 🖋
San Antonio, Texas 78204

INNKEEPERS: Johnny Halpenny and Tammy Hill

ADDRESS/TELEPHONE: 329 Old Guilbeau Street; (210) 229–9422
or (800) 254–4440; fax (210) 229–9422

ROOMS: 11; one handicapped accessible, all with private bath (walk-in
showers), TV, and cable; ceiling fans; fireplaces with gas logs; coffeemaker and refrigerator. No smoking inn.

RATES: $99 to $155, double; EPB.

OPEN: All year.

FACILITIES AND ACTIVITIES: Porches with rocking chairs; bicycles,
off-street parking, conference room. Nearby: downtown, Alamo,
Convention Center, museums, Spanish missions.

There's a perfect reason for this inn's name: It's located right on
San Antonio's famous Paseo del Rio, the Riverwalk, a lovely place
to stroll. The inn consists of a group of log homes transported
log by log from Tennessee, where the inn's owners, Jan and Tracy Hammer,
found them in a state of ruin. "People were making them into fences," Jan
says. "It was sad." First constructed in 1842, the restored cabins fit right into
the inn's philosophy.

"Our mission is to have our guests relive the history of Old San Antonio through the lifestyles of Texas heroes Davy Crockett and James Bowie, who were from Tennessee," says innkeeper Johnny Halpenny. "Of course," he adds with a grin, "with all of today's amenities. We want to have the feel of the old—with the technology of the new."

The five two-story log houses were built from cottonwood trees, in Spanish called *Alamo*, described as an American variety of the poplar. This happy coincidence adds to the flavor of the history enacted every Sunday morning at breakfast, when storytellers make an appearance to entertain the guests.

"They represent Texas characters from the 1840s," Johnny says. "They tell historic tales and answer any questions guests might have. We've had pioneer doctors, horse traders, Davy Crockett . . . we even had Santa Ana!" Santa Ana, of course, was the Mexican general Texans finally routed at the Battle of San Jacinto during the War of Texas Independence.

If all this isn't entertaining enough, refreshments are served every evening, not just on Storytelling Sunday.

Rooms are named in honor of the heroes of the Alamo. Each room is decorated with country antique furniture, and seven of the eleven have views of the river from outside porches or balconies. Fireplaces are of stone, and in many of the rooms you can see the log layers that built the cabins. Many tall pine four-posters, homey quilts, old chests, and comfy armchairs make each room a relaxing and comfortable place to fall apart.

The landscaped Riverwalk parkway gives the aura of being out in the country, yet San Antonio's main attractions are perhaps a five-minute walk away. At night, across green trees and lawn and the river, the bright lights of downtown twinkle and the Tower of Life Building stands out against the night sky.

Breakfast is served in the dining room or out on the porch. This is some porch, 80 feet long and overlooking the Riverwalk. Breakfast is always special: Johnny's specialty is baked French toast served with spiced apples, along with ham and cheese kolaches. Kolaches, a legacy of Central Texas's ethnic pioneer tradition, are wonderful Czech "Danish." Usually filled with fruit—cherry, peach, apple—these are a real treat, too.

HOW TO GET THERE: Take U.S. 281 to exit 140B (Durango Street/Alamo Dome) and turn east on Durango for ⁹⁄₁₀ mile, crossing South Alamo and South St. Mary's Streets. Take the first right, which is Aubrey Street (look for the bridge next to the television station). Aubrey ends in 1 block at Old Guilbeau Street, and the inn is on the corner.

The Royal Swan
San Antonio, Texas 78204

INNKEEPERS: Helen and Curt Skredergard

ADDRESS/TELEPHONE: 236 Madison; (210) 223-3776 or (800) 368-3073

E-MAIL: the swan@cor.com

WEB SITE: www.royalswan.com

ROOMS: 5; all with private bath, telephone, and TV. No smoking inn.

RATES: $85 to $140, double; EPB.

OPEN: All year.

FACILITIES AND ACTIVITIES: Parking. Nearby: downtown San Antonio, with The Alamo, La Villita, Convention Center, museums, RiverCenter Mall, El Mercado.

The name of the original owner, Dr. Jabez Cain, is engraved on the carriage stone of this 1892 home. A dentist, he built two homes in the King William Historic District, and The Royal Swan, happily restored after an interim as an apartment house, is one of them.

The home is a showcase, with a gabled roof, verandas and back and front porches, fireplaces, crystal chandeliers, stained glass, hand-carved woodwork—every decorative embellishment those Victorians could think of. The entry is classic Victorian, the parlor is warm and welcoming, and a full sitdown breakfast is served in the formal dining room at 9:00 A.M. If that's not a good time for you, you may have an expanded continental at your own time.

The Texas Rose Room is decorated in soft rose and yellow; the Crystal Room features a carved mahogany poster bed and a Victorian love seat under the crystal chandelier. The Emerald Room, with a mahogany rice poster bed, opens onto a veranda, as does the Veranda Suite, which has its own sitting room. The Garnet Room offers complete privacy; there's a private entrance off the back deck.

HOW TO GET THERE: From I-35 take 281 south and exit at Durango. Turn right and go through three traffic lights to St. Mary's. Go south on St. Mary's to Madison and turn left to number 236.

Terrell Castle
San Antonio, Texas 78208

INNKEEPERS: Diane and Vic Smilgrin

ADDRESS/TELEPHONE: 950 East Grayson Street; (210) 271–9145 or (800) 481–9732; fax (210) 527–1455

E-MAIL: smilgrin@aol.com

ROOMS: 9; all with private bath and TV. Pets permitted. Smoking permitted.

RATES: $85 to $205, double; $15 extra person; EPB. Cribs free; assorted rates when rooms are booked as suites.

OPEN: All year.

FACILITIES AND ACTIVITIES: Nearby: the Paseo del Rio (River Walk) downtown, lined with restaurants, bars, and boutiques; The Alamo; several fine missions; zoo, horticultural garden, Sea World and Fiesta Texas amusement parks.

*T*errell Castle is quite regal. The magnificent entrance hall has a red-brick fireplace and built-in seats in a "coffin" niche; also restored are the parlor, library, music room, dining room, breakfast room, and enclosed porch. The home was built in 1894 by Edwin Terrell, a San Antonio lawyer and statesman who served under President Benjamin Harrison as ambassador plenipotentiary to Belgium in the early 1890s. He fancied a castle like those he saw in Europe, and as soon as he returned home, he commissioned a local architect to build one.

Well, while the Terrell Castle doesn't particularly remind me of a European castle, it certainly does impress me as a very stately mansion. The front staircase is extraordinary. Antique furniture and lace curtains set off the fine parquet floors and curved windows in the parlor. The dining room has a huge fireplace and a wood-paneled ceiling, the first like it I've seen.

Guest rooms include the Giles Suite and the Terrell Suite, the Colonial Room, the Victorian Room, the Tower Suite, and the Oval Room (with curved windows). The Americana Room has the best view in the house: Its windows face all four directions and offer a grand fourth-floor view of San Antonio. The Ballroom Suite is in what once was the ballroom of the mansion. It has an oriental flair, while retaining the Victorian character of the house. Interesting . . . each room is more lovely than the next, so I leave it to you to make a choice.

All the fireplaces in the house are functional, including one with a green-tiled mantel in the meeting room on the third floor. Breakfast is a feast of bacon or sausage; eggs however you want them, including a wonderful Mexican omelette; crisp hash browns or creamy grits; homemade goodies such as popovers and sticky buns; as well as muffins, raisin bread, biscuits, preserves, dry cereal, juice, coffee, tea, and milk. There's a television in the large library/office, and guests can watch whenever they want.

HOW TO GET THERE: Grayson Street is between Broadway and New Braunfels Street, adjacent to Fort Sam Houston.

A Yellow Rose 📱
San Antonio, Texas 78204

INNKEEPERS: Deb Field-Walker and Kit Walker

ADDRESS/TELEPHONE: 229 Madison; (210) 222–9903; fax (210) 229–1691

E-MAIL: yellowrs@express-news.net

ROOMS: 5; all with private bath, telephones, and TV. No smoking inn.

RATES: $100 to $175; $15 extra person; EPB.

OPEN: All year.

FACILITIES AND ACTIVITIES: Parking. Nearby: downtown, with the Alamo; La Villita; Convention Center; museums; RiverCenter Mall; El Mercado.

BUSINESS TRAVEL: 5 blocks from downtown San Antonio.

The yellow-painted brick Yellow Rose is a fine example of the many homes that were built in San Antonio's King William District more than a century ago. Built in 1879 by Charles Mueller, a German immigrant house painter, the house, like many in the neighborhood, had been a Victorian beauty.

Every room and many of the ceilings are covered with beautiful figured papers. In the Victorian Rose Room the French walnut bed dates from the 1880s. The Green Sage Room is decorated in eighteenth-century design; the Yellow Rose Room is light and airy with French-country pine antiques; the Bluebonnet Room has turn-of-the-century antiques from Massachusetts; the Magnolia Room enjoys a private entance and a porch overlooking the garden.

As for breakfast, Deb says that "everyone raves about our muffins and our coffee. And there are special requests for the blintz soufflé."

HOW TO GET THERE: From I–35 take 281 south and exit at Durango. Go right, then through three traffic lights to St. Mary's. Turn left, and the second right is Madison. The inn is the seventh house down the block on the right, with an American flag out front.

Crystal River Inn 📱
San Marcos, Texas 78666

INNKEEPERS: Cathy and Mike Dillon

ADDRESS/TELEPHONE: 326 West Hopkins Street; (512) 396–3739 or (888) 396–3739; fax (512) 353–3248

WEB SITE: CrystalRiverInn.com

ROOMS: 12; all with private bath, TV, and phone; wheelchair accessible. No smoking in rooms.

RATES: $75 to $110, weekdays; $80 to $130, weekends; EPB.

OPEN: All year.

FACILITIES AND ACTIVITIES: Nearby: San Marcos River for water sports; Southwest State University, LBJ's alma mater; many special events in San Marcos.

Crystal River Inn rooms are named for Texas rivers because "we are river rats," Cathy says. Both she and Mike are pleased to show guests the ropes if they want to take on the nearby San Marcos River. Each guest room has its own watery personality. The Colorado Room reflects the iciness and blue color of the river, while the Pedernales Room, in blue and warm peach, is folksy and friendly. The honeymoon suite is named for the beautiful Medina. The house, designer decorated, is restfully clean and uncluttered, and the rooms carry out this feeling.

"The peace, beauty, history, and happiness of this unique chunk of Texas have been bottled up right here, just waiting to be shared," Cathy says of her

very attractive and relaxing inn. The veranda upstairs is the happy-hour porch. "Usually our guests come breezing in here from Houston or Dallas, and they're all tightly wound. We prop them up on the veranda or in the atrium-sunroom with some wine in their hands, and in an hour the change is just amazing." The Dillons also pamper guests with bed-side brandy and chocolates, although many of them linger in "the library," the lovely parlor with a cozy fireplace and walls lined with bookshelves.

Crystal River Inn is also known for its knockout weekend brunch. I feasted on fruit-filled cantaloupe ring, beer biscuits that Cathy calls "beer-scuits," sausage, and the pièce de résistance, bananas Foster crepes topped with crème fraîche and toasted slivered almonds. Cathy invented the recipe, and when she made the crepes for a Chamber of Commerce fund-raiser, people were lined up and winding out the door waiting for them.

Other great breakfasts are sour cream–apple walnut French toast, *huevos rancheros*, and I could go on and on with a whole assortment of homemade breads such as zucchini-and-apple fritter bread. You can be sure of a gourmet feast to begin the day at the Crystal River Inn.

HOW TO GET THERE: Take exit 205 west off I-35. This is Highway 80, which becomes Hopkins in town. The inn is on the right, just before you come to Rural Route 12 to Wimberley.

Utopia on the River
Utopia, Texas 78884

INNKEEPERS: Polly and Aubrey Smith

ADDRESS/TELEPHONE: Highway 187 (mailing address: P.O. Box 14); (830) 966–2444

ROOMS: 12; all with private bath and TV.

RATES: $59, single; $10 each additional person; EPB.

OPEN: All year.

FACILITIES AND ACTIVITIES: Barbecue grills and picnic tables; refrigerator and microwave in some rooms, $5 extra; gift shop, pool, Jacuzzi, sauna, volleyball, horseshoes, hiking trails, fishing, hunting, tubing on river. Nearby: stables with horses for hire and one restaurant in Utopia; Lost Maples State Park.

*E*arly on, Utopia had several other names, but then a town postmaster happened to read Sir Thomas More's description of Utopia. "This is it!" he cried. "Perfect climate, happy, healthy people—we live in Utopia!" and Utopia it became. That postmaster was not far off base, and he would have felt all the more vindicated if he could have seen today's Utopia on the River, with its large, bright, A-frame lobby and breakfast area. The inn is run by Polly and Aubrey Smith: Aubrey has been busy as sheriff of Uvalde County.

"I had managed property in San Antonio, so I knew what I was getting into," Polly says. "But weekends Aubrey has been in Utopia, and sometimes he even helps cook." The inn is on 650 acres that have been in Polly's family for more than a hundred years, and rooms are named after pioneer settlers of the area. William Ware, an ancestor of Polly's, founded the town, and, of course, he has a plaque on the door of one room; another is named for Polly's grandmother. Rooms are large and airy, with touches such as quilt-pattern bedspreads and colorful duck appliques, sewn by Polly, framed over the beds. The construction of stone with wood floors is typical of this Hill Country area, and the view from each room is a refreshing wilderness of mesquite and pecan trees.

The inn grounds are a veritable animal preserve. To begin with, it's a working ranch; you'll drive through a flock of sheep as you wind into the property. (Just honk your horn to get them off the road.) During nature hikes you might see the likes of such exotica as axis and fallow deer, audads, and black buck antelope. After that the deer, turkeys, sheep, and goats may seem pretty tame by comparison! The place is great for the children—bird-watchers, too. Special as well is the storytelling on the river every Saturday night, March through October—and in front of a cozy fire, November through February.

Breakfast can be fancy, with banana bran pancakes, or hearty, with scrambled eggs and biscuits as well as juice and coffee. Then you can wander down to see the falls on the cool, clean Sabinal River, go rock and driftwood hunting, or marvel at the old cypress tree. "We think it's from 750 to 800 years old," Polly says. "Everyone wants to see it." The huge native pecan trees in front of the inn are something to see, too.

There is a collection of art and craft wares as well as T-shirts and other necessities in the loft above the dining room. Otherwise you'll feel far from the madding crowd. "We enjoy our guests," Aubrey says, "but we want to keep our tranquillity." Tranquillity and serenity are the words he uses to describe Utopia on the River.

HOW TO GET THERE: The inn is approximately 80 miles northwest of San Antonio. Take Highway 90 west to Sabinal, then Highway 187 north to 2 miles south of Utopia. The inn is on the left; there is a sign.

Casa de Leona
Uvalde, Texas 78802

INNKEEPER: Carolyn Durr

ADDRESS/TELEPHONE: 1149 Pearsall Road; (830) 278–8550;
fax (830) 278–8550

E-MAIL: bednbrek@hilconet.com

ROOMS: 6; 4 with private bath, all with telephone and TV.
No smoking inn.

RATES: $55 to $150, double; $15 extra person; EPB.

OPEN: All year.

FACILITIES AND ACTIVITIES: Use of washer and dryer, sundeck,
balcony, gazebo, seventeen acres of wilderness on Leona River with
nature trails, fishing. Nearby: many eating places, Fort Inge Historical
Site, John Nance Garner Museum, First State Bank's "Petit Louvre"
Briscoe collection of art.

Mesquite and Spanish oak border the long drive into Casa de
Leona, and catfish practically jump out of the river alongside
the inn. "A thirty-five-pound catfish was caught in our river,"
Carolyn Durr says, "and recently a ten-and-one-third-pound bass. Wow!"
The inn has two Spanish fountains, one in the garden by the side of the
house and one inside the courtyard.

Carolyn's interests are revealed by all the cookbooks in her kitchen and
all the paintings hanging on the walls. One of the guest rooms, the Picasso
Room, adjoins her bright studio, where china painting and jewelry making
share time with painting on canvas. Business guests can use her typewriter
and desk.

"I started painting in
1972, just to relax," Carolyn
says. "My husband traveled,
back then, and I needed to fill
my time after I'd put the children to bed." She hasn't
stopped; the whole inn is an
art gallery, with her paintings
for sale.

Each guest room is tastefully decorated, and there are some lovely antiques. "I love antiques and I would have more if they weren't so expensive," Carolyn says with a rueful laugh. Interesting decorative touches include needlepoint done by Carolyn and framed on the walls, onyx chess sets, and arrowheads found in the vicinity. In the Bethany Room, named for daughter Bethany, her tiny ruffled flower-girl dress (she was in a wedding when she was three) is framed. Carolyn is a town booster, and you'll find a packet of Uvalde "what to see" brochures, as well as a "good night Tiger" snack of Carolyn's making, in your room.

She enjoys relaxing and sipping thirst quenchers on the sundeck with guests. Some guests bring their own canoes for a float on the Leona River behind the inn, and there's fishing there, too. "We had a guest from Houston who just threw in a line," Carolyn says. "He got a bass, a bream, some perch, and a carp. The carp are the biggest here, like Chinese carp."

Breakfast, for which there is a huge formal dining set—"we bartered two calves for it," she delights in telling—is what Carolyn calls Texican. Sundance eggs are scrambled and served in tortillas with refried beans, or there may be chili rellenos. Carolyn's homemade cinnamon rolls are a tasty ending to the meal, and there's always fresh fruit and juices.

HOW TO GET THERE: From Highway 90 in Uvalde take Highway 117 toward Batesville (post office on corner) for 1 mile to Highway 140, Pearsall Road. Turn left for 1 mile. Casa de Leona is on the right, and there is an inn sign at the driveway.

Texas Stagecoach Inn
Vanderpool, Texas 78885

INNKEEPERS: Karen and David Camp

ADDRESS/TELEPHONE: Highway 187, HC 02 Box 166; (830) 966–6272 or (888) 965–6272

E-MAIL: stageinn@swtexas.net

WEB SITE: www.hat.org/property/west/txstagecoach.html

ROOMS: 5; all with private bath. No smoking inn.

RATES: $85 to $115, double; EPB.

OPEN: All year.

FACILITIES AND ACTIVITIES: Biking, bird-watching, canoeing, fishing, hiking, horseback riding, river tubing. Nearby: Lost Maples State Natural Area, Garner State Park, Bandera ("Cowboy Capital of the World") and Medina ("Apple Capital of Texas").

The name of this lovely white ranch house with black shutters was taken from a history book on Bandera County. Though it wasn't actually on a stageline, travelers passing by at mealtime were often invited to stop, and many times they stayed on for the night. The Camps like to continue this tradition of hospitality along the Sabinal River, which runs along the rear of the property.

The 6,000-square-foot home includes five guest rooms (with fitting names, like Cottonwood, Thompson Peak, Panther Hill, Button Willow

Canyon), common rooms, and a gift shop and art gallery. Among the gallery offerings are paintings by David, cowboy turned artist. The large sunroom overlooking the river is a great place to relax; the upstairs rooms open onto a balcony with a great view of the Hill Country.

HOW TO GET THERE: From I–35 or I–10 take Highway 46 west until the road ends at Highway 16. Go north on Highway 16 through Pipe Creek and Bandera to Medina. From Medina take Highway 337 west to Highway 187, then go south for 4 miles to inn entrance along a white fence on the river side of the road.

Judge Baylor House

Waco, Texas 76706

INNKEEPERS: Dorothy and Bruce Dye

ADDRESS/TELEPHONE: 908 Speight Avenue; (254) 756–0273 or
(888) JBAYLOR; fax (254) 756–0711

E-MAIL: jbaylor@iamerica.net

ROOMS: 5; all with private bath; wheelchair accessible.

RATES: $69 to $89, double; $10 extra person; EPB.

OPEN: All year.

FACILITIES AND ACTIVITIES: Browning Weekend, mule-drawn wagon
tour. Nearby: Dr. Pepper Museum, Texas Sports Hall of Fame, Texas
Ranger Museum, historic homes, Baylor University with Armstrong-
Browning Library.

Dorothy is a vocalist and Bruce is a storyteller, and not only are you
bedded and fed, you can be royally entertained. One of the
charms of this inn is "A Weekend with the Brownings," the English poets Robert and Elizabeth Barrett Browning. (The Armstrong-Browning Library in Waco's Baylor University is internationally renowned.)

There's a swing hanging from the large ash tree on the front lawn, a
player-friendly piano is in the living room, and the Dyers want you to feel at
home in their home. Guest rooms
are named for the Dyers' four children—Alan, Anne, Aaron, and Amy—
identified alongside the door by a
chalk profile of each one, souvenirs
of a family trip to Disneyland back
in 1964.

Breakfast is as full and as
gourmet as Dorothy can make it
(and her powers are considerable),
and although the set times are 8:00
A.M. weekdays and 8:30 on weekends, you can request an earlier time if you
like. You can also elect for lively conversation around the dining room table,
or dine by yourselves at a table-for-two.

HOW TO GET THERE: From I–35 exit at Eighth Street and turn east and right
at the next stop sign, which is Speight Avenue. The inn is at 908 Speight.

Poets in Waco

Waco's Baylor University campus houses the Armstrong-Browning Library with the world's largest collection of memorabilia, and more, of the lives and the world of poets Robert and Elizabeth Barrett Browning.

Fifty-four stained glass windows give you an introduction to both the building, an eighteenth-century Italian Renaissance beauty, and to the poets' works: Each tells the story of a Browning poem. And there's more: The bronze entrance doors depict themes from ten of their poems.

Written works in the collection include all the first editions of both poets, as well as most of the books and other publications written about them. Fascinating, too, are the more than 2,000 of their letters and manuscripts.

Select List of Other Inns
in Central Texas

Carrington's Bluff

1900 David Street
Austin, Texas 78705
(512) 476–4769 or (800) 871–8908

8 guest rooms; all with private bath. Just west of the University of Texas campus.

Citiview Inn and Day Spa

1405 East Riverside Drive
Austin, Texas 78741
(512) 441–2606

4 guest rooms; all with private bath. Menagerie of dogs, birds, llamas, wallabies, goats, and rabbits.

The Inn at Pearl Street

809 West Martin Luther King
Austin, Texas 78720
(512) 477–2233

4 guest rooms; all with private bath. Champagne brunch, complimentary wine.

Lazy Oak Inn

211 Live Oak
Austin, Texas 78704
(512) 447–8873

5 guest rooms; all with private bath. Minutes from downtown, State Capitol, and Convention Center.

Strickland Arms

604 East Forty-seventh Street
Austin, Texas 78751
(512) 454–4426

3 guest rooms; 1 with private bath. Close to Highland Mall, University of Texas, state offices.

Pecan Street Inn

1010 Pecan Street
Bastrop, Texas 78602
(512) 321–3315

4 guest rooms; all with private bath. Elegant turn-of-century landmark home with kitchen privileges.

Boerne Sunday House

911 South Main
Boerne, Texas 78006
(830) 249–9563 or (800) 633–7339

14 guest rooms; all with private bath. Breakfast in a historic Hill Country Sunday House.

Angelsgate

615 East Twenty-ninth Street
Bryan, Texas 77845
(409) 779–1231

3 guest rooms; all with private bath. 1930s building with guardian angels on the front steps.

Main Street Inn
808 North Main Street
Burnet, Texas 78611
(512) 756-2861

3 guest rooms; all with private bath. Great Room with games and music.

The Browning Plantation
Route 1 Box 8
Chappell Hill, Texas 77426
(409) 836-6144 or (888) 912-6144

6 guest rooms; 2 with private bath. Children welcome.

Das College Haus
106 West College Street
Fredericksburg, Texas 78624
(830) 997-9047 or (800) 654-2802

4 guest rooms; all with private bath. Wheelchair accessible.

Claibourne House
912 Forest Street
Georgetown, Texas 78626
(512) 930-3934

4 guest rooms; all with private bath. In the heart of "Old Georgetown."

Stoney Creek Emu Ranch
2879 Cedar Hollow Road
Georgetown, Texas 78628
(512) 863-8635

3 guest rooms; 1 with private bath. Learn about alternative ranching livestock.

Swan & Railway Country Inn
11280 Castro Avenue
LaCoste, Texas 78030
(830) 762-3742

8 guest rooms; all with private bath. An authentic 1911 railway inn.

Albion House
604 West San Antonio Street
Lockhart, Texas 78644
(512) 376-6775

5 guest rooms; each with private bath. Eclectic neoclassical style built of heart pine.

The Woodbine Hotel & Museum

209 North Madison
Madisonville, Texas 77864
(409) 348-3333

8 guest rooms; all with private bath. "Spend a night in a museum," truly.

Oma's & Opa's House

617 El Paso Street
Mason, Texas 76956
(915) 347-6477

4 guest rooms; all share 1 bath. In a unique German town in the Hill Country.

St. Charles Square Bed & Breakfast

8 Chisholm Trail Road
Round Rock, Texas 78664
(512) 244-6850

3 guest rooms share 2 baths. Outlaw Sam Bass territory.

The Rose Mansion

P.O. Box 613
Salado, Texas 76571
(254) 947-8200 and (800) 948-1004

12 guest rooms; 4 in main house, others in cottages. Greek Revival mansion surrounded by cottages and log cabins.

Bed and Breakfast on the River

129 Woodward
San Antonio, Texas 78204
(210) 225-6333

8 guest rooms; all with private bath. On the banks of the famous San Antonio River.

Bullis House Inn

621 Pierce
San Antonio, Texas 78208
(210) 223-9426

7 guest rooms; 2 with private bath. Also an International Youth Hostel.

Classic Charm

302 King William
San Antonio, Texas 78204
(210) 271-7171

5 guest rooms; all with private bath. In the historic King William District close to downtown.

Vieh's B & B

Route 4 Box 75A
San Benito, Texas 78586
(956) 425-4651

3 guest rooms share 2 baths. Down in the heart of the Rio Grande Valley.

The Katy House

201 Ramona
Smithville, Texas 78957
(512) 237-4262 and (800) 843-5289

4 guest rooms; all with private bath. Decorated in American antiques and railroad memorabilia.

Brazos House

1316 Washington Avenue
Waco, Texas 76701
(254) 754-3565 or (800) 729-7313

4 guest rooms; all with private bath. Sunday lunch by reservation.

Colcord House

2211 Colcord Avenue
Waco, Texas 76707
(254) 753-6856

4 guest rooms; 3 with private bath. A 1924 Georgian mansion among Waco's historic homes.

Gulf Coast/ Border Texas

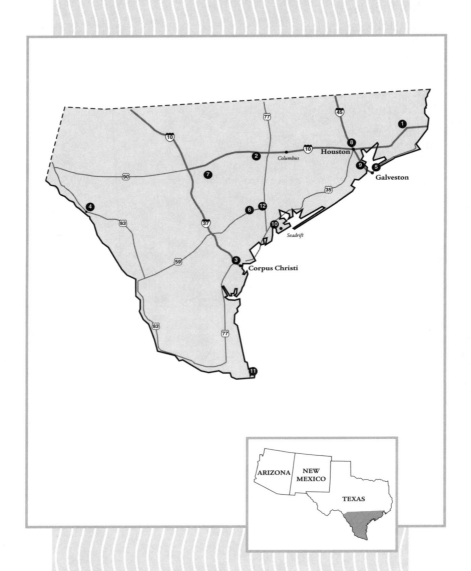

Gulf Coast/Border Texas

Numbers on map refer to towns numbered below.

*Top Pick Inn

Grand Duerr Manor
Beaumont, Texas 77701

INNKEEPERS: Doug and Karl Duerr

ADDRESS/TELEPHONE: 2298 McFaddin; (409) 833–9600 or (409) 839–4558

ROOMS: 4; all with private bath. No smoking inn.

RATES: $99 to $159, double; EPB.

OPEN: All year.

FACILITIES AND ACTIVITIES: Nearby: McFaddin Ward House, Art Museum of Southeast Texas, Babe Zaharias Museum, Julie Rodgers Theatre of Performing Arts, Spindletop Gusher Oil Musuem, Lamar University, fishing on Sam Rayburn and Toledo Bend Lakes.

*T*his father-and-son team are doing a great job with Beaumont's very first country inn. In the town's historic district close to museums, restaurants, and Old Towne Shops, the manor is shaded by lovely old oak, magnolia, and pecan trees within an iron-fenced acre. Built in 1937 for Judge Stephen King, this Victorian home contains a fine antiques collection.

The Master Suite, of Victorian satin and lace, is for the romantically inclined, whether honeymooners, anniversary celebrants, or romantics seeking a getaway. Bluebonnet is a Texas Heritage theme room, decorated, of course, with the state flower. Legends evoke the memory of great entertainers and stars of the Silver Screen with photos and other memorabilia. The Cottage is a separate house in the back courtyard. With its sitting room and kitchen, it's ideal for extended stays.

Breakfast is "expanded continental," with fresh fruits and juices, breakfast meats and breads. Homemade biscuits and croissants are served with specially prepared strawberry jelly.

HOW TO GET THERE: From I–10 take the Seventh Street exit and turn south to McFaddin. The inn is on the corner of Seventh and McFaddin.

Black Gold, Texas Tea

Beaumont is the place that the Texas oil industry got its start. Several promoters were hoping to discover some oil in a salt dome at Spindletop, and in 1889 mining engineer Anthony Lucas made several attempts to complete a well. But it wasn't until a January morning in 1901, when the drillers were actually changing bits, that oil and gas suddenly exploded into the biggest gusher anyone had ever seen.

This put the town that grew up around the Spindletop Oil Field into the big time—except that it grew up in a hurry of flimsy frame buildings and muddy streets called Gladys City. Gladys City has long been replaced by the city of Beaumont, but you can see a replica of the town on the campus of Lamar Tech, near the site of the original gusher. There's a museum, too, with many artifacts from the Spindletop era. There's a monument at the site of the gusher, on Spindletop Avenue on Beaumont's southeast city limits.

Magnolia Oaks
Columbus, Texas 78934

INNKEEPERS: Nancy and Bob Stiles

ADDRESS/TELEPHONE: 634 Spring Street; (409) 732–2726

ROOMS: 5; all with private bath, 2 with phone and TV. No smoking inn.

RATES: $80 to $120, double; $35 extra person; EPB. No credit cards.

OPEN: All year.

FACILITIES AND ACTIVITIES: Bicycles. Nearby: tennis, golf, horseback riding, and canoeing; restaurants; antiques shops; historic homes; Stafford Opera House Theater; Old Water Tower Museum; Walking Tours; Columbus Country Jamboree; Texas Pioneer Trail; Bluebonnet Wildflower Tours; Harris House Museum; Preston Kyle Museum; Santa Claus Museum.

*N*ancy and Bob begin their guests' day with a unique offering: As Nancy serves the hearty meal, Bob accompanies himself on the guitar with an inspiring song. "I'm just a campfire singer, but I love to sing," he says as he gives us a rendition of "What a Wonderful World." "That's what people are here for, to relax. This makes a quiet, peaceful time for people to start out their day." It works, too—we all visibly relaxed as we dug into Nancy's fresh fruit, quiche, and sausage. Relaxing is not hard to do in this lovely Eastlake Victorian home, built in 1890 by a prominent Texan of those times—Marcus Harvey Townsend, the legislator who sponsored the bill for the purchase of the Alamo. Between the Townsends and the Stileses, the home had one other owner, the West family.

"We bought it at the West estate auction," Bob says. "Nancy's son played football with the University of Texas Longhorns, and we kept driving through Columbus (from Houston) to Austin for the games. Nancy looked at a brochure about the sale and just about went crazy. Next Saturday we stopped at the auction, bid for the house, and made the kickoff at one o'clock!"

The lovely color scheme is Nancy's; Bob calls her the color "schemer." She'd never stolen anything in her life, yet somehow a hotel washcloth came home from a trip with her. "I had to have those colors," she says, and the variety of terra-cotta and old rose shades is lovely.

The house was structurally excellent but cosmetically bad, and everything in the interior had to be redone "from head to toe." Did they do it themselves? "Nope," Bob says emphatically. "We're smarter than that! Nancy took forty-five minutes to do an area about yea long, so I said, okay, we're going to get help. In two days we got the whole thing stripped."

Nancy, who is a school principal in nearby Katy, also dabbles in the antiques business, so you'll find lots of interesting furniture in the inn. The Victorian Room has an old display case on the bedside table, lighted to show off the collectibles inside. On the flowered chaise a checkers game is set out and ready to play.

Another small display cabinet, in the Warren Room, is filled with a collection of toys from the attic, which Bob discovered were left by the previous owners, the Wests. The room is named for the inn's carpenter, who moved into this room and set up a cot thirty days before Nancy and Bob arrived, so eager was he to get to work. The large bathroom has a pink wicker chair, which proved to be hiding a toilet seat.

Coffee's out at 7:00 A.M. in the main Magnolia Room, with its polished wood floors, grand piano, and bevy of comfortable wing chairs, two of pale-green velvet in the bay window and two floral ones on the side. You might or might not meet Berkley, "our bed-and-breakfast cat," Bob explains.

The windows in the Magnolia Room are original to the house—hand-blown, it looks like—and all over the outside is the most marvelous ginger-bread trim, also original.

HOW TO GET THERE: From I-10 take the Columbus exit (mile marker 696) and go north. At the *Y* in the road, bear right onto Milam for about ⁹⁄₁₀ mile. Turn left on Spring Street and continue for 2 blocks. The inn is on the right at number 634.

Bay Breeze Inn
Corpus Christi, Texas 78404

INNKEEPERS: Perry and Frank Tomkins

ADDRESS/TELEPHONE: 201 Louisiana; (512) 882-4123

ROOMS: 4; all with private baths. No smoking inn.

RATES: $65 to $90, double; $10 extra person; EPB.

OPEN: All year.

FACILITIES AND ACTIVITIES: Pool table. Nearby: Spohn Hospital, downtown Corpus Christi, seawall, bicycles, fishing, windsurfing, Texas State Aquarium, Art Center, Bayfront Arts and Science Park, Botanical Gardens, Greyhound Race Track, U.S.S. Lexington Museum on the Bay, more.

"We're empty-nesters," Frank says, referring to the grown children who have left the family home. The home means a lot to him; he lived in it during his youth, and even then didn't want to leave it. "I lived in the Tree House in back while I was in college. If I could, I would have stayed there until I was forty!" He bought the house from his mother in

1973. "I've lived all my life within walking distance of the hospital where I was born." He and Perry wanted to justify keeping it even though it was too large for the "empty-nesters," and they were inspired to do that by visiting other inns.

Now, he says, thanks to Perry's culinary arts, "I've not eaten better in all our years of marriage, and I just get to eat in the kitchen." This is hardly a hardship with dishes such as fresh shrimp omelette (in season). Frank is in real estate, and Perry has been the city's most outstanding model, according to her loyal husband. She sings at weddings, too— she's an elegant, talented lady. The house is lovely, with a gorgeous view down to Corpus Christi Bay. "I wouldn't take any- thing for the view," Frank says. The living room has a bookshelf wall of bright yellow behind the sofa

and an antique Steinway piano that belonged to Perry's grandfather. The wall behind the piano is a picture gallery of ancestors, and there's a photo- graph of the Ohio forebear who invented the striking match.

The Sunroom is a real treat. It runs the width of the house and is bright green and yellow, with white wicker furniture, lots of windows, and Perry's mother's childhood dollhouse. Frank says the 1930s pool table at one end of the room was probably in a bar. "I called Brunswick, the manufacturer, to find out if it was authentic; probably it could tell many a story if it could talk."

The Tree House out back is now a large guest room with kitchen and sofa bed in addition to the queen-sized bed. There's a fireplace in the center of the room, and French doors open onto a deck above the treetops. The table is set with pretty blue-and-white china. "That was my mother's," Perry says.

The Nook below the deck is rustic, with wood planking on the floors and a white-painted, scrolled iron bed. "We call it our Elegant Economy Rustic Room." Perry shines in the kitchen, turning out such tasty dishes as Pan- cakes Pierre and a South Texas Omelette. "It's a cheese and egg soufflé, with artichokes and salsa on the bottom." Her decision to make it depends on where people are from, she says of the spicy dish. There might be cinnamon- streusel muffins and quiche, along with seasonal fresh fruit. Empanadas, which are Mexican pastries, are also served, and you'll find a dish of *polvo* (shortbread cookies with sugar) by your bed.

Guests in the Brass Bedroom tend to sleep late, Perry says. "It's so quiet. And there's that view of the water." The Hunt Room is masculine, great for outdoorsmen, with real trophies displaying the wildlife of South Texas. An East Indian axis deer is one such specimen, a pair of antlers is another. The twin beds have pretty paisley spreads. Off the high-ceilinged dining room, the butler's pantry has a lovely stained-glass window.

HOW TO GET THERE: From I–37 turn south on Shoreline Boulevard and go 2³⁄₁₀ miles to Louisiana on the right. The inn is just down the street on the left; there's a sign.

The 1890 House
Del Rio, Texas 78840

INNKEEPERS: Laura and Alberto Galvan

ADDRESS/TELEPHONE: 609 Griner Street; (830) 775-8061; fax (830) 775-4667

ROOMS: 5; all with private baths, telephones, and TV. No smoking inn.

RATES: $89 to $125, double; $10 extra person; continental breakfast.

OPEN: All year.

FACILITIES AND ACTIVITIES: Meeting room, dinner by reservation. Nearby: Roy Bean Historic Site, Alamo Village movie location, Amistad Lake, bicycling, horseback riding, golf, waterskiing, tennis, fishing, hunting, bird-watching; the inn is 3 miles from the border for shopping and dining in Cuidad Acuna, Mexico.

This lovely inn, built around 1890, resembles an antebellum plantation house from the deep South. Huge pecan trees shade the verandas and the garden beside a clear stream. Yet the home is situated in the heart of downtown Del Rio, and the Del Rio Chamber of Commerce has a walking tour brochure of the historic buildings, churches, and homes dating from the 1800s.

The inn has elegant antiques throughout, and stepping into

the large parlor is almost like entering a stage setting for a Victorian drama: windows draped with graceful portieres, Oriental rugs on gleaming polished wood floors. Guest rooms are large and luxurious, with linens from England, hand-crocheted spreads for summer and quilts for winter. Both the Victorian Suite and the Safari Suite have Jacuzzis; all have oversize "soaking" tubs.

The candlelight breakfast includes fresh fruit and juice, homemade breads, and fresh ground coffee and specialty teas.

HOW TO GET THERE: Heading west on Highway 90, enter Del Rio; at the second traffic light turn left over the overpass. Go through four more traffic lights and then left on Griner for one more traffic light. The inn is the third house on the right.

Bayview Inn with Hot Tub and Boat Pier
Galveston, Texas 77553

INNKEEPER: Pat Hazlewood

ADDRESS/TELEPHONE: P.O. Box 1326; (409) 741–0705

ROOMS: 4; all with private bath and TV. No smoking inn.

RATES: $85 to $140, double; $35 to $65 extra person (depending upon where Pat puts them); EPB.

OPEN: All year.

FACILITIES AND ACTIVITIES: Boat pier, beach, hot tub, palm trees, close to golf club. Nearby: the Strand with shops, galleries, and restaurants; Bishop's Palace, Ashton Villa, the Silk Stocking District; Galveston Seawall and Gulf of Mexico beaches; Moody Gardens Rainforest Pyramid; Texas Seaport Museum; Railroad Museum.

*Y*ep, that's the entire name of Pat's new inn, the whole of it. It's right on the waterfront facing Galveston Bay, and there are beautiful sunset and moonrise views from all the rooms and decks of the inn. "Casual elegance and luxury!" Pat exclaims with her usual enthusiasm, and what with Oriental antique furnishings, Oriental rugs, and eclectic artifacts gathered from the far corners of the world—Thailand, India—seeing is believing.

The hot tub on the lower deck is screened from the wind but not the view, and you can have a wonderful waterfront view while lolling in the water. A striped hammock and green director's chairs surround the tub, and the green grass leads down to the boat pier, with palm trees spreading tropical shade on the way to the water. There, you can park your boat at the pier (if you happen to come by water) and have a swim. "There's about 30 feet of sandy-bottom shallow water before it drops off to about 20 feet at the end of the pier," Pat says.

Breakfast is a continental buffet, and you're free to eat when you want and where, either at the breakfast table indoors while enjoying the view of the waterfront or on the upstairs deck, or you can sip your coffee in the Jacuzzi. "Casual" is indeed the watchword at Bayview Inn with Hot Tub and Boat Pier.

HOW TO GET THERE: Go south on I–45 to Galveston; the highway then becomes Broadway. Turn right at Sixty-first Street to Seawall Boulevard and on to Eighty-ninth Street. From there follow the signs to "Bayview."

Coppersmith Inn
Galveston, Texas 77550

INNKEEPERS: Lisa and Mike Page

ADDRESS/TELEPHONE: 1914 Avenue M; (409) 763-7004

ROOMS: 4; 1 with private bath (with more in the works), telephone, and TV. No smoking inn. Rates: $90 to $135, double; $20 extra person; EPB.

OPEN: All year.

FACILITIES AND ACTIVITIES: Deck, herb garden and arbor, fountain. Nearby: the Strand with shops, galleries, and restaurants; Bishop's Palace, Ashton Villa, the Silk Stocking District; Galveston Seawall and Gulf of Mexico beaches; Moody Gardens Rainforest Pyramid; Texas Seaport Museum; Railroad Museum.

The Coppersmith is named not for the man who occupied the house with his family for three-quarters of a century, but for his profession. Paul Shean was a coppersmith, and he created the fine bathroom and other fixtures in the house. The mansion was designed by

Galveston's famed architect Alfred Muller. The house was built in 1887 and is one of the few of Muller's still remaining, no thanks to the hurricane of 1900, which blew an awful lot of Galveston away.

The inn has many fascinating features, beginning with the sky-blue ceiling in the entry, covered with fluffy painted clouds. The French-vermillion living room walls are softly sponge painted, and the Red Leopard fireplace is totally faux marble; the red plush sofa and chair are circa 1880. There's a huge built-in curly-pine cupboard in the hall leading from the entry into the kitchen, and the staircase to the second floor is a beauty, curving and bending under five different woods. The triple stained-glass window on the landing is a knockout, and the painting of angels flying above the panels is another surprise.

Downstairs, the little turret room is the telephone room; upstairs it's a cozy library and television room. And the guest bath downstairs has some of the fancy fixtures that coppersmith Shean specialized in, as well as another beautiful stained-glass window. Many of the walls have stenciled patterns up high just under the tall ceilings, all done by Lisa and an artistic friend. The renovated kitchen has a faux-copper stove hood over the range.

The Rose Room is furnished with inherited family antiques, some from Lisa's grandmother, and there's a picture on the wall of the house just after it somehow made it through the hurricane. Pretty garlands of roses are stenciled high up under the ceiling. Out the back door and across the deck, a complete cottage awaits, with bedroom, bath, kitchen with table and chairs, and a sleeping loft overhead. The wicker love seat strikes a nice note, too. The historic home has been featured on the Galveston Annual Homes Tour, and it may have a ghost, although no one has seen it yet.

HOW TO GET THERE: Go south on I–45 to Galveston; the highway then becomes Broadway. Turn right at Nineteenth and Broadway to Avenue M; the inn is at 1914 Avenue M. There is a sign.

The Wall, Texas Style

It took a really big one to convince the early citizens of Galveston that the Gulf hurricanes could wreak deadly havoc. The town was established as the richest and most important city in Texas—before 1900. That was when the Great Storm swept over the island, killing some 6,000 people, destroying buildings—even the courthouse—and leaving high-water marks on many downtown walls.

Those feisty folks felt that there was too much of the city and the island to be abandoned, but the fury and destruction prompted the city to erect a long, protective seawall. They raised the level of the island behind the seawall by pumping fill from surrounding bays and channels, competing with sand and tide as the engineering feat stretched out 7 miles along the beach on the Gulf of Mexico.

It was a prodigious effort, but one that has paid off. The Seawall along the beaches is a favorite promenade for walkers, joggers, bicyclers, sightseers; a major tourist attraction for Galveston.

The Gilded Thistle
Galveston, Texas 77550

INNKEEPERS: Helen and Pat Hanemann

ADDRESS/TELEPHONE: 1805 Broadway; (409) 763–0194 or (800) 654–9380; fax (409) 7633941

ROOMS: 3; 1 with private bath, all with TV, VCR, telephones and TTD for hearing impaired. No smoking inn.

RATES: $135 to $165; $50 extra person; EPB and snack tray in evening.

OPEN: All year.

FACILITIES AND ACTIVITIES: Walk-in closet with complimentary snacks, soda, water, teas, chocolate; a refrigerator and microwave, videotapes. Nearby: historic Ashton Villa and the Bishop's Palace; the historic Strand, with Galveston Art Center, Galveston County Historical Museum, Railroad Museum, shops and restaurants; the Seawall and Gulf Coast beaches; Moody Gardens Rainforest Pyramid; Texas Seaport Museum.

I asked innkeeper Helen Hanemann to explain The Gilded Thistle's name, because it seemed to me a contradiction. Helen, very much into the island's history, said that like native thistle, sturdy Texas pioneer stock sank deep and lasting roots into the sandy island soil, building a Galveston that flowered into a gilded age of culture and wealth.

Her home was part of those people and their times—in the late 1800s Galveston's Strand was known as the "Wall Street of the West"—and The Gilded Thistle is a lovely memorial to Galveston's past. The beautiful antiques throughout the house make it an exceptionally elegant place to stay, but the atmosphere is so homey that my awe melted away to pure admiration. Helen is on duty at all times, and I joined the other guests in her kitchen, watching her arrange the fresh flowers that fill the rooms.

It wasn't hard to get used to being served on fine china, with coffee or tea from a family silver service. Breakfast, Helen says, is "whenever you want," and I took mine on the L-shaped screened porch around the dining room, especially enjoying Helen's specialty, "nut chewies," and her crispy waffles. Guests might also have Pat's fulsome scrambled eggs, country sausage, spicy baked potatoes, and homemade biscuits. "That'll take them through lunch," he says. There's always a bowl filled with apples or other fruit on the sideboard.

Tea and coffee are available at all times, and I loved it when my morning began with orange juice and a pot of boiling water for coffee or tea at my bedroom door. The evening snack tray could almost take the place of dinner; there are strawberries and grapes and other fruit in season, ham and cheese and roast beef sandwiches, at least four kinds of cheese, and wine.

The Gilded Thistle has been gilded horticulturally: In recent years the inn's landscaping has won two prizes, the Springtime Broadway Beauty Contest and an award for a business in a historic building. And now there's a lovely new gazebo. But the climate never makes it easy and has given rise to the Texas saying (borrowed from Mark Twain) that if you don't like the weather, wait a minute, it'll change. "A few years ago we had that bitter winter," Helen says. "Now we've put in lawn sprinklers and, wouldn't you know, often as not there's too much rain."

I overheard a visitor asking Pat what was so lively about The Gilded Thistle. Pat's answer: "Our guests."

HOW TO GET THERE: Stay on Highway 45 south, which becomes Broadway as soon as you cross the causeway onto Galveston Island. The inn is just beyond Eighteenth Street, on the right.

Michael's
Galveston, Texas 77550

INNKEEPERS: Mikey and Allen Isbell

ADDRESS/TELEPHONE: 1715 Thirty-fifth Street; (409) 763-3760 or (800) 776-8302

ROOMS: 6; 4 with private bath. No smoking inn.

RATES: $85 to $110, double; $15 extra person; EPB.

OPEN: All year.

FACILITIES AND ACTIVITIES: Bicycles, rose garden with fountain. Nearby: the Strand, with shops, galleries, and restaurants; historic Galveston attractions such as the Bishop's Palace, Ashton Villa, the Silk Stocking District; the Galveston Seawall and Gulf beaches; Moody Gardens Rainforest Pyramid; Railroad Museum; Texas Seaport Museum.

*M*ichael's is housed in an impressive red-brick mansion built by Hans Guldmann, cotton exporter and vice-consul to Denmark, as a bulwark against the famous—or infamous—storms that blow in on Galveston from the Gulf of Mexico. The early 1900s hurricane destroyed much of the island but didn't touch the sturdy home, which was not yet inhabited. Even so, Guldmann was so impressed by the furor of the storm that he had the new house torn down and rebuilt atop a sloping terrace formed by storm-damaged bags of concrete. Mikey will take you down in the basement, an oddity on the sea-level island, and show you the wine cellar and the thick concrete walls.

Impressive also is the Isbells' collection of Western art—Remington-inspired bronzes and paintings by Fort Worth artist Jack Bryant. Decoration was planned with an accent on light, enhancing the spaciousness of this

house. The mix of family antiques and contemporary pieces together with original art is pleasing to the eye.

The rose garden, amid the broad green lawns surrounding the house, enables Mikey to fill the house with beautiful blooms and a wonderful scent. "It's great to sit out in the spring and fall, and someday we'll have a greenhouse," she says hopefully. The estate once had tennis courts, a grape arbor, and pergolas covered with roses, and Mrs. Guldmann's greenhouse (now a garden room for winter plants and a party room other times of the year) and fish pond make a charming, nostalgic picture.

All the rooms are extraordinarily large, from the entrance hall with its sweeping center staircase to the glassed-in sunroom, bright with white wicker and green plants. Breakfast is served on Mikey's grandmother's huge dining room table. "My mother made the chair seats," Mikey says, as I admire the rose-and-cream pattern handworked in bargello needlepoint.

The full breakfast varies from Belgian waffles with berries to a delicious egg casserole with homemade bran muffins, and you may have it in the formal dining room or in the cheerful sunroom. Mikey's renowned for her cheesecake, and the Isbells used to serve coffee and dessert at bedtime. "But we've found that most guests come in too late or too full," she says, "so we encourage them to feel free to help themselves to whatever's in the refrigerator or have coffee with us."

Nanny's Room, with a bright-blue iron bedstead, was once the room of the young Guldmann children's nurse and has a small antique student desk from now-defunct Terrell Military Institute. The Schoolroom, with a large green-tiled fireplace, recalls the children's classes with their tutor. The four guest rooms in the main house share a bath; both the attic suite and the carriage house have private baths.

HOW TO GET THERE: Go south on I–45, which becomes Broadway as soon as you cross the causeway onto Galveston Island. Turn right at Thirty-fifth Street, and the inn is on your right in the 1700 block.

Victorian Inn 💙
Galveston, Texas 77550

INNKEEPER: Marcy Hanson

ADDRESS/TELEPHONE: 511 Seventeenth Street; (409) 762–3235

ROOMS: 6; 3 with private bath.

RATES: $100 to $125, double; $25 extra person; EPB.

OPEN: All year.

FACILITIES AND ACTIVITIES: Nearby: the Strand historical district, with shops, galleries, museums, and restaurants; the historic sailing ship *Elissa*; Railroad Museum, Seawall, and beach; restored 1894 opera house; Moody Gardens Rainforest Pyramid; Texas Seaport Museum.

Isaac Heffron, who built the first sewer systems for both Houston and Galveston and the first phase of the famous seawall now protecting the island from hurricanes, built his family a beautiful redbrick residence with a wraparound veranda and a gorgeous circular porch upstairs off the master bedroom. That room is named Mauney's Room, and it was the one for me. Green and yellow, two of my favorite colors, decorate the big room, which is filled with brass, wicker, and antiques. It shares a bath with Isaac's Room, brown and turquoise with patterned cloth wallpaper. Both rooms have recently been redecorated, keeping the original color schemes.

The new Garden Apartment has a full kitchen, living room, and bedroom, all furnished with turn-of-the-century antiques. There's not enough room here to describe all the beautiful things in this house. The entry hall is immense. There is a hand-carved wooden settee by the fireplace, and two more face each other at the end of the room, with a checkerboard set up for guests on the table between them. The parlor has a floor done in a hand-cut-and-laid bird's-eye maple design, a hand-carved mantel, and its original crystal chandelier.

But the best part of this elegant inn is the welcome innkeeper Marcy offers to guests—I just know she loves her job. She has added personal touches and uses her own special recipes for the hearty continental breakfast she serves. In addition to local history lessons, guests get homemade cookies and fresh flowers in their rooms, coffee and tea any time they want in the sunny yellow butler's pantry, and, perhaps, a glass of sherry. Breakfast is orange juice, coffee, tea, milk, fresh fruit in season, cold cereals or hot oatmeal (depending on the temperature outdoors), quiche, French apple pie, a variety of homemade breads, croissants, and granola.

I sat on the curved upstairs porch with a refreshing glass of iced tea in my hand and rocked; a fresh breeze swept off the Gulf. Ryan's Room has a balcony, and Amy's Room has an open porch, so I wasn't the only one savoring the breeze. And, of course, there's always the veranda that wraps around the house, with its view of shady green trees and other grand old houses. The third-floor suite may not have a porch, but it's a favorite hideaway for honeymooners.

The inn is a perfect setting for storybook events, and Marcy loves to plan small business meetings, weddings, and retreats. Romantic, in keeping with the ambience of the inn, is a carriage ride through the historic East End District to view many other late-nineteenth-century homes, neighbors of the 1899 Victorian Inn.

Galveston is synonymous with seafood; there are many wonderful restaurants where you can get your fill of shrimp, soft-shell crab, fresh flounder, and other fruits of the sea.

HOW TO GET THERE: South on I-45 into Galveston; the highway becomes Broadway. Turn left at Seventeenth Street; the inn is on your left when you reach the 500 block.

The Linburg House 📱

Goliad, Texas 77963

INNKEEPERS: Terry and Mike Heskett

ADDRESS/TELEPHONE: 736 N. Jefferson Street; (512) 645–1997; fax (512) 6451997

E-MAIL: mheskett@viptx.net

ROOMS: 3; all with private bath and TV. No smoking inn.

RATES: $65 to $85, double; EPB.

OPEN: All year.

FACILITIES AND ACTIVITIES: Lunch by reservation. Nearby: Fannin Plaza and courthouse with "hanging tree"; General Zaragoza State Historic Site; Goliad State Park with restored Mission Espiritu Santo; Presidio La Bahia; Market House Museum.

*V*ictorian elegance with country comfort is the byword of the Linburg House. The inn, a two-story Victorian Craftsman style, is furnished with lovely antiques, and each of the three guest rooms is pretty and comfortable.

Room names reflect Texas history, and Terry and Mike will answer any questions. The Zaragoza Room has a king-size bed, a large walk-in closet, and a whirlpool tub in the bath. The Goliad Room is large and cheerful, with an old-fashioned iron double bed dating from 1850. The Fannin Room includes a trundle bed, which opens into two twin beds. The private bath is huge.

The country breakfast is made from "scratch." You might be served sour-cream scrambled eggs with onions and garlic, ham hocks and pinto beans, or brown rice cooked in chicken broth—all accompanied by homemade muffins and bread. The formal meal is served in the dining room on fine china and crystal.

HOW TO GET THERE: At the intersection of Highway 183 and 59 go north ¼ mile on Highway 183, which becomes North Jefferson Street. The inn is on the west side of the street at 736.

Spooner-Reese Inn
Gonzales, Texas 78629

INNKEEPERS: Kerry and Noel Reese

ADDRESS/TELEPHONE: 207 St. Francis; (830) 672–8382; fax (830) 672–5125

ROOMS: 5; 4 with private bath. No smoking inn.

RATES: $60 to $90; EPB.

OPEN: All year.

FACILITIES AND ACTIVITIES: Four porches with swings, lunch and dinner by reservation. Nearby: historic walking tour, Gonzales and Old Jail museums, local dinner theater; Palmetto State Park; Independence Park with nine-hole golf course and swimming pool; fishing in Guadalupe River; antiques shops.

*I*n the beginning Gonzales was a rugged pioneer town, but by the late 1800s a new era of prosperity had begun, and in 1875 the elegant Spooner-Reese home was built. Exceptional woodwork, an elegant staircase, and elaborate fireplace mantels are features of the historical home, and the revolving stained-glass window between the foyer and the dining room is quite unusual.

The Master Bedroom is furnished in late-nineteenth-century Victorian with a hunter-green-and-burgundy color scheme. An antique sewing machine gives the Sewing Room its name; a dollhouse adds to the charm of the Doll's Room, with pretty pinks and lace accenting the brass bed. The Cowboy's Den is rustic, of course, in yellows and reds.

Often featured for breakfast are what Kerry calls "French-provincial quiches," while at other times you might enjoy eggs Benedict or homemade waffles, along with Canadian bacon, fresh fruits, and homemade bread and jam.

HOW TO GET THERE: From I–10 take Highway 183 south, which becomes St. Joseph in town. Go south to St. Francis and turn west to 207.

The Buried Cannon

Gonzales is famous for firing the opening shot in the battle for Texas independence from Mexico. And ironically that first shot was fired from a Mexican cannon. Seems that the Mexican authorities lent the cannon to the settlers to discourage Indian attacks. But when the Mexican authorities got wind of the Texans' rebellion, the commander of the Mexican garrison at San Antonio quickly sent a squad of soldiers to take the cannon back.

Well, the citizens of Gonzales weren't about to give that cannon back. They buried it and raised a flag that challenged COME AND TAKE IT. Then they sent out a call for help from other Texans. But before they could get there, the Mexicans arrived. The Gonzales defenders stalled the Mexicans by conversation until help arrived from La Grange. Then they dug up the cannon—and promptly attacked the Mexicans with it.

Although history says it wasn't much of a battle (one Mexican was killed and the others beat it back to San Antonio), this victory encouraged the Texans, starting the chain of events that led to the surrender of Mexican General Santa Ana at San Jacinto on April 21, 1836.

St. James Inn 📱
Gonzales, Texas 78629

INNKEEPERS: Ann and J. R. Covert

ADDRESS/TELEPHONE: 723 St. James Street; (830) 672-7066

ROOMS: 5; all with private bath. No smoking inn.

RATES: $75 to $100; $20 extra person; EPB. Corporate rates available.

OPEN: All year.

FACILITIES AND ACTIVITIES: Picnic baskets, lunches, and dinners by reservation; tandem bicycle. Nearby: historic walking tour, Gonzales and Old Jail museums, local dinner theater; Palmetto State Park; Independence Park with nine-hole golf course and swimming pool; fishing in Guadalupe River; antiques shops.

The St. James Inn occupies a home built in 1914 by a descendant of a family that was involved in Texas history right at the beginning. The first shot of the Texas Revolution was fired right here in Gonzales in October 1835. "Walter Kokernot, who built the house, was the grandson of a merchant seaman who came over from Holland and was the captain of three ships of the Texas Navy," J. R. says. "For that, he was granted several leagues of land, which he turned into the Big Hill Ranch. His oldest son was a 'cattle gatherer.'" Cattle gatherer? J. R. laughs. "Well, he gathered what cattle he could find and made his fortune on the Chisholm Trail, which today goes right by here with the name of Highway 183."

However he came by his fortune, he surely built a beautiful mansion. The house must be about 12,000 to 14,000 square feet—the Coverts aren't sure how large it is if you count the basement and the attic. Downstairs ceilings are 12 feet high, upstairs, 10. The home is absolutely breath-

takingly large, and the guest rooms and baths (and bathtubs!) are about the most spacious I have seen anywhere.

All the rooms are charming as well as huge: The Sunny Meadow Room, the Bluebonnet Room, the Cactus Flower Room, Josephine's Room—it's hard to make a choice. The Children's Playroom on the third floor has all sorts of nooks and crannies under the eaves. A wonderful collection of antique children's toys is in one ell, and Ann's basket collection is under the eaves outside the door. And there are other collections, all interesting, all over the inn, which also has nine fireplaces. "Guests may burn imitation logs," J. R. says, "but not make real fires!"

The Coverts are fugitives from Houston; J. R. is an architect and Ann was executive director of the Republican Party of Harris County. "But I'm among Democrats here," she says with a laugh. "We just got tired of the Houston rat race; we'd been working on an escape plan for seven years."

"We found this place quite by accident," J. R. says. "I said, 'Here we are, this is what we're looking for, what can you say?' Ann said, 'Let's take it!'" Breakfast might be pecan pancakes topped with Ann's special bananas Foster sauce. She also fixes "Treasure Basket" picnics filled with "little surprises"; "I find out something about our guests and put in little mementos. One guest crocheted, another went fishing, we're in a pecan-growing area. . . . it's fun."

You can enter the inn either from the formal front porch or by the side door. Either way, you'll be floored by all the room there is to make yourself comfortable in.

HOW TO GET THERE: Highway 183 becomes St. Joseph in town, and St. James runs parallel to it 1 block west. The huge house is on a southwest corner lot at St. James and St. Andrew.

Angel Arbor Inn
Houston, Texas 77004

INNKEEPERS: Marguerite and Dean Swanson

ADDRESS/TELEPHONE: 848 Heights Boulevard; (713) 868–4654 or (800) 722–8788; fax (713) 861–3189

E-MAIL: b-bhoutx@wt.net

WEB SITE: www.angelarbor.com

ROOMS: 4; all with private bath, telephone, and cable TV. No smoking inn.

RATES: $85 to $125, double; $10 extra person; EPB.

OPEN: All year.

FACILITIES AND ACTIVITIES: Lunch and dinner by reservation during Mystery weekends. Nearby: Houston Heights area of historical interest; George R. Brown Convention Center; Galleria Menil Museum and Museum of Fine Arts; Astrodome, Astroworld; Houston Museum of Natural Science, Space Center, Texas Medical Center; and more.

*T*he Swansons of Durham House have opened a nice, solid red-brick inn with all the amenities and careful coddling that guests enjoyed at Durham House.

"I wanted to accommodate more people," Marguerite says. "And I love angels, and Dean is very fond of arbors, so I combined the two for the inn," Marguerite says. The back garden has for a focal point a large cement angel; on the angel's right, providing privacy from the street, is Dean's arbor, busily supporting growing jasmine vines.

There are angels elsewhere, too; they are not confined to the garden, and you can stay in an angelic room. Gabriel's Room is a restful combination of burgundy, with a bedspread of blues, rose, and green. The room has a cherry-wood four-poster, a writing desk, and a spacious closet, in case you intend to stay for a while.

The Raphael Room has a rice-carved four-poster covered with a pretty pink-and-white brocade spread and, on the posts, a hand-crocheted canopy perfectly draped, each corner even. Behind the secretary desk's glass shelves there is quite a full display of Dean's beer stein collection. Robes are in the closet here, as well as in all the rooms. But they're especially appreciated for this room, which has its own bath—a very large one, but down the hall a little way.

Margaret settled on Angelique for the name of the third guest room, which opens onto a porch shaded by tall pecan trees. Yet you can see the skyscrapers of downtown Houston way off in the distance if you really want to. The room has an antique cherry-wood sleigh bed and a comfortable sofa. A nice touch in all the bathrooms are the shelves, mounted cleverly in front of the windows.

The Michael Suite has a sitting room and private deck, as well as a large bath with whirlpool tub-for-two, and a walk-in shower. Beneath the upstairs porch is the Garden Room, all glassed in with a lovely view of the garden and the angel statue. "The back was a wilderness area," Marguerite says. Now there are trim flower beds, flagstone walks, Marguerite's angel, and Dean's arbor.

As you enter a large foyer, to the left, in the living room, there's a magnificent 200-year-old Chinese hutch of teak, with mother-of-pearl inlays, something to die for. "Dean's mom was an antiques dealer in London, and she wanted to import things like this to the United States when trade was not allowed. But the customs man was so nice; he let her bring this over as long as she promised to keep it in the family!"

The Library is opposite the living room, and what used to be another sun-porch is now a game room, with square glass table and four chairs all ready for the next game. And there's another angel, a crystal cherub, gracing the living room mantel.

Marguerite's breakfasts here are just as sensational as ever. The fruit cup might have fresh strawberries and bananas with a dollop of strawberry yogurt. The three-cheese oven omelette with ginger-peach crisp and lemon-pecan bread are wonderful, as are the apple-nut pancakes, the curried fruit bake . . . ummm. The applesauce-raisin bread is delicious, too.

HOW TO GET THERE: From I-10 take the Heights exit and turn right down Heights Boulevard to 848. The inn is on your right, on the corner of Ninth and Heights Boulevard.

La Colombe d'Or 📅
Houston, Texas 77006

INNKEEPER: Steve Zimmerman

ADDRESS/TELEPHONE: 3410 Montrose Boulevard; (713) 524–7999

ROOMS: 6 suites; all with private bath; wheelchair accessible.

RATES: $195 to $575, per suite; EP.

OPEN: All year.

FACILITIES AND ACTIVITIES: Restaurant, bar. Nearby: within five minutes, Houston central business district, Houston Museum of Fine Arts, Rice University, and Menil Art Foundation; the Astrodome.

*I*t's no surprise to find this exquisite inn so close to two art collections: The inn is patterned after one of the same name in St. Paul de Vence, France, where many famous French painters traded their work for lodging. Houston's La Colombe d'Or ("the golden dove") is hung with fine art, too, and each suite has a name I certainly recognized.

I stayed in the Van Gogh Suite, named for one of my favorite Impressionist painters. Others are named for Degas, Cézanne, Monet, and Renoir; the largest suite, up at the top, is called simply The Penthouse. The suites are decorated with fine art, although there are no original works of the artists.

But I didn't miss them, so swathed in beauty and luxury was I in this prince of an inn. On my coffee table I found fruit, Perrier water, and wine glasses waiting to be filled from my complimentary bottle of the inn's own imported French wine.

Owner Steve Zimmerman has succeeded in bringing to the La Colombe d'Or the casual elegance of the French Riviera. European and American antiques, as well as his own collection of prominent artists' works, are set in the luxurious house that was once the home of Exxon founder Walter Fondren and his family.

The twenty-one-room mansion, built in 1923, is divided into suites. Each consists of a huge bedroom with a sitting area and a glass-enclosed dining  room where Queen Anne furniture, china plates, linen napkins, and cutlery are in readiness for breakfast. As soon as I rang in the morning, a waiter arrived with a tea cart from which he served a very French-style plate of sliced kiwi fruit, raspberries, and strawberries; orange juice; coffee; and croissants with butter and jam. I ate this artistic offering surrounded by the leafy green boughs waving outside my glass room.

You may have lunch or dinner served in your room, too, but I feasted downstairs on meunière of shrimp and lobster, cream of potato and leek soup, the inn's Caesar salad, and capon Daniel; and as if that weren't enough, I ended with crème brûlée!

If you long to visit France, you may decide you don't have to once you've visited La Colombe d'Or. The inn is a member of Relais & Châteaux, a French organization that guarantees excellence, and I absolutely soaked up the hospitality, tranquillity, and luxury.

HOW TO GET THERE: 3410 Montrose Boulevard is between Westheimer and Alabama, both Houston thoroughfares.

The Lovett Inn
Houston, Texas 77006

INNKEEPER: Tom Fricke

ADDRESS/TELEPHONE: 501 Lovett Boulevard; (713) 522–5224; fax (713) 528–6708

E-MAIL: lovettinn@aol.com

ROOMS: 9; 8 with private bath; all with phone, TV, and clock radio. Wheelchair access. Pets permitted. No smoking inn.

RATES: $85 to $150, double; extended continental breakfast. No checks.

OPEN: All year.

FACILITIES AND ACTIVITIES: Swimming pool, Jacuzzi, gazebo, garden, off-street parking. Nearby: Galleria (shopping), the Museum District (Menil and Museum of Fine Art); Astrodome, Astroworld; Houston Museum of Natural Science, Space Center.

On a lovely tree-lined boulevard in Houston's Museum District, the Lovett Inn is a stately mansion on a well-landscaped corner lot. The shaded, fenced pool is hidden behind green trees and shrubs, and pretty soft-red umbrellas offer shade from the sun. The Lovett Inn, built in 1924, was the home of Houston Mayor and Federal Court Judge Joseph C. Hutcheson. Tom is a developer who likes to restore old homes. The formal entry hall opens onto the large living room on the left (unfurnished and ready for whatever is needed for meetings and banquets); the formal dining room is to the right.

Breakfast, an extended continental, offers juice and coffee; cereal, both cold and warm (oatmeal); and muffins—sometimes chocolate chip, sometimes bran, sometimes blueberry. Fruits of the season, such as fresh strawberries with banana, make a nice combination.

The guest rooms have elegant four-poster beds, lounge chairs, armoires or chests, and desks for serious work. Four are in the main house; two are in the Carriage House at the rear of the property; and the seventh, next to the Carriage House, is a regular little townhouse. It has two bedrooms, one with a king-sized bed, the other with a queen, and a living room, dining room, kitchen, and private patio.

HOW TO GET THERE:
From Highway 59 (Southwest Freeway) exit at Elgin and go west; Elgin becomes Westheimer. From Westheimer turn left on Montrose Boulevard. Go 1 block, then turn left again, onto Lovett Boulevard. The inn is on the right; there is a sign.

The Patrician 📱
Houston, Texas 77004

INNKEEPER: Pat Thomas

ADDRESS/TELEPHONE: 1200 Southmore Boulevard; (713) 523–1114; fax (713) 523–0790

ROOMS: 5; all with private bath, phone, and TV. No smoking inn.

RATES: $85 to $145, double; $20 extra person; EPB.

OPEN: All year.

FACILITIES AND ACTIVITIES: Gazebo and deck, solarium for parties and meetings, off-the-street parking, ten minutes from business district, capabilities for audio/visual presentations and fax service. Nearby: the Museum District (Menil Museum, Museum of Fine Arts, and Contemporary Arts Museum, Rothko Chapel); Astrodome, Astroworld; Houston Museum of Natural Science, Space Center; Texas Medical Center; Hermann Park and Zoo; Hermann Municipal Golf Course; Rice University; shopping, restaurants, and nightclubs.

As a business manager in a doctor's office, Pat dreamed of owning a big old house, and when she and the doctor's office parted company, she made that dream come true. The large Colonial Revival mansion, built in 1919, was owned originally by a prominent Houston attorney, and Pat has lovingly restored the home to all its former glory.

"A girlfriend suggested the name, since the house is patrician," Pat says, and it's a happy coincidence that Patricia is her name. The house contains

5,000 square feet and the rooms are large and light, with windows on all sides. The living room sports a gorgeous coromandel screen, and two niches in the fireplace walls have little sitting Chinese Mandarins tucked inside, results of Pat's worldwide travels.

But that's the end of the Oriental touches. The dining room has a large maple hutch: "I was into Early American ages ago," Pat says. Luckily she has kept some very nice pieces. The solarium is a window-enclosed porch with an unusual Early American bench, and that's where the television is, too.

Guest rooms are very large, with lots of space to put things—a plus, I think. Kathleen's Room, named for Pat's sister, has emerald-green walls with white trim, lovely flowered linens, and a bright red Oriental-patterned rug on the gleaming hardwood floor. There are both an easy chair and a love seat to sink into, as well as a desk and an early 1900s oak bed, converted into a queen.

Blue-and-white Lottie Dee's Room honors a daughter of the original owner, and her room has an antique burled-walnut bed, an unusual dressing table, and a love seat. A door leads outside onto a lower portion of the roof, fine for desperate smokers who won't mind viewing downtown alongside the air-conditioner compressor!

The Ivey Room's name is taken from the pretty wallpaper covered with vines. Interesting here is the huge northern-rock-maple armoire that practically had to be built into the wall. The Margaret Rose Room has antique East-lake furniture and two perfectly wonderful Tiffany lamps with beaded fringe hanging from the colorful glass shades. A sunroom opens off this room, with a flowered queen-sized sleeper sofa and two comfortable lounge chairs.

Down in the dining room, a portrait of a very proper and prim ancestor hangs on the wall. But Pat says, no, he's none of hers. "It's a pseudoancestor!" Guests can breakfast here at the large table or in the sunny solarium. Pat's breakfast specialty is French toast "slathered with cream cheese and marmalade" and covered with nuts. She also serves a chocolate banana bread, a

poppyseed bread, and almost-too-pretty-to-eat individual cherry cheesecakes. There are doggy bags for guests who can't eat everything at one sitting!

HOW TO GET THERE: From U.S. 59 south take the Fannin exit just past downtown Houston. Turn left at the second light, which is Southmore. Go 1 block farther, crossing San Jacinto. The inn is on the southeast corner of Southmore and San Jacinto.

Sara's Bed & Breakfast Inn
Houston, Texas 77008

INNKEEPERS: Donna and Tillman Arledge

ADDRESS/TELEPHONE: 941 Heights Boulevard; (713) 868–1130 or (800) 593–1130; fax (713) 868–1160

E-MAIL: stay@saras.com

ROOMS: 14; 12 with private bath, all with TV and VCR. No smoking inn.

RATES: $55 to $150, per room; $15 extra person; continental breakfast.

OPEN: All year.

FACILITIES AND ACTIVITIES: Deck, sun balcony and widow's walk, television room, games. Nearby: Houston Heights area of historical interest, Farmers' Market, George R. Brown Convention Center, Galleria (shopping); the Museum District (Menil Museum and Museum of Fine Arts); Astrodome, Astroworld; Houston Museum of Natural Science, Space Center; Texas Medical Center.

*N*amed for the innkeeper's daughter, this pretty-as-a-picture Victorian is easy to love. But it wasn't always so. "To give you an idea," Donna says, "the house had no front door, no back door, and all the wood had been pulled out." It was Tillman who fell in love with the house, and every day he would say to Donna, "Just look what we could do with it." Donna gave in. "I finally said anybody who would want something that bad ought to have it." It's hard to believe that Sara's began life in 1910 as a small, one-story Victorian cottage. The downstairs parlor is "ready to encourage guests to relax and feel right at home," Donna says, while bright bedrooms are furnished with antiques and collectibles. A circular stairway leads up to the third-floor widow's walk and a great view of the Houston skyline. Sunrise cheers early risers from the front balcony, and the large covered deck out back is a favorite lounging spot any time.

Rooms have books and luggage racks. Downstairs bedrooms have washbasins. The garden sitting area on the second floor is furnished with white wicker, and the four windows of the cupola shower the entire house with light. The Heights neighborhood has a small-town feeling, great to walk around (or jog) in, in spite of the big city only 5 miles away.

Each charming room is named after a Texas town, with decor to suit. The Galveston Room has nautical beds, the Tyler Room is white wicker, the San Antonio Room is Spanish. One guest surprised his wife by telling her they were going to Austin (Texas's capital city) for the weekend, and she was certainly surprised by the Austin Room at Sara's! (She loved it.)

I was intrigued by the plate collection on the dining room walls. "That's my grandmother's collection," Donna said. "We keep adding to it." Breakfast of hot bread or muffins, fresh fruit cup, juice, and coffee is a friendly gathering in the dining room, with the plate collection for an icebreaker if need be. But many guests are repeaters, which makes them old friends.

HOW TO GET THERE: From I–10 east take Shepherd Drive and turn right to Eleventh, then right on Heights Boulevard for 1½ blocks. The inn is on the right. From I–10 west take the Studemont exit. Make a U-turn just before Studemont and turn right at Heights Boulevard. (This is necessary because of interminable road construction.) Sara's is on the left in about 6 blocks.

Captain's Quarters 📱
Kemah, Texas 77565

INNKEEPER: Mary Patterson

ADDRESS/TELEPHONE: 701 Bay Avenue; (281) 334–4141 or (800) 309–2177

ROOMS: 15; 5 in the main house, others in two separate buildings nearby, all with private bath and telephones. No smoking inn.

RATES: $40 to $140, double; $10 extra person; EPB.

OPEN: All year.

FACILITIES AND ACTIVITIES: Elevator, bicycles, pier, use of Yacht Club pool and tennis courts. Nearby: Kemah is known as the boating capital of Texas: private charters, dinner boats, excursions, water taxi to waterfront restaurants, sailboat races; shopping in the Gaslight District.

*M*ary likes to compare the Captain's Quarters to an early American whaler's home on the rugged New England coast. It's built on a bluff overlooking Galveston Bay, but it offers true Southern hospitality. And although you won't see any whaling ships on the horizon, from the veranda you can watch pretty sailboats passing by. Better yet, enjoy the view from the widow's walk atop the inn, the highest point in all of Kemah.

The five-story nineteenth-century building, with 8,500 square feet, is only 30 feet from the water's edge. The grand stairway outdoors leads to the grounds and a private pier. Rooms, of course, have nautical names. The Constitution has a king-size bed, a fireplace, and a front water view. The America's Cup, with a queen-size bed, also faces the waterfront. The Cutty Sark offers a side view of the bay, as does The Flying Cloud, while the Endeavour has to do without any water at all. The inn ceilings are 10 feet high, with beams, there are stained-glass windows, and antiques and collectors' art fill the rooms.

The dining room table seats twenty, and Mary likes everyone to eat formally together. Breakfast is served on fine china, and you'll have a full meal, perhaps of New England baked eggs along with meat and potatoes, cereal, and breads. But if that doesn't satisfy you, Mary says "we are a town known for its restaurants—within 6 blocks of the inn there are 4,400 restaurant seats!"

HOW TO GET THERE: Go south on I-45 from Houston and turn east on NASA Road I for 7½ miles to Highway 146. Go right on 146 for a mile to Kemah. Turn left on Seventh Street and the inn is the last building, on the water's edge.

Hotel Lafitte 📱
Seadrift, Texas 77983

INNKEEPERS: Frances and Weyman Harding

ADDRESS/TELEPHONE: 302 Bay Avenue; (512) 785-2319; fax (512) 785-7381

ROOMS: 10; 4 with private bath. Smoking permitted.

RATES: $60 to $115, double; $15 extra person; EPB.

OPEN: All year.

FACILITIES AND ACTIVITIES: Downstairs and upstairs verandas right on San Antonio Bay. Nearby: fishing, swimming, walking on the Seawall; Matagorda Island; Aransas Wildlife Refuge.

This long, white wooden building is a treasure tucked away almost where Highway 185 ends at the Gulf of Mexico. It fronts right on the water, and you may just want to sit out on the veranda and rock, lazing the day away. It was built in 1909 as a railroad hotel. Hospitality begins in the parlor, where a wooden holder displays three kegs of wine for guests to help themselves. Rosé, Chablis, what is your pleasure? Other pleasures of the parlor are rose-colored wing chairs flanking an organ, a soft flowered sofa, and old-fashioned lace curtains. There's a fireplace, and the walls as well as the floors are constructed of planks of wood.

Guest rooms are airy and roomy, and those facing the front have a gorgeous ocean view. Rooms are all large and decorated becomingly, reflecting

the inn's turn-of-the-century mood. Number 5 has a flapper dress of the 1920s hanging on the armoire. Room number 6 not only contains the original hotel furniture, but there's also an antique wedding dress hanging up, a gift from a friend whose grandmother wore the gown.

The two large suites are on the third floor, and the Honeymoon Suite has a rose satin bedspread, an inlaid-wood card-table set, a Jacuzzi, and not one but two chaise longues. Hedonistic luxury!

Breakfast might be a ham-and-egg casserole or a quiche, along with bran muffins, fruit, and juice. For lunch and dinner the Hardings will be delighted to direct you to the family restaurant, Barkett's, where seafood specialties abound. After all, here you are on the famous Texas Gulf Coast.

HOW TO GET THERE: From I-10 take Highway 77 south to Victoria and Highway 185 south to Seadrift, a small town approximately 35 miles southeast of Victoria. Bay Avenue is, of course, on the bay.

Brown Pelican Inn
South Padre Island, Texas 78597

INNKEEPERS: Vicky and Ken Conway

ADDRESS/TELEPHONE: 207 West Aries (mailing address: P.O. Box 2667); (956) 761–2722; fax (956) 761–1273

ROOMS: 8; all with private bath; wheelchair accessible. No smoking inn.

RATES: $69 to $120; $15 extra person.

OPEN: All year.

FACILITIES AND ACTIVITIES: Nearby: birding, fly-fishing, windsurfing, beachcombing, bicycling; close to Laguna Madre Nature Trail and half an hour from the Border and Matamoros, Mexico.

Overlooking Laguna Madre Bay and set in the center of the wetlands, this inn is a birder's paradise. Just sitting on the covered porch, you can count the brown pelicans and the other shore birds as they go about their business.

The Laguna Madre Nature Trail is just outside the door. The 1,500-foot boardwalk crosses four acres of wetlands, and with informative signs about dune systems and prevalent bird species, it offers an opportunity to observe brown and white pelicans, seagulls, great blue herons, egrets, and other wildlife in a natural habitat.

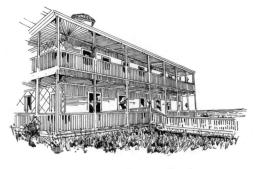

The guest rooms are named for areas of Texas, such as Big Bend, Davis Mountains, Hill Country, Guadalupe Mountains, Laguna Atascosa, and the Big Thicket, and are decorated accordingly.

Breakfast includes hot breads or muffins, fresh fruit, cereal, and juice— and then you can be off to a day of sunshine and water, or shopping and dining.

HOW TO GET THERE: From Highway 77 south take Highway 100 east south of Harlingen to Port Isabel and cross over the Queen Isabella Causeway onto the island. Go north on Padre Boulevard to Aries and turn west to 207.

Beauty in the Deep

South Padre Island, a narrow strip of land and sea and sun on the tropical tip of Texas, is the place to save as well as savor nature. Along with the miles of beautiful white sand beaches, windswept dunes and balmy air, there's a new dive spot where corals, barnacles, sea fans, and sponges can find a home and grow; a Whaling Wall to open peoples' eyes to the necessity of saving the earth's oceans; and a nature trail over the wetlands to observe birds and wildlife.

There are two artificial reef systems off the blue waters of South Padre. The reefs have been established to benefit the environment by creating habitats for marine organisms and, not incidentally, to provide areas for sport diving and fishing opportunities. Divers may see colorful damsel fish, blennies, and butterflyfish, as well as countless invertebrates and the big ones: amberjack; tarpon; grouper; and blacktip, tiger, and hammerhead sharks. Anglers have the opportunity of catching the amberjack and tarpon the divers see in the deep.

"I believe that if people see the beauty in nature, they will work to preserve it before it's too late," says Wyland, the environmental artist who painted the huge Whaling Wall mural of whales on outside walls of Padre Island's convention center. The 153-foot mural covers three walls and can be seen clearly well before you arrive at the center. Part of a project by the artist of completing one hundred such walls by 2011, it's currently the largest art project in the world.

Naturalist Ed Hawkins conceived the idea of the 1,500-foot boardwalk crossing four acres of wetlands near the South Padre Island Convention Centre. With informative signs about dune systems and prevalent bird species, it also offers a fine opportunity to observe many species of birds such as brown and white pelicans, seagulls, great blue herons, egrets, and other wildlife in a natural habitat.

Friendly Oaks 📱
Victoria, Texas 77901

INNKEEPERS: CeeBee and Bill McLeod

ADDRESS/TELEPHONE: 210 Juan Linn Street; phone and fax (512) 575–0000

E-MAIL: innkprbill@aol.com

ROOMS: 4; all with private bath; wheelchair accessible. No smoking inn.

RATES: $55 to $75, double; EPB.

OPEN: All year.

FACILITIES AND ACTIVITIES: Conference room, lunch and dinner available by reservation, exercise equipment. Nearby: historic area of restored Victorian homes; McNamara Historical Museum; Texas Zoo; Victoria Memorial Square; Riverside Park on the Guadalupe River; the Gulf Coast (30 miles).

*L*ocated on the historic Street of Ten Friends, the inn was built in 1915 in historic Victoria, established in 1824, which is pretty long ago for Texas. CeeBee and Bill love to tell about local history, so you're sure to be entertained.

Each guest room is a different treat, beginning with The Boudoir, large, airy and romantic, with a queen-size rice bed topped with pinecone posters and an adjoining wicker-furnished sitting area. The Ranch offers an entirely different mood, with its thick log canopy bed and a horse-collar-framed mirror. Preservation Room honor's Victoria's historic preservation with pencil-post bed and turn-of-the-century memorabilia. And should you happen to be of Scottish descent, you'll feel at home in the Thrifty Scot.

The Royal Scottish pancakes are a signature breakfast dish with bangers (sausage) and a fruit plate starter.

HOW TO GET THERE: From the junction of Highways 87, 59 and 77 (Navarro and Rio Grande Streets) go south on Navarro for 1 mile to third traffic light. Turn right and go 3 blocks; the inn is the only house at the intersection of Juan Linn and William Streets.

Select List of Other Inns
in Gulf Coast/Border Texas

Bailey House
1704 Third Street
Bay City,Texas 77414
(409) 245–8479

3 guest rooms; 1 with private bath. Quilts are an attraction in this classic Revival mansion.

The Queen Anne
1915 Sealy Avenue
Galveston, Texas 77550
(800) 472–0930

6 guest roooms; 4 with private bath. Only 6 blocks from The Strand.

The Whistler
906 Avenue M
Huntsville, Texas 77340
(409) 295–2834 or (800) 404–2834

5 guest rooms; 4 with private bath. Sam Houston territory: home, burial site, statue, and museum.

Moonlight Bay
506 South Bay Boulevard
Palacios, Texas 77465
(512) 972–2232

7 guest rooms; all with private bath. A 1910 Frank Lloyd Wright Prairie house on the water.

Hoope's House

417 North Broadway
Rockport, Texas 78382
(512) 729–8424 or (800) 924–1008

8 guest rooms; all with private bath. With a panoramic view of Rockport Harbor and the beach.

The Pelican House

1302 First Street
Seabrook, Texas 77586
(281) 474–5295

4 guest rooms; all with private bath. Great views of the bay under the pecan and live oak trees.

Our Guest House

406 East Hugo Street
Yoakum, Texas 77995
(512) 293–3482 or (800) 762–1475

4 guest rooms; all with private bath. Historic Yoakum claims title of Leather Capital of Texas.

West Texas

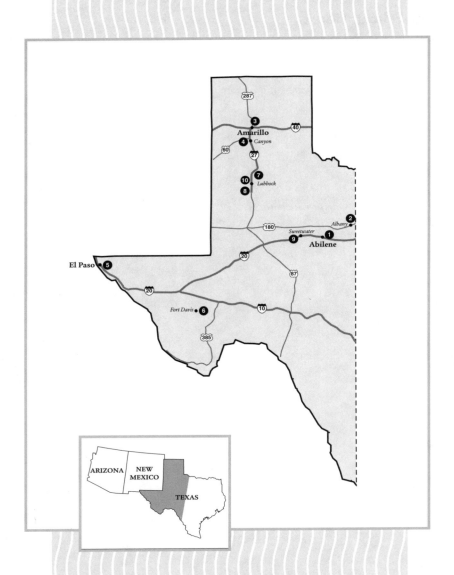

West Texas

Numbers on map refer to towns numbered below.

Top Pick Inn

Bolin's Prairie House
Abilene, Texas 79601

INNKEEPERS: Ginny and Sam Bolin

ADDRESS/TELEPHONE: 508 Mulberry Street; (915) 675-5855 or
(800) 673-5855

ROOMS: 4; 2 with private bath. No smoking inn.

RATES: $50 to $65, double; EPB.

OPEN: All year.

FACILITIES AND ACTIVITIES: Nearby: restaurants, fine arts museum,
Grace Cultural Museum, zoo, three universities, historic Buffalo
Gap Historic Village.

This large and airy Prairie house was once a Victorian mansion,
home of an Abilene pioneer whose name was Colonel Christmas
Comfort. "He never was a colonel," Ginny says. "That was just his
name." Not only names but styles change, too, and new owners in 1920
decided they preferred a simpler style. They remodeled the story-and-a-half
house into a full two-story,
smoothing the lines along the
way. The inn's color scheme is
mainly red, white, and blue—
pale, royal, and navy blue. The
living room has an old wood-
burning stove, pale-blue woodwork, and shutters behind airy,
white-lace curtains. Fabric is
striped navy-and-white ticking.

Guest rooms are spacious
and light corner rooms with lots of windows and distinctive color schemes.
Love is decorated in blue and beige and has comfortable wing chairs; Joy is
furnished with Mamma Bolin's old bedroom set, and Ginny has used a riot
of pink roses, quilted roses, striped roses (wallpaper), and rose-covered pillows in rose-colored rocking chairs. Peace now has an ornate 1920s bedroom
suite, refurnished to look brand new, and Patience, instead of two twin beds
now has one twin and one full size, "for those too long or too wide for a
twin," says Ginny.

Breakfast is plentiful. There are Dutch Babies (oven-baked pancakes),
grits, sausage, hash browns, baked egg dishes, homemade bread, and oatmeal
with apples and cinnamon if you don't want eggs.

Old Nail House Inn
Albany, Texas 76430

INNKEEPER: Joie Parsons

ADDRESS/TELEPHONE: 329 South Third Street (mailing address: P.O. Box 632); (915) 762–2928 or (800) 245–5163

ROOMS: 3; all with private bath. No smoking inn.

RATES: $60 to $75, double; $15 extra person; EPB.

OPEN: All year.

FACILITIES AND ACTIVITIES: Nearby: restaurants, antiques and gift shops, Shackleford County Courthouse, Old Jail Art Center, Fort Griffin State Park, Fort Griffin Fandangle Festival (June).

The Nail House was built in 1914 for Robert Nail, playwright and creator of the Fort Griffin Fandangle. All that remains of Fort Griffin, a wild, Wild West settlement in the 1870s and '80s, are the ruins of several old buildings, three restored buildings, and the yearly Fort Griffin Fandangle.

The Fandangle is a show put on by the townsfolk the last two weekends in June. It's an outdoor show, a musical blend of history, hoedown, ballet, spectacles, "and a good time for everybody—those who are in the Fandangle and those who come to see it."

"I've been in real estate for years, and I was looking for an office" is how Joie got into innkeeping. "Years ago we had a restaurant, I guess maybe twenty-five years." Joie laughs. "Been a day or two."

But she hasn't lost her touch with food. The Nail House's breakfast is beautiful to behold as well as to eat: a Southwest Casserole with turkey breast and herbed tomatoes, served with oven potatoes, chips, and salsa. Mixed-fruit yogurt topped with peaches or strawberries, maybe pecan waffles—it's all delicious, whether you eat it in the formal dining room downstairs or on the sunporch. The time you want it is your choice, too.

"Sometimes I get industrious," Joie says, as if all the aforementioned food does not require industry. "Then I also make cinnamon blintzes, a cream cheese breakfast dessert." The two-story home is right across the street from the historic Shackleford County Courthouse, the oldest courthouse in Texas "still working," she says. The living room boasts a pale-green Victorian love seat; the dining room has a window seat and an old grandfather's clock, a gift of Joie and Bill's three sons.

The guest rooms, on the second floor, offer a picturesque view of downtown Albany (population about 2,000). Two of them, the Oak Bedroom and the White Bedroom, open off the sunporch, which has a trundle bed to accommodate two additional guests.

The White Bedroom has white half-paneling with pretty, small-patterned blue wallpaper above, a white quilted spread on the antique bed, and two rust-red wing chairs in a corner. Joie says a little lady who moved to Albany from Abilene (about 36 miles southwest) told her about the joys of innkeeping. "She actually told me how; it was fascinating." But friends and family were not so sure. "You're going to let strangers stay in your house?" they asked.

"Luckily, my oldest son, Mike, had stayed in various inns, and he was very encouraging," Joie says. Special touches, such as fruit baskets in your room, embroidered gowns for the ladies, plush terry robes for everyone, potted plants, and fresh flowers (in season), make the Old Nail House Inn a delightful place to stop.

HOW TO GET THERE: Off I–20 take Highway 6 north to Albany and follow it into town to Main Street (Highway 180). The inn is on the corner of Main and South Third Streets, across the street from the Shackleford County Courthouse.

Galbraith House
Amarillo, Texas 79102

INNKEEPER: Martha Shaw

ADDRESS/TELEPHONE: 1710 South Polk Street; (806) 374–0237

ROOMS: 4; all with private bath. Pets in garage. No smoking inn.

RATES: $85, double; EPB.

OPEN: All year.

FACILITIES AND ACTIVITIES: Bicycles, hot tub, use of exercise facilities at health club, dinner by reservation. Nearby: Amarillo College, Plemons-Eakle Historic District, Amarillo Art Center, Palo Duro Canyon, *Texas* (musical drama).

Galbraith House was built in 1912 by a lumberman, and you should see the woodwork in this 4,000-square-foot mansion; the construction cost the princely, back then, sum of $25,000. Oh, the beautiful hand-rubbed mahogany, walnut, and oak—rich! "People go around with their mouths hanging open at the woodwork," Martha says. They're also awed at the Bukhara Oriental rugs and antiques and collectibles that fill the mansion. The home is managed by Martha, and she is dedicated to pleasing her guests.

Breakfast? "I do a really good breakfast," she says, and I doubt she could find any dissenters. Egg casseroles, omelettes, "and though I try to give guests light and heathful food that remains flavorful, the men like my Southern-style biscuits and gravy. . . . It just depends on who my guests are that morning." With only three or four guests, she'll cook to order, happy as a lark in the large, sunny kitchen of the big house. When guests come in there are soda and  chips; in fact, "they're welcome to what's in the refrigerator! Carrot sticks, microwave popcorn—they can do their own thing; they have free use of the kitchen, the entire house, as long as they don't swing from the chandeliers!" she adds with a laugh.

"We're not strict or rigid on check-in or out." That, says Martha firmly, is one of the advantages of an inn. I like her philosophy: "We're flexible; we cater to our guests. We're in the hospitality business, and the people who are the nicest get the nicest guests and the best business."

All the guest rooms are spacious and comfortable. The Christmas Room is the most popular; a king-sized bed, a pair of lounge chairs, a large dressing table, and family photographs make it very homey. Guests have full use of the home's other rooms: living room, dining room, library, solarium, three balconies, even a butler's pantry.

An unusual feature of the home is the Gentlemen's Smoking Porch, a tiny outside balcony off the upstairs hall, where even back in 1912 smokers were sent. Quilts handmade by local artisans are on all the beds and many of the walls, and so are works of art by local artists.

"There's been an ever-increasing emphasis on the Palo Duro Canyon and real-life ranching heritage experiences," says Martha, "like the Creekwood Ranch Old West Show and Chuck Wagon, the Cowboy Morning Breakfast, and the American Quarter Horse Heritage Center and Museum." Not surprising—this is the West, after all!

HOW TO GET THERE: Take the Washington Street exit off I-40; go to Seventeenth Street, turn east, and go 2 blocks to Polk Street. Turn right; the inn is on the right at 1710.

Parkview House 📱
Amarillo, Texas 79101

INNKEEPER: Carol Dia

ADDRESS/TELEPHONE: 1311 South Jefferson Street; (806) 373-9464; fax (806) 373-3166

E-MAIL: parkviewbb@aol.com

WEB SITE: Members.aol.com/Parkviewbb

ROOMS: 5; 3 with private bath. No smoking inn.

RATES: $65 to $85; cottage $150; EBP.

OPEN: All year.

FACILITIES AND ACTIVITIES: Hot tub, bicycles, Victorian rose and herb garden. Nearby: Amarillo College, Plemons-Eakle Historic District, Amarillo Art Center, Palo Duro Canyon, *Texas* (musical drama).

*L*ocated in the Texas Panhandle and at the edge of Amarillo's historic district, Parkview House offers both contemporary charm and a touch of the Old West. There's a lovely garden beyond the breakfast room French doors, with grape arbors, a Victorian gazing ball, and an herbal garden. Wander among the roses and grape arbors, lounge in the hammock or soak in the hot tub under the blue Texas sky. (It's cooler at night, under the stars!)

The French Room has an ornate French satinwood queen-size bed under a crystal chandelier; the Colonial Room boasts a mahogany four-poster and a drop-leaf desk, while in the Victorian Rose Suite a good-size guardian angel floats overhead. There's a nice niche here to sit and look over the treetops and relax. All three have a private bath; the English County, with a cozy reading nook, and the Dutch Room, tucked under the eaves, share a bath.

Breakfast includes homemade breads and muffins "dripping with butter," Carol's granola, and herb omelettes seasoned with fresh herbs from the inn Herbal Garden.

HOW TO GET THERE: From I–27 take the Washington Street exit, go north about 2 miles to Fourteenth Street (passing Amarillo College). At Fourteenth Street turn east and travel 1 block. The inn is on the corner of Fourteenth and Jefferson Streets.

Country Home
Canyon, Texas 79015

INNKEEPER: Tammy Money-Brooks

ADDRESS/TELEPHONE: Route 1, Box 447; (806) 655–7636

ROOMS: 4; 2 with private bath. No smoking inn.

RATES: $55 to $95 double; EPB.

OPEN: All year.

FACILITIES AND ACTIVITIES: Swimming pool, garden with gazebo and picnic tables, dinners by reservation, horse and carriage rides, special massage. Nearby: Palo Duro Canyon State Park and *Texas* outdoor drama in Pioneer Amphitheater, Panhandle-Plains Historical Museum, Buffalo Lake National Wildlife Refuge.

*J*ust walking up the front walk, edged with flower beds, of this pretty little cottage makes you feel like you've come to a happy place. The white Victorian lampposts on the green lawn on each side look as if they ought to be gaslit. The front door is Victorian to match, and the wide foyer opens onto a living room with a totally unexpected tall cathedral ceiling and picture windows opening up the rear wall.

The old dresser in the foyer has a pretty collection of plates. The dining room, on the right, is filled with plants and Depression chairs. But it's the two-story living room that is such a pleasant surprise. There's an antique mantel over the fireplace, one of Tammy's handmade quilts, and Tammy's paintings on the wall. She's a teacher as well as an artist. Her grandmother gave her an acre to build on, and she saved all her teaching money to fulfill her dream house, and a dream it is.

The inn is furnished with antiques, many of which have been passed down through the family. In the Oak Room you'll see Grandma Money's wedding dress from 1907, Grandma Jones's childhood rocker, and Great-Grandmother Fortner's treadle sewing machine. The Honeymoon Suite downstairs has a mahogany four-poster and a whirlpool bath in its private bathroom. Upstairs, the two guest rooms share a bath with an old-fashioned claw-footed tub. They also share a loft, with a sitting area perfect for viewing clear West Texas sunsets.

Breakfast might be puffed pancakes with a hot fruit compote and sausage, or sausage quiche made with Country Home's own farm-fresh eggs, and blueberry muffins. To cap off a perfect day, perhaps touring Palo Duro Canyon and taking in the famous musical *Texas*, performed under starry

skies in the canyon, snacks will be brought to your room. Every night when *Texas* is playing out at Palo Duro, Canyon can host up to 1,300 tourists.

HOW TO GET THERE: From I–27 turn west on Fourth Avenue and go to Eighth Street. Turn left for 1 mile. The inn is on the right; there's a sign.

Hudspeth House
Canyon, Texas 79015

INNKEEPERS: Mary and Mark Clark

ADDRESS/TELEPHONE: 1905 Fourth Avenue; (806) 655–9800

WEB SITE: www.hudspethinn.com

ROOMS: 8; all with private bath, phone, and cable TV; 5 with fireplace. No smoking inn.

RATES: $60, double; EPB.

OPEN: All year.

FACILITIES AND ACTIVITIES: Hot tub, dinner by reservation. Nearby: hiking, biking, horseback riding in Palo Duro Canyon State Park; *Texas* (musical drama); Panhandle-Plains Historical Museum; West Texas A&M University; seven golf courses within 25 miles; antiques shops and restaurants on The Square within walking distance.

Mark says that with his engineering, house building, and remodeling, he and Hudspeth were a perfect match when he and Mary took over the historic property from their Haynie friends who had operated the inn for several years. "Lots of restoration," he says: windows, doors, oak floors, and plumbing so that now the inn's eight guest rooms all have private baths. "And since the Haynies took everything with them, we have furnished each room completely differently. It's hard for us to say the rooms are beautiful," Mark says modestly, "but our visitors say they are really beautiful and find it hard to pick a favorite."

All the Clarks have had inning experience; they've lived in California, Greece, Spain, Colorado, and now Texas. "We've lived all over the world and stayed in many B&Bs, so we know what guests want in an inn," Mary says. "Mary loves to cook, clean (!), and remodel/decorate," her husband reveals.

Mark loves to play the guitar, and he plays for guests occasionally, but during romantic candlelight dinners he definitely sets the mood with the dessert.

Mary does something clever with her breakfast fruit when she serves bananas: She rolls them in sugar and cinnamon, which keeps them from turning brown. With this (and other fruit in season) she serves French toast, bacon, orange juice, and coffee. "And that's whenever our guests want it," she says. "We've served anytime from 3:00 A.M. to 10:30 A.M.!"

When they're asked what's the hardest part of having an inn, Mary always answers: "Naming the rooms!" In fact, they had a contest when they first opened, and the prize for the guest who won was a free night's lodging.

The Hideaway is at the back of the house; so is the Prairie Maid. "We think it was the original maid's room. It's all slatted wood, even the ceiling, so it has a prairie look." The Presidential has a gold invitation to Ronald Reagan's inauguration framed on the wall. The Royal is very Victorian; the

Empire is lovely art deco, all gray and black, with etchings and a black-metal canopy bed. In the 1940s Room you'll see *Life* magazine photos of World War II and a big green overstuffed chair in front of the fire to contemplate them in.

For the upstairs Loft, the Clarks gutted the whole third floor, and now the room is a refreshing garden, with walls and sloping ceiling a restful sea green-blue, a bed with a white picket-fence headboard (made by Mark), and Georgia O'Keeffe flower prints on the walls.

The most fun is Prohibition. "When we were remodeling, I pulled down the drywall ceiling and got hit with dozens of hidden beer cans!" Mary says. Have the Clarks show you yet another hidden treasure in the room!

HOW TO GET THERE: From either I-40 to I-27 Business or I-27 south, take exit 106 (Fourth Avenue) and go 7 blocks, turning right at the third traffic light. Go 3 blocks west; the inn is on the right.

Sunset Heights Inn ▢
El Paso, Texas 79902

INNKEEPER: Consuelo (Grandma) Martinez

ADDRESS/TELEPHONE: 717 West Yandell; (919) 544–1743;
fax (915) 544–5119

ROOMS: 4; all with private bath, phone, and TV; wheelchair accessible
(electric chairlift from first to second floor). No smoking inn.

RATES: $75 to $150, double; $20 extra person; EPB.

OPEN: All year.

FACILITIES AND ACTIVITIES: Dinner by reservation; pool and Jacuzzi.
Nearby: many museums and historic fort, old Spanish missions, Tigua
Indian Reservation, zoo, scenic drive; Ciudad Juarez in Mexico, just
across the Rio Grande.

*B*uilt in 1905 up in the high and mighty area of El Paso overlooking downtown, this inn on the National Register of Historic
Homes is a three-story corner house of dark-yellow brick surrounded by an iron fence. Tall
palm trees wave over it, and the
large grounds of almost an acre
are graced by roses blooming
much of the year.

The inn is a decorator's
dream, with beautifully coordinated fabrics and wall coverings, mirrored doors, and
sybaritic bathrooms. The Oriental Room has another coromandel screen as well as a brass
bed. The bathroom, with brass fixtures and a huge bathtub, is on what was
once a porch. But not to worry: All the windows are now one-way mirrors.

HOW TO GET THERE: From I–10 west take the Porfiro Diaz exit and turn
right. Go 2 blocks to Yandell, turn right and go 6 blocks (count the ones on
the right, not the left) to Randolph; the inn is on the far corner to the left.

Before Plymouth and Turkey, There Were Berries in El Paso

El Paso has been giving Plymouth, Massachusetts, a hard time. The town is trying to persuade the proprietors of Plymouth Rock that the first Thanksgiving took place not there, but on the banks of the Rio Grande twenty-two years before the *Mayflower* landed. According to Texas historians, hundreds of Spanish colonists led by Don Juan de Onate arrived near El Paso on April 20, 1598. Ten days after the Spanish arrived, Onate claimed the land for Spain and ordered the colonists to dress in their best and gather for a feast of thanksgiving.

"This is very typical Texas, no question; they'd have a better chance getting hold of Plymouth Rock" comment the Massachusetts legislators, but that hasn't stopped El Pasoans from celebrating Texas's very own April Thanksgiving. Crowds picnic on the grassy slopes of Chamizal National Memorial on the banks of the Rio Grande to watch a pageant with more than ninety men, women, and children costumed in the dress of the 1590s—conquistadores in steel-plated armor and helmets and men and women in their best finery, depicting the thankfulness of the colonists in finding water after four months of wandering in the desert, eating roots and berries.

While the folks in El Paso don't really want to do away with football and turkey in November, they just want to be sure America has its history straight on just when and where the first Thanksgiving took place.

The Veranda Inn
Fort Davis, Texas 79734

INNKEEPERS: Kathie and Paul Woods

ADDRESS/TELEPHONE: 210 Court Avenue (mailing address: P. O. Box 1238); (915) 426-2233 or (888) 383-2847

E-MAIL: veranda@overland.net

WEB SITE: www.theveranda.com

ROOMS: 8 in the main house, 2 in the Carriage House just behind the main building; all with private bath, plus 3 "extra" for guest use. No smoking inn.

RATES: $60 to $70, double; $10 extra person; EPB.

OPEN: All year.

FACILITIES AND ACTIVITIES: Courtyards, walled garden, orchards, rocking chairs on the verandas. Nearby: restaurants in the Limpia Hotel and The Drug Store, Fort Davis National Historic Site, Overland Trail Museum, Neill Doll Museum, Davis Mountain State Park, McDonald Observatory, Big Bend National Park.

If you're really serious about getting away, this Texas outpost is the perfect place. Fort Davis is set in the Davis Mountains of far West Texas, and the Wild West ruins of Fort Davis are there to haunt you—in a nice way, of course, by reminding you of more simple times gone by (but more dangerous, too!).

"We find we're sort of a refuge," Kathie Woods says of the very small town. "Professionals from the hectic life actually tear up when they tell us what a pleasant weekend they've had! Many of them work sixteen hours a day, and they really need a place to relax and rest."

The Woods know whereof they speak: For twenty-five years Kathie was a director with the Texas Department of Human Services as well as a computer specifications writer. Paul taught architecture at Texas A&M University, which came in handy with the remodeling and reopening of the inn.

The inn was called the Lempert Hotel back in 1883 when it was built by W. S. Lempert, who was a mail guard and scout for the Overland Trail. "By 1880 the area was considered free of the 'Indian menace,'" Kathie says. Evidently so, since in 1884 the new hotel hosted Quannah Parker, son of

Comanche Chief Peta Nocona and white captive Cynthia Ann Parker (one of the colorful episodes in Texas history).

Kathie and Paul have restored many of the features of the old adobe building, preserving the pine floors, the 14-foot-high ceilings, and the transom windows of the original hotel. The adobe walls are 2 feet thick, making air-conditioning in the cool mountain air totally unnecessary.

The Veranda of the inn's name is the place to relax. "Our guests often spend hours out there in the cool of the evening, rocking away and watching the stars—our sky here is famous," Kathie says. But there are also two secluded walled courtyards, with large shade trees, lilac bushes, and irises. The entire grounds take up a city block, and there are roses and other flowering plants, as well as an herb and a vegetable garden. There's even an orchard, with apples and figs, peaches, and apricots, as well as grape and blackberry vines.

Much of this good gardening turns up at breakfast. Scotch eggs are a favorite: hardboiled and wrapped in sausage, rolled in breadcrumbs, and then browned. Or Kathie's special German farmer's omelette, which won Kathie a first prize at the Alpine Fair, served at the inn with homemade biscuits and sour-cream coffee cake. There's always fresh fruit—remember the orchard!—yogurt, and both dry and hot cereal for lighter eaters.

Rooms are roomy, and although baths are private to each room, many had to be built across the hall because of the building's age. But thick, soft Egyptian-cotton robes are provided for those whose bath is not attached to the room. Half the baths have large "soaking tubs"; the rest have showers, so take your pick. Linens are hung outside to dry in the fresh mountain air—think how deliciously fragrant that makes them!

HOW TO GET THERE: 1 block west of the Courthouse. (Kathie says, "We do not describe our location in terms of the Overland Trail, because all streets in Fort Davis are unmarked, and people cannot readily locate the Overland Trail.")

Frontier Fort

You can hear the haunting sounds of a nineteenth-century military parade—of bugles and hoofbeats, the jangle of spurs and swords of mounted troops, echoing over the empty parade ground of the Fort Davis National Historic Site. It's a ghostly experience, as the music from band manuals of 1875 drifts through the air of the empty parade ground, ringed round with the rugged Davis Mountains.

Fort Davis was a military post, established to guard the nearly 600 miles of wilderness that stretched beween El Paso and San Antonio. It was built to protect wagon trains from falling prey to hostile Indians and to offer haven along the waters of Limpia Creek.

Today the fort is a fine example of the frontier forts of those days, with buildings both in ruins and restored. The museum in a reconstructed barracks gives a true picture of frontier military life.

Woodrow House
Lubbock, Texas 79410

INNKEEPERS: Dawn and David Fleming

ADDRESS/TELEPHONE: 2629 Nineteenth Street; (806) 793-3330; fax (806) 793-7676

WEB SITE: www.woodrowhouse.com

ROOMS: 8 in the main house; with private bath; wheelchair accessible. Children welcome. No smoking inn.

RATES: $85 to $105, double; $10 extra person; EPB.

OPEN: All year.

FACILITIES AND ACTIVITIES: Laundry. Nearby: Texas Tech University with music, theater, and game activities.

Here's a novelty, an inn built to be just that, a bed-and-breakfast inn. The Flemings spent four years dreaming, planning, researching, and designing, and the result is a comfortable modern inn with old-fashioned hospitality.

Room decor reflects the room names: Victorian Room, President's Room, Alumni Room, '50s Room, Equestrian Room, Granny's Attic, the Lone Star Room; all are furnished with authentic furniture of yesteryear. Granny's Attic, for instance, has a 1917 telephone that belonged to David's great-grandparents, and the bedroom suite in the Equestrian Room is furnished with a 1917 Sears Roebuck and Company suite.

Breakfast, served buffet style on an antique sideboard handmade in Scotland, might be sweet potato pancakes, French toast with bacon, a breakfast casserole, even *migas* with sausage and biscuits and gravy, and fresh fruit and juice. Enjoy it on a 130-foot mahogany table that easily seats sixteen breakfasters.

HOW TO GET THERE: Across the street from Texas Tech University, on Nineteenth Street between Boston and University Avenues.

The Bones of Lubbock

Archaeologists have not only found bones of extinct animals in Lubbock but also man-made stone tools. Excavations have revealed remains of extinct mammoth, horse, camel, giant bison, and even a 6-foot-long armadillo. Carefully excavated stratigraphic and artifactual records also identify prehistoric cultures, leading to the probability of continuous human occupation from approximately 12,000 B.C. to the present. Prehistoric cultures identified include Clovis, Folsom, Plainview, and Firtview peoples.

An Interpretive Center exhibits fossils and artifacts from the site, but access to the archaeological areas is by guided tours only, organized by the Museum of Texas Tech University and offered only during actual archaeological work. But excavations continue all summer, with crews often made up of students from all over the world.

Mcnabb's Green Acres
Ropesville, Texas 79358

INNKEEPERS: Sandra and Ronnie McNabb

ADDRESS/TELEPHONE: Route 1, Box 14; (806) 562–4411

ROOMS: 4; 1 with private bath. Children welcome. No smoking inn.

RATES: $60 to $75, double; $15 extra person; EPB. No credit cards.

OPEN: All year.

FACILITIES AND ACTIVITIES: Lunch and dinner by reservation, farm tour. Nearby: Buddy Holly Statue and Walk of Fame, Lubbock County Museum, Lubbock Fine Arts Center, Mackenzie State Park, Lubbock Lake Landmark State Historical Park, Texas Tech University campus, National Ranching Heritage Center, Llano Estacado Winery, Meadow Musical (country music) second Saturday each month.

"Come on over," Sandra says. "We'll leave the porch light on." More than that, she'll let you help with the chores. For McNabb's Green Acres is a real working cotton farm. "West Texas is the major cotton area for the United States," Sandra says. "We like people, and what we would truly like is for the general public to see firsthand what farming is really like," says Sandra, full of enthusiastic missionary zeal.

The McNabbs are deeply entrenched in Ropesville and Texas, and Ronnie and Sandra have published a booklet on the history of the area. They moved their house from Lubbock, set it down alongside the road in the middle of 700 acres of cotton, rebricked it, and added a room. It's furnished family-style, with an English tea cabinet from Waco in the living  room, topped by a pewter tea service from Ronnie's mother. The hutch in the dining room belonged to Ronnie's great-grandfather, and the family clock and decorative glassware came from forebears in Marble Falls.

The wonderful old kitchen cabinet, with a flour cabinet and sifter, was going to be burned, until "I rushed over and rescued it," Sandra says. Breakfast, as is to be expected on a real farm, is hearty. Sandy's Cotton Farm Breakfast includes quiche, sausage and salsa, sourdough biscuits and gravy, grapes from the grape arbor, and apricots from the backyard. The jam is made from wild plums. "They grow around Post and we go and pick 'em ourselves," Ronnie says—just in case they're not busy enough with the cotton.

HOW TO GET THERE: From Lubbock take Highway 82/62 to Ropesville and turn left at the blinking light at FM 41. Go east for 4 miles; McNabb's, a pink house with white columns, is on the left in the middle of the curve. There is a sign.

Mulberry Manor 📱 💚
Sweetwater, Texas 79556

INNKEEPERS: Beverly and Raymond Stone

ADDRESS/TELEPHONE: 1400 Sam Houston Street; (915) 235–3811 or (800) 235–3811; fax (915) 235–4701

ROOMS: 6; 5 with private bath, all with phone, TV, and VCR; wheelchair accessible. Children welcome; pets welcome.

RATES: $70 to $225, double; $15 extra person; EPB, afternoon snacks and open bar.

OPEN: All year.

FACILITIES AND ACTIVITIES: Lunch and dinner by reservation, hot tub, shuffleboard, chess table, games and game table, touring in 1929 Model A touring car, beauty stylist by appointment. Nearby: horseback riding; golf; Pioneer City-County Museum; lakes Sweetwater, Trammell, and Oak Creek Reservoir with fishing, boating, and water sports; World's Largest Rattlesnake Roundup (March).

BUSINESS TRAVEL: Office available with computer and fax; phones in rooms.

*I*t's a surprise to discover a mansion like Mulberry Manor in a town the size of Sweetwater (about 12,000 population). It was built in 1913 for banker, businessman, and rancher Thomas Trammell—and the architect was John Young, father of movie star Loretta Young.

This may account for the Hollywood glamor of this showplace. The focal point of the mansion is a glass-domed atrium, filled with plants and sunshine, in the center of the house. A white slatted fence encloses this, the heart of the house, and the inn's rooms surround it. The formal French parlor to the right of the entry is furnished in authentic Louis Quinze; the tailored parlor on the left also contains lovely pieces, garnered from all over.

"Just about everything is from estate sales and antiques shops," Beverly says. "We bought everything in this house on weekends." This gave them something to do while the house was being restored. "Auctions are really the best buy," is her advice.

"It was an old duplex, and it took thirteen months to remodel." The house had a checkered life after the Trammells were gone. To give you some idea of the scale, in 1923 it became Sweetwater and Nolan County's only hospital. Then, like many old homes, the 9,800-square-foot house was divided into apartments. Eventually, it somehow became part of the estate of the brother of General Clair Chennault of the famous Flying Tigers.

Beverly had retired from Southwestern Bell; the Stones were living across the street, restoring that house, when this one came on the market. They sold the other and bought this. The house has three downstairs guest rooms plus a vast suite upstairs. The separate barroom has an oversize television screen and a sitting area. The formal dining room is impressive, but so is the so-called breakfast room, with its brocaded French chairs, a beautiful mirrored sideboard, and an Oriental rug on the polished wood floor.

But most exotic is the upstairs suite, which Beverly describes as "neoclassical." To give you an idea of the size, originally it was a ballroom. "It was an apartment, and it was horrible," Beverly shudders. Now, on the huge expanse of white carpet, the furniture is gold and black, and there are plants (there's even a fern behind the king headboard). A statuary group, busts of classical figures, occupies a corner. The adjoining bath is suitably sybaritic.

Breakfast is as opulent as the manor: fresh fruit compote, eggs Benedict or quiche, hash browns, sausage or ham, biscuits and gravy, cinnamon raisin biscuits, strawberry cream cheese on croissants. And afternoons there's a big snack tray with the beverage of your choice; our snack was cream puffs filled with ham salad. Who does all this? "Me. I'm the cook!" Beverly says. Her dinners are spectacular seven-course meals, too. And to cap it all off, Raymond takes guests for a fun ride in that shiny 1929 Model A Ford out front.

HOW TO GET THERE: Take exit 244 off I-20 and go north 4 blocks to Sam Houston Street and number 1400. There's a sign on the Model A Ford out in front.

Filet o' Snake— Hold the Mayo

Sweetwater's rattlesnake roundup is not a rattlesnake appreciation festival—after all, who really loves rattlesnakes? Nope, this unique event in Sweetwater began as an attempt by West Texas ranchers and farmers to get rid of the abundance of the critters that were plaguing them and their livestock. Ever since its inception in 1958, more than a hundred tons of Western Diamondbacks have been turned in at the roundup.

What's to do at a snake festival? You can meet up with the stars of the celebration in person if you register for the Snake Hunts on Friday, Saturday, or Sunday. Not to worry, they're led by guides, experienced snake hunters who assist in hunting and handling the rattlesnakes. The hunt lasts from four hours to all day, and you've gotta bring a container to hold live rattlesnakes, a hand mirror, high-top boots (you bet!), snake hooks or tongs, and, just in case—a snakebite kit. This is serious business, subject to Texas Hunting Laws, and absolutely no firearms are allowed.

What does this critter taste like? Rattlesnake meat is considered a delicacy in many parts of the world, and at the Jaycees Cook Shack you can taste Deep-fried Western Diamondback Rattlesnake to your heart's content: More than 4,000 pounds of rattlesnake meat is served each year.

Country Place
Wolfforth, Texas 79382

INNKEEPER: Pat Conover

ADDRESS/TELEPHONE: South Upland Avenue; Route 1, Box 459; (806) 863-2030; fax (806) 863-2030

ROOMS: 5; 1 with private bath, 1 with TV. No smoking inn.

RATES: $70 to $100, double; EPB and snacks. Wheelchair accessible.

OPEN: All year.

FACILITIES AND ACTIVITIES: Lunch and dinner by reservation, swimming pool, hot tub, barbecue grill, bicycles, horses. Nearby: Buddy Holly Statue and Walk of Fame, Lubbock Country Museum, Lubbock Fine Arts Center, Mackenzie State Park, Lubbock Lake Landmark State Historical Park, Texas Tech University campus, National Ranching Heritage Center, Llano Estacado Winery.

"These are the things I like doing," Pat says: "Cooking, entertaining, meeting people—I enjoy hostessing, and I really enjoy cooking. Actually, I felt raising the children was just practice, and whenever they come home to visit, I get to practice more!"

Guests feel like family, too, what with the way Pat makes you feel at home. In the wet bar next to the refrigerator, there are always snacks such as cheese balls and fruit and soft drinks. "Guests can use the fridge, make their own waffles if they want to," Pat says.

Inky, a small black dog who likes to steal socks, came out to greet me, looking hopeful. "He's a party animal," Pat says, but he was content with a few pats before wandering off, maybe looking for some socks? Pat also has a horse named "Horse."

The two-story ranch house is modern and new. Both living room and dining room are large and open, with light woods. The Sun Room was designed to gather heat from the West Texas sun. For entertainment there's a piano for those who can play and board games for other kinds of play.

The Country Place is really out in the country, and it's hard to remember that Lubbock is just minutes away. I wandered outside to the big yard. I could hear the horses neighing—Pat boards them—and I saw the lovely P-shaped pool and the covered patio with hot tub and barbecue grill. Big towels, robes, books, easy chairs . . . all very easy to take.

"The country roads are ideal for walking, jogging, or bicycling," Pat says. "The neighboring farms have a variety of exotic animals, which can make it pretty interesting." Up the wide staircase, the walls are hung with family photographs. "That's my mother as a young girl," Pat points out. Windows have clean white shutters, and the color scheme of the Wicker Room is maroon and beige, complementing the wicker furniture.

In the Walnut Room, Pat likes to show off the walnut furniture, which is the set she grew up with, back in Iowa. "First my mother had it in her house, then my boys had it in college, then I got it—and had it redone." Both Wicker and Walnut share a bath. "It's easy," Pat explains. "You have the pink towels, the others have the maroon." The Striped Room and the Rosy Room share another bath. The Striped Room is named for the striped wallpaper and quilted spread on the queen-sized bed. The Rosy Room has soft-pink walls, a rosy carpet, white French provincial furniture, and white quilts, covered with rose and pink poppies, on the twin beds.

Breakfast, says Pat, "depends on the mood of the cook but is always gourmet." We had a Southwestern omelette with crispy hash browns and sausage and Pat's special bran muffins and homemade cinnamon rolls. The cook was in a good mood!

HOW TO GET THERE: From Lubbock take Highway 82/62 (Brownfield Highway) southwest ¾ miles to Upland Avenue (Hayloft Restaurant sign), turn left, and go 6 miles. The inn is the last house on the right; there is a sign, and the Conover name is on the mailbox.

Select List of Other Inns
in West Texas

Adaberry Inn

6818 Plum Creek Drive
Amarillo, Texas 79124
(806) 352–0022

*9 suites; all with private bath. Newly constructed to accommodate
business travelers.*

Auntie's House

1712 South Polk
Amarillo, Texas 79102
(806) 371–8054

*3 guest rooms; all with private bath. Historic home twenty minutes
from Palo Duro Canyon.*

House of Kathleen

RR 3, Box 661
Canyon, Texas 79015
(806) 655–9436

3 guest rooms; 1 with private bath. On ten acres of "very quiet" land.

Broughton Guest House

215 Patricia
Junction, Texas 76849
(914) 446–2112 or (915) 446–3055

*3 guest rooms; 2 baths. Just $^8/_{10}$ mile out of town, along the clear
South Llano River.*

Mellie Van Horn's Historic Inn

903 North Sam Houston
Odessa, Texas 79761
(915) 337–3000

16 guest rooms; all with private bath. Step back to the 1930s here.

Indexes

Alphabetical Index to Inns

Inns with Restaurants

Inns Serving Meals by Reservation Only

Inns with, or with Access to, Swimming Pools, Hot Tubs, or Spas

Inns with, or with Access to, Golf or Tennis Facilities

Inns with Downhill or Cross-Country Skiing Nearby

Inns Where Pets Are Accepted with or without Restrictions

Inns That Especially Welcome Children

Inns with Wheelchair Access

Inns for Business Travelers